DELIVER US

Peacekeepers, Warlords and

William

FROM EVIL

a World of Endless Conflict

Shawcross

SIMON & SCHUSTER

NEW YORK   LONDON   TORONTO   SYDNEY   SINGAPORE

SIMON & SCHUSTER
Rockefeller Center
1230 Avenue of the Americas
New York, NY 10020
Copyright © 2000 by William Shawcross
All rights reserved,
including the right of reproduction
in whole or in part in any form.

SIMON & SCHUSTER and colophon are registered trademarks
of Simon & Schuster, Inc.

Designed by Karolina Harris

Manufactured in the United States of America

1   3   5   7   9   10   8   6   4   2

Library of Congress Cataloging-in-Publication Data
Shawcross, William.
Deliver us from evil : peacekeepers, warlords and
a world of endless conflict / William Shawcross.
p.   cm.
Includes bibliographical references and index.
1. World politics—1989–   2. History, Military—
20th century.   I. Title.
D860.S48 2000
909.82'5—dc21   99-058915

ISBN 0-684-83233-X

To Alice Mayhew, wonderful friend

Contents

DELIVER US FROM EVIL

THE ONLY THING NECESSARY FOR THE TRIUMPH OF EVIL IS
FOR GOOD MEN TO DO NOTHING.

—Edmund Burke

LONG IS THE WAY
AND HARD, THAT OUT OF HELL LEADS UP TO LIGHT.

—John Milton, Paradise Lost

Prologue

The World's Texan

O N a dark evening at the end of 1993, the international aid worker Fred Cuny drove me up a hill in Sarajevo into a road tunnel, one lane of which was filled with more than two hundred yards of gleaming new machinery. Workmen were crawling over it to the sound of jackhammers digging up the road.

Cuny was a well-built, articulate and delightful Texas engineer who had a rare combination of strategic, engineering and analytical faculties. I first came across him when he installed sanitation in Cambodian refugee camps in Thailand in 1979. Now he was working for the International Rescue Committee on projects funded by George Soros, the financier and philanthropist.

Water was one of the most precious commodities in Sarajevo, a city besieged by the Bosnian Serbs. Thousands of people now had to draw it from the river in buckets every day. Often they were shot down by Serb snipers as they did so. Cuny wanted to stop that.

When we arrived at the tunnel, the jackhammers were still pounding, the arc lights were still lit, workmen were still crawling over the machine. I saw a fantastic structure, a thing of beauty, which looked like the engine room of an aircraft carrier. The pumps were all bought off the shelf in Texas; the tanks had to be designed not only for the tunnel, but also so that they would just fit into a C-130 transport plane. The whole plant came in twelve C-130 loads, fitting the fuselage with half-inch tolerance. Cuny showed me detailed drawings of how each huge section of the plant was slid off the plane onto truck transporters. He devised it so that each plane could be unloaded in only seven minutes, thus minimizing the risk of being hit on the runway by the Serb gunfire which always rendered the airport hazardous and sometimes closed it.

The water was pumped up from the river below the road. In the tunnel it passed first through a skid consisting of three chemical containers that added a flocculant, which bonded to the suspended particles in the water. This was sprayed onto a clarifier, where the heavier material was separated off into a sludge line, then pumped into the storm sewer system and back into the river. The clarified water passed through three filters—anthracite, sand and garnet—and was then chlorinated and pumped up the hill to an old reservoir built in the days of the Austro-Hungarian Empire that had been abandoned for years until Cuny rediscovered it. It then ran by gravity through the city. So the project was a happy combination of ancient and modern. It cost only $2.5 million.

Cuny said that by the time the plant was finished, "Sixty thousand people will have water twenty-four hours a day. Another sixty thousand for a few hours a day." Altogether, just under half the population of Sarajevo should benefit. He was outraged when the local mafiosi who controlled many of the resources of the besieged city beat the humanitarians; a combination of politics and corruption on the side of the Bosnian Muslim government delayed turning on the system for many months.

FREDERICK C. Cuny, six feet four in his Texas boots, was an American original. He was not a quiet American; he was a loquacious one. I see him as a great American—a sort of universal Schindler, a man with lists of millions of people in Asia, Africa, Latin America and Europe whose lives he succored or saved.

He was one of the outstanding people with whom I traveled through hideous crises around the world in an attempt to understand how "the international community," the amorphous creature to which the *New York Times* refers (without caps) in editorials as not being able to cope with disorder, has dealt with it in the decade since the Berlin wall came down.

I write about Cuny not just because he became a friend who touched all who knew him, but because his world was the world in which I am interested here, and his engagements on some of the battlefields of what is often called post-modern warfare show the scope and complexity of finding international solutions to local or regional crises. His life and his work epitomized the story of humanitarian endeavor.

At the University of Houston, he studied urban planning. In the late sixties he worked in small towns along the Texas-Mexico border where there were often serious sanitation problems, mosquitoes and disease. His involvement in international humanitarianism began in 1968 during the civil war in Nigeria, when the region of Biafra attempted to secede from the federal republic. Images of starving children, displayed on front pages of newspapers and on television for the first time in a sustained manner, girded the first great international response to humanitarian disaster.

Many of the veterans of Biafra, like Cuny himself, went on to try to help in other disasters through the seventies and eighties. "Biafra was where we first came to grips with dealing with famines, and the different ways of dealing with them—either food aid or market interventions," Cuny explained. Ways of targeting supplementary feeding were developed then, as were measurements of malnutrition. "We still use the yardstick of Biafra to measure our performance," Cuny told me. "It's the defining moment."

In 1969, at the height of that war, he had flown to Lagos to find out what it was about. He went to see the minister of the interior. "I said," Cuny related, " 'I'm from Texas and I'm here to study your war and tell you what you can do when it's over to get humanitarian aid in.' "

The minister said, "That's interesting. Let's see your passport." He thumbed through to find the Nigerian visa and ripped it out, saying, "We don't want anything to do with these damned Biafrans and all you Americans and others that are helping them. I want you out of here in twenty-four hours."

Cuny was flown out of Lagos under armed guard. He went to the other side and helped organize the airlift which kept Biafra alive. The planes included ancient Constellations, C-97s, DC-3s, DC-4s, DC-6s, some from the Korean War or even World War II. "Spare parts flying together in close formation, we used to say," Cuny reminisced.

The pilots numbered mercenaries, CIA fliers from Air America, the agency's covert airline in Indochina, who had come "to redeem themselves," idealists and war protestors. They were, in Cuny's words, "a real mixed bag, the world's largest flying zoo. . . . Even in the crew of one airplane, you'd find five different reasons why people were there. Some guys were there simply for the adrenaline rush; that was big when you were flying in at night, turning the plane around under fire."

The aid groups included the International Committee of the Red Cross, the best organized, Interchurch Aid, CARE. Motives, as always, differed. There was the idealism of saving the Biafran Ibos, who were thought to be facing genocide. But behind the humanitarianism some governments and companies had their eyes on the Biafran oil fields and were eager to see the secession succeed and Nigeria break up.

Cuny quickly understood what has been evident in disasters since, that food distribution acts, as he said, as "a gigantic magnet pulling people out of the fields into the towns and out of the towns to the airport." Aid workers and agencies had to turn the system around and get people back into the countryside away from the airfield. In those days most aid workers and agencies were inexperienced. According to Cuny, "They focused on the most obvious things, like giving out food, rather than discovering how people normally got food and how that could best be supported. It was an assumption that we had to bring everything in for them."

One of his first surprises was to find how much food there was in the markets. "There's always food in famines," Cuny stated. "The problem was that people in the rural areas couldn't afford to eat the food they were producing. They had to sell it to speculators and food was being hoarded."

The other huge problem was, as always, public health. "I kept thinking, if we could just get people to start building better drains and focus on planning, far fewer people would be sick," Cuny told me. There were few engineers in the relief agencies in those days. "Aid workers would say, 'We don't know how to dig latrines,' " Cuny went on. "I'd say, 'Well, the armies of the world have millions of manuals on latrine digging. Can't you get some of those?' "

Gradually an anguished debate developed among aid workers as to whether the airlift was helping the Biafrans or harming them by prolonging the war. (The same debate has occurred in almost every comparable emergency since, certainly over Bosnia.) The real unknown was whether Biafran propaganda was right—that the Nigerians would commit genocide if they won.

Cuny became convinced that the food lift was indeed merely sustaining the fighting and that the rumors of genocide were exaggerated. He came to see that it was the intransigent demand of the Biafran leadership for independence that prevented compromise and increased the starvation. He left—and lost a lot of friends whose emotional commitment to the Biafran cause would not allow them to see this. Their single-minded belief in the Biafran cause led them to misjudge, if not vilify, the government of Nigeria, which was, in fact, pursuing a policy of reintegration, not genocide.

In 1970 the Nigerian army, under General Yakubu Gowon, won and, despite the Biafrans' and humanitarians' fearsome predictions, was merciful. The error of the humanitarians appeared to have prolonged the conflict, and that, said Cuny, colored relief workers' views later: "In Cambodia, in 1975, as the anti-communist government was collapsing, we all felt at the end, 'Let's shut everything down and pull out. Let the government collapse. The Khmer Rouge can't be that bad.' " The Khmer Rouge then killed between one and two million Cambodians in their three-and-a-half-year rule.

After Biafra, Cuny set up a small company in Dallas, Intertect Relief and Reconstruction, to specialize in technical assistance, research and training services for voluntary agencies and the United Nations in disaster relief. In the seventies Intertect was involved in many disasters, including in Bangladesh, Cambodia and the Guatemala earthquake of 1976. In 1988, Cuny went to Armenia after the earthquake and surprised the U.S. disaster chief, Julia Taft, who was with him, when he insisted that the plastic sheeting they had brought be used for stabling animals rather than sheltering people. Livestock was the only asset people had left, he said; it must be protected.

At the end of the Gulf war, Cuny was in southern Iraq attempting to rescue some of the Shia Muslims who, with Western encouragement, had risen against Saddam Hussein only to have the West stand by as he crushed their revolt. When wounded Shias arrived in desperation at Allied lines, they were pushed back until Cuny, with one brave junior U.S. officer, insisted on the lines being opened. "Americans should be helping these people, not turning them away," he shouted.

He then went to Kuwait to help restore the city's water operation, and on to northern Iraq to help deal with the 500,000 Kurdish refugees who had fled into the mountains along the Turkish border after their own uprising against Saddam had failed. There he met Morton Abramowitz, the American ambassador to Turkey. Abramowitz was incredulous when Cuny told him that the Kurds could be returned to their own homes in two months. "I told him, 'Fred, you're full of crap.' "

Cuny just went on talking nonstop, as he often did. After two hours he convinced the ambassador it could be done, and with the help of the U.S. military, under General John Shalikashvili, he went on to do it. "Fred Cuny was the expert on almost everything we did. To me he was the hero of that operation," Shalikashvili said later. Since then Cuny had had connections at almost every level of the U.S. government—in the White House, the Pentagon, the Central Intelligence Agency, the Agency for International Development.

In summer 1992, Cuny went to Somalia and reported that the situation was "one of the worst that relief agencies have ever faced." He examined the clans' wars, the state of the markets in provincial towns and the international response. The feeding stations established by the agencies were acting as a magnet, Mogadishu's population had exploded and food had become currency. He recommended a U.S. military intervention to help a wider distribution of food so that people would not be drawn into the cities.

Cuny also warned against the dangers of sending in too much food and too large a force. Above all, he cautioned the military to stay out of "the concrete snakepit" of Mogadishu, the capital. Such advice was ignored. Pentagon logisticians insisted that the U.S. Army had to control Mogadishu.

N o w , at the end of 1993, Cuny was in Bosnia, where the brutal war of ethnic cleansing between Serbs, Croats and the Muslim-dominated Bosnian government was in its second winter. Hundreds of thousands of civilians, either driven from their homes or cowering within them, were being kept alive by food convoys and an airlift into Muslim-controlled Sarajevo organized by what was now the world's largest relief agency, the United Nations High Commissioner for Refugees, UNHCR. (In 1987, UNHCR had assisted 12 million people around the world; by 1993 this figure had doubled to some 25 million. At the same time the agency's expenditures had tripled from $500 million to $1.3 billion.)

Soros had pledged $50 million to Bosnia. Cuny had advised that the money would best be spent on restoring the utilities in Sarajevo. Soros had flown into Sarajevo on an old Russian Ilyushin-76 cargo plane rented to the United Nations. Accompanying him were Aryeh Neier, the president of one of Soros's philanthropic vehicles, the Open Society Fund, and Lionel Rosenblatt, the head of Refugees International, an effective Washington advocacy group for refugees which Soros supported. Our feet rested on some thirty tons of gas piping, paid for by Soros. Cuny met us at the airport and, as he gave a calm description of the hazards of life, drove us swiftly in an armored Land-Rover through heavily shelled streets, whose pulverized houses reminded me of Cambodia, to the government's presidency building, where the Bosnian branch of Open Society had an office.

The quarter million or so people in Sarajevo were virtually imprisoned there—by Serbs, by Croats, by their own government and by rules the UN had been forced to agree to as the price of its relief operation. They had almost no light, water or heat, and were almost entirely dependent on food brought in by UNHCR convoys and airlift. And they were target practice for Serb gunners in the surrounding hills.

Today was a quiet day in Sarajevo for snipers and mortars and shells, Cuny told us. People knew which streets were safe from snipers; these were filled with pedestrians, cyclists and some people pulling little carts laden with water containers. Other people were lining up for cigarettes, still made in Sarajevo, which they traded for bread.

Winter had now come to Bosnia, and the plight of the people seemed far grimmer than the previous year, when winter was exceptionally mild. Most of the trees around Sarajevo had already been cut down for fuel. After twenty months of siege, people were more depleted and demoralized. Last year 75 percent of supplies had come on commercial trucks. Now the roads were blocked by warring armies. The villages and small towns of central Bosnia were in even worse shape than Sarajevo; almost no UN convoys had got through for weeks.

At the presidency building, we were hustled upstairs through cold, darkened passages to meet with the local people whose work in the independent media or relief effort Soros was financing. Everyone sat in clouds of cigarette smoke, bundled in their overcoats; the cracks of more intense sniping could be heard outside. A psychologist from the hospital said the incarceration in Sarajevo was causing serious stress disorders: "We don't know what long-term impact that will have. Maybe I'll be a fat man in the future, but I don't know about my mental state." Probably most Sarajevans would have liked to leave, but they could not. The airport divided them from other parts of Bosnia and separated them from the world; neither the Serbs nor the Bosnian government would allow ordinary Bosnians to leave on the UN planes and, to protect its humanitarian airlift, the United Nations rigidly enforced this embargo. The airlift did not break the siege; it dented it.

We drove to see General Francis Briquemont, the Belgian UN force commander in Sarajevo. The general was disillusioned by his time in Bosnia. He said that the Croats were just as brutal as the Serbs. Like many UN officials in Bosnia, he had also come to distrust the Muslim-dominated government. As we left, General Briquemont said that if he ever wrote his memoirs he would call it, "General, something must be done."

In the late afternoon Soros and his team met with representatives of the principal humanitarian agencies in Sarajevo at the Holiday Inn, the only functioning hotel, whose shattered windows were covered with UN-supplied plastic sheeting. The conference room was lit by candles on long tables; again everyone sat around in their coats. The scene resembled a seventeenth-century Dutch oil painting, a meeting of conspirators in a war. And in one sense that was indeed what it was—an open conspiracy to try to bring help. But how to direct help to the victims rather than to those responsible for the conflict was always the problem.

Soros asked them all to tell him what they thought Sarajevo

needed. Someone said that the problem was not of money but of access. A man from UNICEF said he would make himself unpopular, but he was still going to say that all sides, including the Muslim government, had abused and betrayed the people. In other words, not just the Serbs were to blame, but also the Croats and the Muslims.

That night surgeons, theater directors, writers, engineers and other prominent Sarajevans came through the dark streets to dinner at the Holiday Inn. It was an extraordinary occasion. Everyone came smartly dressed; despite the lack of water and electricity, the women were beautifully coiffed and turned out. The effort was remarkable.

One UNHCR official charged with protecting human rights and often lives argued that the war in Bosnia was now a series of battles for money and power, sustained by violent mafias whose control over the black market was absolute and whose influence over the armies was enormous. "The mafias fight for turf and finance their battles from the booty they steal from the civilian population," this official said. "They stoke the fires of nationalism and ethnicity in order to create an environment of fear and vulnerability."

Soros ended his visit to Sarajevo denouncing the United Nations. "Sarajevo is a concentration camp and the UN is part of the system that maintains it," he said. The UN was "allowing the Serbs to decide what humanitarian aid should be brought in to enable the concentration camp to survive at the absolutely minimum level. The only justification of the UN's presence here would be if it was lifting the siege. If not, then the UN and especially the European Community must accept responsibility for preserving the concentration camp."

This stark accusation carried truth, but it did not reflect the complexity of Bosnia. It was under pressure from the humanitarian community and the media that one Security Council resolution after another had driven the United Nations deeper and deeper into the conflict. Originally charged only with protecting humanitarian convoys, it was now supposed to protect whole Muslim communities known as safe areas, including Sarajevo. "Humanitarianism" was forcing governments to act, and it was also being exploited by governments as a cover for their political failures. UN humanitarian aid to Bosnia had undoubtedly kept many people alive, but it had also sustained the war which had killed many others. Intervention was prolonging the conflict. It had also led to serious splits within NATO

and with Russia. As in Somalia and elsewhere, peacekeepers, humanitarian workers, refugees and the internally displaced were now all
pawns to be played by the warlords and their minions. The European
Union's chief negotiator, David Owen, had recently suggested that
there was a danger that any sort of intervention in civil wars did just
that. "We can help with humanitarian aid. But let us not forget that
we are feeding the warriors, we are interfering with the dynamics of
war."

As we left the Holiday Inn for the airport, a rare water tanker was
filling the hotel's own tanks. Around it were dozens of people—children, old people, well-dressed middle-aged women—waiting with
plastic cans and buckets to catch the water leaking from the hoses.
They were remarkably patient; no one fought to the front. Those
who managed to fill their containers lugged them away, avoiding the
line of Serb sniper fire just yards from the hotel. So did those whose
jars were still empty.

That evening we heard that a Serb mortar had just crashed
through the roof of a school killing three children and their teacher
and grievously wounding many more. The dead were taken to the
morgue with labels tied to their toes. It was a quiet day in Sarajevo.

It would not be a quiet winter. The intransigence of the combatants, the mistakes combined with the moral purpose of the international community and the limits of humanitarianism meant that it
would be grotesque.

A few weeks later, I visited Sarajevo again—just after the appalling
mortar attack on the central marketplace in which sixty-eight people
were slaughtered. I stayed with Cuny.

I took notes of Fred talking, talking, talking, endlessly as ever:
"Need to rethink entire system. Present-day relief organizations all
started after World War II. After Europe, caseloads shifted to warm
Third World. Now shifting back again. Back to Europe, Russia and its
former satellites. What are the implications? Costs are greater. Need
more calories in cold weather. More food, heavier food. Not just
blankets, sleeping bags. Need heating oil. Probably costs ten times as
much to care for a Bosnian as a Cambodian. Also far fewer markets;
in former USSR can't just go out and buy things.

"Breakdown in neutrality. Growth of factions. Growth of mafias. More and more need for military protection of humanitarian operations. Politicians don't understand peacekeeping. In Bosnia the West wanted the UN to create 'safe areas' like the Allies had done in northern Iraq. Impossible. UN can't do that—it doesn't have the resources, structures, chain of command. Somalia went bad because they moved from fighting the famine to trying to rebuild the nation. Voluntary agency staff often too young and inexperienced. No institutional memory.

"Major field operations almost always hampered by slow deployment. In Bosnia it took the UN High Commissioner for Refugees (in many ways the best UN agency today) 8 months to mobilize nongovernmental organizations; inadequate logistics support; poor military cohesion; bad relations between the UN and NGOs. In northern Iraq things worked well so long as the U.S. military was in charge—after that, quarrels developed; inadequate rules of engagement. In Bosnia, UN restricted to protecting UN personnel and equipment rather than civilians. No strategies from international community."

AFTER Bosnia, Cuny went to Albania, where he tried to help rebuild the school system, and then to one of those wars from which the West deliberately averted its eyes—Russia's assault on its satellite Chechnya, to stop its lunge for independence under its warlord, Czhokar Dudayev. In this case, the Western calculus was that it was more important to preserve Boris Yeltsin's government in Moscow than to protect Chechens seeking self-determination.

On his second trip, in April 1995, Cuny set off into Chechnya with two Russian Red Cross doctors and a young Russian woman interpreter. They all vanished. His disappearance led to an extraordinary search led by his family and by his friend Lionel Rosenblatt of Refugees International. The search was joined by American and European aid workers, Russians, Chechens, American diplomats, FBI agents, CIA agents, the White House, people from the Soros Foundation, UN officials, journalists and friends from all over the world. President Bill Clinton even asked President Yeltsin to help find the missing aid workers.

To no avail. Cuny had become one of the hundreds of aid workers killed in the last decade in the crises they tried to alleviate. Four and a half years later a group of Chechens produced what they said was Fred Cuny's body and offered it for ransom to his family.

o

IN the course of writing this book, I made a number of trips to Bosnia, Kosovo and other states of the former Yugoslavia, to Cambodia, Sierra Leone, New York, Washington, Paris, Rwanda, Burundi, Algeria, Nigeria, Albania and Afghanistan. I tried to choose places that represent different sorts of provocation to war and different levels of response and commitment by the international community.

Some of my trips were made in the company of Kofi Annan, first when he was head of the UN's peacekeeping department and later after he became UN secretary general. When he was elected to the position at the end of 1996, I said to him that he had been given a job from hell. That was not quite accurate, but as his tenure lengthened I wondered at his predicament—a good and uncommon man invested with the hopes and moral authority of the world, charged to deal with evil, and at the same time buffeted and limited in that task by the world's principalities and powers.

One way of looking at that, suggested by U.S. Deputy Secretary of State Strobe Talbott, is that in the last ten years we have seen the interaction of four forces—three benign but not yet employed to best effect, one malign and daunting. The malign force has been most visible in the warlords who have dominated the 1990s. The two who stand out are Saddam Hussein and Slobodan Milosevic, but their behavior is aped by many lesser warlords, satraps, dictators and demagogues around the world.

The three benign forces are the nongovernmental organizations, represented here by Fred Cuny; the United Nations and its ideals, which Kofi Annan has come to personify more than any other international official for decades; and the liberal democracies, led (or not) by the United States, which, largely under the Clinton administration, has had a difficult time in adjusting to the new demands upon it as the sole remaining superpower or, as its critics see it, the Great Hegemon.

Among those I met along my journeys were lightly armed UN

peacekeepers with ambitious mandates, unarmed monitors, humanitarian aid workers from nongovernmental organizations, election officials and UN volunteers—all trying to deal with the chaos and the suffering caused by failed states, by tribalism and by warlordism in the post–Cold War world. I also talked with some of the protagonists of the wars, and collected, according to my bad habit, thousands of pages of documents from different agencies and individuals dealing with or thinking about these issues.

Some of the places I visited were bathed by the light of the West's concern—Bosnia and Kosovo, for example; others were obscured by our lack of interest. Afghanistan was one of the latter. During the last decade of the Cold War, Afghanistan was an important proxy war zone, with CIA-supplied mujahideen guerrillas fighting Soviet tanks and helicopters. After the fall of the Soviet-backed government in 1992, the country became a battleground for various groups of mujahideen struggling against each other. The capital, Kabul, was half destroyed in the fighting; the countryside was lawless. Since 1996 order, of a sort, has been imposed by the Taliban, a ruthless group of fundamentalist zealots who suppressed women and were backed by Pakistan. For the most part, the continuing warfare in Afghanistan was now obscured by Western indifference.

On a brief trip there in fall 1997, I drove east of the mountains of rubble in Kabul before dawn with a CNN television crew to visit a tank position of the Taliban armed forces defending the capital. CNN had visited it a few months before. One of the tank crew they had met then had apparently since been killed; the others were happy to have an audience. The CNN men were careful not to request it, but the Afghan gunners obligingly shot their tank cannon across the valley at their unseen enemy many miles away. I wondered if anyone had died because of our prurient interest in seeing smoke and hearing noise coming out of the barrel of a gun again.

Less than a year later, the Taliban massacred up to eight thousand of their enemies in the town of Mazar-i-Sharif. They were killed because they were Hazara men, ethnic enemies of the Taliban. Many were shot in the streets or in their homes or in hospital beds; others were boiled or asphyxiated, crammed into metal containers in the relentless August sun. Victims were left in the streets as a warning, to be eaten by dogs.

The crime was remote and unseen, but it was quickly documented by Amnesty International in London, by Human Rights Watch in New York and by the UN Commission on Human Rights. None of these reports caused any stir. The Western media was preoccupied with the Monica Lewinsky scandal, the U.S. bombing of a chemical factory in Khartoum and the deteriorating situation in Kosovo, where deaths were then numbered in the scores, not the thousands.

One can say that in the last fifty years there have been three different periods, three different kinds of warfare. First, during and just after the Second World War, conflict was classical—states fighting each other. Second, during the Cold War and the period of decolonization, governments fought guerrilla liberation movements, which were often based on the desire for independence and on some form of political morality. But the central dynamic of the Cold War established sides: parties were usually identified as pro-Soviet or pro-West.

With the end of the Cold War, established patterns vanished. In many of the new conflicts there were multiple parties or interlocutors, and often none had real authority or decisive force. In this new, third period, which started after the fall of the Berlin wall, the world was now in a period of nonstructured or destructured conflict, sometimes called "identity based." Now there was something approaching chaos in some parts of the world. Others have weathered storms with relative success.

Where previously the parties, guerrillas and governments, received assistance from their Cold War patrons, now they needed to raise money for weapons. This had created closer links between political aims and crime in Somalia, Liberia and Bosnia. Now, more than ever, war was often made by local warlords or bandits setting their own policies. Mafias multiplied.

By the mid-nineties, the International Committee of the Red Cross judged that the human costs of disasters—mostly manmade—were overwhelming the world's ability to respond. There were fifty-six wars being waged around the world; there were at least 17 million refugees and 26 million who had lost their homes, plus another 300 million affected by disasters unrelated to war. The Red Cross urged a massive review of the way the world responds to disaster and to suffering.

★ ★ ★

I often feel that writing books about even recent historical events is like archaeology. It is a question of collecting a few thousand pieces of a vast mosaic. The full design would be one of the world depicting, as with gods blowing winds across the sky, all the forces that play upon man and geography.

I know that I have managed to find, collect and assemble only fragments or at best segments of the entire picture of keeping peace in the post–Cold War world. But I hope that, as with a partially reassembled mosaic from Ephesus or Pompeii, these fragments give an adequately accurate portrayal of the whole.

In the fragments I have tried to reconstruct, some characters emerge dimly, others with great clarity. The clearest and most obvious of all are the warlords who have dominated this decade. Indeed, at one level the history of the nineties is the story of how the international community has attempted to confront and control warlords—Saddam Hussein; Slobodan Milosevic, Franjo Tudjman and Radovan Karadzic in the former Yugoslavia; Pol Pot and Hun Sen in Cambodia; Mohammed Aideed in Somalia; Foday Sankoh, the terrorist rebel leader in Sierra Leone; General Raoul Cédras of Haiti; Jonas Savimbi, the leader of the UNITA rebels in Angola; Laurent Kabila, the successor to Marshal Mobutu in Zaire/Congo; and many others from Kabul to Kurdistan whose names have not, perhaps fortunately, become members of the international household, but who have nonetheless held autocratic and destructive if not criminal sway over the peoples they control.

The warlords are easy to identify. Much more difficult to discern, let alone describe, are the men and women, often anonymous, whom the international community sends to corral them. What are the particular problems faced by a Japanese UN official in the Balkans, a Canadian general caught in genocide in Rwanda, a French volunteer in Cambodia, a Brazilian refugee official in Congo—or a Ghanaian international civil servant charged with the moral leadership of the world?

I hope this book shows in some part how difficult, if not impossible, their decisions are, faced with the conflicting demands of politicians at home, members of the Security Council, generals on the ground and the evil which they attempt to face down.

And beyond all that there is the question of whether intervention, often demanded for emotional reasons, is necessarily wise. Consider an older example—the American Civil War and the demands for intervention it created in Europe.

After the war began in 1861, its carnage and its threat to international stability, and particularly to the cotton trade on which millions of people in France and Britain depended, were greeted with horror in Europe. As is almost always the case in matters of international diplomacy, motives were mixed, but as well as mercantile concern, there was genuine dismay that the most important experiment in democracy in the world had broken down. By 1862, Britain and the United States were almost at war. The French and Russian governments seriously discussed intervention.

When the war finally ended with the defeat of the Confederacy in April 1865, 620,000 Americans had been killed—more Americans than were to die in the First and Second World Wars combined. By then European opinion had shifted in favor of the North and the Union that had survived. The notion of self-determination for the South had been killed forever.

How different it might have been if dispatches from Bull Run had traveled instantly through the air rather than slowly by ship across the ocean. Imagine what the effect on Europe might have been if CNN camera crews had been showing Europeans every night the prison camps of Andersonville, the Battle of Gettysburg, the burning of Atlanta or Sherman's march through the South. European opinion would have been even more aroused, and it might have reinforced the inclinations of the French and British governments to intervene to "manage" the conflict. Would they have sent an occupying force of "peacekeepers"? How long would it have stayed? What would have been the effect of such an intervention? Professor Michael Howard, a former professor of war at Oxford, has said, with well-chosen understatement, "I think we can agree that it would have been adverse." Imagine Abraham Lincoln and Jefferson Davis shaking hands on the lawn at 10 Downing Street or the Elysée Palace under the benevolent eyes of Lord Palmerston and Napoléon III. Such an intervention would not have been very welcome to many people in the United States. By what "right" would they have intervened? What good would it have done?

If the prospect of having their conflict "managed" for them by foreigners (however well intentioned) would have been unwelcome to the American people then, why should it be more acceptable to other peoples in the world today just because the motives of those who believe fervently that "something must be done" are often decent?

Today "humanitarianism" often rules. It becomes a sop to international concern, and then it can be dangerous. Reconciliation is much favored in today's peacekeeping efforts, but sometimes the desire for it is unrealistic. After the American Civil War, reconciliation took decades—some would say much longer—to develop between the North and South. Today we demand instant reconciliation. The examples of Bosnia, Rwanda and Kosovo show that that often just cannot happen.

1

Another World War

O N a dark afternoon in January 1999, with the wind chill factor down to minus ten and snow rushing around outside the thirty-eighth floor of the United Nations headquarters in New York, the secretary general, Kofi Annan, could be forgiven for feeling beleaguered. Nineteen ninety-eight, he said to me, "was a hell of a year. But I think 1999 will be worse."

Eleven months before, he had been hailed in much of the world as a savior after persuading Saddam Hussein to permit UN inspectors to resume their search for Iraqi weapons of mass destruction, thus stopping the United States and Great Britain from bombing Iraq. One newspaper called him "the world's secular pope," a phrase which recalls Joseph Stalin's mocking question, "How many divisions has the pope?"

But within weeks Saddam had reneged on his agreement with Annan; Iraq continued to flout countless resolutions of the Security Council. For months Annan had continued to try to be the peacemaker, and in November 1998 he finessed another delay in a U.S. attack aimed at forcing Iraq to comply with the resolutions, to the fury of some American policymakers. But in December the United States and Britain lost patience and responded to Iraqi intransigence with four days of bombing just before Ramadan and Christmas.

The Anglo-American action split the Security Council. There was no precise warning when it began on December 16. Members of the council were debating the crisis when their cell phones started ringing almost in unison. Some, particularly the Russian ambassador, Sergei Lavrov, and the French ambassador, Alain Dejammet, were furious. Annan made a short statement: "This is a sad day for the United Nations, and for the world. . . . It is also a very sad day for me personally."

Annan tried to find a way of reuniting the council. It was not easy. He had continual calls or visits from the Russians and the French to complain about the attacks. The French were especially bitter; from President Jacques Chirac down, they denounced *"les anglo-saxons,"* by whom they meant not only the United States and Britain but also Richard Butler, the tough and sometimes undiplomatic Australian chairman of the UN's Iraq arms inspectors, UNSCOM—the United Nations Special Commission, which had been set up to disarm Iraq completely of its weapons of mass destruction after the Gulf war in 1991. Butler's December 1998 report alleging continued Iraqi obstruction had been the casus belli for the bombing. Butler must go, Chirac said several times to Annan. The Russians said the same, more brutally and more publicly.

In early January 1999, articles in the *Washington Post* and the *Boston Globe* quoted "confidants" of the secretary general complaining that the United States had placed spies on Butler's teams to collect information not just for the UN but also for Washington. The Iraqis had alleged this of UNSCOM all along, and a dissident American inspector, Scott Ritter, who had resigned from UNSCOM in 1998, had made similar allegations.

Publicly Annan responded that there was no evidence for such allegations, but he added, "Obviously, were these charges true, it would be damaging to the United Nations' disarmament work in Iraq and elsewhere." These remarks aroused the fury of the *Washington Post,* which accused him of "the sly undermining" of the UN's own inspectors. In the *New York Times,* the columnist A. M. Rosenthal, who had characterized Annan's policy toward Saddam as "diligent appeasement," now described the secretary general as "Saddam's greatest single asset at the UN." A long profile in *The New Republic* by David Rieff, the author of *Slaughterhouse,* a swinging attack on the United Nations in Bosnia, castigated Annan as "The Indecent Decent Man" and said that he refused "to regard the evil in the world realistically." The UN Secretariat under Annan, Rieff charged, was "in principle and in practice committed to the peaceful resolution of conflicts almost at any price."

Other articles asserted that Annan was as eager to rid himself of the turbulent Richard Butler as the French, Russians and Chinese. It was certainly true that among many of Annan's staff, Butler was about as popular as a whore in a nunnery. They saw him as too close to the United States and too publicly belligerent toward Iraq. Annan insisted to me, however, that Butler was not the problem, and that since the United States and Britain had justified their recent bombing by his report, there was no way Butler could be quickly eased aside, whatever the French and the Russians demanded.

At the Council on Foreign Relations in mid-January 1999, Annan defended himself publicly against the attacks: "Whatever means I have employed in my efforts in dealing with Iraq, my ends have never been in question." These included disarming Iraq and reintegrating its people into the international community. "By precedent, by principle, by charter and by duty, I am bound to seek those ends through peaceful diplomacy," Annan said.

Annan was calling attention to the limits of his role. Miracles are rare; in the end he was seen merely to have delayed war and was now being accused by some of having played into Saddam's hands. Annan insisted that a UN secretary general cannot be judged by the same standards as a head of state because he is bound by the demands and interests of the UN's 185 members (188 by the end of 1999). "With no enforcement capacity and no executive power beyond the organization," Annan told his audience at the Council on Foreign Relations, "a secretary general is armed only with tools of his own making. He is invested only with the power that a united Security Council may wish to bestow, and the moral authority entrusted to him by the charter."

There is a vast gulf between what millions around the world believe about the United Nations and the reality. The idealized belief is that the UN is an independent and objective body of nations, gathered under one blue flag, to bring peace, perfect justice and economic development. Annan, a practicing Christian, shares some of this quasi-religious belief in the institution.

What the idealists often fail to reckon with is both the power of and the divisions within the Security Council, particularly its permanent five members, who have the power of veto. Back in 1945, the five major powers had been given the veto to guarantee their commitment to the new world body and to enable them to prevent the council from authorizing force against them. Otherwise, they were supposed to exercise collective responsibility for "the maintenance of international peace and security." They did not treat the veto with such reserve, and during the Cold War it was constantly invoked and abused—especially by the Soviet Union.

It is a relic of World War II that the United States, Russia, China, Britain and France dominate the impossible but probably essential world body. But they do, and attempts to change the membership to reflect more accurately the world on the edge of the millennium have always foundered. None of the permanent five wishes to leave the council, and too many of the other members of the UN wish to join. So the agreements or the divisions between the victors of 1945 still determine much of the direction of the world. They can either project the power of the United Nations or tie its hands. That is the reality, as against the ideal.

Annan was invested with the moral authority of the charter of the United Nations, but this did not and could not override the realities of power as displayed in the council. The expectations of the secretary general were always great, but his ability to deliver was never as broad.

IRAQ was not the only crisis at this time. There was the continued emergency in Kosovo, a province of Serbia, the dominant republic in what remained of Yugoslavia. There the Serbs and the Kosovo Liberation Army (KLA) were held in an uneasy truce by the presence of unarmed Western monitors from the Organization for Security and Cooperation in Europe (OSCE), backed up by the threat of NATO bombing of the Serbs.

Annan had just received a briefing paper from his senior staff which warned him that the human crisis in Kosovo was getting worse and worse. The KLA was spreading its power in the countryside; the level of violence was increasing and moving into urban areas. "There is a strong apprehension that the KLA may be moving towards IRA tactics," read this report. There was a real fear that clashes would escalate out of control. The government in Belgrade considered that the KLA was preparing for war, and was itself again on the offensive against KLA strongholds and neighboring civilians alike; local Serbs were arming themselves. There was no dialogue between the two sides; in the face of Serb repression, the moderate Albanian leadership had been sidelined by the KLA radicals. (For years, those concerned about Kosovo had warned that the confrontation could turn violent; for years, the West had failed to act on those warnings.)

In an agreement of October 1998, the American negotiator Richard Holbrooke had managed to persuade President Milosevic of Yugoslavia to accept these unarmed observers from the OSCE to monitor a partial withdrawal of Serb troops from Kosovo. The deal had then been seen as an achievement. But ten weeks later the monitors were still not fully deployed. Originally, two thousand had been envisaged, but recruitment was not easy, and so far only eight hundred were on the ground. They were being dragged into the conflict beyond their mandate. Recently, for example, they had mediated the release of Yugoslav soldiers captured by the KLA. Annan was warned by his staff, "With the accumulation of such extra tasks the KVM [the monitors] could face the same problems as UNPROFOR in Bosnia." This was a warning with substance. UNPROFOR, the United Nations Protection Force in Bosnia from 1992 to 1995, was one of the unhappiest UN peacekeeping missions in recent times.

As with Iraq, the Security Council was divided on Kosovo, with Russia being, as always, more sympathetic to the Serbs than other members. China, always fearing that Tibet, whose independence it has crushed since the 1950s, could be next, was unsympathetic to any intervention in other nations' affairs. The council's division meant that it was often unable to react to developments on the ground. It had even failed to agree to a statement on the capture of the Yugoslav soldiers. There was no reason to believe that it would be able to agree on any course of action if the situation deteriorated and international involvement was urgently needed. "The UN has little leverage on events and is not getting any guidance from the Council," Annan was told.

Talks on an interim arrangement for autonomy for Kosovo were getting nowhere. By January 1999, the KLA had reoccupied parts of the province from which the Serbs had driven them in 1998. Armed incidents were increasing wherever Serbs and Albanians were in contact. In mid-January the bodies of forty-five Albanian Kosovar villagers, including three women and a twelve-year-old boy, were found on a hillside around the village of Racak, fifteen miles south of the capital, Pristina.

Kofi Annan called for a full investigation. The international observers blamed the Yugoslav security forces. Yugoslav officials accused the KLA of staging the massacre with its own dead and said the international monitors were party to the lie. The Yugoslav army's mobile anti-aircraft cannon pounded Racak. The Belgrade government then ordered the head of the observers, the American diplomat William Walker, out of the country. Louise Arbour, the UN prosecutor for war crimes in the former Yugoslavia, was turned back from the border when she tried to enter the country to carry out an investigation.

Even though the Russians condemned both the massacre and Walker's expulsion by Belgrade (later suspended), the Security Council remained divided. Some members feared that only NATO air strikes against the Serbs would stop the growing Serbian abuse of the Albanian population. Other members were afraid of NATO becoming, in effect, "the air force of the KLA." There were cruel echoes of the dilemmas the UN had faced in Bosnia in the early nineties.

AND there were many other issues crowding the secretary general's agenda with greater or lesser urgency that January.

In Haiti, the poorest country in the Western Hemisphere, the 1994 UN intervention to restore democracy, backed if not controlled by the United States, had at first been thought of as a success. But when I went there in January 1999, there seemed to be almost no government at all; the country was spiraling down into greater impoverishment and anarchy and the outside world—especially the United States—had no policy whatsoever beyond somehow preventing Haitians from fleeing in boats to Florida.

In Cambodia, over which the United Nations had established a form of trusteeship in the early 1990s, there was now fierce debate over the fate of Khmer Rouge leaders who had been involved in the mass murder of over a million Cambodians in the 1970s, and who had never been brought to trial. Over the past few months, the

Khmer Rouge guerrilla movement had finally collapsed. Pol Pot, the movement's principal leader, had died in 1998, but other leaders had been given amnesties by the Cambodian government. To add insult to injury one group of senior Khmer Rouge who had returned from their border redoubts had just been treated by the government to a tourist trip around the country. Why, more and more Westerners, if not Cambodians, were asking, when international tribunals had been established to try alleged war criminals from Yugoslavia and Rwanda, was nothing being done about the Khmer Rouge?

The gloomy backdrop to these and other crises was Africa. Indeed, Annan said that the Security Council was now spending 60 percent of its time on Africa.

In Angola, which had been torn by civil war for almost a quarter of a century, the UN peacekeeping process, which had continued through alternating periods of war and peace since 1991, had collapsed; all-out war began again in December 1998; the country was on the cusp of another disaster. The return to war marked the end of the difficult, incomplete peace process that had begun with the Lusaka Protocol of November 1994. The process had been overseen by two UN peacekeeping missions, which had cost the international community about $1.5 billion. Two UN planes had just been shot down over Angola, with all twenty-three people on board killed. (On board the second plane was the son of the pilot of the first, who had gone to search for the wreckage of his father's flight.)

Annan's senior staff warned him that "heavy fighting is taking place in several regions of the country, with dire humanitarian consequences." The government had launched a major attack against the rebel UNITA forces led by Jonas Savimbi, whose belligerence was one of the main reasons for the return to war. At the same time the government had embarked on a propaganda campaign against the UN because of its failure to induce UNITA to remain in the peace process.

The Angolan government wanted the current UN mission, MONUA, to leave when its mandate expired at the end of February. But some African countries were urging the UN to stay and were complaining about "double standards" if the UN left Angola but stayed in equally difficult environments such as the former Yugoslavia. Annan, however, told the Security Council that there was no longer any basis on which the UN could remain in Angola and recommended that its armed thousand-man force of peacekeepers be gradually reduced and then removed.

Angola was not the only African country at war. For several months at least fourteen countries had been fighting in Congo, defending or attacking the regime of President Laurent Kabila, who had been pushed into power by many of them less than two years before. This conflict was sometimes called Africa's Great War. Kabila was aided by Zimbabwe, Angola, Namibia and Chad. The rebels were supported by Uganda, Rwanda, Zambia, Burundi, Kenya, Sudan, Ethiopia, Republic of Congo and others. There was a real threat that regional ambitions and hatreds could tear apart the postcolonial map of Central Africa. Wars between (rather than within) African countries had hardly happened after independence and during the Cold War. Now they were becoming commonplace.

Farther north the UN was still coordinating Operation Lifeline Sudan, a relief operation for the starving victims of the Sudanese civil war. It cost $1 million a day to fly in seventeen thousand tons of food. This was keeping alive many hundreds of thousands, but once again and inevitably, there were questions about how far the aid also helped to sustain the government forces or the rebels of the south who had been fighting them for years.

To the east of Sudan more war loomed. Annan had just dispatched one of his senior staff, Mohammed Sahnoun, a seasoned Algerian diplomat, to Eritrea and Ethiopia, where a border war, which had begun just after Annan had visited both countries in May 1998, threatened to become a full-scale conflict. In December, the Organization of African Unity had come up with a framework agreement to try to settle the dispute, but Eritrea had still not accepted it. On January 12, Eritrea announced that it had received intelligence reports that Ethiopia was planning to launch new attacks. Ethiopia dismissed this announcement as a diversionary tactic to shift international attention from Eritrea's "aggression against Ethiopia." The language of both sides was becoming more vitriolic. Escalation of the war was imminent, Annan was warned. At a meeting in his office with Ethiopia's permanent representative at the UN, Annan stressed that a resort to force would have disastrous consequences. It happened nonetheless. In the next few weeks tens of thousands died, untelevised and unremarked by the world.

And of the African crises confronting Annan in January 1999 none was more immediately horrible than Sierra Leone, which was consumed by a savage civil war between an elected but ineffective government and a rebel group. In 1996, after decades of corrupt military dictatorship, elections had been held and a civilian government created under a former UN official, Ahmad Tejan Kabbah. In 1997 he was overthrown by the rebels and then restored to power by a West African peacekeeping force led by Nigeria, which had been unsuccessfully trying to defeat the rebels ever since. In recent weeks the country had imploded as political and moral order collapsed.

The rebels were known as the Revolutionary United Front (RUF); their leader, Corporal Foday Sankoh, was now in jail in Freetown, the ramshackle capital. The RUF seemed to have no ideology; their trademark was to chop off the hands of peasants in the countryside. "Short sleeves or long?" the rebels would ask the peasants, and then hack at the elbow or wrist accordingly. Tens of thousands had been mutilated in this way. Over 400,000 people had fled into neighboring countries to escape.

The Nigerian role now bitterly divided the six countries of West Africa—largely along the fault line of British Commonwealth versus Francophone countries. Kabbah and the governments supporting him thought that the rebels had to be fought to the death. The Ivory Coast and Togo believed that a compromise settlement had to be negotiated. That was also Annan's belief. Senior Nigerian officials, furious that the Ivory Coast and Togo were calling them warmongers, told Annan that they thought these countries were giving the rebels clandestine support. So, perhaps, were the French, in support of their allies in those two French-speaking countries.

On January 6 the rebels fought their way into Freetown. They were under the command of Sam Bockarie, a former dancer and hairdresser, and they ran amok. They burned down the statehouse and the Nigerian embassy. Government officials and UN workers fled. Most people could not. Thousands lost their hands to the rebels' insane chopping. Food and water became scarce. Freetown's Connaught Hospital was described as "overflowing with dead." Rebel soldiers invaded the wards, shot patients and climbed into beds themselves, demanding that they be treated.

Rampaging around the city, the rebels exulted that they were punishing the people for supporting President Kabbah. Allieu, a fifty-year-old civil servant, said later, "They ordered me to put my arm in

a tree trunk and they swung an axe from behind and hacked it off;
they kept talking about Kabbah and I screamed. I didn't know anything about politics, and so they hacked off my other arm . . . blood
was spurting out, and I kept falling. They spat on me and took a
hammer and started knocking my teeth out—they danced around
me, saying, 'We've really got you now, here you will die.' " The
writer and photographer Stuart Freedman reported that Hasan Fu-
fona, whose left hand was paralyzed by polio, had his good hand
chopped off. Two sisters, Mariamatu and Aminata, were gang-raped
and both were doubly amputated. There were thousands of such victims.

The Nigerians rushed in reinforcements. The rebels killed and
burned as they were pushed back into the suburbs. Bodies littered
the streets, fed upon by vultures. Kabbah announced a cease-fire, but
Bockarie demanded the release of Foday Sankoh before he would
agree to it. He rejoiced: "We have made Freetown ungovernable."

Francis Okelo, Annan's special representative to Sierra Leone, was
shuttling between Sierra Leone and its neighbors. On January 10 he
flew into Freetown to see both Kabbah and Foday Sankoh. Okelo
urged Kabbah to compromise with Sankoh, but the president was reluctant to deal with the rebels whom, with good reason, he reckoned
to be mere murderers.

On January 14, Annan was woken by an early morning call from
President Charles Taylor of Liberia. Taylor insisted (despite all the
evidence to the contrary) that he was not arming the rebels. Taylor
claimed that he had persuaded Sam Bockarie to accept a cease-fire
and that he would announce it that day.

Later that morning President Kabbah called Annan to tell him
that the rebels were now trapped, and that was why the Liberians
were urging a cease-fire.

Kabbah told the *Times* of London that the UN and the West were
guilty of double standards. They were fighting for democracy in Iraq
and "doing nothing to defend democracy in my country." He wanted
more than "lip service" to the UN resolutions condemning the
rebels; he wanted military assistance. "I'm not asking for special
favours. I am saying that the UN should apply the same principles
across the world. If the world believes in democracy then it should
come to our aid."

His finance minister, James Jonah, similarly accused the West of double standards. It was true, he said, that more than two thousand people had died in Kosovo over the past year, but over two thousand people had been murdered by the rebels in Freetown since Christmas. Many more had had their hands and feet cut off. So why was the West concerned only with Kosovo?

It was not only in Sierra Leone that such questions were asked. Similar concerns had been expressed in or about parts of Southeast Asia, Afghanistan, Chechnya and Tajikistan, and many countries of Africa. Peace and security, the responsibilities of the United Nations, were absent in dozens of countries around the world. But in only a few of them was the UN actively engaged in finding solutions.

There is never an easy answer as to why the spotlight of international concern focuses on some conflicts more than others. Sometimes it is due to access by television, sometimes to the consequent public demand that "something must be done," sometimes to traditional national interests on the part of at least some of the permanent five. But increasingly among the rich West there is a belief that humanitarianism must now be part of national policymaking in a way which it has never been before. That conviction bestows a right to interference which cannot always be carried out, but sometimes should be. It is an ambitious doctrine, both morally and politically.

IN the early 1990s the world faced the collapse of empire for the third time this century. The first such earthquake occurred at the end of World War I. The second came with the end of colonialism after World War II. The third was caused by the death of the Soviet Union; Russia and its satellite states from the Baltic to the Black Sea and beyond were sent spinning off on independent trajectories. The world was irrevocably changed by all three ends of empire; only the third left one great power triumphant in the world.

In one way, at the end of the Cold War, the world went back to normal. For decades responses to international crises had been governed by ideology, alliance pressures and a nuclear stalemate. Now national and local interests came, once again, to the fore.

The consequences of this astonishing upheaval have been overwhelmingly beneficial, but not exclusively so. In some places, the end of the Cold War has caused political, social and humanitarian turbulence. The forces unleashed by the implosion have brought about both the creation and destruction of states. Since the early 1990s, just as those seeking the destruction of states wave the banners of ethnicity and identity, those who seek to alleviate the suffering and end the conflicts that result wave the banners of world order, humanitarianism and the international community—without always fully understanding what those concepts mean.

Perhaps one way of looking at what has happened is to remember that in political and diplomatic discourse the state has been a given. We address and attempt to understand the world at the level of states. Maps are drawn to define them and to contain them. For centuries nation-states have been the principal actors on the world stage. During a half century of Cold War the integrity of nation-states was a fundamental principle of international order. Since the end of that period the reality of the nation-state has been challenged in countries as different as Russia, Somalia, Yugoslavia, Haiti, Angola, Rwanda and many others.

States are not nations, or vice versa. Nations are social or cultural entities, groups of people who share common language, history, ethnic background, religion or culture. Senator Daniel Patrick Moynihan, a former U.S. ambassador to the United Nations, has proposed that "the nation is the 'highest' form of the ethnic group, denoting a subjective state of mind as regards to ancestry." The historian Christopher Liptak has pointed out that individuals tend to identify more with their nationality or ethnicity than with their government. This means that, if allowed, nations may become more powerful than states. Most states comprise several nations. Eric Morris of the United Nations High Commissioner for Refugees, whose responsibilities have grown a thousandfold in this period, caring for the victims of the clash of the banners, has attempted better than most I know to try to explore what has happened. He points out in a distinguished study of this bloody period, *The Limits of Mercy*, that no one really knows what "ethnicity" and "world order" actually mean. Nonetheless, they are at the center of debate about international relationships after the end of the Cold War.

How we now deal with the disjunction between statehood and nationality is one of the subjects of this book. And that means that I deal with intervention and peacekeeping. In a world that is at the same time more tightly bound by what is called globalization and yet also more broken asunder, how can states which fail and their populations be aided? And at what level—humanitarian aid by UN and nongovernmental agencies, peacekeeping by lightly armed UN soldiers in blue berets and soft-topped white vehicles, or war waged by the rich world's private army, NATO?

o

IN the second half of January 1999, the secretary general went on a trip to Europe. The most congenial stop was Ireland. The Irish government has always contributed generously to UN peacekeeping efforts and Annan was welcomed warmly. The same could not be said of Brussels, where he landed a few days later. He was there to see senior officials of the European Union and of NATO to discuss, in particular, NATO's threat to intervene in Kosovo if the Serb and Kosovar leadership could not reach an agreement which would stop the killing. He was greeted by Belgian and Rwandan families who had lost relatives in the 1994 Rwandan genocide, in which close to a million people had been murdered. They were demanding further inquiries, in particular into the failure of the UN peacekeeping department, which Annan then headed, to have done more to prevent the genocide. Shortly thereafter, Annan agreed to just such an inquiry.

At the World Economic Forum in Davos, Switzerland, at the end of January, Annan urged business to do more for its workers and to help the UN press for human rights and good governance around the world. The world pursued him. Richard Butler had just accused the Russian ambassador to the UN, Sergei Lavrov, of not telling the truth. The Russian prime minister, Yevgeni Primakov, took Annan aside and said, "If Butler stays, we leave the game."

At the beginning of the last year of the decade, there was little trace of the euphoria with which the decade had opened as the Berlin wall came tumbling down. But Annan, an optimist, saw reasons for hope. U.S. Secretary of State Madeleine Albright had called the United States "the indispensable country"; Annan said the United Nations was "the indispensable institution." He thought there was now "a new diplomacy" in which nongovernmental organizations, the International Committee of the Red Cross and the citizens of many countries could push issues on governments much more effectively than before.

I spoke to Annan in his hotel room overlooking the mountains. After discussing the crises of Kosovo, Sierra Leone and Iraq, I said, "You're negotiating all the time between different levels of evil, aren't you?"

"This is the problem and they are constantly shifting," he replied.

"You are almost halfway through your term now. It looks like a terrifying ride," I said.

"It is a terrifying ride!"

"What do you think is the most important thing the secretary general can do? What's the best way to use your last two years?"

"Everything I touch is a race against time—to save lives, to stop killing. One of the areas where we have really tried to make a difference is to really get the governments and public to get engaged in [the] issue of good governance, to respect [the] rule of law and human rights—to let people know they do have rights and not everything is at the beck and call of governments.

"The other area is to try to make a difference in people's lives by focusing on development—health, clean water, etc. The difficulty is that the strategy is not only to get increased assistance but also investment. But no one is going to invest in Africa with all its crises and divisions. I hammer this home to African leaders whenever I have a chance. They listen and they say, 'You are right,' but then they go home and do nothing about it—they carry on their wars."

In the last decade the international community has edged toward new solutions, half a step at a time, and some steps backward. A new global architecture is being created through many initiatives of which the secretary general is, when the international community agrees, the standard-bearer. This architecture includes the international ban on land mines, the war crimes tribunals in the former Yugoslavia and Rwanda and the International Criminal Court. Popular consensus can be formed on all of these despite reluctance or even opposition from governments.

"Is there any such thing as an international community anymore?" I asked Annan. "How does it use you?"

"It's interesting. For small governments it does exist because they realize they have to band together to tackle issues around the world. The big boys move in and out of the concept of the international community. When it suits them, they go along with the others—otherwise they go it alone.

"I think there is another sort of international community," he said. "In many countries a public consensus has developed to fight on matters of international concern like land mines and to push for an international criminal court. It's much more solid in some ways than governments banding together, and often leaders cannot ignore it."

But he acknowledged that public opinion can be fickle. "It was public pressure that forced governments to go into Somalia and Bosnia and then forced them out again." Television audiences in the rich industrial countries, appalled by the suffering, demand that "something be done," but they or their governments are often unwilling to meet the necessary costs. That paradox is at the heart of many attempts to make peace in the last decade. It can be harmful.

2

From Phnom Penh to Sarajevo

EUPHORIA followed the end of the Gulf war and the success of the U.S.-led UN mission to evict Iraq from Kuwait. President George Bush spoke (briefly) of a new world order. Even though that very quickly came to be seen as optimistic, in the years after the Gulf war there was a belief that now much of the world could be put to right. With the Cold War over, reason, not politics, might prevail. No longer was the world divided into blocs led by the rationale of MAD (Mutually Assured Destruction).

Since the Gulf war the Security Council has consistently expanded what it regards as "threats to the peace, breaches of the peace and acts of aggression" to allow it to take action under Chapter VII, the enforcement chapter of the UN Charter. Thus in Resolution 687, after the end of the Gulf war, the Security Council acted in order to restrain Iraq's *future* behavior and declared the flow of refugees caused by Iraq's persecution of its minorities to be threats to peace. Resolution 687 set up the UN Special Commission to eliminate Iraq's weapons of mass destruction and to control future nuclear, chemical and biological weapons; it established a mechanism for demarcating the border between Iraq and Kuwait; and it provided for payment of war reparations out of future Iraqi oil revenues. Resolution 688 did not call specifically for intervention, but it led to the establishment of safe havens and no-fly zones in northern and southern Iraq intended to protect the Kurdish population in the north and the Shia Muslims in the south.

In the first flush of post–Cold War enthusiasm, the Security Council became more and more assertive. The number of resolutions increased exponentially: in 1993 alone there were ninety-three resolutions, compared to an average of fifteen a year during the Cold War years of 1945–88.

There has been much more for the council to be concerned with. Civil wars or internal conflicts have been a growth industry in the 1990s. The alliances (sometimes harsh, but restricting) of the Cold War system have been replaced by much more traditional politics as usual. The post–Cold War world has exaggerated ethnic hatreds, encouraged the failure of states, exacerbated internal conflicts (or at least prolonged them) and led to more global disorder. Rivalries within states and between states and transborder ethnic, tribal and religious groups are now more powerful. In 1996, about forty-two million people were said to be affected by internal conflicts or civil wars. At the height of international involvement in 1994 some $7.2 billion a year was being spent on aid to the victims of violence.

At the same time, with the Security Council's expansion of what it regarded as "threats to peace," there was a sudden and massive growth in UN peacekeeping missions. In the first forty-three years of the UN, till the end of 1988, there were thirteen peacekeeping missions. In the next three and a half years there were five new operations, and by the end of 1994, a further seventeen peacekeeping missions had been launched around the world, with some eighty thousand peacekeepers serving in them—an extraordinary explosion.

Since 1990 the word "humanitarian" has featured in more and more resolutions that deal with the effects or the residue of war. This is in part because, as the British historian Adam Roberts has pointed out, it is often much easier to reach agreement on humanitarian than on strictly political or strategic ends. Satellite broadcasting has brought many, though by no means all, conflicts to much wider attention. Global audiences of these outrages demand that "something must be done." That "something" has often been done in the name of humanitarianism or neutrality.

A British scholar, Hugo Slim, reminds us that in Dante's Inferno there is a special place of torment reserved for those who have been neutral in life. Their sin is considered so grave that they are not even allowed into hell, only its vestibule, separated from hell by the river Acheron. For their sin of indecision and vacillation, Dante has devised an appropriate and awful torment: they are condemned to rush forever behind a banner "which whirls with aimless speed as though it would never take a stand, while also being stung by swarms of pursuing hornets."

As Slim points out, and I hope to show, UN peacekeepers and relief workers often see themselves in this particular predicament. On many occasions the international humanitarian system might be accurately described by Dante's image: a great number of international agencies rush frantically behind the whirling banner of international concern, which seldom takes a definite stand by planting itself firmly on the ground.

THROUGHOUT this troubled period two men have presided, at least in a titular sense, over the lack of order in the post–Cold War world: UN Secretary General Boutros Boutros-Ghali and his successor, Kofi Annan. They have played the same role, in very different manners.

Boutros Boutros-Ghali, a Coptic Christian and the minister of state for foreign affairs in Egypt, was a distinguished diplomat and academic. He had had an important part in the success of the Camp David agreement of 1978, but the United States was not enthusiastic about his candidacy. On November 21, 1991, with the U.S. initially abstaining, Boutros-Ghali was voted in as the sixth secretary general on the sixth ballot. He remained until the end of 1996, when the United States used its veto to deny him a second term.

His first serious peacekeeping crisis, and one which haunted his entire term, was Bosnia. Yugoslavia was disintegrating into violence as he was elected. But the UN was already gearing up for a huge mission in Cambodia. A few weeks before Boutros-Ghali's election, the foreign ministers or other officials of nineteen nations had gathered in Paris to sign up for one of the most ambitious interventions ever—the Paris peace agreement. It was the most comprehensive and audacious peacekeeping operation the UN had ever mounted. It intended to place Cambodia under the virtual trusteeship of the UN as the world rescued it from itself, and from the world.

Cambodia is a victim of its geography and of its political under-development. It is a small country (now some nine million people) overshadowed by two huge and threatening neighbors—sixty million Thais to the west and seventy million overcrowded Vietnamese to the east.

The French rescued Cambodia from its neighbors when they im-posed a protectorate on the kingdom in 1864, and kept the country isolated as an underdeveloped rural backwater for the next hundred years. After Prince Norodom Sihanouk won Cambodia's indepen-dence from France in 1953, the country's neutrality and sovereignty were challenged frequently. With its eastern border only thirty-five miles from Saigon, it was inevitably dragged into the Vietnam War, despite Sihanouk's professions of neutrality. By the late sixties the Vietnamese communists had established substantial bases along the border. The United States started to bomb these in secret, and in 1970, after Sihanouk and his autocracy were overthrown in a coup d'état, a new military regime brought Cambodia into the anti-communist camp on the side of South Vietnam and the United States.

From Beijing, the angry prince decided to side with the North Vietnamese and the small group of Cambodian communists, whom he had hitherto fought and denigrated as "les Khmers Rouges." Si-hanouk's endorsement immediately provided the communists with the nationalist appeal they could not otherwise have won. Over the next five years Cambodia was a sideshow to Vietnam. Warfare de-stroyed Cambodian society as only the Khmer Rouge prospered. U.S. bombing and the growing cruelty of the Khmer Rouge combined to drive peasants off the land.

In April 1975, a few days before the fall of Saigon, the Khmer Rouge captured Phnom Penh. They began at once to empty the cap-ital and all other towns, and embarked on their radical, murderous revolution—one of the most terrible of the twentieth century. They brought Sihanouk back to a deserted city, and for the next three and a half years, while the people labored under harsh conditions in the countryside, they kept him under house arrest in the palace and mur-dered several of his children. No one knows exactly how many peo-ple died from execution, forced labor, malnutrition or disease under the Khmer Rouge. Between one and two million is the widely accepted estimate. The "killing fields" display some of their remains in and around the provinces today.

Khmer Rouge decisions were grounded in both a grotesque communist philosophy which carried Stalinism and Maoism to extremes and an obsessional fear and hatred of Vietnam. At the end of 1978, Hanoi invaded, drove the Khmer Rouge out of Phnom Penh and installed its own client regime.

Khmer Rouge misrule has since been called a form of autogenocide conducted by the regime against both minorities and the majority Khmer alike; it left the country and the people in ruins. Vietnam's invasion was a liberation for almost all Cambodians, but it became an occupation that the Vietnamese insisted was "irreversible." Hanoi's motives were strategic rather than humanitarian; it had long nurtured ambitions of dominating an Indochinese federation. The Vietnamese leaders had the full support of their major ally, the Soviet Union, and incurred the enmity of China, the United States and the noncommunist states of Southeast Asia.

Throughout the eighties Hanoi controlled Cambodia, but the United Nations refused to ratify its invasion; Vietnam's client regime was shunned by most of the world. Cambodia's UN seat was held by a coalition led by Prince Sihanouk. It included three armed resistance groups based along the Thai-Cambodian border—the Khmer Rouge; Sihanouk's political party, Funcinpec; and the noncommunist Khmer People's National Liberation Front (KPNLF). The Chinese armed the Khmer Rouge, while the United States, Britain and France helped the Association of Southeast Asian Nations (ASEAN) build up the noncommunist groups. Thailand helped all groups, especially the Khmer Rouge. Prince Sihanouk became a familiar figure at the UN General Assembly's opening sessions.

Meanwhile the regime in Phnom Penh, the People's Republic of Kampuchea (PRK), remained in limbo. Not nearly as brutal as the Khmer Rouge, it was nonetheless a hard-line, one-party state which tolerated no dissent, frequently imprisoning and torturing its political opponents. The regime was supported only by the Soviet bloc and India. Starved of UN or other development funds, Cambodia decayed as an adjunct of Vietnam. The UN was criticized for its inaction, but the dictates of the Cold War and the overriding principle of sovereignty, which Vietnam had clearly abused by its occupation, prevailed over the notion of justice.

In the mid-1980s, with the rise of Mikhail Gorbachev, Soviet support for Vietnam's occupation began to wane. In 1986, ASEAN and Vietnam began to discuss political compromise. In December 1986, Prince Sihanouk met for the first time with Hun Sen, the former Khmer Rouge soldier whom Vietnam had installed as prime minister in Phnom Penh.

Though the first talks broke down, the Vietnamese withdrew their troops just as the communist regimes in Eastern Europe collapsed in 1989. The government of Hun Sen, while attempting to move from a command to a market economy, was still dogmatic, corrupt, cruel to its enemies and (to many Cambodians) tainted by its association with Vietnam. The civil war continued. At the end of the 1980s it seemed that the Khmer Rouge might be able to seize more territory than they already occupied.

The Australian foreign minister, Gareth Evans, took the initiative, adopting an idea put forward by U.S. Congressman Stephen Solarz to create "an international control mechanism" that would rule Cambodia temporarily. In February 1990, Australia produced the first draft of a plan for an international peacekeeping operation in Cambodia that ultimately led to the Paris peace agreement of October 1991.

The agreement had many purposes, some of them unspoken and certainly unwritten. One was to remove an impediment to U.S.-Soviet-Chinese détente. Another was to get the international community off the hook of recognizing the Khmer Rouge and their allies as the legitimate government of Cambodia. At the same time the agreement distanced the Khmer Rouge from their principal sponsor, China. In return for allowing their Khmer Rouge clients into the political process, the Chinese agreed to stop supplying them with weapons. The Chinese saw the agreement as a means of ending Vietnamese hegemony over Indochina, restoring Prince Sihanouk to Phnom Penh and allowing Beijing to resume a position in Cambodia.

To include the Khmer Rouge, rather than attempt to try them for crimes against humanity, was a distasteful solution. It reflected Western reluctance to stage a sustained confrontation with the Chinese and Thai governments on the issue. But, if cynical, it was also pragmatic. (There were later similarities in Sierra Leone, where in 1999 the government was forced to deal with the murderous rebels.) The alternative was a continuation of the war, no international recognition for Cambodia and no chance of peace. Many Western diplomats argued that the peace process would in itself marginalize the Khmer Rouge.

The agreement was signed by all four Cambodian factions—the State of Cambodia (SOC—the renamed PRK), the Khmer Rouge (known as the Party of Democratic Kampuchea), Prince Sihanouk's Funcinpec and the Khmer People's National Liberation Front. Events would demonstrate how differently each faction saw and planned to use the peace process.

The agreement created the United Nations Transitional Authority in Cambodia, UNTAC, which was to control the administration of the country. Cambodian sovereignty was embodied in a Supreme National Council (SNC) which Prince Sihanouk would chair and on which the four Cambodian factions would sit, and which was supposed to delegate all necessary power to UNTAC. In theory, the UN Security Council endowed UNTAC with wider powers than any previous UN peacekeeping operation. Its mandate included the supervision of a nationwide cease-fire; cantonment and disarmament of the troops of all four factions; repatriation of 370,000 refugees from the Thai border camps; monitoring of human and civil rights; and the creation of a neutral political environment through direct control over the areas of foreign affairs, defense, national security, finance and information. Free and fair elections would also be held for a Constituent Assembly. UNTAC was to help commence the rehabilitation and development of the country and to promote "reconciliation."

By the end of 1991, UN planners had decided UNTAC would cost nearly $2 billion, to be spent on a force of twelve infantry battalions and support units—some fifteen thousand men—plus five thousand civilians. Where were they to be found? No one knew, when the Paris agreement was signed. Then the restoration of Cambodia clashed with the destruction of Yugoslavia.

The UN was slow in deploying UNTAC's elements and advance planning in New York was fragmented. Yugoslavia was obviously distracting to the Secretariat. But it quickly became evident in any case that the UN was ill prepared to mount such a large and complex peacekeeping operation as Cambodia. It was clear also that since, unlike in Yugoslavia, the operation in Cambodia had been anticipated for years, more could and should have been done to prepare for it before the end of 1991.

Boutros-Ghali chose a Japanese career UN official, Yasushi Akashi,

the under secretary general for disarmament, to be his special representative in charge of the Cambodia mission. (The job had been
turned down by Rafruddin Ahmed, a Palestinian UN official who
had been deeply involved in all the Paris negotiations.) Boutros-Ghali
had decided to abolish the department of disarmament affairs in his
first restructuring, so Akashi needed a suitable new post. Since Japan
was heavily involved in the preparation of the Paris peace agreement
and was a large-scale investor in Cambodia and in UNTAC, this position seemed appropriate. When Boutros-Ghali offered it to him
Akashi replied, "I am a samurai. Accordingly, I must accept this
challenge."

Akashi was a slim man with a ready smile and an active, often surprising, sense of humor. His management skills were not his most
obvious asset and he was not used to leading a large team in the field,
let alone one that in the end would grow to twenty thousand people.
But he had great tenacity. He arrived in Phnom Penh on March 15,
1992—almost five months after the Paris peace agreement was
signed. With him came the force commander, Australian Lieutenant
General John Sanderson, and the heads of some of UNTAC's various
components—human rights, civil affairs, electoral, information and
so on. Some of these officials had been recruited only at the last
minute, and most of them had never met each other before, still less
discussed their mandate and mission in Cambodia. Some of them
knew the area well; others had no experience of it.

Akashi was shocked by the wretched state of the country, which
had been through over twenty years of war, revolution and isolation.
Everything was wrecked. The roads were like twisted ribbons,
cratered and often impassable. In Phnom Penh, office space and supplies were just not available. Akashi thought the governments involved were quite unrealistic about what the UN faced in Cambodia.
He cabled back to New York: "There is simply no infrastructure to
speak of in Cambodia and to speak of our inducing the local authorities to provide us services, materials, facilities is quite unrealistic. The
fact is, the Cambodians quite openly beg such things from us at every
turn, and their need for them is quite clear."

Akashi had the first of many meetings with the half dozen ambassadors who had grouped in Phnom Penh as "friends of the Paris
agreement" and who would provide crucial unity over the next two

years. They comprised the United States, France, Britain, Japan, Russia and China. He looked at the state guesthouse offered by Prince Sihanouk for UNTAC's headquarters, and he went to see the prince himself in his palace on the banks of the Mekong. Sihanouk's attitude toward the UN was always unpredictable, but his support was essential. He told Akashi what he knew and believed about the various leaders of the Khmer Rouge.

The prince said Pol Pot was still "le maître" of the movement. Khieu Samphan, the Khmer Rouge's public face, who had signed the Paris peace agreement and often represented the Khmer Rouge at meetings in Phnom Penh, was merely "a noncommissioned officer."

Sihanouk said that the Khmer Rouge were hiding in various mountainous regions, but they felt safe only in Thailand, where Pol Pot was under the protection and pressure of General Suchinda Kraprayoon, the Thai supreme commander. The prince was outspoken on the traditional ambitions of Thailand and Vietnam in Cambodia. He said that the Thais were still pursuing a dual policy of working through the State of Cambodia (Hun Sen's regime) to foster their economic expansion into the country, while also helping the Khmer Rouge in case Hun Sen should fail. The Vietnamese were still backing their protégé Hun Sen. Sihanouk thought that the most important elements of rehabilitation were raising the standards of the rural people, restoring bridges and roads, providing education and protecting the environment, especially forests (which were by now being systematically ravaged and sold by all sides).

At the first meeting of the Supreme National Council after UNTAC was established, Sihanouk welcomed Akashi graciously. Akashi made a long speech in which he said that $200 million had already been authorized to UNTAC as start-up capital, but it would not be easy to obtain the full budget.

Hun Sen proposed that UNTAC employ ex-soldiers to clear mines as well as rebuild bridges and roads. Akashi thought this was a good idea because they would be cheaper than troops from other countries and because clearing mines was a dangerous business. Referring to the central paradox of peacekeeping, he said, "Loss of life among volunteers from troop-contributing countries will have a very chilling effect on their willingness to participate in peacekeeping operations and risks to them must be kept to an absolute minimum."

There was debate over the economy, as there would be for the next few years. The picture was bleak, with the Phnom Penh administration slowly collapsing under grave financial stress, faced with a large budget deficit and caught in a vicious cycle of inflation nearing 100 percent a year. Three means of relief were suggested: direct budget support, local cost of financing projects and balance-of-payments support. Akashi said that UNTAC's mandate to control and supervise the Cambodian bureaucracy was moot since many civil servants were not being paid and were employed at other jobs much of the time. They must be paid, but UNTAC could not do this.

The UN military component, led by an Indonesian battalion, began to arrive in the fourth week of March. The Indonesians were stationed in the northern province of Kompong Thom, one of the wildest, poorest and most dangerous areas of the country where Khmer Rouge infiltration was heaviest. Fighting between the Hun Sen troops and Khmer Rouge was worse here than anywhere else. Akashi told his superiors in New York that until the Indonesians arrived Kompong Thom was "set fair to be Cambodia's last battleground."

Deployment of the fifteen thousand multinational troops lagged further and further behind schedule. As of the end of March, the UN had had positive replies from eight of the twelve countries asked to provide an infantry battalion. General Sanderson directed that infantry and other line units should arrive with sixty days' supplies so that they could operate independently until external logistics support arrived. (The civilian police and civil administration components of UNTAC did not take similar initiatives and, as a result, they arrived even later.) The Malaysian battalion followed the arrival of the Indonesians. An engineer battalion from Thailand arrived. All the others were still to come. Vehicles were in very short supply and conditions throughout the country were harsh. Member governments of the UN often proved equally reluctant to release administrators, arguing that they were themselves short of qualified staff. Akashi later acknowledged that the UN must have seemed very inefficient to the Cambodian factions.

On April 1, Akashi handed over the draft electoral law to Sihanouk. He would have preferred to give copies to all SNC members, but UNTAC had only one suitcase-sized photocopier, and, what with power cuts, it took about half an hour to make just one copy of the fifty-six-page document which the electoral component had just completed.

On April 6, at the Supreme National Council, Akashi, supported by Sihanouk, made a direct appeal to the Khmer Rouge to allow UNTAC access to their territory to find cantonment sites in which their soldiers could be grouped and disarmed. Khieu Samphan appeared to agree, but Akashi warned New York that "there is doubt as to Mr. Khieu Samphan's ability to deliver on promises he makes." He was, after all, only Pol Pot's spokesman. The Khmer Rouge had come very well prepared to the meeting "and clearly tried to take it over," said Akashi.

Akashi warned Boutros-Ghali that both the politics and the logistics of the UN operation were proving difficult; there were doubts about the cooperation of the Khmer Rouge. Moreover, the timetable was tight. Elections had to be held by May 1993 at the latest. Cantonment of the four factions' troops and the return of refugees must begin before this year's rains started at the end of May. And that meant that the bulk of the military component and a substantial number of police must be deployed by then. This tall order was made more difficult by the fact that governments that had agreed in principle to send troops were now arguing about exactly where they should be deployed.

The French minister of defense complained about the French battalion to UNTAC being sent to northeast Cambodia, the most remote area of the country, along the border with Vietnam. There was a risk of confrontation with the Vietnamese, with whom France was trying to improve relations. The French had been chosen for that sector because the Khmer Rouge—paranoid about Vietnamese infiltration—were insisting that the area be patrolled well, or they would not allow the UN access to their own areas. They were claiming that tens of thousands of Vietnamese infiltrators and soldiers were still in the country, and that until they were removed, the Khmer Rouge were under no obligation to abide by other aspects of the Paris peace plan. The French battalion was one of the few which was already fully equipped and highly professional, and could be deployed immediately. But Paris wanted them deployed around Kompong Som, the port area in the southwest of the country. It was closer to Phnom

Penh, much more developed than the wild northeast and much more visible. The French had their way. The Uruguayans were sent to the remote northeast.

Other troop contributors were also becoming nervous about deploying their men. Boutros-Ghali had to write to the Dutch foreign minister, Hans van den Broek, to protest that Holland was delaying the dispatch of its battalion to Cambodia. The battalion was supposed to go to the northwest, an area rife with Khmer Rouge. Boutros-Ghali said he shared the Dutch concern over the Khmer Rouge's attitude, but the international community was determined to implement the Paris agreement. "The Netherlands government's decision will unfortunately convey the opposite impression and could lead the KR to believe that the international community will give in to pressure from them."

The Dutch tried to compromise by sending just one company of men to the sector prescribed for the Dutch battalion. The UN's peacekeeping department told them that was not acceptable—that the full Dutch battalion should be deployed as soon as possible, and that its precise deployment was a matter to be decided by the force commander. Eventually the Dutch came.

By April it was clear that UNTAC's governing bodies—the Supreme National Council and the Mixed Military Working Group—were not working properly. The Khmer Rouge prevented them from making decisions. The Khmer Rouge were still denying the UN access to their areas and refusing to mark their minefields. They had seized the town of Kompong Thom, and they had fired on at least one UN helicopter. They justified such behavior on the grounds that the UN had not taken control of the Phnom Penh administration as the Paris agreement required.

Akashi was increasingly angry with their lack of cooperation, but Boutros-Ghali was anxious to avoid any showdown with the Khmer Rouge. On a visit to Phnom Penh in April he saw all the factions and advised caution. One of the most contentious issues during his visit was whether or not to set up an UNTAC radio station to broadcast news of UNTAC in Khmer. This was being strongly urged by the information component of UNTAC, led by Tim Carney, an American diplomat with long experience in Cambodia. He persuaded Akashi that a Radio UNTAC was the only way to disseminate the UN's message free of interference from the factions. There was no more effective means of communication in a poor rural country with terrible communications between the capital and the countryside. Boutros-Ghali was not at first impressed. But eventually the radio was allowed.

On May 9 the UNTAC force commander, General Sanderson, announced that Phase Two of the cease-fire agreement—regroupment and cantonment—would begin on May 13. The Khmer Rouge were not prepared to allow this to happen. They argued that Phase Two should be postponed on the grounds that Vietnamese forces had not all withdrawn.

On May 30 an incident took place which demonstrated the limits of UN power in a way which was both humiliating and portentous. Akashi attempted, with General Sanderson, to drive into the Khmer Rouge zone around the western town of Pailin. The convoy came to a checkpoint manned by just a couple of young Khmer Rouge soldiers with a thin bamboo pole across the road. They refused to let the secretary general's special representative pass.

This flimsy roadblock was not heavily defended. Akashi and Sanderson could have insisted on the UN's right, under the treaty that the Khmer Rouge had signed in Paris, to enter the Khmer Rouge zone, like any other. They could have demanded that the UN troops with them open the way ahead. Akashi and Sanderson decided to make no such attempt. By turning back they created an image, flashed throughout the world, of UN impotence.

There were those, especially outside UNTAC, who felt the UN should have called the Khmer Rouge's bluff and sent UN troops into their areas at once. But Sanderson believed that such pressure might at once result in wider warfare. Moreover, most of the countries that had sent troops would not tolerate their use in battle against the Khmer Rouge. On a practical level, the UN battalions were not positioned for such offensive action. Sanderson pointed out that UNTAC was a peacekeeping mission that could not engage in peace enforcement. From now on Akashi, and the UN generally, would be tarred, at least by the laptop generals in the press corps, with being soft on the Khmer Rouge—but in New York there were concerns that he was being too confrontational with them.

* * *

THE UN's problems in Cambodia grew in parallel to its difficulties in Yugoslavia. The roots and the conduct of the 1990s wars in the Balkans have been explored elsewhere exhaustively. The emergence of fierce Serbian nationalism at the end of the eighties, exacerbated and exploited by Slobodan Milosevic, was followed by the emergence of a nationalist regime in Croatia. In June 1991, discouraged by the United States but encouraged by Germany, its traditional ally, Croatia seceded, along with Slovenia, from the Yugoslav federation. The Serb-controlled Yugoslav National Army (JNA) let Slovenia go after a ten-day battle but entered Krajina, an eastern and central area of Croatia which was populated by Serbs, in order to protect the Serb minority under new Croat rule, and to build a Serb state on the territory.

Javier Perez de Cuellar, Boutros-Ghali's predecessor, in his last days as UN secretary general, had appointed the former U.S. secretary of state Cyrus Vance to try to devise a cease-fire agreement between the Serbs and the Croats. In October 1991, a week after the Paris agreement on Cambodia was signed, de Cuellar appointed the UN High Commissioner for Refugees as the lead agency for humanitarian relief in the former Yugoslavia.

At that time UNHCR had a small office in Belgrade and no presence in either Croatia or Bosnia. Just what the organization was supposed to do and how were never clearly spelled out. Nonetheless the high commissioner, Sadako Ogata, and her staff grasped the opportunity. UNHCR's new role brought money and (at first) cachet. Its global budget rose from $883 million in 1991 to $1.1 billion in 1992.

UNHCR considered its mandate as lead agency to include "prime responsibility for logistics/transport, food monitoring, domestic needs, shelter, community services, health, emergency transition activities in agriculture and income generation, protection/legal assistance, and assistance to other agencies in sectors under their responsibility." The first special envoy of UNHCR arrived in the Balkans in November 1991 with just one assistant and a laptop computer. There were only 19 UNHCR staff in Yugoslavia that December, but 337 a year later—and even more thereafter. Ogata took to calling herself "the desk officer for the former Yugoslavia." As war consumed the former Yugoslavia, and the humanitarian catastrophe caused by ethnic cleansing grew, more and more UNHCR resources were switched there—inevitably at the expense of other crises, perhaps particularly in Africa.

The humanitarian needs in the Balkans were already great. Villages were being burned, men murdered, women and children driven away. The Croatian resort of Dubrovnik was under siege from Serb artillery. More merciless was the prolonged Serb assault on the Croat town of Vukovar. The population had to live underground for weeks. When the town finally fell to the Serbs in mid-November, the inhabitants emerged from the cellars into ruins. "Corpses of people and animals littered the streets," Laura Silber and Allan Little wrote in their fine history of the death of Yugoslavia. "Grisly skeletons of buildings still burned. . . . Serbian volunteers, wild-eyed, roared down the streets, their pockets full of looted treasures." The Serbs separated the male survivors from the women and children and took the men away, in a pattern that was to be repeated again and again over the next four years. Hundreds of the men were incarcerated in grotesque detention camps. Hundreds more were shot dead.

With hindsight, Vukovar can be seen as the last moment at which NATO forces might have intervened to stop the fighting and to halt Yugoslavia's fall into the abyss. Calls for such intervention were made at the time by some, including the former British prime minister Margaret Thatcher. There was no political will to undertake such difficult action. Instead the paths of diplomacy and humanitarianism were followed.

The frustrations of the UN and any other intermediaries were already very obvious. The U.S. had passed the ball to Europe, with Secretary of State James Baker memorably announcing, "We don't have a dog in that fight." The Europeans had tried to rise to the occasion, with one senior European Union diplomat declaring grandiosely, "The hour of Europe has come." The chief EU negotiator, Lord Carrington, almost succeeded in getting all sides to agree on a plan to end the war. It collapsed in part because Milosevic refused to give Albanians in Kosovo the same rights he was demanding for Serbs in Croatia. Then came Cyrus Vance with proposals for a UN peacekeeping force in Croatia. All in all, said Carrington, the warring parties were offered mediation "à la carte." They exploited the differences in the menus offered them by different mediators, made agreements they had no intention of keeping and expanded the wars. The UN official in charge of peacekeeping was then Marrack Goulding, the senior British UN employee. A glimpse at his diary for the time shows the nature of the problem.

On November 16, 1991, Goulding flew with Cyrus Vance to Amsterdam (Holland was chairing the European Union at the time), where they met the Dutch foreign minister, Hans van den Broek. Van den Broek said that a UN peacekeeping operation was essential to get the Yugoslav army to withdraw from Croatia, and thus establish calm to allow negotiations to proceed between Zagreb and Belgrade. He also wanted the EU monitoring mission to continue alongside the UN mission. Cyrus Vance resisted, but in the end it did happen.

From Amsterdam, Vance and Goulding flew on to Belgrade in a plane provided by the Swiss government as a voluntary contribution to the UN, arriving on the day that Vukovar fell.

Goulding met an old colleague, a senior Yugoslav army officer who had served in UNIIMOG, the UN military observer group sent to monitor the cease-fire between Iran and Iraq in 1988. Goulding knew him quite well and had been impressed with him in the Middle East. The UN peacekeeper certainly was not prepared for the officer's attitude to peacekeeping in the Balkans and to the Croats in particular. "The Yugoslav National Army should be using flame-throwers to get the rats out of the cellars of Vukovar," the officer said. If it were not for his heart condition he would have gone off to fight as a volunteer. If the Croats would not agree to a sensible settlement, the Serbs would have to kill them all. Goulding did not find this attitude of a man trained in UN peacekeeping reassuring.

Vance and Goulding asked to visit Vukovar in the hope of deterring atrocities against the twelve thousand to fifteen thousand civilians left in the town. They were told they could not go. They met with Milosevic and proposed "inkblot" deployment of UN peacekeepers. This meant UN military and police deployment in crisis areas where intercommunal tensions were high and fighting had been taking place. Milosevic, expert at running rings around foreign diplomats, appeared to like the idea, explaining that Croatia's boundaries were only "administrative" and that once Croatia had decided to secede, the federal army had a right to intervene to protect the Serb residents who were being attacked by the Croatian authorities.

Eventually, the two were taken to Vukovar in an armored personnel carrier. APCs have slits for windows, so they could see almost nothing. They were not shown the parts of the town that had been most badly damaged by Serb shelling. Goulding felt that everything was being done to waste their time. They were taken to an army reception center for displaced people; the civilians were dazed and hopeless, the soldiers triumphant, the Serbian irregulars, in their rag-tag uniforms, were threatening. Army officers kept bringing to Vance people "who want to talk to you, Mr. Vance"—and who invariably told him what a wonderful humanitarian job the army was doing.

Vance had repeatedly asked to visit the hospital in Vukovar, but Goulding and he were driven in the opposite direction. They halted the convoy to complain in front of the TV cameras. They had a fierce argument with a Serb major who was later charged by the war crimes tribunal in The Hague with a massacre at Vukovar. He told them the road to the hospital was mined. When Goulding remonstrated, the major flew into a rage, complaining that Goulding had accused him of lying. They were still not allowed to go to the hospital, from which patients had been dragged off to be murdered by the Serbs. Finally they had to give in and drive back to Belgrade. "It had been a sobering visit, giving us our first taste of the violence and hatred of this civil war," wrote Goulding.

Vance and Goulding then flew to Croatia to see President Franjo Tudjman, who spoke at length of "Serbian imperialism" and described the Serb-dominated Yugoslav army as the largest communist army in Europe after the Soviet Union. They persuaded him to accept the "inkblot" deployment concept, saying that the demilitarization of the crisis areas was the best way to get the Yugoslav National Army out of Croatia.

On November 21, Vance and Goulding flew to Sarajevo, where they called on President Alija Izetbegovic and his foreign minister, Haris Silajdzic. Izetbegovic spoke of the danger of fighting between the Serb and Croat communities in Bosnia-Herzegovina and asked for a peacekeeping operation there also. Vance agreed to consider it. In Belgrade, Milosevic said he did not like the idea. Nonetheless at a meeting in Geneva on November 23 he and Tudjman agreed to a cease-fire and appeared to agree in principle to a UN peacekeeping mission. Goulding and Vance then flew to Rome to see the outgoing secretary general, Perez de Cuellar. He was wary about the whole idea of peacekeeping in such a murderous and volatile environment.

The Italian foreign minister, Gianni de Michelis, was much more gung ho. He urged Perez to press on with the peacekeeping plan. When Goulding said that the UN had to check that the protagonists could control their extremists, and that there were procedures to be followed in New York on the cost of any such operation, de Michelis apparently castigated him as "another bureaucrat."

In Belgrade on December 1, Milosevic repeated that he was strongly opposed to any UN deployment in Bosnia. He was also worried about the German promise to recognize Slovenia and Croatia by December 19 and the threat of tighter EU sanctions on Serbia. Milosevic asked if the European Union was still capable of playing a mediatory role. Goulding thought it was a fair question. As for the UN, Milosevic was very much against Goulding's intention to set up its headquarters in Sarajevo. He thought Izetbegovic would exploit the UN in order to promote Bosnian separatism. There were other objections. Behrooz Sadry, a senior Iranian UN official who was in charge of administration, logistics and personnel for UN peacekeeping operations, arrived in Belgrade and said he thought that Goulding's inkblot approach was unworkable. Moreover, he said, Cambodia was looming over the UN, and the Secretariat simply could not take on another operation. Goulding could not disagree.

The cease-fire agreed in Geneva on November 23 seemed to be holding and on December 6, Goulding and Vance flew back into Sarajevo, where they found Izetbegovic and Silajdzic much more anxious than two weeks before. They were afraid that the German and EU rush to recognize Croatia and Slovenia would precipitate a war in Bosnia. The Yugoslav army would intervene to prevent the republic from seceding.

Goulding then met with leaders of the Muslim, Serb and Croatian parties in Bosnia. The Muslims and Croats were strongly in favor of UN deployment; the Bosnian Serbs were against it. All three blamed one another for past genocides. When one of them suddenly opened his briefcase, Goulding feared for a second that he was looking for his gun. In fact he produced a book of photographs of World War II atrocities. The atmosphere was very grim. That day news came in of synchronized and heavy Serb bombardment of Dubrovnik and

Osijek, in the extreme southwest and northeast corners of Croatia, respectively.

In Belgrade, Vance told Milosevic how shocked he was by this. In a fashion that was to become a pattern, Milosevic said he too was shocked. He placated Vance and Goulding by saying that he wanted a peacekeeping operation in the Serb area of Croatia, Krajina. He asked them to prepare a paper. They did so, now calling the disputed areas of Croatia UN-protected areas (UNPAs).

Then Boutros-Ghali, about to assume his new position as secretary general, made no secret of his misgivings about UN involvement. Quite apart from the difficulties and dangers of the operation on the ground, he was concerned about the impact on the UN's standing. "We are probably onto a loser already," he told one of his new colleagues. "If we recommend against an operation, we will be accused of spinelessness by France and others, and terrible things will happen in Yugoslavia. If we say yes, and the council agrees, the operation will almost certainly fail, possibly after being expanded to other parts of Yugoslavia, and the UN would have to withdraw in ignominy."

His concerns were well placed.

Germany was still pushing for the European Union to recognize the independence of Croatia. Other members of the EU were urging patience, fearing, like the Bosnian leaders, that premature recognition would result in deadly fighting over borders. But German pressure on behalf of its traditional Croat ally was implacable.

On Monday, December 16, the European Union announced that it would recognize Slovenia and Croatia in January subject to their giving guarantees on the rights of minorities within their borders. Germany then declared it would recognize them anyway—with or without such guarantees. It became clear that Germany was also pressuring Macedonia and Bosnia to apply for international recognition. On December 19, Macedonia applied. Bosnia followed the next day. By the end of the week, wrote Goulding in his diary, "the drums of war were sounding loudly from Bosnia and the EU, with astonishing effrontery, was pushing the UN ever more insistently to recommend the deployment of military observers to that republic."

The rush to recognition was one of the most dangerous foreign interventions of the period. The international community never defined a political objective for the former Yugoslavia. As the American historian Charles King has pointed out, the international community "ignored the real driving forces behind the country's bloody demise." Just what was the Yugoslav federation created by Tito? he asked. Was it a union of sovereign territories each of which had its own legitimate authority? Or was it "a union of distinct and semisovereign peoples *(narodi)* that were scattered through the federation's six republics and two provinces"? If the first, then recognition of each state made sense; if the second, then separation would be very messy indeed. In the first case, claims by one territory on another would look like international aggression. In the second, they could seem predictable disputes over how to divide the remnants of a failed state. Premature recognition, Lord Carrington pointed out, deprived him and other mediators of the most powerful lever to extract commitments for the safeguarding of minorities within the new states.

At the end of 1991 and in early 1992 the international community allowed Yugoslavia to be dissolved on the basis of two conflicting principles—that the republican, administrative borders of the federal state were international borders and that the new states were based on the right of national self-determination. The violence in the former Yugoslavia over the next few years stemmed in good part from the definition of borders of the hastily formed and hastily recognized states.

T H E new year at the United Nations began with the arrival of Boutros-Ghali and new crises in Yugoslavia. By the end of his first week, Boutros-Ghali had come to the reluctant conclusion that there would have to be some sort of UN peacekeeping operation in Yugoslavia.

Cyrus Vance had managed a negotiated cease-fire over the disputed areas of Croatia. They were to become UN protected areas, patrolled by a traditional UN peacekeeping force—which is to say, a lightly armed force policing an agreed cease-fire. This was meant to be a temporary arrangement until an overall political settlement could be devised for all of the former Yugoslavia. But the EU's recognition of Croatia meant that the Tudjman government was in no hurry to accept any such settlement.

Boutros-Ghali realized that the pressure from the United States and Europe (though it was by no means consistent) meant that the UN had to become more widely involved. Despite misgivings he sent the first of the UN blue helmets, the peacekeepers, into Croatia. They were known as UNPROFOR, UN Protection Force, and their task was to police the areas where there were substantial Serb populations—eastern and western Slavonia and Krajina. From that first commitment of UN troops all else followed.

In March 1992, despite the advice of the U.S. State Department and others, President Alija Izetbegovic of Bosnia declared independence. This followed a referendum in which a majority of those voting had opted for such independence. The Bosnian constitution required that any such decision be agreed to by all three constituent nations of Bosnia—Muslims, Croats and Serbs. The Bosnian Serbs had refused to take part in the referendum. So they now claimed that they were being forced to leave the Yugoslav federation against their will. The Bosnian Serb leader, Radovan Karadzic, declared a Bosnian Serb republic within Bosnia. Its capital was Pale, a skiing resort just outside Sarajevo. Fighting in Bosnia spread, as the Bosnian Serbs tried to create "ethnically pure" areas by murdering Muslims and Croats or expelling them from their new statelet. They began to shell Sarajevo and to kill its inhabitants by sniper fire from the hills around.

By this time the UN had established its regional headquarters in Sarajevo because it was seen as neutral in the Croatian conflict, the UN's first responsibility in the area. By April there was talk on the Security Council of extending the peacekeeping mandate to cover Bosnia as well. Boutros-Ghali sent Goulding to Bosnia to advise him. He returned very gloomy. Unlike Croatia, where there was an agreement for the UN to police, in Bosnia there was widening war.

The Bosnian government wanted a UN peacekeeping mission; the Bosnian Serbs did not. Boutros-Ghali reported to the Security Council that peacekeeping was not possible unless all the parties respected the United Nations, its personnel and its mandate. None of the three Bosnian parties—Muslims, Serbs or Croats—really did so. Boutros-Ghali later wrote that wicked though the Bosnian Serbs were, "I felt that no party in Bosnia was free of at least some of the blame for the cruel conflict."

The vulnerability of the UN was shown in an incident during Goulding's fact-finding trip there. He and Shashi Tharoor, an astute

Indian novelist who worked for the UN's peacekeeping department, could not fly into Sarajevo because of the fighting and so went first to Belgrade. The Yugoslavs agreed to give them a helicopter to fly to Pale. The commander of UN troops based at Sarajevo airport, General Satish Nambiar, was then to pick them up from Pale in a convoy of armored personnel carriers to drive them to Sarajevo to meet Bosnian president Izetbegovic. Nambiar, a highly decorated Indian general, was on close terms with Shashi Tharoor. In their international telephone calls they talked in Malayalam, a southern Indian dialect, which they believed with some reason would defeat any Serb or Croat eavesdroppers.

When Goulding and Tharoor landed on a football field in Pale, they waited and they waited. The general and his seven APCs had been stopped on the road up the hill from Sarajevo by one Serb with a pole across the road. After Tharoor and Goulding sat for an hour or two in their hot helicopter on the football field, the minister of information of the newly declared Republika Srpska came to see them. Goulding and Tharoor told him they could not deal with illegal authorities.

The head of the Serbian news agency, Todor Dutina, came and offered them the hospitality of his offices. While there, Dutina offered a meeting with Karadzic. When Goulding said he had to meet Izetbegovic first, the Bosnian Serbs kept the two senior UN officials waiting all day before they allowed Nambiar up the road to pick them up. Nambiar said he could have lifted the pole with one finger. He was far more attuned to fighting than to peacekeeping, yet he did not confront the Serbs. As with Akashi in front of the Khmer Rouge pole in Cambodia, the Serbs had proved a point to the UN soldiers in Bosnia: you are here on our sufferance, you are not here to fight, we can stop you when we wish, there is no real freedom, you have no power.

But the Security Council was not prepared to heed warnings from Boutros-Ghali and others. Resolution 752 of May 15 enlarged UNPROFOR's role into Bosnia; it required UNPROFOR to provide armed escorts for humanitarian convoys in Bosnia and demanded that "all irregular forces . . . be disbanded and disarmed" and cooperate with the United Nations. This was totally unrealistic, and within a fortnight the fighting had got so fierce that Boutros-Ghali had to order the evacuation of most UN officials from Bosnia. He reported to the council that the disarming called for in Resolution 752 would not happen without an overall political settlement in Bosnia.

Resolution 752 was the first of more than 150 Security Council resolutions and statements on Bosnia, as the demand for action dragged the UN further and further into the conflict without the means to limit, let alone stop it. The whirling banner of international concern did not lead toward any kind of peace.

"This is diplomacy," Boutros-Ghali later told the author Stanley Meisler. "The U.N. has been created to help the member states solve their problems. If you will solve problems by adopting certain resolutions that are more spectacular than practical, if this can help diffuse tension, why not? I don't say that it doesn't hurt the U.N. I am saying that the U.N. has been created to do this. It can hurt the U.N., certainly. If you adopt a very practical resolution and the U.N., for different reasons, is not able to implement it, this will hurt the U.N." It did.

Divided at its heart between Europe and the United States, the international community responded to the war in Bosnia with an arms embargo, humanitarian aid and the deployment of a peacekeeping force. A self-critical report published by Kofi Annan in 1999 noted that "these measures were poor substitutes for more decisive and forceful action to prevent the unfolding horror."

When the embargo was imposed, Bosnia was not yet an independent member of the United Nations. But after it became so, the embargo deprived it of its right to self-defense and maintained the Serbs' military dominance in the former Yugoslavia. Thereafter, despite the spreading fury of war and ethnic cleansing, "the international community still could not find the political will to confront the menace defying it. . . . This was not a problem with a humanitarian solution."

Between 1992 and 1995, Boutros-Ghali pointed out time and again that UNPROFOR could not bring peace to Bosnia. None of the conditions for peacekeeping had been met. There was not even a functioning cease-fire, let alone a peace agreement; there was no will to peace and no clear consent by the belligerents. Nonetheless, the council insisted that UNPROFOR was the only answer. As Annan's report noted, "Lightly armed, highly visible in their white vehicles, scattered across the country in numerous indefensible observation posts, they were able to confirm the obvious: there was no peace to keep."

Remaking Cambodia

I n the village of Snuol, set in rubber plantations and forests in eastern Cambodia, and on the invasion route from Vietnam, people were lining up patiently outside an old blue painted building at the end of 1992. Snuol had always been a poor town. Pigs and cows rooted around the market, where many of the goods came across the border from Vietnam. The town was destroyed during the 1970 American invasion supposed to root out the Vietnamese communist sanctuaries in the area. Eight years later Vietnamese tanks had roared along the narrow, rutted dirt road as Hanoi invaded Cambodia, liberated it from the Khmer Rouge and then established a ten-year occupation.

Inside the building I watched Cambodian farmers and their families stand stiffly in front of an old sheet while a Polaroid photo was taken of each of them. They were then interviewed by the UN's Cambodian registration team, to make sure that they were born in Cambodia of Cambodian parents. Their particulars were written on the next page in a book of small printed vouchers. The page was then torn out for them to sign—or, in many cases, mark with their thumb. With the photograph attached, it was passed through a laminating machine. The villagers were then given the registration cards which would entitle them to vote in the elections that the United Nations was planning to hold in May 1993.

In towns and villages throughout most of Cambodia, millions of people had been registering in the last few weeks. Their participation was one of the greatest successes so far of the huge UN presence, the United Nations Transitional Authority in Cambodia, or UNTAC. Snuol was a microcosm of the UNTAC effort. Among the military and policemen here to protect the electoral process and try to ensure civil order were Ghanaians, Malaysians, Indians, Chinese, Australians, Uruguayans, Bangladeshis, Nepalese, Nigerians, Kenyans and Filipinos.

The actual electoral process was run by UN volunteers. In Snuol they were Jeff Bloor, a young Canadian, and Marina Ahl, a young Swede. Their job was dangerous; the previous team had been withdrawn after they had survived a land mine that blew up their car. Cambodia is littered with millions of mines sowed recklessly by all factions in the long civil war; they pose a terrible threat to everyone, above all to Cambodian farmers. The number of amputees in the country is pitiful.

By the end of November 1992 the electoral teams in Snuol had registered about half the twelve thousand voters thought to be in the district. Mobile electoral teams were still out in remote villages. Bloor said that government officials and police had tried to intimidate officials of other parties, but the registration here had been rather straightforward.

Throughout the country the electoral process was impressive and moving. Everywhere I went the UN volunteers, who were paid $700 a month, were enthusiastic. Close to Angkor Wat, the fabulous eleventh-to-thirteenth-century temple complex which Cambodians take as a symbol of national identity, villager voters watched on a television powered by a generator UNTAC films explaining democracy. According to Sajjad A. Gul, a Pakistani volunteer, people said they really did want to vote, though some of them hoped they could vote for UNTAC. In a village on the Mekong east of Phnom Penh, Charlie Bowers, an Australian, tempered the optimism by saying that people were worried about instability after the vote—and after UNTAC left. "We take on the fears of those we work with," he said. In Kompong Cham province, Carol Garrison, an American, had registered 85 percent of the possible voters by early December. She said that the election office had become the welfare office for the district.

By early December, 3 million of the estimated 4.8 million prospective voters in Cambodia had been registered. Reg Austin, a veteran of the Zimbabwe elections of 1980, who now ran the electoral component of UNTAC, hoped that when the process ended, over 80 percent of the potential electorate would be registered. (Most of the other 20 percent were inaccessible, in areas controlled by the Khmer Rouge. In June 1992 the Khmer Rouge had decided to withdraw from the peace process, refusing to demobilize or to allow UNTAC troops, registration teams or anyone else into their areas.) At the end of December an ominous development occurred in Kompong Thom, a northern province where the Khmer Rouge were strong. They went into villages they did not control, tore down UNTAC election posters, confiscated the radios UNTAC had distributed so that people could listen to Radio UNTAC and—most frightening of all—cut people's registration cards in half, keeping the piece with their names on. For the villagers the threat was clear and terrifying.

Whether and how the elections would take place in May 1993 now depended in good part on Khmer Rouge intentions—and on how well the UNTAC military could limit them. Both they and the authorities in Phnom Penh, the State of Cambodia, could lose in the elections. Each could prevent UNTAC from creating the "neutral political environment" which the Paris agreement deemed essential to the process. As so often in Cambodia, nothing was very clear.

Understanding Cambodia had always seemed a bit like trying to put together a three-dimensional jigsaw puzzle of morality, politics and geography. Some pieces of the puzzle were missing, some were scuffed and torn beyond recognition, others were bent completely out of shape and fitted nowhere at all. The picture showed a maze through which a small people had been stalked for over twenty years by successive monsters—a military coup followed by brutal civil war, strategic bombing, a Marxist revolution so bloody that it had been called autogenocide, international and regional power politics, liberation and occupation by a hated neighbor, famine, decay and renewed civil war.

By the end of 1992, Cambodia was in the middle of its strangest phase of all. And it was the only phase that could really be said to have benign intent. In the last few months the country had been oc-cupied by about twenty thousand men and women in white cars, white trucks, white airplanes and white helicopters—UNTAC. They were supposed to be giving Cambodia something it had never had—democracy—along with something it had not known for twenty-two years—peace. The stakes were high. For Cambodia itself, the UN plan represented the last and the best hope to escape the maze. For the UN, the plan was a test case of whether the international organi-zation could adapt to the new realities of the postwar world and im-plement what are sometimes called second-generation multinational operations. It was not at all clear that either could succeed.

Long neglected and with many of its services disintegrating, by the end of 1992 Phnom Penh was a boomtown, where vast commer-cial billboards lined the road from the airport, where UNTAC's white Toyotas made huge traffic jams vying with the bicycle rickshaws, par-ticularly outside the restaurants where the UNTAC people dined with dollars, where even the roof of the 1930s covered market was decorated with the logo of 555 cigarettes, where ugly new hotels fi-nanced by Thai and Chinese businessmen were being thrown up next to wrecked villas (the Thais were trying to buy everything they could in Cambodia), where the rubbish was never collected, where women and kids sold stolen gasoline in soft drink bottles.

By now UNTAC's full force of twelve battalions—some fifteen thousand men—plus five thousand civilians, working on refugee repatriation, civilian administration, reconstruction and so on, had finally arrived. Costs had soared. The program was now expected to cost over $2 billion. Most of this would be spent outside Cambodia, much of it on salaries and four-wheel-drive cars for the expatriate UN officials. Salaries for the military and international staff were esti-mated to reach $118.5 million, and their travel costs alone would be $62 million. Nearly nine thousand new vehicles had been purchased (almost all from Japan) at a cost of $81 million. Most controversial of all, senior UN bureaucrats in New York and Geneva were refusing to come unless they were given a hardship daily cost-of-living allowance of $145.

In Cambodia, the average annual income was only about $130. In other words, most country people earned less in a year than the $145 that international officials were being given as pocket money—or "mission subsistence allowance"—every day. The per diems alone were expected to cost the UN some $230 million.

To Cambodians the arrival of UNTAC's massive and hugely rich force and all its white vehicles was quite astonishing. It caused serious inflation which made life even more difficult for the poor, social dislocation and a big rise in prostitution and AIDS cases in Phnom Penh. Cambodians had to jump out of the way as one of the thousands of new Toyota Land Cruisers and pickup trucks was barreled far too fast down the road by an UNTAC official. Many of the worst drivers seemed to be members of CivPol, the UN's civilian police, who were on loan from national police forces, some of them from Third World dictatorships. One comment on their behavior came from an UNTAC human rights worker in Kompong Cham: "They behave here just as they do in their own countries."

In Phnom Penh, there was a political as well as a commercial boom. After seventeen years of communist rule of various kinds, now, in the shade of the UNTAC umbrella, at least fourteen different political parties had sprung up to contest the election. It was not just politics which was flourishing. At the UNTAC human rights office in Phnom Penh, I watched as a Cameroonian lecturer taught basic human rights law to the first group of Cambodians training to be defenders and prosecutors. The first class graduated at the end of November 1992.

At this time the Khmer Institute for Democracy was opened in Phnom Penh by a young Chilean-Australian, Julio Jeldres, who had been a fan of Prince Sihanouk since the early seventies and had devoted his life to Cambodia. The institute was intended to spread ideas of democracy as far as possible throughout the country.

The human rights component of UNTAC worked hard under a New Zealander from UNHCR, Dennis McNamara. They had an uphill job in trying to temper the brutal authoritarianism of the Phnom Penh authorities and no luck at all with the Khmer Rouge. They managed to free some political prisoners and others detained for long periods without trial. They had the use of leg irons in prisons banned. And they fostered the growth of indigenous human rights groups in Cambodia. By the end of 1992, helped by UNTAC, they distributed ideas and literature around the country. Several hundreds of thousands of people joined these groups. They were extraordinarily brave. Outside Phnom Penh there were not even telephones. A human rights campaigner in the provinces was truly alone facing the wrath of either the Khmer Rouge or the secret police and army of the Phnom Penh regime.

The teaching of English, outlawed under the previous regime, became very popular. Almost every other house in Phnom Penh seemed to have a handwritten chalked sign outside the gate, advertising English lessons. (French diplomats and aid workers were often displeased.) The number of uncensored newspapers began to grow. In a state where politics had always included thuggish brutality, UNTAC's civic education program and Radio UNTAC, when it was finally established, in late 1992, taught the virtues of free speech and democratic behavior.

In some ways the ferment and enthusiasm in Cambodia in 1992 reminded me of the Prague Spring of 1968. Here, too, people were finally being offered political freedom. But here, as in Prague, there was the threat that spring could be plunged into winter.

Despite all its horsepower and all its men and women, UNTAC had failed to take control of the Phnom Penh administration as Article 6 of the Paris agreement demanded. In many provincial capitals UNTAC arrived late, often because accommodations were not good enough. In the provinces there were sometimes two or three civil servants from UN headquarters in New York facing an entrenched local communist apparat backed by all the resources (police included) of the state.

In Siem Reap, the senior UN provincial official, Benny Widyono, an Indonesian, told me, "When I arrived, I went to see the communist governor of the province and told him I had come to take over. He stared at me, I stared at him, we stared at each other. Finally I blinked first. That was it." The idea that a small group of foreign civil servants could take over and supplant a well-entrenched communist regime was absurd. The Khmer Rouge could well claim that their mortal enemy, the Phnom Penh government, had survived Paris almost intact and that UNTAC had not met its obligations.

In Siem Reap, I talked to Brigadier General Somcheet, a Khmer Rouge liaison officer, at the run-down house he shared with officers of the other resistance groups which during the eighties had fought in alliance against the Vietnamese—the Khmer People's National

Liberation Front, and the Armée Nationale Khmer, of Prince Si-hanouk. As we talked, the Sihanoukist officer sat and listened, wearing what looked like pink satin women's pajamas. What I wanted to know was why the Khmer Rouge had left the peace process and were threatening to wreck it. Somcheet's response was that the Khmer Rouge could never rejoin the peace process until UNTAC had removed all Vietnamese troops from Cambodia and had taken full control of the administration in Phnom Penh.

As I traveled around Cambodia, hitching lifts on UNTAC helicopters or cars, hearing the complaints, fears and thrills of UNTAC personnel, I was continually amazed by the presence of the United Nations here in such force. Why Cambodia? Many other countries are equally benighted but have failed to capture the conscience of the world.

Guilt, I think, is one reason. Guilt that the world stood by, unremarking, as the Khmer Rouge embarked on the holocaust in which they killed well over one million people when they were in power from 1975 to 1978. "Never again" had been the promise after the genocide of European Jewry in the Second World War, but that promise appeared to have been broken in Cambodia. The images of mass graves that were published in 1979 after the Vietnamese invasion caused horror. Yet the response of the rest of the world to the intransigent Vietnamese occupation after 1979 involved rebuilding the Khmer Rouge. For these and other reasons, the Paris accords had been devised and signed. Now there was a danger that too much of the UN's credibility had been invested in Cambodia. UNTAC could fail if there was not the will on the part of enough of the Cambodian factions to see it succeed. And an election would not in itself constitute success. It would be a stage, not an end.

The problems were evident in the province of Kompong Thom, on the northwestern shore of the Great Lake. The Khmer Rouge were seen as a serious threat here.

In July 1992, two British UN military observers, Major George Jones and Major James Gray, and a French observer, Captain Pierre Prieto, were stationed at the village of Kraya in the north of the province. The Khmer Rouge then started to increase the infiltration of men and supplies down the so-called Pol Pot Trail, all-weather jungle tracks which reached down from Thailand to the north. Kraya was on their route.

In August the local Khmer Rouge commander, General Men Ron, the deputy commander of Division 616, told the UNTAC observers in Kraya, "Get out or I will kill you." After consultations with Phnom Penh, the Khmer Rouge order was in effect obeyed and the observers were not redeployed to Kraya until the end of September. Since then, despite his obligations under the Paris agreement, Men Ron had refused to discuss any problems with the observers, always answering, "There are Vietnamese in the country. I will not deal with UNTAC."

General Men Ron demanded that a cantonment of 450 Sihanoukist soldiers be moved from another village on a Khmer Rouge infiltration route, Ta Prok. He also demanded that an UNTAC election registration team be withdrawn from the district. When it was not done Men Ron threatened to move it out by force.

Nonetheless the UN military observers believed that in Kompong Thom (as in other provinces) the Khmer Rouge were a much weaker military force than was often thought. They could and did inspire terror among ordinary people. But they did not have the means to mount large-scale assaults. They could be contained.

"Our initial briefing made the Khmer Rouge sound ten feet tall. It was several months before we realized that it was absurd; they were far weaker than we were led to believe," said Major Jones. Others in UNTAC never recovered from such initial briefings.

In Kompong Thom, the predicament was complicated by the collaboration between the Khmer Rouge and the Indonesian UNTAC battalion stationed in the province. The Indonesian commander, Colonel Ryamizard, said he thought his battalion had better relations with the Khmer Rouge than any other foreign troops in Cambodia. Other UNTAC officials in Kompong Thom believed that was part of the problem. There was discussion in UNTAC over whether the Indonesians were following a separate mandate. The battalion was supposed to be deployed to protect election teams, and should have been on constant investigative patrol throughout the province. But the Indonesians did little of that. "It was two months before they wore their [UN] blue berets and blue sashes. They have a special relationship with the Khmer Rouge," one UNTAC military observer remarked to me. "They won't move." Another observer asked the Indonesians to transport him on one of their Zodiac rubber boats to verify reports of troop and tank movements a few miles down a river. The Indonesians refused, saying first that the water was too shallow and second that the boats were broken. Neither was true.

Rudi Warjiri, an Indian Foreign Service officer who was deputy head of the civilian branch of UNTAC in Kompong Thom, said that the Indonesians treated the Cambodian population well. "But what benefit is there for UNTAC's mission that they are so close to the Khmer Rouge? It has not helped the electoral components, or human rights or anything else." A particularly sore point was the abduction of eight Vietnamese fishermen—four men, one woman and three young boys from a fishing village on the Great Lake, the Tonle Sap. General Men Ron at first acknowledged that his men had abducted the Vietnamese, but claimed that they were soldiers. Subsequently he denied that his men had abducted them.

The case was taken up by the UNTAC Human Rights Office in Kompong Thom. The Indonesian battalion was asked to tell the Khmer Rouge to hand over the Vietnamese. The Indonesians were slow to do so. General Sanderson, the UNTAC force commander, wrote to Son Sen, the Khmer Rouge defense minister, to demand their release and to warn that any harm done to them would be punishable under law.

In Kompong Thom, I asked Colonel Ryamizard about the fishermen's fate. He said that he thought they were still alive and that General Men Ron had stated this. But UN military observers had already seen and photographed bodies which they believed to be of the Vietnamese. The bodies were never retrieved.

It is sometimes hard for peacekeeping troops to be truly neutral, to observe only the commands of the UN and not the priorities of their own governments. Indonesia, an important Southeast Asian regional power, felt able to behave as it wished. The Indonesian government had long-term strategic interests in Indochina which would remain long after UNTAC left. It wished to maintain good relations with all Cambodian factions so as not to jeopardize its relations with a possible coalition government. All of these factors affected the behavior of its battalion.

ONE day in late November, I flew with Yasushi Akashi, the civilian head of UNTAC, by helicopter to inspect several of the outposts of his empire. UNTAC was served by Russian helicopters crewed by Russians whose uniform was blue boxer shorts, blue undershirts and flip-flops. (This informal attire was taken as an insult by one Thai general, who refused to board the helicopter sent for him unless the crew were properly dressed.) Our first stop was a UN post on the border with Vietnam.

The Khmer Rouge were still exploiting the issue of the Vietnamese presence in Cambodia. This had resonance since most Cambodians have always feared Vietnamese domination. There was no evidence to support the Khmer Rouge claim that Vietnamese military forces were still in the country. But there were undoubtedly still Vietnamese civilian advisers to the Phnom Penh regime, and there had been a huge influx of Vietnamese emigrants in recent months, many of them demobilized soldiers looking for work. As artisans they had been invaluable in the rebuilding now taking place in Phnom Penh. There were also thousands of Vietnamese small traders here, as well as Vietnamese prostitutes catering to UNTAC.

To show that it took the issue seriously, UNTAC had installed new control posts along the frontier. After passing over beautiful waterlogged country crisscrossed by canals, rivers and streams, our helicopter landed on a narrow dike between two paddy fields in the Kiri Vong district of Prey Veng province. In a small wooden house on the dike, a crisp Bangladeshi officer gave us an efficient briefing and revealed that after its 1978 invasion, Vietnam had arbitrarily shifted the border here some two and a half miles into Cambodia; scores of villagers had been cut out of their country. Many such border changes had been imposed by Vietnam, and they remained a source of anger to Cambodians. The officer pointed out that there were so many footpaths through the woods and the fields here, and elsewhere, that the border was almost impossible to control. On the dike outside, a UN volunteer from Sri Lanka, Ranjit Jayesingha, said that there were serious problems of intimidation of election teams by the Cambodian army.

After another border post on the Mekong itself, the pomp and circumstance of the UN were in proud display when we dropped out of the sky at the UN civil administration headquarters in Svay Rieng. The helicopter was greeted at the playing field where it landed by a fleet of fourteen white Toyota Land Cruisers, each of which was to drive one of Akashi's party the couple of hundred yards to the provincial headquarters.

Akashi was late. There was time only for a very hurried but determinedly optimistic briefing from the UN's civil administrator of the province, a long-serving UN official. When the human rights worker, Philip Ramaga, from Uganda, tried to speak about intimidation of other political parties by the State of Cambodia, he was brushed aside by senior UN officials. The party then dashed downstairs for formal speeches and lunch under a gazebo especially constructed for this occasion and lavishly decorated with flowers and bunches of bananas.

A visit to the headquarters of the Bulgarian battalion stationed in Svay Rieng was canceled, but this perhaps was not critical. Of the foreign troops stationed here in UNTAC, the Bulgarians were deemed the worst, said to be more interested in organizing prostitution rings than in monitoring cease-fire violations.

At the next town, Prey Veng, the pomp and reverence with which UN officials treat their superiors was again on display. A French UN official made a speech in which he said that until now Akashi was a distant personality. "Now here I am in front of you, your devoted servant. You can imagine my satisfaction but also my apprehension at being your interlocutor." But there was also time to air grievances about the UN bureaucracy. Of these, the most scandalous was that thousands of UNTAC's Cambodian staff had not been paid for months. The international staff had all been receiving their salaries plus their per diem payments on time, but not the Cambodians, who were supposed to be paid up to $140 a month, with no per diem. In many provinces the international staff had been paying their Cambodian workers out of their own pockets. At the end of November some of the international staff threatened to stage a sit-in at UNTAC headquarters in protest.

At each stop, Akashi emphasized the need for the UN to create a neutral political atmosphere for the election. To Cambodian local politicians, he said, "UNTAC is here to help Cambodians exercise their full democratic rights, respecting the rights and liberties of others." He acknowledged that getting used to the idea of competing political parties was difficult, especially for the Hun Sen regime, which was used to ruling through brute force.

Akashi and General Sanderson then flew to Thailand to try to persuade the Thai government to observe Security Council resolutions on restricting the Khmer Rouge border traffic and imposing an oil blockade on them. As usual, the Thais were unable to give any such guarantees. "The Thai government is obviously under great pressure from its military and from business interests," said Akashi.

Much of Cambodia's border with Thailand was inaccessible to the UN. An appalling assault upon the environment was being conducted by a combination of the Khmer Rouge, communists who disavowed private enterprise more completely than other Marxists, and Thai businessmen, who were abetted by the Thai military and government. Hundreds of thousands of trees were being felled over large areas of forestland. Thousands of truckloads of earth had been driven out of the country to be sifted for the gems that it contained. As a result, rivers had become polluted and Sihanouk himself had warned that the assault threatened the ecology of the Great Lake, from which Cambodia derives much of its natural wealth. The UN had made an aerial film of the devastation. It was a piece of environmental pornography.

B y the end of 1992, some Western commentators had written off UNTAC, the most common complaint being that the UN was too soft on the Khmer Rouge. But it was not UNTAC's mandate to fight the Khmer Rouge. If UNTAC had declared war and if some of its peacekeeping soldiers had been killed, the troop-contributing countries would soon have demanded a change or have withdrawn their men. General Sanderson's policy of containing the Khmer Rouge and allowing them to wither in isolation seemed the only sensible course. The downside to that policy, not all of it the fault of UNTAC, was different.

UNTAC had shied away from facing the truth that the overall Paris agreement as such was now dead. The UN was reduced to staging an election with only three of the four main factions taking part. There had been little progress on the rehabilitation of the country. Donors had pledged $880 million at a conference in Tokyo in June, but almost none of that had arrived by the end of 1992. The economy and the country's infrastructure were still in ruins. Indeed, the economy probably functioned at all only because Cambodia was still a country of subsistence farmers and fishermen.

On the positive side, many UNTAC officials worked hard for their money and had secured notable achievements. The electoral process was, so far, a remarkable success. The human rights component was spreading important ideas around the country.

Under UNTAC's umbrella, the UN High Commissioner for Refugees had been relatively successful in repatriating the 370,000 refugees along the Thai border. So far over 200,000 had come home safely. There were 170,000 more to come. One problem had been finding land for them which was free of mines. UNHCR originally promised them either agricultural land or a cash payment. When it became clear that not enough land was available, there was a risk that the whole repatriation program might collapse, but UNHCR officials persuaded the refugees to opt for the cash instead. They were repatriated, but many were cast into awful poverty.

The original mission of the UN battalions—cantonment and disarmament of all the troops—was now abandoned, but some of the foreign soldiers were doing fine work in bringing public health and other services to villagers (the Uruguayans and the Bangladeshis were widely praised).

It seemed to me at the end of 1992 that if, despite the threats from the Khmer Rouge and from the State of Cambodia, the election could be held in most of the country, UNTAC would have given Cambodians an opportunity to move toward a more decent, accountable government. After UNTAC, in the end the leadership could come only from Cambodians. The long-term success of the UNTAC investment would depend on whether, at last, Cambodian political leaders could cooperate with goodwill to address the huge underlying problems of the country. UNTAC, Yasushi Akashi pointed out, "cannot force Cambodians to be free." Perhaps he should have said UNTAC could not force Cambodian leaders to give their people freedom. Dealing with warlords, whether in Cambodia, the former Yugoslavia, Somalia or anywhere, that is nearly always so.

4

Crossing the
Mogadishu Line

M AYBE it was, in the end, "the economy, stupid," but keeping the peace and the way in which the world should respond to post–Cold War human disasters was an important theme of the 1992 U.S. presidential election campaign. Two countries in dire need of assistance, Bosnia and Somalia, were intertwined, both rhetorically and militarily, in a way which ultimately helped neither.

In August 1992, Western reporters discovered what some called the concentration camps the Bosnian Serbs had created to imprison Bosnian Muslim men. Although "concentration camp" was not an accurate description, the conditions were grotesque, and the images of emaciated men from the camps at Omarska and Keraterm were deeply shocking when they were broadcast around the world. President George Bush denounced the camps and demanded that they be closed. Some were, but the Serbs continued with their brutal policies of ethnic cleansing—raping, beating, mutilating, murdering, expelling people from their homes.

Public outcry grew more intense. Calling for a more active response, candidate Bill Clinton said, "President Bush's policy towards the former Yugoslavia mirrors his indifference to the massacre at

Tiananmen Square and his coddling of Saddam Hussein. . . . Once again, the administration is turning its back on violations of basic human rights and our own democratic values." He made it clear that he would be prepared to lift the arms embargo on Bosnia, which had been imposed on all of the former Yugoslavia in September 1991. He said he would sanction air strikes against Serbian targets—not only in Bosnia but also in Serbia itself.

During the campaign Clinton also said that troops should be sent to Somalia to alleviate the appalling starvation that was seen on television through much of 1992. He even endorsed the idea, around for many years but never seriously considered by the United States, of a standing UN army, of a small "rapid deployment force" which could conduct such operations as "standing guard at the borders of countries threatened by aggression, preventing mass violence against civilian population, providing humanitarian relief and combating terrorism."

Human rights officials and advocates strove to get Washington to agree that what was happening in Yugoslavia was genocide. The Bush administration did everything it could to distance itself from any mention of the term. If Serbian atrocities were accepted as "genocide," international law would come into full play. Governments would no longer be able to refer to "warring factions" which must be separated. "Genocide" would create a moral, political and legal demand for decisive intervention. And that was what the U.S. government felt it could not afford.

Just before the election General Colin Powell, the chairman of the Joint Chiefs of Staff, took the offensive against those who were urging intervention. As well as lobbying within the administration against a U.S. commitment, he stated in an article in the *New York Times* that objectives must be clear before military force is projected. "You bet I get a little nervous when so-called experts suggest that all we need is a little surgical bombing or a limited attack. When the desired result isn't obtained, a new set of experts comes forward with talk of a little escalation. History has not been kind to this approach," he wrote, invoking the ghost of Vietnam. The same ghost was summoned by Radovan Karadzic, who proclaimed that Bosnia would become "a new Vietnam" if the West intervened.

Instead of risking another "quagmire" in the Balkans, Bush decided to send American troops to another place where help was desperately needed, but where he was told the risks would be fewer—Somalia. As Lawrence Eagleburger, a former U.S. ambassador to Yugoslavia who was briefly secretary of state, said, "We knew the costs weren't so great and there were some potential benefits." General Powell himself was said to have predicated his support for U.S. intervention in Somalia on the condition that the United States would make no such effort in Bosnia. As Elizabeth Drew, the well-known political writer, pointed out, "Bosnia and Somalia were to continue to have reciprocal effects on each other."

o

THE Somalis are a culturally, linguistically and religiously similar people, divided into six distinct clans who live scattered sparsely over harsh, dry land. People identify with their clan, not with the state, and the state has often been weak. Three fifths of the five million people live as nomads or semi-nomads in the deserts, herding animals. Only about 10 percent of the population live in the cities, most in the capital, Mogadishu.

The state of Somalia was created in 1960 by combining the former British and Italian colonies in the Horn of Africa. After the state's nine difficult years as a Muslim republic, attempting a form of pluralism, a coup d'état was staged by Major General Mohammed Siad Barre, who began to establish a Marxist-Leninist dictatorship as a client state of the Soviet Union. He outlawed all political opposition and attacked the clan system. But at the same time he favored his own clan in appointments, and his autocracy actually increased the strength of clan structures.

By the end of the eighties, as Gorbachev cut back aid to distant outposts of the Soviet empire, including Somalia, the state which Barre was trying to create lost strength to clan power. In January 1991 he was deposed by rival clans, including the Somali National Alliance (SNA) led by Mohammed Aideed.

Bad government was replaced by no government. The clans which took over had no concept of a nation-state. Throughout 1991 they fought among themselves as government, civil society and basic services collapsed. Law and order disintegrated, and by the end of the year there was anarchy. Gangs of heavily armed thugs careered along the roads on "technicals," light trucks or jeeps fitted with machine guns, terrorizing, killing, looting food and other aid provided by the international community. It was, as Secretary General Boutros-Ghali pointed out, "a war of all against all." By 1992, Somalia was more a geographical expression than a country.

Then the rains failed. As a result, the nomadic, pastoral people of the interior—the vast majority of the population—began to starve to death. Some believe that more than half a million Somalis died in the course of 1992. In Mogadishu and other towns, clan warlords and the military terrorized and exploited refugee populations and the Western nongovernmental agencies which came in to try to alleviate the suffering.

During the Cold War, Somalia and the rest of the Horn of Africa had been the focus of intense strategic competition between East and West. Now, at least at first, there was indifference. Far more resources were already being committed to Bosnia where, for all the horrors, far fewer people were dying. This contrast led Boutros-Ghali to make one of his more famous and challenging aphorisms, accusing the Security Council of "fighting a rich man's war in Yugoslavia while not lifting a finger to Somalia. . . ." He complained to the British ambassador to the United Nations that the crises in Bosnia and Somalia were similar "except for the fact that the parties in Somalia are not sophisticated and did not wish the UN to become involved, whereas those in Bosnia are sophisticated, welcome the UN, but violate the agreements the UN helps them to conclude."

Western television news cameras and print journalists began to pay some attention to Somalia. The images of death captured the attention of the international community. The first of three spasms of international involvement began with Security Council Resolution 751 of April 24, 1992. Its wording was significant and illustrated both post–Cold War euphoria and the unwillingness of the council to take political action. Its basis was purely humanitarian. The council decided that "the magnitude of human suffering" in Somalia constituted a threat to peace and security. This was a significant extension of the concept. Until now a threat to international peace and security had always involved some kind of cross-border dispute involving at least two sovereign states. This was no longer so. A purely humanitarian response met the popular Western demand that "something must be done" at, it was hoped, relatively little cost to the main powers. In the absence of a feasible political plan, it had little hope of reversing Somalia's spiral of disintegration, but it is fair to ask whether any such plan could be devised, let alone imposed.

The resolution created UNOSOM I and authorized the secretary general to appoint a special representative; deploy an observer group to monitor a cease-fire in Mogadishu; and establish a security force, only five hundred strong, to protect the delivery of humanitarian assistance in the country. It was not mandated to use force; it depended entirely on the consent of the warring factions, and so none of its aims was met. Boutros-Ghali chose as his special representative Mohammed Sahnoun, a gifted Algerian diplomat, who was to try to reconcile the clans; he later resigned in a policy dispute with Boutros-Ghali. There was never a real cease-fire in Mogadishu, and the security force was unable to protect the aid and see that it went only to the starving. Instead, a lot of it went straight to clan fighters.

The troops of UNOSOM I were Pakistanis; authorized in April, they did not arrive till September—largely because Mohammed Aideed refused till then to allow them. They were supposed to safeguard food shipments arriving at the airport and escort food convoys. Instead, their rules of engagement meant that they remained virtual prisoners at the airport, humiliated and abused by armed gangs of looters who made it impossible for them to carry out their mission. Subsequently, the Security Council authorized another three thousand Belgian and Canadian troops. These never arrived.

As in Biafra at the end of the 1960s, in Cambodia after 1979, in Ethiopia in the mid-eighties and as it was beginning to do in Bosnia in the nineties, humanitarian assistance saved lives but also provided the warlords with currency to expand the conflict. As one writer has put it, "Far from there being protection for the delivery of humanitarian assistance, the assistance itself gave rise to protection rackets throughout Somalia."

By the end of the year, the Bush administration determined that the only organization capable of meeting the needs of the country was the U.S. military. Force must be used. In December 1992 the Security Council passed Resolution 794, which declared that "the situation in Somalia is intolerable" and authorized "all necessary means" to establish a secure environment for the delivery of aid. The Security Council welcomed a U.S. offer to send in troops.

What the resolution created was not a UN peacekeeping mission but a multinational mission of "armed humanitarianism." It was called UNITAF and was known in Washington as Restore Hope. The force was to be large—thirty-seven thousand in all, of whom twenty-eight thousand were to be Americans. Washington ultimately limited the duration of its troop commitment to May 1993, when the UN should take over again. Resolution 794 allowed the U.S. military to use force to achieve security and stability. But it miscalculated the impact the U.S. Army would have. When a massive U.S. armed force appeared in a country where there were no institutions, they became in effect the state. If they were to withdraw, they first had to create a new state to succeed them. That was not possible.

Washington declared the mission nonpolitical, but there is no such thing as a vast military intervention which has no political impact or subtext. The secretary general insisted that UNITAF must disarm the factions by force if necessary. This was very dangerous and the Pentagon demurred but eventually made efforts to get factions to disarm voluntarily. Even this altered the balance of power between the factions. And the fact that U.S. commanders had to negotiate with faction leaders to move supplies into the worst affected areas of the country gave those leaders stature and power that they had never before enjoyed.

Within its terms of reference Restore Hope had important successes. It may not have restored hope over the long term, but it certainly did so for a while; above all, it restored life to many hundreds of thousands of starving people. But the mission was meant as more than a mere food drop. It was supposed to help rebuild this classic "failed state" so that it did not simply tumble into another cycle of chaos, warlordism and famine. The real problem came a few months into the Clinton administration when Restore Hope was replaced by UNOSOM II. This was a UN mission but still one very much under American control, and it was ambitious.

o

I N the early days of his administration, Clinton emphasized the importance of the United Nations in his strategic views. The ambassador to the UN was to be Madeleine Albright; she was also made a member of the Cabinet and of the National Security Council. Agencies were restructured in order to give greater weight to the UN. The new administration seemed enthusiastic about the possibilities of peacekeeping. A new post was created—assistant secretary for peace-keeping and democracy in the Department of Defense, as were new offices for peacekeeping in the State Department. In his inaugural address Clinton said that the United States was ready to use force "if the will and conscience of the international community is defied." But there always seemed to be a disjuncture between the administration's rhetoric and its practice. It was a catastrophic disjuncture for Bosnia.

At this stage UNPROFOR's mandate still centered on the protection of humanitarian assistance, but more and more responsibilities were being added by a Security Council that remained fundamentally divided on whether Bosnia was experiencing a civil war or an external invasion, and that still felt forced, from time to time, to respond to public opinion at home. Military flights (by Serb aircraft in particular) were now banned over Bosnia and the ban was to be monitored; UNPROFOR was also supposed to monitor adherence to cease-fires and to set up and police weapons-exclusion zones. But none of these would be as fateful for the UN in general and for UNPROFOR in particular as the creation of "safe areas" out of the Muslim enclaves in eastern Bosnia, which nonaligned states sympathetic to Bosnia had begun to suggest at the end of 1992.

Clinton's new national security team—Secretary of State Warren Christopher, Secretary of Defense Les Aspin and National Security Adviser Tony Lake—disagreed on Bosnia. Lake wanted a tough response toward Serb aggression. Aspin thought Bosnia was "a loser from the start"—that no intervention would be successful unless massive military force was applied. The best that could happen would be a divided Bosnia with the Serbs maintaining what they had already seized. Secretary of State Christopher was ambivalent on Bosnia policy.

Clinton had promised forceful action during the campaign. Christopher now stated that if the problem of Bosnia was not solved, "you may well have the entire Balkans involved . . . and it could draw in Greece and Turkey. . . . The United States has an interest in preventing the world going up in flames." But his firefighting tactics were limited. Washington would appoint a special envoy to the talks; it would tell all parties that the only solution lay through negotiations; it would strengthen sanctions. In other words, it would do virtually nothing. Zbigniew Brzezinski, Jimmy Carter's national security adviser, pointed out that "the powerful rhetoric used by Secretary Christopher to justify U.S. engagement was . . . refuted by the toothless and essentially procedural steps that emanated from the rhetoric."

The administration's first attempt at a Bosnia policy was to reject the peace plan prepared in great detail and after arduous negotiations by the former secretary of state Cyrus Vance and David Owen, the former British foreign secretary, who was now representing the European Union. For the last few months Vance and Owen had conducted an exhausting shuttle between the Balkan warlords. Their plan was based on a new map of a united Bosnia divided into ten cantonments drawn as closely as possible on ethnic lines. It provided for a constitutional agreement, a cease-fire within seventy-two hours followed by a fifteen-day withdrawal of forces from Sarajevo, followed by forty-five days for the separation of forces. It defined Bosnia as a decentralized state with the cantons having substantial local autonomy. It required the Serbs to surrender a great deal of conquered territory and to return the property they had seized.

Vance was close to many members of the new administration and believed they would accept his work. Not so. As soon as he and Lord Owen had presented the plan privately in Washington, they realized they would have trouble. When they briefed Warren Christopher, Owen wrote later, it became "painfully apparent" that the secretary had barely studied their proposals. It seemed that "he had not had time to read even a short factual information sheet on what was the essence of our plan. I was baffled as to how Christopher could come so badly briefed to meet his old boss, Cy, who was under virulent public attack over a plan his critics claimed favoured ethnic cleansing."

Clinton's advisers decided, or at least they said, that the plan rewarded the Bosnian Serbs by giving them too much territory in the new cantonment structure. They refused Boutros-Ghali's request to endorse the plan. Instead, officials of the new administration began to propose that they push for the lifting of the arms embargo on all the parties and nations of the former Yugoslavia—an embargo that hurt the Bosnians most. And they would encourage the use of airpower against the Serbs. Both these proposals were opposed by the countries contributing troops to UNPROFOR, in particular Britain and France. They feared their men and women would be under even greater threat of retaliation if the Serbs were bombed. They would not be able to protect themselves.

Washington's public rhetoric and private assurances encouraged the Bosnian government to believe that the United States would intervene on its side. The Bosnians stalled on signing on to the Vance-Owen plan. Owen was furious about charges that his plan rewarded the Serbs: he pointed out that it required them to give up 38.6 percent of the territory they had gained, keeping only 43 percent of the country. (The Dayton peace plan devised and imposed by the United States in 1995 gave the Serbs more—49 percent.)

What the administration did not or would not understand was that the Vance-Owen plan did not pretend to be a "just settlement." It was, in fact, designed as an imperfect alternative to war which reflected basic political realities, including the unwillingness of Western powers, above all the United States, to commit their forces to impose a settlement of which they approved. Owen had warned the Bosnians in Sarajevo, "Don't, don't, don't live under this dream that the West is going to come in and sort this problem out. Don't dream dreams." The plea fell on deaf ears then and for some time to come. The new American president had promised strong action time and time again—and the Bosnians now expected it. But having encouraged Bosnian hopes and military adventurism—and thus cost more Bosnian lives—Clinton shied further and further away from the real commitment of U.S. resolve that he had promised.

As a result of congressional pressure for more decisive action, the administration increased its commitment to the "lift and strike" option—lifting the arms embargo and striking the Serbs—and further criticized its European allies. They were castigated for callousness and faintheartedness as U.S. officials attempted to shift the blame for the administration's failure to live up to its campaign promises onto the Europeans. In fact, the advice from the Pentagon—as opposed to that from some State Department officials—was as cautious as that of the Europeans.

The administration remained deeply divided throughout 1993. Colin Powell, the chairman of the Joint Chiefs, recalls in his memoirs that the discussions that "the principals" had over America's role in the world "wasn't policy making, it was group therapy. . . . [T]he discussions [meandered] like graduate-student bull sessions or the think-tank seminars in which many of my new colleagues had spent the last twelve years while their party was out of power." Powell was more determined than anyone else to see that "Vietnam" was not "repeated" by foolish, incautious or ignorant politicians.

On May 18, Secretary Christopher, having undercut Vance-Owen, told Congress of the administration's determination to enhance the UN's peacekeeping capabilities. He described the tragedies of Somalia and Bosnia as "grim witness to the price of international delay" and said that in the future, "International peacekeeping—especially by the UN—can and must play a critical role. Capabilities must be enhanced to permit prompt, effective, preventive action. And the U.S. must be prepared to pay its fair share. Millions invested in peacekeeping now may save hundreds of millions in relief later."

This was echoed by Albright when she told Congress a few weeks later that it was for the United States a "top priority this year to work with the UN Secretariat and key peacekeeping contributors to ensure that the UN is equipped with a robust capacity to plan, organize, lead and service peacekeeping activities." Albright said that the U.S. was "pushing" for particular UN reforms, such as the creation of an operations center in New York and a revolving stock of peacekeeping equipment; a register of peacekeeping forces available from member states at any time; and the development of standardized procedures which would enable more effective coordination. This was all supportive in tone, but otherwise not a great change from the proposals outlined by President George Bush to the General Assembly in September 1992.

o

B Y early 1993 in Cambodia the election campaign was in full force. The months since UNTAC's deployment had been an extraordinarily difficult, dangerous and frightening time for UN officials in UNTAC and for many ordinary Cambodians. By the end of 1992, UNTAC had, in effect, stopped trying to pursue the comprehensive political settlement spelled out in the Paris agreement. Instead, it was attempting merely to create a new Cambodian government with domestic and international legitimacy. It had agreed to a de facto reduction of the mandate conferred by the Paris agreement; this had been accepted in a series of UN Security Council resolutions.

UNTAC's electoral component, working with its seven hundred UN volunteers, had managed to register a phenomenal number of voters by the end of 1992. The enthusiasm the Cambodian people brought to voter registration was a welcome surprise to all UNTAC officials. Meanwhile, the UN High Commissioner for Refugees was still proceeding with the repatriation of refugees from their ten-year exile in camps along the Thai border.

Throughout this period Prince Sihanouk was supposed to chair the Supreme National Council, but he spent large amounts of time out of the country. Sometimes he was at one of his favorite homes in exile in North Korea, where poor communications kept him almost completely out of touch with Phnom Penh, or in Beijing, where several meetings of the Supreme National Council actually had to be held.

From Beijing, Sihanouk issued a stream of faxes and statements, some on the poor state of his health, which, he said, required him to remain in China, and others on the poor state of Cambodia. He became increasingly critical of UNTAC and insisted that he would bring the Khmer Rouge back into government whatever the results of the "UNTACist" election. At the end of 1992 he tried to arrange for presidential elections to be held before those for the Constituent Assembly. He was supported by France, but the proposal ultimately foundered.

Altogether twenty different parties registered to compete in the election scheduled for May 1993. Some UN officials hoped right up to the registration deadline in early February 1993 that the Khmer Rouge would return to the process. But despite several Security Council resolutions insisting that all sides comply with the Paris agreement, the Khmer Rouge did not do so. Instead, secure along the Thai border, they were now making as much as $20 million a month from the sale of gems and timber. The Supreme National Council banned the export of logs, but the Khmer Rouge and the Thais evaded the restrictions by setting up sawmills just inside the Cambodian border so that they could export planks rather than logs. The Phnom Penh regime also exported large amounts of timber. Powerful men made a lot of money.

There was escalating violence in the months leading up to the election. The Khmer Rouge fired on UNTAC helicopters and detained UNTAC personnel, sometimes for days at a time. Much worse, they continued murderous attacks upon Vietnamese residents of Cambodia, hoping to turn their presence into a major election issue. More than one hundred Vietnamese civilians were murdered in different incidents. Few Cambodian politicians denounced the attacks outright, and Sihanouk advised ethnic Vietnamese to leave Cambodia for their own safety. For its part, the Phnom Penh regime embarked on a policy of harassing and physically attacking all its political opponents, especially the royalist party, Funcinpec. The regime employed what it called reaction forces and A-groups, often vigilante thugs.

UNTAC responded with one of its bolder initiatives. Its control teams mounted investigations into the activities of these groups in three provinces, Prey Veng, Kompong Cham and Takeo, and managed to seize provincial government working papers and even notebooks. Its "UN-Confidential" reports revealed that the regime was sabotaging and intimidating political parties wherever it could. One provincial police report from Prey Veng boasted of "preventing utterly the work of other parties." It revealed: "We have assigned forces to . . . prevent [other parties from] engaging in their activities. We have broken their internal forces. . . . We have sent good forces to attack and break them in a timely manner. . . ." Government officials handpicked troublemakers, "persons with foul mouths," to carry out attacks on its opponents.

By early 1993, after government agents had killed or wounded at least a hundred Funcinpec officials, Prince Ranariddh, the leader of Funcinpec and son of Prince Sihanouk, came under great pressure from within his own party and from his former Khmer Rouge allies to withdraw from the election. That would have destroyed the election entirely. He refused to do it.

The broadcasts of Radio UNTAC helped offset the political impact of the violence of the regime and the threats of the Khmer Rouge. They became one of the most successful components of the UN's operations in Cambodia. For the first time Cambodians had a free and unbiased source of information, and nearly the entire population became avid listeners. Along with UNTAC's civic education programs, Radio UNTAC was crucial in convincing ordinary voters that they could ignore intimidation and vote secretly. Even Khmer Rouge soldiers became loyal listeners. Independent radio stations may well prove essential to future UN peacekeeping operations.

The weeks leading up to the election of May 23 were increasingly tense for UNTAC and war-weary Cambodians. Violence from both the Khmer Rouge and the government's People's Party increased. When a twenty-year-old Japanese volunteer, Atsuhito Nakata, was murdered in Kompong Thom province, many people feared that it marked the beginning of an all-out Khmer Rouge assault upon the UN workers who were so crucial to the electoral process.*

After Nakata's death, eighteen of the thirty UN volunteers in Kompong Thom left, though they had already decided to do so before his murder, citing concerns over the security arrangements in this dangerous province. Throughout the rest of the country, most volunteers remained at their often isolated electoral posts in the countryside. They were very brave. In the remote eastern town of Snuol, Jeff Bloor, a Canadian UN volunteer, wrote in his diary: "All of us are dismayed at Atsu's death and it's sapped us of much of our enthusiasm, motivation and cheer. I'm still fairly certain that Snuol is safe but it's impossible to be sure, now that the KR have left the process entirely."

Fears mounted when, at the end of April, the Khmer Rouge pulled their last remaining representatives from Phnom Penh. This seemed to presage attacks on Phnom Penh itself. Some senior UNTAC officials felt that the Paris agreement's precondition for a "neutral political environment" did not exist, and the election should be postponed or even canceled. But that, of course, was just what the Khmer Rouge sought.

On May 3 in Snuol, Jeff Bloor was told that the Khmer Rouge were about to attack the town. "Thirty more Uruguayans are on their way to Snuol tomorrow and two helicopters are to be made ready in case we have to beat a hasty retreat." The attack did not happen, but throughout the country Cambodians and UN workers alike

---

* Subsequently, a UN investigation revealed that the Khmer Rouge did not, in fact, carry out Nakata's murder. He was apparently killed by a senior officer of the Phnom Penh regime. Following their son's death, Nakata's parents dedicated themselves in a very moving manner to promoting the cause of peaceful reconciliation. At the end of 1998, Kofi Annan awarded Nakata a posthumous peace prize.

waited, often in terror, for Khmer Rouge assaults. Their courage was remarkable.

On May 21, two days before the election was due to begin, two Chinese engineers serving with UNTAC were killed in a Khmer Rouge attack. The Security Council unanimously condemned the murders and also expressed its determination that the election take place as planned. By that point, China was no longer prepared to give any political support to its former Khmer Rouge client. UNTAC's approach had succeeded in isolating the Khmer Rouge.

From Beijing, whence he continued to alternate grudging praise and denunciations of the UNTAC plans, Sihanouk insisted that if the election was canceled, he would form a quadripartite administration including the Khmer Rouge. Khmer Rouge leaders tried to persuade him to sit out the election in China, and, until the very last moment, it seemed likely that he would do so. In the week before the election he received letters urging his return from both Boutros-Ghali and French president François Mitterrand. Reminding the prince that the world had invested much, including lives, in UNTAC, Mitterrand warned that no one would understand if he failed to go home and support the electoral process.

Sihanouk arrived in Phnom Penh with his customary North Korean bodyguards the day before the election. Some believe that his presence had a decisive effect, deterring Khmer Rouge attacks and instilling in the electorate the courage to vote. His return was certainly a significant blow to the Khmer Rouge.

o

I T was now, in spring 1993, as Clinton floundered for a Bosnia policy that both sounded courageous and was yet free of risk, that the names Srebrenica, Zepa and Gorazde began to flash across the consciousness and, to some extent, the conscience of the international community. These were traditional Muslim towns in eastern Bosnia close to the Drina River and the border with Serbia. They were now under sustained and vicious attack by Bosnian Serb forces determined to "ethnically cleanse" them and to drive the Muslims from their homes in order to make the hills along the border with Serbia a pure Serb heartland.

Srebrenica had been a relatively rich and rather pleasant silver and bauxite mining town. By now it was a prison crammed with Muslim refugees—those who had survived "cleansing" elsewhere—surrounded by Serbian-controlled mountains. The place was filthy with refuse and excrement in the streets and had almost no food.

But Srebrenica had held out against the Serb onslaught. Its defense was led by Naser Oric, an effective and ruthless guerrilla commander. He would muster large groups of starving Muslim refugees who would follow his soldiers into battle, descend on Serb villages and run amok, knifing, killing, looting, sparing no one. In one such attack on the village of Kravica on January 7, 1993, Orthodox Christmas, about three thousand Muslim soldiers and civilians swooped on the town, murdered forty-five people—soldiers, women, children—set fire to the houses and carted all the Christmas foods they found back to Srebrenica. A week later, as Oric and his men seized a bridge across the Drina in the town of Skelani, Serb women and children were machine-gunned as they fled. General Ratko Mladic, the Bosnian Serb commander, drove Oric and his men back toward Srebrenica.

By the spring of 1993 the hills around Srebrenica were filled with Serb artillery and mortars trained upon the Muslim citizens. Shells were set for air bursts to cause the maximum carnage. In one attack on Srebrenica, sixty-four people were killed and over a hundred wounded in just one hour; many of them were children playing in their schoolyard. Ham radio operators in Srebrenica begged for help, as NATO jets screamed above in futile shows of their presence but not their strength. The government in Sarajevo abused the UN for being "a passive witness and accomplice in tragedy" and requested the deployment of NATO ground troops.

The fighting now was a real test of international resolve. Warren Christopher declared: "Bold tyrants and fearful minorities are watching to see whether 'ethnic cleansing' is a policy the world will tolerate. If we hope to promote the spread of freedom or if we hope to encourage the emergence of peaceful multiethnic democracies, our answer must be a resounding no." But there was little resounding in U.S. policy.

UN officials were convinced that the Bosnian government was determined to exploit the suffering in order to force the United States to take stronger action against the Serbs. The Bosnian Muslims did this even to the extent of launching offensives that would delay aid convoys to starving enclaves, on the grounds that this would place even greater pressure on the UN mandate and increase the demands for more robust international intervention. They timed attacks to follow delivery of UN supplies; this made it appear as if they were being helped directly by the UN, which led the Serbs to disrupt future convoys—which led once more to calls for stronger intervention.

On March 10, 1993, UNPROFOR's Bosnia commander, General Philippe Morillon, managed to drive through Serb lines into Srebrenica, though the Serbs refused to let him take in a convoy of food and medicine. As soon as he arrived the Serb shelling eased—Mladic did not want to kill the UN general.

The local Bosnian authorities then decided that Morillon should not leave. Oric arranged for him to be surrounded by women and children who sat in front of his car, carrying posters reading, "Don't abandon us" and "If you leave, they will kill us." Morillon tried to slip out unseen at night; they stopped him again. So he decided to make a virtue of his dilemma; standing in the center of the town, with the blue flag of the United Nations in his hand, he declared, "You are now under the protection of the UN forces. I will never abandon you."

On March 19 the Serbs finally allowed an aid convoy into Srebrenica; it was mobbed by starving, desperate people, and after it had been emptied about seven hundred women and children fought their way aboard to be taken out of the town. When they arrived in Tuzla doctors found them in terrible condition.

Morillon then met in Belgrade with Milosevic and Mladic, and obtained their agreement for another convoy to bring supplies into Srebrenica and take people out. But after this second crammed exodus, the Bosnian authorities (and some UN officials) became concerned that the UN was carrying out the Serbs' own policy of ethnic cleansing. (Mladic agreed; he suggested three hundred trucks a day go in to take people out.) The government in Sarajevo wanted Srebrenica and other enclaves to be declared safe havens, protected by UN forces. If too many civilians were evacuated, no one would be there for the UN to protect. By the end of March, Bosnian forces were actually blocking all efforts to evacuate their people from the enclaves.

Mladic renewed his assault on Srebrenica, and Morillon, by now dedicated to if not obsessed with the town, set off there once again. But this time it was Serb women who besieged his cars in the town of Zvornik; he had to be saved from the crowd by Mladic's chief of staff, who flew in by helicopter, breaching the UN's no-fly zone to rescue the UN's force commander. The artillery assaults on Srebrenica increased in ferocity, and by the end of the second week in April the town was about to fall. It was saved, for the time being, by a demilitarization agreement between the Serbs and the Muslims sponsored by UNPROFOR, and then by the Security Council's safe areas resolution.

The idea of designating Sarajevo and the remote Muslim enclaves as safe areas had been discussed in the Security Council for months. Pakistan and some of the nonaligned were initially enthusiastic about the idea. UNPROFOR generals and UN peacekeeping officials were very much opposed. Sadako Ogata, the high commissioner for refugees, sent the secretary general a long paper detailing UNHCR's objections. She said that the real question was how to end the fighting and that creating safe areas might distract attention from that. She thought safe areas should be only a last resort and pointed out that all sides were either opposed to the idea or wanted to use safe havens to further their own military objectives. And, since there were almost no areas in Bosnia which were mono-ethnic, it would be almost impossible to make sure that any "safe area" was really safe. In addition, safe areas could consolidate front-line and territorial conquests, and thus have serious political consequences. It was also clear that UNPROFOR's existing mandates and resources did not fit the idea of safe areas. It would require a new mandate and greatly expanded forces.

UNPROFOR command shared all these and other reservations. They pointed out that the Kurdish area of northern Iraq—from which the safe areas model came—and Bosnia were very different. "The Kurds are at least partly nomadic and they were threatened by one side. In Bosnia Herzegovina we have a 3-sided civil war in which the population is, notwithstanding the ethnic cleansing, still very intermingled. The people of Bosnia are not nomadic. They will only leave their homes in the case of utmost emergency. Furthermore the consent of all sides would be needed."

But by April, with the appalling visions of Srebrenica on the nightly news, such reservations were set aside. On April 16 the Security Council passed Resolution 819, which demanded that all parties treat Srebrenica as a safe area and that the Bosnian Serbs cease their attacks and withdraw. The resolution required the secretary general to deploy UNPROFOR troops to Srebrenica in order to monitor the humanitarian situation there.

The next day Mladic and Bosnian general Sefer Halilovic agreed to a cease-fire in Srebrenica in the presence of the UNPROFOR commander, General Lars Eric Wahlgren, acting as mediator. All weapons inside Srebrenica would be handed over to UNPROFOR. The town would be demilitarized. A small contingent of UN troops was allowed in to start disarming the citizens who had endured such appalling assault and deprivation. This was not popular either in the ruined town itself or abroad among those who saw the defenders as innocent victims—which the vast bulk of them were.

Kofi Annan, who had succeeded Marrack Goulding as head of the UN's peacekeeping department, realized the implications, and in a cable to UNPROFOR headquarters a few days later he accepted that UNPROFOR was "lending its good offices to help both parties fulfil the commitments they have made to each other. This includes receiving weapons from the defenders of Srebrenica for the purpose of demonstrating to the attackers that they have no reason to attack. In doing so, however, UNPROFOR takes on a moral responsibility for the safety of the disarmed that it clearly does not have the military resources to honour beyond a point." He therefore discouraged disarmament. "Given your public statements that say Srebrenica is fully demilitarised, we see no need for UNPROFOR to participate in house-to-house searches for weapons. You will undoubtedly be made aware by the visiting Security Council delegation of the strong feeling amongst several member states that UNPROFOR should not participate too actively in 'disarming the victims.' "

The next relevant resolution, 824, of May 6 declared Sarajevo, Tuzla, Zepa, Gorazde and Bihac to be safe areas. The U.S. ambassador to the UN, Madeleine Albright, said that the conduct of the Bosnian Serbs following this resolution "will determine whether the use of force is inevitable."

Resolution 824 made no mention of disarming the populations of the safe areas. It embodied a fundamental, indeed fatal contradiction. The towns could either be demilitarized or not. If not, the Serbs were bound to continue to regard them as legitimate targets.

Moreover, as Annan informed Wahlgren, the nonaligned sponsors of the resolution were aware of UNPROFOR's "resource limitations" and intended it to deploy only some twenty to thirty soldiers to each town "as a symbol of the United Nations' commitment to the well-being of its inhabitants. The idea would not be to physically protect the town but raise the political price of any aggression."

Wahlgren replied that he understood the purpose of the symbolic commitment, but "the problem for the men on the ground will be if the safe area is utilized for military purposes by the owners especially because it's a safe area." Spreading UN platoons around the safe areas was acceptable in a peacekeeping mission in cooperation with all the parties, but "not as a military concept."

And resources were a real problem. Wahlgren believed that a platoon would not be enough—a company was the smallest unit that should be sent to each safe area. But the deployment of these troops would lessen UNPROFOR's ability to escort UNHCR aid convoys, still its main mandate. Moreover, there was no point in putting troops into the areas unless they had proper communications, and UNPROFOR had no spare equipment. "We had to strip one [communications] system out of this HQ today to enable an UNMO [UN military observer] team to deploy to Zepa," Wahlgren said.

These and other practical considerations continued to preoccupy the soldiers on the ground. They were overridden by the diplomats in New York. In Europe, David Owen, who had serious reservations about the safe areas concept, called on the United States to demonstrate its commitment to ending the war in Bosnia by contributing its own ground troops to UNPROFOR. In fact, as Owen well knew, the U.S. would do nothing of the sort.

THE mood of the moment was set by a journey Warren Christopher made in May through the capitals of Washington's European allies to discuss Bosnia. It was a failure. The administration had tried to bury the Vance-Owen peace plan, though the Bosnian parties were still discussing it. They pressed even harder to "lift" the arms embargo against the Bosnians and "strike" Serb targets with NATO fighter bombers until the Bosnians had time to absorb their new weapons. (How these weapons were actually to be delivered to the Bosnians quickly was not made clear.)

But Christopher and the other principals in Washington well understood that so long as the Europeans had "troops on the ground," unlike the Americans, they would not be likely to favor lift and strike. After all, it was their men and women who would be at risk from it, caught between a newly armed Bosnian army and a further enraged Serbian one. Christopher did not make much of a hard sell. On his return he told Clinton that the allies would not agree to lift and strike unless pushed very hard. He did not recommend it. Christopher told Congress that the conflict had "evolved into a war of all against all . . . a struggle between three groups . . . each possessing deep distrust and ancient hatreds for each other." He believed that the Bosnian combatants were not ready to make peace and that it would therefore be dangerous for Clinton to insert U.S. troops between them. The Europeans could be blamed for destroying the lift and strike option by their cowardice, and they duly were. In the words of the American journalist Mark Danner, "Bill Clinton had thus managed to shape the perfect policy; a rhetorical policy, one consisting solely of words. It brought moral credit; it carried no risk." Or, as Boutros-Ghali put it in his memoirs, "Washington had devised a way to gain domestic political benefit from tough talk about air strikes, knowing that it was shielded from acting because its European allies would never agree to put their personnel serving with the UN in Bosnia in danger."

At the same time the United States fully embraced the nonaligned caucus's idea of safe areas for the Muslims. In the week of May 17 the Russian foreign minister, Andrei Kozyrev, suggested that safe areas should be given international protection. The French agreed and suggested that the U.S. should also provide troops. Clinton said during a photo-op that he would not send U.S. troops into a "shooting gallery." On May 18, Christopher testified on Capitol Hill that Bosnia was "a problem from hell," "a morass" of ancient hatreds which had caused "atrocities on all sides," and declared that "at heart, this is a European problem."

Christopher invited the foreign ministers of Britain, France, Japan and Russia to Washington. On Saturday, May 22, the five foreign ministers committed themselves to "protecting" the six safe areas in Bosnia; the U.S. commitment was to provide airpower alone, in support of UNPROFOR troops. It was another minimalist approach, presented as the Bosnian policy.

Morillon then told Mladic that forces around the safe areas must be separated and weapons around them withdrawn. Mladic refused on the grounds that Srebrenica, among others, had not been disarmed. He warned Morillon that if the Muslims did not stop their attacks and if U.S. planes bombed the Serbs for defending themselves, then the Serb relationship with UNPROFOR would change. "We will become enemies."

In New York, Annan and his staff were still troubled about the agreement between the Bosnian Serbs and the government in Sarajevo that the Muslims disarm in the safe areas. Yet he understood that if UNPROFOR was expected to connive in continued Muslim arming of the areas, this would pose a huge danger of further attack and would indeed mean, as Mladic warned Morillon, that the United Nations would become the enemy of the Serbs. A comment from the UN's Situation Center in New York pointed out that the resolution "has been drafted to satisfy a multiplicity of concerns and interests of the diplomatic community and does not translate into an easily implementable instruction for the military." Notwithstanding such objections, the Security Council proceeded with preparing a new resolution.

On the afternoon of Tuesday, June 1, the Security Council held its 3,226th meeting. After it unanimously passed Resolution 834, which was intended to put further pressure on "the warring parties" in Angola to return to the UN-sponsored peace talks, the council informally discussed a revised draft of the safe areas resolution. Cape Verde, on behalf of the nonaligned caucus, said, in effect, that the present plans for the safe areas were far too little too late. The UK and U.S. disagreed. New Zealand believed it was essential that the resolution be adopted by consensus, and that it be crystal clear what it was intended to achieve. Hungary argued that the "modest and timid" response of the international community would not produce the intended result. The council should not just contain the situation but repel aggression.

They then moved on to discuss one of the other great current preoccupations of the United Nations—Cambodia, where the UN-run elections had just taken place. They had been an unexpected success, but what followed was not.

W H E N thunder broke over Phnom Penh early on the morning of Sunday, May 23, many people awoke fearing that it was a Khmer Rouge barrage. It was not. That morning hundreds of thousands of people arrived at ballot stations in the rain, on the first day in a week's voting. The political mood of Phnom Penh was epitomized by the responses awaiting first Chea Sim, the hard-line former Khmer Rouge who was now chairman of the communist-controlled People's Party (CPP), and Prince Ranariddh when they arrived at the Olympic Stadium to vote. Chea Sim was greeted by silence from thousands of voters; Ranariddh was given a rapturous welcome. Ranariddh easily won Phnom Penh.

Throughout the country people flocked to the polls in their best clothes. UN volunteers and Cambodian electoral workers checked voters' UN-issued ID cards, dipped their fingers in indelible invisible ink and handed each voter a large folded ballot paper with the symbols of the twenty participating parties. Voters went behind the cardboard booths, made their marks and often came out smiling. (Despite Cambodia's high illiteracy rate, the number of invalid papers was remarkably low, only about 4 percent.) This author has rarely seen anything so moving as the joy with which ordinary Cambodians defied violence and intimidation and seized the opportunity the world gave them to express their wishes. Nonetheless, the government's influence was clearly felt. In some areas turnout was high because government officials ordered people to vote. In some districts officials allegedly gave voters money to vote for the People's Party. In others people were reportedly forced to take fearsome oaths that they would do so. Truck drivers were threatened for renting to Funcinpec officials.

In Kompong Cham, Prime Minister Hun Sen was a candidate of the People's Party and enjoyed the support of his brother, whom many believed to be a notably corrupt governor. The regime had divided the population into groups of ten, with one party member controlling each group and responsible for getting them to the polls, ordering them how to vote as they went in and interrogating them as they came out. Nonetheless, Kompong Cham went to Funcinpec.

In some areas Khmer Rouge officers warned people that to vote would be to commit suicide. Before the election Khieu Samphan, the Khmer Rouge president, had insisted that no one would take part in what he called "this stinking farce." His speech was repeated on

Khmer Rouge radio throughout the election. After the voting began Khmer Rouge radio claimed that no one was going to the polls. As it became clear that the turnout was enormous, the radio was forced to acknowledge higher numbers, but never the truly startling figure of 90 percent turnout nationwide. Indeed, in one of his letters to Sihanouk, Khieu Samphan actually protested that such a high turnout was impossible. UNTAC officials would have been happy if 75 percent of the electorate had turned out to vote, but the overwhelming response represented a ringing endorsement of the process and a serious rebuff of the men of violence.

Theories abound about why the Khmer Rouge did not attack polling stations throughout the country. Some military analysts argue that they did as much as they could, and that their inaction reflected above all the logistical and manpower constraints upon them. General John Sanderson, UNTAC's force commander, believed that in much of the country, UNTAC's battalions and CPAF, the government forces, had managed to push the Khmer Rouge back from the main areas of population and polling.

Some Khmer Rouge defectors later said that a few days before the election, they had been instructed to cancel the planned attacks. Others in Kompong Thom province told journalist Nate Thayer of the *Phnom Penh Post* that their orders were to attack throughout the election. There was clear disarray. Perhaps the leadership finally decided that it could not enforce a complete boycott of the election, and believed that a victory by the Phnom Penh regime was not inevitable. Toward the end of the election week, as the massive size of the national turnout became obvious, some Khmer Rouge commanders in the northwest even trucked their people to the polls, where they presumably voted for Funcinpec.

Other intelligence reports assert that the Khmer Rouge's few allies—in the Thai and Chinese leaderships—warned them against destroying the election. The international community had invested so much that disruption would elicit such international obloquy that they could never have any hope of being included in any future coalition government.

Essentially, the Khmer Rouge effort to disrupt the elections foundered because of its basic political and ideological weaknesses. Steve Heder, one of the foremost Western scholars of Cambodia, who was working for UNTAC's information arm, argued that Pol

Pot lived in a fantasy world in which he believed that the Khmer Rouge had vast popular support and assumed that they would be able to mobilize the peasantry to attack the whole of Hun Sen's local political structure and the UNTAC-organized network of polling stations. He also believed that his troops had such good relations with the people that they would be able to pinpoint polling stations with attacks that would be sufficiently violent to scare UNTAC away but would not adversely affect "the masses."

"In fact," said Heder, "the Khmer Rouge had no such popular support and could not sustain a war against SOC [the State of Cambodia] in the villages, much less extend it to polling stations. The more people hated the Hun Sen regime, the more they wanted to vote, and the less they wanted to support the Khmer Rouge. Instead of boycotting the elections, as Pol Pot had presumed they would, the people boycotted the Khmer Rouge and used the elections to hand Hun Sen a stunning, peaceful defeat. Instead of a political opportunity, the Paris Agreements were the political death knell for Pol Pot." Both the international community and the Cambodians themselves had called the Khmer Rouge's bluff.

On Saturday, May 29, after polling ended, Yasushi Akashi declared UNTAC satisfied that the elections were free and fair. At a Supreme National Council meeting chaired by Prince Sihanouk at the palace that morning, Funcinpec promised to accept the results, whatever they were. But, speaking for the People's Party, Hun Sen refused to offer any such assurance.

After the ballot counting began on May 29, Radio UNTAC began to broadcast rolling totals of the votes as counted. The count went much more slowly than hoped. But by Tuesday, June 1, it appeared that the ruling People's Party was more widely hated than outside observers had realized—the party would not win even a plurality of seats in the new assembly. When the final results were declared, the Cambodian People's Party leaders found that intimidation had won them only 38 percent of the vote, whereas Funcinpec had 45 percent. In provinces like Kompong Cham where the intimidation was most serious, the people were most defiant. The eighteen or so smaller parties were virtually wiped out; the Buddhist Liberal Democrats (the renamed party of Son Sann, one of the doughtiest noncommunist resistance leaders) gained 3.8 percent of the vote. In terms of seats in the new Constituent Assembly, Funcinpec had fifty-eight, the

People's Party fifty-one, the BLDP ten and a fourth party, Molinaka, one. Over most of the country, people had voted for peace, for reconciliation, for Sihanouk and, perhaps above all, for change.

Power in Cambodia had never before been peacefully transferred as the result of free and fair elections. As soon as the unexpected results became known, there was a clear danger that the leaders of the People's Party would invoke the old, brutal traditions. The intense internecine maneuvering that followed illustrated the unchanged nature of politics in Cambodia.

The Paris peace agreement did not have much to say about the period of transition after the election. Annex 3, paragraph 1 of the agreement stated merely that within three months of the election the newly elected Constituent Assembly would complete its task of drafting and adopting a new constitution "and transform itself into a legislative Assembly which will form a new Cambodian Government."

This brevity was commendable and, perhaps, in view of Cambodia's tortuous political processes, wise. It did not, however, leave UNTAC with much guidance. Until the end of May 1993, UNTAC personnel were understandably preoccupied with the election. Many had also assumed that the People's Party would win. Now as power was divided, UNTAC was left very much a bystander. The political parties and Sihanouk himself seized the initiative. As soon as the voting trends had become clear, rumors began to circulate that army generals and hard-line communists in the administration were organizing a coup. Government spokesmen denounced election "irregularities," but these were, in fact, inconsequential. The next day Chea Sim, the People's Party leader, visited Sihanouk and asked him to negotiate a compromise with Ranariddh, but Ranariddh had left Phnom Penh saying he feared for his life.

Under pressure from Hun Sen, Sihanouk declared that he was forming his own government. UN officials in Phnom Penh described Sihanouk's action as a constitutional coup and a violation of the Paris agreement. Infuriated by the criticism, Sihanouk tore up his plan and on June 4 said that Ranariddh and the Hun Sen regime would now be responsible "for whatever bloody and tragic events that could happen to our hapless country and unfortunate people." He also attacked UNTAC for its "colonialism." The People's Party kept up the pressure. In what was a piece of theater—a frightening one—a faction of the party announced an "autonomous zone" in the eastern provinces of Prey Veng, Svay Rieng and Kompong Cham. Two days later five more provinces in eastern Cambodia were said to have seceded.

The "autonomous zone" was a farce with a serious purpose. The State of Cambodia regime unleashed its "A-group" and "reaction force" thugs. They smashed local offices of UNTAC, Funcinpec and other parties opposing the CPP. Opposition party workers were threatened, many were badly beaten and some were murdered. About four thousand people fled to Phnom Penh, and others went to Khmer Rouge areas. Demonstrations took place against UNTAC itself, and on June 12, Sihanouk demanded UNTAC's withdrawal from the area. UNTAC did evacuate some civilian staff but left its military and civilian police in place. Many of them were terrified and did little to help, but the Indian battalion serving with UNTAC in Kompong Cham remained calm and prevented the situation from degenerating further.

In an attempt to reverse the election results, the People's Party used the secession to blackmail both Funcinpec and UNTAC. The peacekeepers of UNTAC were shown to be unable to stop it. Akashi reminded the Phnom Penh regime of its responsibility to keep order and declared that the announcements of secession were "in violation of international law, the territorial integrity of Cambodia and the Paris peace accords."

The Constituent Assembly met for the first time on June 14, and in an almost surreal first act, declared null and void the March 1970 overthrow of Prince Sihanouk. The assembly thus expunged the act of lese majesty which had obsessed Sihanouk for twenty-three years. Recognizing him as true head of state through all the travails since 1970, it endowed him with unspecified "full and special powers."

On June 15 the People's Party secession ploy effectively ended. No punishment awaited the plotters. Funcinpec now realized that it would have to compromise with the People's Party if it was to gain any power by peaceful means. The reality of the emerging deal became apparent on June 16 when Sihanouk broadcast an announcement that a "Provisional National Government of Cambodia" would be formed at once. The interim government would run Cambodia until the constitution was approved. Sihanouk would serve as head of state with two co–prime ministers, one from Funcinpec and one from the CPP.

Believing that the CPP would never hand over full power, Ranariddh returned to Phnom Penh and agreed without enthusiasm to accept the conceit that the election had produced "no winners and no losers" and accepted parity with the People's Party in the provisional administration. He agreed that there should be both co–prime ministers and co-ministers of defense and interior. The division of portfolios reflected Sihanouk's suggestion: 45 percent Funcinpec, 45 percent CPP and 10 percent to the smaller parties. The Constituent Assembly then endorsed the provisional administration. The new arrangements did not reflect the margin of Funcinpec's election victory. Some of its officials were aghast that Ranariddh had conceded so much. But the compromise aptly reflected the administrative, military and even financial muscle of the CPP.

At the end of June, in his palace in Phnom Penh, Sihanouk assailed the People's Party for blackmailing him into cooperation. He told me that the party oppressed, intimidated and murdered people and served as "a champion of corruption." He blamed its members for trying to protect their own interests rather than those of Cambodia. They had given an ultimatum to Funcinpec, saying, "If you don't share power, there will be secession and civil war." The UN was powerless to stop this.

o

WHILE Cambodia teetered on the edge of a new era, UN officials in Bosnia and New York continued to wrestle with the safe areas resolution. It boiled down to what extra duties it would oblige the United Nations to undertake, and what extra "resources"—usually a euphemism for troops—would be provided. Operative paragraph 5 specifically exempted the Bosnian army from the requirement to withdraw its forces from safe areas. But paragraph 9 authorized UNPROFOR "to take the necessary measures, including the use of force, in reply to bombardments against the safe areas by any of the parties."

Kofi Annan thought that this was a recipe for dragging UNPROFOR deeper into the war. UNPROFOR's commander, General Wahlgren, agreed. He warned that under the resolution the Bosnians would be able to use the safe areas as havens in which to refit, rearm, train and prepare for further action. He was also worried about airpower being added as a further tool for UNPROFOR to achieve its mandate. He feared that NATO air strikes would bring humanitarian action to an end, as Karadzic had threatened. He doubted if the troop-contributing nations would wish to leave their contingents in UNPROFOR under the proposed mandate. "One cannot make peace and war at the same time," Wahlgren said.

Because of such concerns, the sponsors agreed to change the wording of the operative paragraphs. But by no means all of the military objections were taken into account. The drafters inserted into paragraph 9 the phrase "acting in self-defence," which had the effect of limiting UNPROFOR's scope of action. Thus it now authorized UNPROFOR "acting in self-defence, to take the necessary measures, including the use of force." But military and paramilitary units of the Bosnian government were still not required to withdraw from the safe areas. At the same time, the idea that the UN would "defend" the safe areas was dropped; now its job under paragraph 5 became simply "to deter attacks." Similarly, UNPROFOR was "to promote withdrawal" of hostile forces from around the safe areas, rather than "to ensure or enforce" such withdrawal.

These changes of language were crucial—and would prove disastrous. They may have been brilliant drafting which satisfied the diplomats at the UN, whose governments were not prepared to send troops to "defend" the safe areas. But it is doubtful whether many of the inhabitants of the proposed areas knew that the new resolution was not, after all, intended to defend them. On June 4, Resolution 836 was adopted by the Security Council. Thirteen of the fifteen votes were in favor; Pakistan and Venezuela abstained.

The safe areas debate was taking place against a background of many crises in which the UN was deeply involved, Somalia and Cambodia being among the most pressing. The day after 836 was passed, on June 5, twenty-six Pakistani peacekeepers were killed in Somalia and another fifty-six were wounded. This atrocity brought home once more the dangers of peacekeeping and the risks to the troops provided by member states.

In terms of the Bosnian safe areas, it was nonetheless extraordinary that for many members of the Security Council adoption of the resolution was enough. Implementation was a detail with which they seemed less concerned. On June 7, Annan held a meeting of the principal sponsors—France, Russia, Spain, Britain, the United States, plus Canada. All would have a heavy involvement in implementing 836.

Not one of the co-sponsors was willing to contribute any more troops for this vast and dangerous expansion of UNPROFOR's work that they had just mandated. Annan reminded them that UNPRO-FOR's preliminary military staff study had suggested that thirty-four thousand more troops would be needed if the safe areas were to be defended credibly. The secretary general gave similar warnings to the full council.

The British ambassador insisted that the French proposal of a "light option," involving only some seven thousand troops, was the preferred approach. He reminded Annan that the Security Council had deliberately chosen the words "to deter attacks on" and "to pro-mote" withdrawal of forces from around the safe areas. This meant many fewer troops than if UNPROFOR was to provide real defense and ensure withdrawal.

Knowing that it would be hard to find a large number of troops quickly, the co-sponsors said they preferred a gradual, incremental approach, starting with the redeployment of troops already in Bosnia. But how this was to be done was not clear; they agreed that UNPROFOR was already stretched to the limit. To Annan's relief, they agreed that the authority to initiate air strikes should rest with the force commander in Bosnia. They encouraged the peacekeeping department to work out arrangements with NATO to that effect. But despite the rhetoric accompanying 836, none of them seemed to en-visage a force capable of effectively defending the areas.

Throughout June and July, Annan repeatedly requested members of the Security Council and the usual troop-contributing countries to try to muster the extra seven thousand or so troops needed just for the "light option." Some of the poorer countries Annan contacted said they might be able to provide men but not equipment. Annan suggested that the UN ask countries unwilling to provide men to pro-vide equipment and air transport. Without proper military support, he was worried that the whole purpose of the resolution would be undermined.

Meanwhile the situation in the new "safe areas" became worse and worse. On June 16 the Bosnian UN ambassador, Muhamed Sacir-bey, told the president of the Security Council that Gorazde re-mained under constant heavy artillery attacks from all directions by Serb forces. At the Vienna Human Rights Conference, Boutros-Ghali asked almost every foreign minister and other representative with whom he met for troops for both Bosnia and Somalia. Algeria said it would study the request, but was unlikely to react positively in the short term. China said it would refer the request to Beijing. Tunisia agreed to provide two thousand troops in principle. Kuwait would refer the request to the emir. Spain said it had already added two hundred troops to its UNPROFOR contingent. Saudi Arabia would refer the request to the king for decision. Indonesia would refer to its president; it had men but not enough vehicles or equipment. Senegal said the request would be immediately forwarded to President Abdou Diouf. Bangladesh pledged an infantry battalion of 1,200 men. Yemen promised to get back to the secretary general next week.

By June 20 only Bangladesh was firm and substantial in its commitment. The Netherlands said they would send a maintenance unit and forward air controllers. Indonesia, seven hundred troops, not confirmed. Pakistan, a brigade, not confirmed, without equipment. Sweden, a mechanized battalion, not confirmed. Tunisia, a brigade of two thousand, not confirmed. Belarus, no reply. Chile, no reply. Colombia, no reply. Malaysia, no reply. Morocco, no reply. Czech Republic, no reply. Ukraine, Egypt, Germany, Russia, no reply. Australia, no. India, no. Venezuela, no.

The United States agreed to provide transport for any troops offered, but would not supply troops.

On June 19 a UN military observer was wounded in Gorazde. Because of the intensity of the Serb artillery barrage, it was nine hours before he could be medevaced out by helicopter. General Mladic wrote to UNPROFOR command, full of sympathy over "the act of the Muslims, who want to provoke the international intervention against the Serbs for such criminal acts. . . ."

At this time, Boutros-Ghali ordered the removal of General Wahlgren—simply because the French demanded that they have a general of their own as force commander. The secretary general did it without consultation, and the French defense minister announced it on television before the Secretariat, the Swedish government or Wahlgren himself had been informed. The Swedish government complained.

Before he left, Wahlgren proposed that UNPROFOR place a renewed emphasis on humanitarian relief in Bosnia because this was still its primary mandate. He pointed out that with the spread of fighting, not just between Bosnians and Serbs in the east, but also between Bosnians and Croats in the center, "The stark realities are that there is little prospect for implementing the safe areas over the next weeks before the new resources arrive, and that the civilian population will face devastating hardship next winter unless we now focus as first priority on a package of diplomatic, military, engineering and logistical efforts to restore utilities and humanitarian relief. . . ."

Winter was looming for UNHCR as well, and Sadako Ogata was worried about the way funds were dropping off. "I believe we are now at a turning point in the humanitarian effort," she said. "The intensification of war, the absence of a decisive political breakthrough, the restrictions on asylum in other countries and the virtual depletion of resources for the humanitarian efforts constitute an explosive mixture which if allowed to continue would provoke a massive humanitarian disaster with even greater consequences."

And so it went on. Gradually, Annan's peacekeeping department built up the promises of enough men to fulfill the "light option" for the safe areas. Even when men were available they were not always good enough. The additional Ukrainian battalion could have been deployed to Gorazde that July, but it was poorly motivated and poorly equipped. Indeed the Ukrainians had by now obtained the reputation of being the foremost black marketeers in UNPROFOR.

By this stage the Secretariat was in the odd position of having received pledges of 24,000 troops of all ranks, far more than the 7,600 authorized by the Security Council. But as Annan pointed out, most of these troops would be coming without equipment; the Secretariat was trying to match the men with equipment offered from such countries as Belgium, Germany, the UK and the U.S. The troops needed to be trained on the equipment. Germany offered equipment and training for a Pakistani battalion, but then withdrew the offer on the grounds that its laws did not allow it to train foreign troops on German soil. Austria then offered to train the Pakistanis, but it too changed its mind. "Finally," said Annan, "we moved the equipment from Germany to Slovakia, trained the Pakistanis there and then deployed them to Bosnia—about a year late."

In August, Bangladesh withdrew its offer of 1,200 troops. It had been contingent on the UN's ability to find armored personnel carriers. No other country would help, so the Bangladeshis would not come. Similarly, the prime minister of Tunisia had made an oral commitment of troops, and Annan's department had asked France to help equip them. But France would not.

What all this meant was further delay—and more horrors in the "safe areas" themselves, where attacks continued in brutal, bloody and deadly fashion. On July 24, President Izetbegovic wrote to the president of the Security Council to say that the Bosnian government "finds the activities of the Security Council and the Secretary-General of the United Nations slow, inconsistent and indecisive. As a result almost nothing has been accomplished on the ground." On July 29, Thadeusz Mazowiecki, the UN's human rights rapporteur, warned that the people in the safe areas "are fast being drawn into a catastrophe while their elementary human rights are constantly being violated."

For the next two years, until the Serbs overran Srebrenica and massacred thousands of Bosnians in summer 1995, the areas were never safe. Many became squalid, overcrowded refugee camps, controlled by ruthless Muslim troops for the political purposes of the Bosnian government, rife with black markets, violence and robbery, and under constant threat of Serb attack. The presence of a handful of lightly armed UN troops—Srebrenica's first group were 140 Canadians, who were followed by 570 Dutchmen—was meant, in the careful words of the Security Council, to "deter" Serb attack rather than to "defend" the areas. They did that in a sense and for a time, but their isolated dotting over the countryside made them hostages to the Serbs. So what they really deterred was any effective UN response by force to Serb assaults anywhere throughout the country. By extending UNPROFOR's mandate in this ill-considered manner, the Security Council actually severely restricted its own scope for action.

By midsummer 1993 the United States appeared to have forgotten that Warren Christopher had said in February that the U.S. must prevent the world "from going up in flames" in Bosnia. Now Christopher argued that while Bosnia was "a human tragedy, just a grotesque humanitarian situation. . . . [i]t does not affect our vital national interests except as we're concerned about humanitarian matters and except as we're trying to contain it."

The administration's position on Bosnia reflected a conflict between the moral imperative to act and the need to identify a national interest which could mobilize domestic support. There was a disjunction between expressions of moral indignation and the unwillingness to risk American lives. It was hard for the administration to have it both ways, but it made a valiant effort to do so. It objected to the partition of Bosnia by force, but behind the rhetoric there was no real policy—and U.S. attitudes actually served to worsen the situation. In April and later in July, U.S. references to "surgical air strikes" were seen by the Bosnian Serbs as preparations for direct military intervention and led to an escalation of the fighting, which in turn led to significant civilian casualties around Sarajevo. But in the long run nothing was so terrible as the way in which the rhetorical support for the safe areas fell so far short of real commitment.

o

I N mid-July, Prince Sihanouk left Phnom Penh to spend two months in Pyongyang, North Korea (where he planned to make a film, his favorite pastime), and Beijing (where he would have medical checkups). His departure evoked dismay among those in Phnom Penh who deemed his continued brokerage essential. During his absence from Cambodia the interim coalition government functioned surprisingly well, at least on the surface and at the upper level. The People's Party retained control of all the provinces, even those it had lost in the election; the police remained firmly in the hands of the party, and in many ministries key personnel and policies remained unchanged.

In one key area, however, there were important changes, of a kind which were unimaginable in the former Yugoslavia. Under the supervision of UNTAC's military component, the armies of the three new partners began the difficult process of amalgamation. On August 18 the new combined army attacked Khmer Rouge positions in several provinces. This marked a huge change: The Khmer Rouge's former allies (Funcinpec and the Khmer People's National Liberation Front) were now fighting with their old enemy (the CPP) against the Khmer Rouge. Close to the Thai border, they captured the important Khmer Rouge base of Phnom Chat. Many Khmer Rouge fled into Thailand. Over both Radio UNTAC and the official government channel Ranariddh broadcast an appeal to all Khmer Rouge soldiers to lay down their arms. He promised defectors that they would be integrated into the new army. By early October almost two thousand Khmer Rouge soldiers were thought to have responded to this appeal out of an esti- mated ten thousand total fighting strength.

Defectors said they no longer saw any purpose in fighting; they had hoped that the Paris agreement would bring peace and they had hoped to take part in the election. They did not believe their leaders' claims that they were fighting Vietnamese; the only bodies they ever saw were Cambodian and they wanted to go home.

During this period, after some argument among the donor coun- tries as to the precedents, UNTAC launched Operation Paymaster, a scheme whereby the United Nations provided the funds for the pro- visional administration to pay salaries of active soldiers and civil ser- vants. UNTAC hoped thereby to give the absurdly underpaid officials and soldiers some stake in the new political process. The program was a success.

Meanwhile, a thirteen-member committee of the Constituent As- sembly continued to draft a constitution in secret. UNTAC offered support and advice, but it was rejected. At the end of August, UNTAC was finally allowed to see a draft, which appeared to give undue power to the chief of state and too little protection to the rights of cit- izens and foreign residents of the country. Also missing were provi- sions for an independent judiciary and the specific prohibition of torture. UNTAC submitted suggestions, and some were accepted.

The secrecy surrounding the process was disappointing. But UNTAC's success in cultivating greater political freedoms was be- coming clear. One of Cambodia's new indigenous human rights groups, Ponleu Khmer, a Citizen's Coalition for the Constitution, felt bold enough to criticize the draft constitution publicly. It was espe- cially concerned by the powers given to the head of state, who would inevitably be Sihanouk. A few months earlier such boldness would have been unthinkable.

Sihanouk announced that he would be a king "who will reign and not govern." He emphasized that "in order to avoid civil war and se- cessions," the new permanent government must retain both Ra- nariddh and Hun Sen as co–prime ministers. (Ranariddh had been arguing that once the interim period was over, he should be sole prime minister.) The constitution, Sihanouk promised, "will be one of the most liberal in the world, with a multi-party system, a market and free enterprise economic system, a clear separation of powers (legislative, executive and judiciary), an independent judiciary, an absolutely free press without any censorship, and the free circulation of books and other publications." Cambodia, he pledged, "will become one of the most advanced democracies in the Third World, the total opposite of the Khmer Rouge Polpotism which wanted Cambodia to be the most 'advanced Communist state in the world.' "

In mid-September a five-day debate on the constitution took place in the assembly. Outside, about six hundred monks, nuns and civilians demonstrated to demand an open discussion. Inside, the debate was surprisingly spirited. While deputies quickly agreed to restore the monarchy, the main source of contention was whether a two-thirds majority should be required to pass all legislation. The People's Party demanded this in order to ensure that it continue to hold the balance of power. The People's Party also insisted that the system of two prime ministers be preserved. Funcinpec resisted both demands, but the People's Party had its way.

On September 25, Sihanouk signed the new constitution and, in a simple but ancient ceremony, took the oath of office. By his side was his wife, Monique, who was invested as queen. Buddhist monks intoned prayers, servants beat a gong, and the once and future king dabbed holy water behind his ears, bowing and beaming to all the audience. Among the spectators at the palace were former Khmer Rouge soldiers who had recently defected. Sihanouk embraced them while Prince Ranariddh said, "There are no more red or yellow Khmers. There are just Khmers."

It was, by any standards, an extraordinary moment. It came fifty-two years after Sihanouk's first coronation under French rule in 1941. Since then, he had been king, chief of state, prime minister, political leader, musician, filmmaker, magazine editor and exile. He had been vain, petulant, autocratic and unpredictable. He had sometimes made catastrophic errors, in particular by allying himself with the Khmer Rouge in 1970. He had also often acted astutely. His principal and interrelated ambitions had been to protect Cambodia from further encroachment by its neighbors and to preserve his own political power and place in history. Whatever irritation he aroused abroad, in Cambodia he was still viewed by millions of people as he saw himself, as "the father of the nation."

On the weekend of September 26, General Sanderson and Yasushi Akashi left the country. The Khmer Rouge radio denounced them, declaring that UNTAC had brought nothing but AIDS to Cambodia and asking the Cambodian people to "throw feces" at Akashi as he left. Instead, Akashi was widely praised for his stewardship of Cambodia. It was his misfortune that a few months later Boutros-Ghali decided to put him in charge of UNPROFOR.

UNTAC had by no means achieved everything that the Paris agreement had mandated, but it had encouraged a brief and very welcome social revolution. "Cambodia," said Akashi, "is a striking demonstration to the world that an intractable conflict can be resolved and seemingly irreconcilable views can be reconciled. Cambodia will thus stand as a model and a shining example for other UN member states."

Model or not, the successes of UNTAC were both real and fragile. When the United Nations struck its tents, Cambodia still lacked security, a viable economy and a civil society. The United Nations had not had the strength to give the people what they had voted for—the end of People's Party rule. The coalition which the party's brutality had imposed was unstable and undemocratic, and after a few years it collapsed. But UNTAC had pointed the country toward more open and accountable government; the beneficial effect of the UN's experiment in trusteeship were profound. It was based on the existence of a political center which showed itself in the people's vote for Funcinpec and against the forces of extremism. The problem was that the political center still faced an authoritarian state which UNTAC had not been able to dismantle.

In neither Yugoslavia nor Somalia was there even any such political center—in Yugoslavia there was no nation and in Somalia there was no state.

o

IN May 1993 the United States handed Somalia back to the United Nations, after the Security Council adopted a resolution which set up UNOSOM II and, in effect, involved the UN in an attempt at nation building. Madeleine Albright wanted Somalia to be a test case in multinational peacekeeping. As far as Clinton was concerned the U.S. mission there was now "over." It was not.

Boutros-Ghali chose a Turkish general, Cevik Bir, as force commander, but UNOSOM II was dominated by U.S. officers. The secretary general's special representative was retired U.S. Admiral Jonathan Howe. Close to thirty other American officers were in key positions, including UNOSOM's deputy force commander, Army Major General Thomas Montgomery, who was also direct tactical commander of the Quick Reaction Force which began to carry out military operations against the Habar-Gedir clan of Mohammed Aideed. The only U.S. forces in Somalia that were under UN control were the logistics component of some 2,700 men and women. All American combat forces were under direct U.S. command.

Much, though not all, of what went wrong in Somalia during UNOSOM II was the result of decisions made by U.S. commanders, not UN officials as American officials subsequently alleged. There were serious command and control problems with the handover from UNITAF to UNOSOM II. The U.S. Marines pulled out so quickly that the UN forces remaining were taken by surprise. In weeks the number of troops was reduced from thirty-eight thousand to twenty-eight thousand. More difficulties arose because previously the troops had come from the United States, Pakistan, France, Belgium, Canada, New Zealand and Norway, and now they came from thirty-one countries. Many were from developing countries. Some sent troops to gain national prestige, others for the training provided. In theory, the UN paid governments $950 per soldier per month, but because of arrears, principally on the part of the U.S., such payments were usually long delayed.

These new soldiers were often ill prepared, but they had much harder tasks than the more powerful mission they replaced. UNITAF, with thirty-seven thousand men and a very strong logistics component, had been expected to reestablish a secure environment for the unimpeded delivery of humanitarian assistance. It did not create a secure environment because it did not undertake the fearfully difficult and dangerous task of disarming the factions. Now UNOSOM II, with twenty-eight thousand people of all ranks, and with troops essentially from Africa and Asia, was asked, in the words of Elisabeth Lindenmayer, a UN official serving there at some of the most dangerous times, "to put Humpty Dumpty together again. In addition to protecting the delivery of humanitarian assistance, it was asked to disarm the factions, assist in the establishment of a police force and a judicial system, repatriate refugees and lead the country to national reconciliation." In a country where every teenager seemed to be armed and happy to threaten violence, and where the clan leaders were still at each other's throats, this was truly mission impossible, and Boutros-Ghali was understandably reluctant to have the UN take it on.

On June 5 a contingent of Pakistani troops inspecting a weapons site had been killed in Mogadishu, and another contingent helping distribute food was attacked. Twenty-six men were killed and another fifty-six were wounded. The faction of Mohammed Aideed was blamed. There was understandable horror at UN headquarters when the news came in. Next day, on June 6, just two days after the fateful Safe Areas Resolution 836, the Security Council passed Resolution 837, which authorized the secretary general to take "all necessary precautions against all those responsible for the armed attacks."

From this moment on the UN's mission was dominated by the imperative to capture Aideed. The policy had clear dangers and was criticized for abandoning UNOSOM's humanitarian mission in order to pursue a renegade warlord. Boutros-Ghali agreed with Washington that it was necessary, but it meant that for the first time since Korea, UN forces were ordered to conduct military operations against an enemy named by the Security Council.

Jonathan Howe put up notices around Mogadishu offering a $25,000 reward for the capture of the warlord. Aideed responded by putting up posters of Howe. Aideed may have been a monster, but he was extremely skillful at exploiting tensions, and he understood the nature of clan warfare in Somalia far better than any UN or U.S. official. Over the summer Howe asked for an increase in U.S. forces and, in particular, for the Delta Force, composed of U.S. Army Rangers and special commandos, to be sent to Somalia. Senior State Department officials, including Christopher and Albright, made the same pitch. Les Aspin and Pentagon leaders were more cautious.

On July 12, with President Clinton's specific authority, sixteen TOW missiles were fired by the U.S. Quick Reaction Force at the so-called Abdi House, which was described as a "major SNA/Aideed militia command and control center." No warning had been given. The victims were not militiamen but unsuspecting clan leaders and religious elders who had been meeting.

On August 8 a remote-controlled land mine was detonated under an American vehicle and four soldiers were killed. Six more Americans were wounded by a land mine on August 22. There were immediate calls in Congress for a U.S. withdrawal. Senator Robert Byrd, the chairman of the Appropriations Committee, said that these deaths showed that the "operation was crumbling . . . [and] that it was not worth the American lives lost and injuries sustained." Instead, General Powell reluctantly changed his mind and agreed to send the Delta Force. They arrived in Somalia on August 27. The very next day they attacked a house where they thought they would find Aideed. In fact it housed officials of the UN. They then captured a former police chief. When they realized he was not Aideed, they beat him up.

The wisdom of pursuing Aideed in this manner was open to question. Boutros-Ghali was accused of having an obsession with catching Aideed at the risk of destabilizing the overall mission. The U.S., in fact, began to reconsider the policy, and in September Warren Christopher, to his credit, sent Boutros-Ghali a paper suggesting a new approach and an end to the hunt for Aideed. Boutros-Ghali rejected the proposal. The subsequent UN Commission of Inquiry, whose report Boutros-Ghali initially tried to suppress, noted quizzically that it was "arguable whether Resolution 837 really envisaged the bombing of houses, garages and meetings."

On October 3, U.S. Rangers and Delta Force launched an airborne assault against a suspected stronghold of General Aideed. Two Black Hawk helicopters were shot down. The Americans were pinned down in a brutal firefight that lasted into the next day. Between five hundred and a thousand Somalis are thought to have been killed. Among the peacekeepers, one Malaysian, one Moroccan and eighteen American soldiers died. One American body was dragged through the streets in an appalling humiliation, shown over and over on American television.

The decision to launch the attack had been made in Florida—at the headquarters of the Special Operations Command. It was relayed directly to the contingent in Mogadishu. Not even Admiral Howe was informed of the operation, and the UNOSOM II force commander, General Cevik Bir, was told only just before it was launched. Bir's troops rescued the surviving Americans. Nonetheless American politicians were quick to blame the disaster on the United Nations. This was fair to the extent that Boutros-Ghali had been the strongest supporter of the policy of capturing Aideed, but combat decisions on this day had been made entirely by U.S. commanders.

The effects were momentous throughout the world. Within days,

Clinton announced that all U.S. troops would be withdrawn from Somalia by the end of March 1994. But the administration also withdrew even further from the whole concept of multilateralism.
Clinton had already been moving in that direction and away from his
early embrace of the UN; indeed, in his first speech to the UN General Assembly just a week before the disaster in Mogadishu, he had
said, "The UN must know when to say no to peacekeeping." This
statement reflected a confusion of the Security Council and the Secretariat. As we have seen, the Secretariat and UN soldiers were often
trying to say no, but they were frequently overruled by the United
States and other members of the Security Council, most obviously
on the Bosnian safe areas.

"Crossing the Mogadishu line" and the disasters that lay therein
now became a fixation in Washington. Not to cross that notional line
became the overriding determination of the Clinton administration
everywhere in the world. U.S. peacekeepers must never again become party to a conflict; their protection must be the overriding priority of U.S. policy. One senior U.S. official said to me later that the
loss of American lives in Somalia was "the defining trauma, the consequences of which the U.S. military will live with (and impose on
the political leadership) long after the Clinton administration is gone.
'Mogadishu' and 'Somalia' are not place names now—they are cau-
tionary slogans for disasters to be avoided at all costs."

The debacle in Somalia prompted the U.S. to return to principles
put forward by then–Defense Secretary Caspar Weinberger in 1984,
which insisted that the U.S. should not enter a war unless doing so
served its national interests and the conflict could be won. In spring
1994, Presidential Decision Directive 25 stated that U.S. support for
peacekeeping operations must be contingent on a conflict's threat to
international peace and security, or on a determination that the operation "serves U.S. interests."

Whatever the administration did, it was not enough for Congress.
At the end of October 1993, legislative support for a continuing U.S.
role in Somalia collapsed totally, and Congress canceled a proposed
$175 million contingency fund to cover immediate UN peacekeeping
costs. Congress also abandoned a special payment planned by President Bush to cover existing arrears and informed the president that
the U.S. share of peacekeeping costs should be cut from 31.7 percent
to 25 percent. The House of Representatives even rejected a Penta-

gon request for $10 million to strengthen the UN Situation Center in New York, which the administration had declared a priority. Right-wing critics such as former U.S. ambassador to the UN Jeane Kirk-patrick began to assert, plausibly if wholly inaccurately, that the Clinton administration had surrendered leadership to the United Nations.

In his desperation never again to cross the Mogadishu line, Clin-ton began to retreat from all lines. The first casualty was Haiti. In June the Security Council had unanimously adopted Resolution 841, which placed an arms and fuel embargo on Haiti in order to try to oust the military regime which had overthrown the democratically elected president, Jean-Bertrand Aristide. The shock of these manda-tory sanctions brought the military leader, General Raoul Cédras, to talks on Governors Island in New York harbor.

An agreement was reached to deploy UN troops and police, and for General Cédras to step down and Aristide to return. Although sanctions were lifted, this deal was not popular among opponents of Aristide and supporters of the military in Haiti. On October 11 the first sizable deployment of troops (two hundred U.S. and twenty-five Canadian) arrived off Port-au-Prince harbor on board the USS *Harlan County*. Waiting on the dockside were a bunch of thugs, the *attachés*, as the successors to the Duvalier regime's famously feared thugs, the Tontons Macoutes, were known. They shook their fists, waved plac-ards and shouted threats at the U.S. ship. They were hooligans who undoubtedly would have dispersed at the first sign of the well-armed U.S. troops. But among their slogans was one in particular: "We are going to turn this into another Somalia."

News of the "welcome party" and its curses was flashed to Wash-ington, where it provoked a panic. Without even consulting the United Nations, the Clinton administration immediately ordered the *Harlan County* to withdraw from Haitian waters and to sail back to the United States. As a direct result, the Governors Island agreement collapsed, violence continued with many opponents of the military killed, and it was almost a year before any further solution to the cri-sis was attempted. That was serious enough. Much worse was to come as a result of the administration's terror of venturing too close to the Mogadishu line. In Rwanda, where the crisis and the dangers were much greater, it helped to condemn hundreds of thousands of people to death by genocide.

5

Genocide in Our Time

O n the evening of April 6, 1994, the plane carrying the president of Rwanda, together with the president of Burundi, was shot down as it prepared to land at Kigali, Rwanda's capital. Everyone aboard was killed. The assassinations proved the signal if not the cause of the third terrible genocide of the century—first Armenians, then Jews, now Rwandan Tutsis. (The mass murder of over a million Cambodians was committed by other Cambodians, the Khmer Rouge. "Autogenocide" was an extralegal term invented to describe this pathology.)

Outside of intelligence agencies and the killers themselves, no one knows who fired the missile that brought down the presidents' plane. Among those who have since been blamed are the Rwandan Patriotic Front (RPF)—the Tutsi-dominated rebel army—the Belgian government, the Hutu Presidential Guard and senior figures from the Rwandan army. In any case, the crash was used as an excuse by Hutu extremists to embark on their well-planned genocide of Tutsis and moderate Hutus. The next twelve weeks were among the most bloody in human history. One calculation is that the daily killing rate was five times that of the Nazi death camps.

In the grotesque final act of a four-year civil war, close to a million

Tutsis are thought to have been murdered in brutal hand-to-hand attacks by Hutu soldiers and police and by their Hutu neighbors; the Rwandan Patriotic Front recommenced its war against the regime in Kigali.

Looked at another way, into these few weeks in Rwanda more human tragedy and far more deaths were compressed than had occurred in four years in the former Yugoslavia. This time the response of the outside world was even more restricted. Once again the United Nations appeared to stand by, impotent.

As in Yugoslavia, the world was quick to assign "ancient ethnic hatreds" or similar explanations to the genocide. But as in Yugoslavia, such shorthand was often misleading. The violence in Yugoslavia and Rwanda may have had historical ethnic components, but it also had political drivers. Leaders exploited existing problems, attempted to transform them into crises and drove their countries deliberately to destruction for their own political ends. Violence was chosen; it was not inevitable.

Rwanda is about the size of Vermont—some ten thousand square miles—and is one of the most densely populated countries in sub-Saharan Africa. Its two principal peoples are the Tutsis and the Hutus, who share a common language, culture and political system. The Tutsis make up only about 10 percent of the population, but for centuries they had ruled over the Hutu majority. The Tutsis inevitably felt superior to the Hutus, but distinctions between the two groups were not rigid and there was intermarriage between them. In the early twentieth century the Germans set up a colonial administration based on the existing hierarchy. The Belgians, who replaced the defeated Germans after World War I, did the same, and the Tutsis used the levers of colonial authority to extend their hold over the Hutus. The Belgians allowed only Tutsis to hold official posts and obtain higher education, and introduced a system of identity cards showing ethnic affiliation. Hutu resentment grew, and after the death of an esteemed king in 1959 it exploded into violence; the Hutus overturned the monarchy, killed thousands of Tutsis and drove tens of thousands of Tutsis into exile.

After Rwanda gained independence from Belgium in 1962, exiled Tutsis tried to fight their way back into the country. The Hutu government used the attacks as a pretext to kill and drive away more Tutsis. The incursions and the killings ended in the late 1960s, but the government carried out the same sort of discrimination against the Tutsis as the monarchy had previously used against the Hutus. During the next thirty years the regime became more and more totalitarian and dedicated to excluding Tutsis from all positions of power. For twenty years from 1973 the regime was led by Juvénal Habyarimana, who set up a political movement called MRND (Mouvement Républicain National pour le Développement, later called MRNDD, Mouvement Républicain National pour la Démocratie et le Développement) which was devoted to the promotion of the Hutus. In 1986, Tutsi exiles in neighboring Uganda helped Yoweri Museveni overthrow the government of Milton Obote. Museveni then encouraged the Tutsis to set up the rebel army called the Rwandan Patriotic Front in the refugee camps; in 1990 it invaded a corner of northeastern Rwanda and declared war on the regime in Kigali.

President Habyarimana had developed a close relationship with French president François Mitterrand. By the early nineties, hundreds of well-armed and well-equipped French paratroopers were fighting alongside the mainly Hutu Rwandan army keeping the mainly Tutsi rebel army at bay. Among French motives was that the rebels, coming out of Uganda, were seen as part of an Anglo-Saxon attack on Francophone Africa. Rivalry between *la francophonie* and *"les anglo-saxons,"* promoted by Paris, was an important subtext to the tragedy.

Cease-fires were honored mostly in the breach. The Rwandan army began training militias and paramilitaries. The government repressed opposition and the press. The Organization of African Unity supported regional talks designed to persuade the Hutu-controlled government to deal with the Tutsi rebels and with moderate Hutus in Rwanda itself. The government bought arms from Egypt—underwritten by France—and from South Africa. In February 1993 the rebels launched a major offensive which was stopped outside Kigali with the help of the French troops stationed there.

That August the two sides finally seemed to come to a power-sharing agreement signed in Arusha, a small town in Tanzania. Under the Arusha accords they agreed to a cessation of hostilities, the repatriation of refugees and the installation of what was called a Broad Based Transitional Government (BBTG), in which Habyarimana agreed to share power with the Hutu moderate opposition and the Tutsi-led RPF. The transitional government was to be set up within thirty-seven days. The rebel forces would be merged with the

Rwandan army. The agreement also called for the deployment of a neutral international peacekeeping force within five weeks. The problem with the accord was that it carried little political support, particularly on the government side. The rebel delegation at Arusha had been much more effective and united than that sent by President Habyarimana. Hard-line Hutu groups in Rwanda saw Arusha as a setback that they should reject. Tensions remained high.

When human rights groups urged France and Uganda to cut off their arms supplies to the belligerents, France defended its role and Uganda denied it. Boutros-Ghali sent a team to Rwanda to assess how best to set up the peace force envisioned by Arusha. Its report, recommending two battalions of about five thousand men, took weeks to find its way to the top of the UN hierarchy. The Security Council, preoccupied with both Bosnia and Somalia, displayed no more sense of urgency. Resolution 872, setting up UNAMIR, the UN Assistance Mission to Rwanda, was passed by the Security Council on October 5, two days after the deaths of the eighteen American soldiers in Mogadishu. The U.S. now suggested a force of just five hundred for Rwanda. The council compromised and authorized the secretary general to deploy only one of the two battalions he had requested.

Soon after, Tutsi rebels in neighboring Burundi staged an abortive coup and killed the Hutu president. Tens of thousands of Hutus and Tutsis were killed by each other, and about 350,000 fled into southern Rwanda during a drought, adding enormously to that country's problems. All this increased Hutu paranoia against the Tutsis in Rwanda and reinforced the often odious and inciteful propaganda against the Tutsis on Hutu radio stations such as Radio Mille Collines. Some of the new refugees were recruited into the Interahamwe, the militia of the MRNDD Party, which became part of Hutu Power, the ideology of ethnic solidarity.

Boutros-Ghali appointed Jacques-Roger Booh-Booh of Cameroon as his special representative in Rwanda. The UNAMIR force commander was a Canadian general, Roméo Dallaire. A good-looking, ramrod-straight soldier with short graying hair and a gray mustache, he arrived in mid-October. He was to become a lonely, brave and tragic hero in the drama of the coming months.

UNAMIR was from the start a poor relation of UNPROFOR in the former Yugoslavia. Dallaire wrote later that he was told by UN officials that Rwanda was not a strategic interest of any nation and that UNAMIR was to be conducted "on the cheap." The Security Council mandate itself ordered the secretary general to seek economies in personnel and funding. "We never had sufficient funding to conduct our mission," Dallaire said. Five weeks was the deadline set by the Arusha accords for the deployment of a neutral international force. Five months later the required force was still not there. Dallaire was appalled.

From the start UNAMIR was hampered by serious shortcomings in equipment, personnel, training, intelligence and planning. Civilian staff took a long time to hire, let alone deploy; six months after the mission began they were still trickling in. The UN Development Program's resident coordinator was also supposed to coordinate humanitarian efforts, reintegrate demobilized soldiers and oversee national reconstruction. In Dallaire's view, he and his staff were unable to do so much. There were tensions among the UN civilian hierarchy, the major funding agencies and some nongovernmental organizations. All in all UNAMIR was much less proactive than it should have been; like UNTAC, its credibility was damaged by its tardiness, and it was unable to win the confidence of the various parties.

Worst of all was what Dallaire saw as "international indifference" to the Rwandan crisis. The peacekeeping operation was mandated but it was never adequately equipped. Dallaire was sent half battalions from Bangladesh and Belgium and a battallion from Ghana. This meant a command and control structure which was totally inefficient; far too few troops were available for operations. Such was the need for men that the Ghanaian battalion had to be deployed for two months without their equipment. The Bangladeshi transport company was short of trucks, and its engineer company had less than a third of the equipment it needed to carry out mine clearance and road repair. Its troops were unable to sustain themselves. They did not even have a kitchen. The Bangladeshis were unable to move themselves, let alone the Tunisian company attached to them. They were supposed to have twenty armored personnel carriers, but had only five in working order. There were no spare parts, manuals or mechanics to service these vehicles and the crews had never even fired their main weapons. UNAMIR's military observers deployed around the country had almost no communications.

UNAMIR's command was consumed by the daily logistics of sustaining both itself and the rebel battalion which arrived in the capital at the end of 1993. Under the Arusha accords, this battalion was to protect the Tutsi political leaders who were to be part of the Broad Based Transitional Government. The command was also severely taxed by the turmoil in Burundi and the resulting refugee crisis. Detailed planning and implementation were delayed.

The mission had no stocks of water, food, ammunition, fuel, lubricants or spare parts. Dallaire could not call up enough skilled mechanics or logisticians. National and local bureaucracies spent a lot of time negotiating pay rates. "Logistics," said Kofi Annan, "are the glue which binds fighting forces and makes them effective—or not." All in all, UNAMIR's logistics problems seriously hampered its operations. The Security Council had dispatched men from several nations in a state of readiness that was close to a shambles and in which no nation would or should have ever deployed its forces. It was, Dallaire thought, bound to lead to disaster in the face of violence. He kept asking for help and so, he said, did Kofi Annan's peacekeeeping department at the UN in New York. It was not forthcoming. Since the resources provided were so desperately unmatched to the gravity of the growing crisis, Dallaire wondered whether it would have been better for the mission to withdraw rather than stay on, pretending it was effective.

O N December 30, 1993, the secretary general reported to the Security Council that the parties had failed to establish the Broad Based Transitional Government and that the situation was very fragile. He urged that UNAMIR's second proposed battalion be deployed and stressed that if resources were not increased, UNAMIR's credibility would be damaged and the peace process jeopardized. On January 6, 1994, the council agreed to the second battalion.

Obstacles to progress grew all the time. Violence always seemed to disrupt any deadline for progress. There was always a pretext for one or the other side to balk at implementing the process. Years later one particular cable from Dallaire became controversial after it was published by Philip Gourevitch, a writer for *The New Yorker*. On January 11, 1994, Dallaire reported to Annan's office in New York that "a very, very important government politician" had put him in touch with a Hutu informant, who said that he had been in charge of the previous Saturday's demonstrations, which had been intended to target deputies of opposition parties and Belgian soldiers; deputies were to be killed and the Belgians provoked and killed in the belief that this would lead to Belgian withdrawal from Rwanda, as had happened with the Americans in Somalia. According to the informant, the demonstrations were organized by government officials who also participated in them.

The informant was a former security guard of the president and was apparently paid handsomely to train the Interahamwe militia to kill Tutsis. They had 1,700 men in the capital. Since UNAMIR arrived he had trained about three hundred people in discipline, weapons, explosives and close combat tactics. "Since UNAMIR mandate he has been ordered to register all Tutsis in Kigali," Dallaire cabled. "He suspects it is for their extermination. The example he gave was that in 20 minutes his personnel could kill up to 1000 Tutsis." The informant supported the opposition to the Rwandan Patriotic Front but not the killing of innocent people. He also said he believed the president did not have full control over all the factions in his party.

Dallaire wrote that the informant was prepared to reveal a cache of about 135 weapons. He had already distributed 110 others. He wanted a UN guarantee of protection for himself, his wife and four children. Dallaire said he was going to act within the next thirty-six hours, and though he admitted he had some reservations about the informant's sudden change of heart, and the accuracy of his information, he recommended that the informant be given protection.

In New York, there was reluctance. UNOSOM had been destroyed in Somalia by its attempts to seize arms. Iqbal Riza, who was handling Rwanda for Annan, sent an immediate response: "Information is cause for concern but there are certain inconsistencies. We must handle this information with caution." In a second cable he wrote that New York could not agree to the action Dallaire proposed "as it clearly goes beyond the mandate entrusted to UNAMIR under Res 872." Instead he instructed Dallaire and Booh-Booh to inform President Habyarimana of the threats by the Interahamwe: "You should assume he is NOT aware of these activities, but insist that he must immediately look into the situation and take the necessary action to ensure that these subversive activities are immediately discontinued and inform you within 48 hours of the measures taken in this regard, including the recovery of the arms which have been distributed."

Before seeing the president, Riza advised, Dallaire and Booh-Booh should see the ambassadors of Belgium, France and the United States and suggest that they make a similar *démarche* to the president. Dallaire was asked to consult New York "if you have major problems with the guidance provided above. We wish to stress however that the overriding consideration is the need to avoid entering into a course of action that might lead to the use of force and unanticipated repercussions."

Dallaire and Booh-Booh met with the ambassadors the next morning. Dallaire reported back to New York, "They expressed serious concern and indicated they would consult with their capitals for instructions." The two men then went to see the Rwandan president to tell him that they assumed he was unaware of such activities and must look into them to make sure they were discontinued. They told him if there was any violence they would bring the matter to the attention of the Security Council immediately.

The president appeared alarmed, denied knowledge of the alleged activities of the militia and promised to investigate. Dallaire also complained about the harassment of both UNAMIR personnel and Rwandan civilians by the Hutu Power militia at the demonstrations on January 8.

For his part the president said how difficult it was proving to set up the Broad Based Transitional Government called for in the Arusha accords. He was very worried about the country's precarious finances.

Later that day Dallaire and his colleagues met again with the president and the national secretary of the MRNDD. Once again the UN officials shared their information about the threats from subversive groups in Kigali "as well as the storage and distribution of weapons to those groups. They both denied it. . . ." Dallaire had the impression that they were bewildered and unnerved that the UN had obtained so much specific information, and he thought that as a result the weapons had been quickly distributed. But he also thought that confronting those accused by the informer was sensible and might force them to think of alternative ways of disrupting the peace process, particularly in the Kigali area. In an interoffice memo of January 21, Dallaire wrote that the political impasse in the country was raising ethnic tensions: "The vast amounts of weapons which have been freely distributed in the past are seemingly readily available. No overt offensive action has been taken [by UNAMIR] as of yet against these weapons caches, due to the ongoing political initiatives."

UNAMIR, he wrote, could not sustain even its current level of operations because all troops had been on duty since mid-December and were exhausted; vehicles were overused and undermaintained; VIPs on both sides needed extra protection. He thought things would get only worse and he expected more aggressive demonstrations which might "be aimed against UNAMIR as a good third party scapegoat." He feared that "UNAMIR does not have the size of force to cope with this scenario, nor does it have a logistics base to sustain such operations. . . . The overall situation . . . is ripe for increased turmoil and potential open conflict."

On February 2, Annan's office cabled Dallaire to agree that there was a "need for some concrete initiative to facilitate the recovery of illegal weapons" in Kigali. But they were concerned that any attempt to recover them throughout the country would be "ambitious if not unrealistic"—and perhaps not consistent with the mandate under Resolution 872.* Dallaire was told, "We are prepared to authorize UNAMIR to respond positively on a case by case basis to requests by the government and the RPF for assistance in illegal arms recovery operations. It should be clearly understood however that while UNAMIR may provide guidance/advice for the planning of such operations, it cannot repeat cannot take an active role in their execution. UNAMIR's role during the execution phase should be limited to a monitoring function." Crossing the Mogadishu line held too many risks.

On February 3, Dallaire informed the military adviser to the secretary general, his compatriot General Maurice Baril, at UN headquarters that grenade attacks by militias, banditry and illegal small demonstrations were causing unusual unrest in the capital, and as a result the defense and interior ministers had just asked that UNAMIR

---

* Paragraph 2a of Resolution 872 instructed UNAMIR "to contribute to the security of the city of Kigali inter alia within a weapons-secure area established by the parties in and around the city."

support the gendarmerie in collecting illegal arms and ammunition. They felt it was "high time to stop the indiscriminate banditry. . . ."

Dallaire wrote that as force commander he had a healthy skepticism of Rwandans bearing gifts, but the fact that all those involved in security matters had publicly asked for UNAMIR's help in supporting their efforts to crush the violence and banditry in Kigali meant that he should be given the authority to support the recovery of illegal arms and ammunition. He was not.

Years later, the Secretariat published an explanation of its failure to allow Dallaire to seize the arms and to inform the Security Council itself. It acknowledged, "With hindsight, the Secretariat perhaps could have sounded the alarm bells more loudly. The Security Council could have been requested in January 1994 to reinforce UNAMIR and endow it with the appropriate mandate to undertake operations such as the one envisaged by General Dallaire." But it also pointed out again that the basic problem was not lack of information but lack of will on the council.

Boutros-Ghali writes in his memoirs that he was not informed about Dallaire's cable at the time. He states that the Secretariat did not make more of it because "such situations and alarming reports from the field, though considered with utmost seriousness by United Nations officials, are not uncommon within the context of peacekeeping operations." But, he asserts, the fact that Dallaire had informed the U.S., French and Belgian ambassadors meant that "the powers that could have acted to prevent the ensuing massacre . . . had indisputably and immediately been informed by the United Nations of the severity of the threat."

Iqbal Riza told Philip Gourevitch in 1998, "We get hyperbole in many reports. If we had gone to the Security Council three months after Somalia, I can assure you no government would have said, 'Yes, here are our boys for an offensive operation in Rwanda.' "

Annan was criticized in newspaper articles for not doing more about Dallaire's information. He said later that no UN peacekeeping mission—not even the NATO force in Bosnia—had ever been given a disarmament mandate. "When a general is going to take an action he has first to make sure that he has the capacity—because if not, he will risk the lives of a lot of people including his own soldiers," Annan contended.

In any case, on February 10, 1994, Boutros-Ghali's senior political adviser, Chinmaya Gharekhan, informed the Security Council that the failure of the Rwandan parties to agree on the establishment of the transitional institutions had created a climate of tension and a worsening of the security situation. He said this raised questions about the commitment of the parties to the Arusha accords. The council took no action. Rwanda remained in a state of tension.

O N April 6, within an hour of President Habyarimana's plane being shot down, the genocide began. It had been well prepared. The Presidential Guard and Hutu militiamen immediately set up roadblocks all over Kigali and started murdering Tutsis. Radio Mille Collines, the radio station of the Habyarimana clique which for months had been broadcasting hate propaganda against the Tutsis, immediately announced that the president had been killed by the Tutsi Rwandan Patriotic Front and by UNAMIR. Regardless of who killed Habyarimana, the fact remains that the organizers of the genocide were primed to exploit his death instantaneously. (In Burundi, whose president had also been killed in the crash, the army broadcast appeals for calm—and there was no explosion.)

The Presidential Guard had lists of people to kill. Their first targets were moderate Hutus who did not subscribe to the racist paranoia of Hutu Power. Early on the morning of April 7, the house of the Hutu prime minister, Agathe Uwilingiyimana, was surrounded; she tried to jump over a garden wall but was caught and murdered.

At this moment another awful event, one which was crucial to the outside world and the international community, occurred. Ten Belgian soldiers had attempted vainly to protect the prime minister. They were captured and disarmed by hostile troops. They were then driven by soldiers to an army camp, tortured, murdered and mutilated. When the news reached Belgium a few hours later there was an understandable outcry and demands for the withdrawal of the rest of the Belgian contingent. This was just what Hutu Power had intended.

Gangs of Hutu assassins went on killing leading politicians, civil servants, journalists, human rights workers and other leaders of what is often today called civil society. Then they began the general attacks on all Tutsis, starting with men, youths and even the youngest boys. Educated Tutsis were in especial danger, just as educated Cambodians were attacked by the Khmer Rouge. But the killings were not discriminate; Hutu killers attempted to murder all Tutsis they could find. "You cockroaches must know you are made of flesh," declared one radio broadcaster quoted by Philip Gourevitch in his book, *We wish to inform you that tomorrow we will be killed with our families.* "We won't let you kill; we will kill you," exulted the radio. By the hundreds, by the thousands, by the tens of thousands, Tutsis were macheted to death, burned alive, thrown dead or alive into pits and latrines, forced to murder their own friends and relatives.

Roadblocks were set up, telephone lines were cut, and disinformation as well as hatred was spewed forth by the radio stations controlled by Hutu organizers of the genocide. Early press reports accurately described the horror, though some of them ascribed it more to "ancient tribal hatreds" than to a carefully organized criminal campaign of genocide. After foreign journalists left the country and UNAMIR observers were evacuated from outlying areas, refugees were the principal source of information and press coverage was sporadic. But there were enough reports through April for the international community to be well aware of the scale of the disaster.

The Belgian foreign minister, Mark Eyskens, rushed to see Boutros-Ghali in Bonn. According to the secretary general, Eyskens said Belgium had decided to withdraw all its forces and he wanted the secretary general to withdraw all other UN troops as well. "Belgium was afflicted with 'the American syndrome': pull out at the first encounter with serious trouble," Boutros-Ghali wrote in his memoirs. The secretary general asked the Belgians to change their minds or, if they insisted on pulling out, to leave behind their heavy weapons for the use of other UNAMIR forces. Belgium refused to do even that. Boutros-Ghali wrote to the Security Council that the Belgian decision would make it very hard for UNAMIR to carry out its tasks effectively. He asked the council to replace the Belgians; otherwise UNAMIR might have to withdraw altogether.

Caution ruled. With the important exception of Ghana, governments ordered their troops to protect themselves first of all, even if that meant standing by and watching as lightly armed drunken thugs hacked women and children to death. (Some Tutsis who had cash managed to purchase a quicker death by firearm.)

Dallaire was particularly distressed that within a week of the genocide, 1,500 well-trained French, Italian and Belgian troops, with several hundred U.S. Marines standing by in Burundi, flew into Kigali to evacuate expatriates and a few Rwandans, then left again at once. That the "emasculated" UN force had to face the clear and present dangers alone was, in Dallaire's view, "inexcusable by any human criteria."

He felt that both Rwanda and UNAMIR had been abandoned; UNAMIR had neither the mandate nor the supplies to face the disaster. He said later that he lacked defensive stores, ammunition, medical supplies and water, and had only survival rations that he called rotten or inedible. All of this, he thought, was "a description of inexcusable apathy by the sovereign states that made up the UN that is completely beyond comprehension and moral acceptability."

Definitions were important. It was clear to Dallaire, to other UN officials and to those few journalists in Rwanda that what was happening was a planned and deliberate campaign by Hutu Power to terrorize and murder Tutsis. It was genocide. Western human rights organizations such as Human Rights Watch and then Amnesty International declared it so. Boutros Boutros-Ghali and the pope did so, though more slowly than some human rights organizations wished. But major heads of state refused to follow suit.

Their reluctance was easy to explain. The 1949 UN Convention on the Prevention and Punishment of the Crime of Genocide requires its signatories to "prevent and punish" genocide—defined as acts committed with the intent to destroy, in whole or in part, a national, ethnic, racial or religious group—as a crime against humanity. Among the many states party to the genocide convention are all the permanent members of the Security Council and Rwanda itself. The major powers continually shied away from any mention of genocide and the implications thereof.

On April 17, Dallaire reported that the young Hutu militia were killing "to their own unruly/drugged tune. They are a very large, dangerous, and totally irrational group of people. Force commander considers them to be a most dangerous threat." He asked for a new mandate, arguing that the UN "cannot continue to sit on the fence in the face of all these morally legitimate demands for assistance/protection." But with his present troop numbers he could do nothing. He urged the quick reinforcement of UNAMIR to five thousand men and a change in its mandate that would allow him to enforce peace. The troops would be directed to stop the genocide, to assist refugees to re-turn from Tanzania and Zaire, to deliver humanitarian aid, to assist in obtaining a cease-fire. A strengthened UNAMIR should in formal terms "re-establish peace and security, thereby facilitating a return to the Peace Process of the Arusha Accord and assisting in the establish-ment of a Broad Based Transitional Government," Dallaire wrote.

This was undoubtedly a tall order in the midst of the bloodletting but Dallaire believed that with five battalions it would be possible. A subsequent study by the Carnegie Commission on Preventing Deadly Conflict agreed with him. There would undoubtedly be op-position by government forces or the Rwandan Patriotic Front, or perhaps even both, but Dallaire considered that it would be intermit-tent and sporadic rather than fully organized opposition by main force units of either side. The Carnegie group later suggested that the Division Ready Brigade of the American 101st Airborne Division (Air Assault) possessed the firepower, staff capability, and combat support and logistics functions required.

Speed was of the essence to save lives. Any outside intervention would have had to take place before the end of April; after that the massacres had expanded across the countryside and far more troops would have been needed to stop them. If sufficient combat forces could have been introduced before the end of April and authorized to seize critical points throughout the country, the political calcula-tions of the participants would have been changed completely. But no such force could have been created without at least the United States taking the lead to generate resources and at least transporting the troops to Rwanda. The United States was interested in doing no such thing.

In the third week of April, as the killings increased, Boutros-Ghali sent a report to the Security Council outlining three options: Dal-laire's choice of immediate and massive reinforcement of UNAMIR with Chapter VII enforcement powers to stop the killing; downsizing of UNAMIR to 270 so that it would just act as an intermediary be-tween the two sides and seek a cease-fire; and complete withdrawal. The secretary general's spokesman said he preferred massive rein-forcement. But it was already late in the day for this.

There was no enthusiasm for real intervention. The British per-manent representative, Sir David Hannay, said at one Security Coun-cil meeting that reinforcing UNAMIR would only mean "a repetition of Somalia with its well-known and dire consequences." He was against pulling out the whole mission as this would have "a negative impact on public opinion." The U.S. delegate, Ambassador Karl Inderfurth, spoke of "a strong feeling in Washington" that the peacekeeping force "was not appropriate now and never will be." By contrast, the Nigerian ambassador, Ibrahim Gambari, said that tens of thousands of civilians were dying. "Has Africa dropped from the map of moral concern?" he asked.

Kofi Annan and others in the peacekeeping department spent many hours on the telephone and in meetings with delegates trying to persuade countries to contribute troops. Later Annan said that he had spoken to representatives of about one hundred different governments at this time. The replies were not encouraging. He agreed that Dallaire could save hundreds of thousands of lives with five thousand troops. "He did not have the capacity not because it did not exist but because the will to provide men, the will to act was not there," Annan stated in 1998.

On April 21 the Security Council met to decide the fate of UNAMIR. The council, by macabre coincidence, included the government of Rwanda at this time. Its representative continued to serve the self-proclaimed regime which took power on the death of Habyarimana. He was allowed to speak and to vote on resolutions concerning Rwanda, despite the convention that representatives should not play an active role in considering conflicts in their own states. By this stage the regime was in favor of the return of UN forces to enforce a cease-fire; the rebels, on the other hand, were advancing on Kigali and wanted no intervention of UN troops between the two armies.

Madeleine Albright and other U.S. officials argued that the mass killings were being caused by renewed warfare. In fact, the genocide had led the Rwandan Patriotic Front to renew its attack upon the government precisely in order to try to end the mass killing. In the end, Washington compromised and argued for a token UN force to remain. This was largely because the public relations implications of total withdrawal in the face of what was now being widely called genocide (even while U.S. officials squirmed to avoid the word) were so awful. The Security Council rejected the idea of reinforcements, ordered UNAMIR cut down to a token force of 270 men and restricted its mandate to mediation and humanitarian aid.

On April 29, Boutros-Ghali wrote to the Security Council stressing that UNAMIR's revised mandate would not enable it to bring the massacres under control. He urged the council to reexamine its decision of April 21 and to consider what action, including forceful action, the council could take, or authorize member states to take, in order to restore law and order and to end the massacres.

Still the killing went on, with its organized nature now clear to the outside world. Hutus were exhorted by the leaders of Hutu Power and by the radio to kill. "Take your spears, clubs, guns, swords, stones, everything," said a typical broadcast. "Sharpen them, hack them, those enemies, those cockroaches. . . . Hunt out the Tutsi. Who will fill up the half-empty graves? There is no way the rebels should find alive any of the people they claim as their own." A secret U.S. Defense Intelligence Agency report stated: "There is an organized effort of genocide being implemented." Washington and London still turned away. In response to the horror, other members of the Security Council—Czechoslovakia, New Zealand and Spain— began to urge that UNAMIR be reinforced.

On May 9, Boutros-Ghali submitted a "nonpaper" (a deniable discussion paper printed without identification of the author) to the Security Council proposing to expand UNAMIR to 5,500 troops along the lines Dallaire had urged weeks before. A vote was scheduled for May 13. Albright had it postponed. She said on May 11, "We have serious reservations about proposals to establish a large peace enforcement mission," and said it was unclear what it was to do. Boutros-Ghali later commented, "Of course, Albright and everyone else knew perfectly well that the mission was to stop the genocide then in progress. The behavior of the Security Council was shocking; it meekly followed the United States lead in denying the reality of the genocide."

On May 17—almost six weeks after the mass murders began—the Security Council did vote through Resolution 918, which would enlarge UNAMIR to 5,500 men, but at U.S. insistence it authorized the secretary general to deploy only one infantry battalion (800 men). The council indicated that it would further review the situation before authorizing the deployment of the rest of the force. From then on, the United States acted to delay deployment. A group of African countries offered to send an intervention force, and the UN asked Washington to provide fifty armored personnel carriers. The Clinton administration eventually agreed, but demanded that the UN pay $15 million to Washington. Boutros-Ghali asked Washington to jam the inflammatory broadcasts of Radio Mille Collines; he said he was told that it would be too expensive.

Meanwhile Dallaire and his few men were, Dallaire wrote later, "standing knee deep in mutilated bodies, surrounded by the guttural moans of dying people, looking into the eyes of children bleeding to death with their wounds burning in the sun and being invaded by maggots and flies. I found myself walking through villages where the only sign of life was a goat, or a chicken, or songbird, as all the people were dead, their bodies being eaten by voracious packs of wild dogs." For the first crucial eight weeks he had had an inadequate mandate, no reinforcement and only one unreliable phone line to the outside world. "I felt the ghost of Gordon of Khartoum watching over me," Dallaire wrote. "Dying in Rwanda without sign or sight of relief was a reality we faced on a daily basis."

The Security Council, Dallaire said, "floundered in the face of mounting heaps of bodies growing daily. . . . As long as these states procrastinated, bickered, and cynically pursued their own selfish foreign policies, the UN and UNAMIR could do little to stop the killing. . . ."

The French intervened. Through April and May reinforcements of the Tutsi rebel army, the Rwandan Patriotic Front, fought their way toward Kigali. In mid-June they neared the capital and total victory. France's traditional Hutu allies faced total defeat. Paris had always seen the Tutsi-led RPF as a stooge of Uganda's president, Yoweri Museveni, and, through him, of Washington and of the wider "Anglo-Saxon world." The prospect of an RPF victory dismayed many French officials, who argued that Rwanda would be only the first domino to fall to *"les anglo-saxons,"* and that Burundi and Zaire would be toppled next. Central Africa could become a Trojan horse projecting "Anglo-Saxon" influence throughout France's client regimes, known as *la francophonie.*

The French now proposed a unilateral Chapter VII enforcement mission to the Security Council. There was reluctance among some members of the council, and others elsewhere who were wary of France's involvement with the Hutu leadership. Nonetheless, a majority of the council, aware of how little anyone had done for Rwanda so far, approved France's "humanitarian" mission.

The 2,500 French troops of Operation Turquoise arrived in southwest Rwanda in early July, after most of the killings, but they may have saved up to 15,000 Tutsis. Leaders of the RPF were convinced that the French were at least as interested in saving the remnants of the Hutu regime, from whose extremist wing the genocide sprang, as in saving innocent lives. Indeed, the French made few bones about it; they declared the area of southwest Rwanda that they with their Senegalese partners occupied a "safe zone." Even former French president Valéry Giscard d'Estaing asked, "Safe for whom?" and accused the government in Paris of "protecting some of those who had carried out the massacres."

In Kigali, with only five hundred UN troops, General Dallaire watched the French deployment with incredulity if not dismay. After all, until quite recently the French had been helping the Rwandan army fight the RPF. Operation Turquoise and UNAMIR had the same master—the Security Council—and Franco-African soldiers served in both forces. Predictably, the RPF reacted violently against UNAMIR troops, who were now entirely deployed behind RPF lines. Dallaire had to evacuate his Franco-African troops as fast as he could from Rwanda, thus further weakening UNAMIR. He thought the fact that the UN had sanctioned two operations, one peacekeeping and one peace enforcement, in the same country at the same time and with almost no coordination showed, above all, "individual states running roughshod over the Secretariat and even the Security Council."

B y August the Tutsi Rwandan Patriotic Front army had swept through most of Rwanda and was able to set up a government in Kigali. The Hutu leaders of the genocide fled across the borders into Burundi, Tanzania and then Zaire, forcing or encouraging the population of hundreds of villages and towns to come with them. The motive was clear: one senior army officer said, "The RPF will rule over a desert," and the leader of an extremist party declared, "Even if the RPF has won a military victory, it will not have the power. It has only the bullets; we have the population."

The flood of refugees captured international attention and concern in a way which the unseen massacres inside Rwanda never did. By mid-July there were some two million people squatting in appalling conditions just outside Rwanda. Almost a million people crossed into Tanzania over four horrible weeks in July. Cholera broke out in several camps, and in one, in Goma, Zaire, fifty thousand people had to be buried.

The exiles fell under the care of the United Nations High Commissioner for Refugees and hundreds of Western nongovernmental organizations, which swooped down into eastern Zaire and Tanzania to set up their tents and their banners to save lives. For the next two and a half years these camps were sustained by the same world which had proved incapable of intervening in Rwanda to stop the genocide.

The Hutus in effect built a government in exile in the camps; Hutu towns and villages had been transplanted across the border. Shops, discos, brothels all operated in the camps much as they had at home in Rwanda. Arms trafficking was better; the Hutu militias sold international aid on the black market to buy weapons, they recruited troops from among the camp populations they terrorized and they mounted increasingly fierce attacks into Rwanda.

In November, fifteen of the more serious nongovernmental organizations in the camps in Goma complained that UNHCR was quite unable to fulfill its mandate of protecting and assisting refugees because everyone in the camps was hostage to the extremist leadership.

Médecins sans Frontières (France) was one of the first nongovernmental organizations actually to pull out, saying, "The continued diversion of humanitarian aid by the same leaders who orchestrated the genocide, the lack of effective international action regarding impunity, and the fact that the refugee population was being held hostage, presented a situation contradictory with the principles of humanitarian assistance."

Other agencies left also, but there were always new ones to take their place. Humanitarianism has a commercial imperative. "The humanitarian machinery was running at top speed, and I think everyone enjoyed that," Romy Brauman, the former head of Médecins sans Frontières, told John Pomfret of the *Washington Post*. "The problem was that we were bringing massive help to the criminals. All of our resources went through their hands, allowing them to strengthen their power over the refugees. This humanitarian operation was a total ethical disaster."

The International Rescue Committee, an American organization, also pulled out—the first time in its sixty-four-year history it had done such a thing. Roy Williams, a senior vice president of IRC, said it was a terrible decision to make because it cost innocent lives in the camps. "Still, the whole aid community has been overtaken by a new reality. Humanitarianism has become a resource . . . and people are manipulating it as never before. Sometimes we just shouldn't show up for a disaster."

Sadako Ogata argued that UNHCR did not have the luxury of leaving. "So long as there were people who had crossed an international border in an asylum situation, I didn't have the freedom to leave them, however complicated the group was," she said. But UNHCR officials became more and more desperate.

The Hutu leaders in the camps spread propaganda about real and alleged atrocities committed by the new Rwandan government against the Hutus, and threatened those who nonetheless still expressed an interest in returning home. There were grounds for criticism of the new RPF government in Kigali. It sometimes seemed that it ignored revenge killings; a UNHCR report that detailed the extent of these was suppressed because Western governments, guilty over their failure to prevent the genocide, were reluctant to criticize the new regime. Inevitably, the regime was composed almost exclusively of Tutsi exiles, many of whom had either lived outside the country since the 1960s or had been born abroad. It was very much a minority regime, whose members had never known government before, attempting to restore a shocked, mutilated society. The economy had collapsed; there was no local or central administration because a large proportion of those who had run it had been murdered or were gone. On top of that, 800,000 Tutsi exiles had come back home with the victorious RPF. They all needed homes. Property rights became a major and contentious issue. Apart from the two million in refugee camps, another million Hutus were in camps for displaced people inside Rwanda.

There was no functioning judicial system, so while tens of thousands of Hutus were held in horrific prisons and detention centers, no trials of those guilty of the genocide took place. In November 1994 an international war crimes tribunal on Rwanda was established in Arusha. Important though its symbolism was, it could deal with only a tiny fraction of those responsible for the mass murder of the Tutsis and moderate Hutus.

The Hutu-run camps were clearly a "threat to peace and security," but for two years the Security Council did nothing about them.

Boutros-Ghali informed the council that a force of up to twelve thousand men would be needed to separate the genuine refugees from the murderous leaders. Just to try to establish minimal security without separation would take between three thousand and five thousand men. Only Bangladesh offered to send troops for even this lesser option. In desperation, Kofi Annan commissioned a study from ADL, a British company, on subcontracting a private security service to control the camps. A group of South African mercenaries, Executive Outcomes, was a possibility. This suggestion could have been quickly implemented, but Annan was told that the United Nations could not subcontract in this manner. Eventually UNHCR employed a Zairean police contingent, but it was hardly adequate.

The dilemma for UNHCR, and indeed for the UN in general, was a familiar one. As Mrs. Ogata pointed out, international responses to internal conflicts and the resulting humanitarian crises are usually of a reactive and ad hoc nature: "As a refugee crisis fades from the front pages of the newspapers and CNN, we witness an evaporation of international concern, financial contributions and political involvement. No international humanitarian organization or NGO can solve political conflicts. . . . We need political will, the involvement of governments and their leaders, of the UN and regional organizations, to maintain and build peace." On the borders of Rwanda they did not get it.

The way in which the world responded at all stages—before the genocide, during the genocide and after the genocide—was not just partial, it was counterproductive. Halfhearted and ineffectual intervention and the deliberate confusion of humanitarianism and politics kill. Boutros-Ghali pointed out later that not so long ago the world had said "never again" to genocide. "But here was genocide once more; in Cambodia, where more than a million victims fell to the Khmer Rouge; in the former Yugoslavia, where genocide was called 'ethnic cleansing'; in Somalia, where genocide by starvation resulted when warlords deliberately withheld food aid from the starving and sick and where 350,000 died before the Security Council decided to step in. In Rwanda close to a million people were killed in what was genocide without doubt; yet the Security Council did nothing."

In early 1999 Annan commissioned a report on the United Nations' role in the genocide, which was due to be published at the end of that year. Till then the most comprehensive study was the eight-hundred-page report written for Human Rights Watch by Alison Des Forges and published in spring 1999. Des Forges documented conclusively both the organized nature of the genocide and the sloth with which the world reacted. "The Americans were interested in saving money, the Belgians were interested in saving face, and the French were interested in saving their ally, the genocidal government," wrote Des Forges. "All that took priority over saving lives." She pointed out that, to be effective, "international interventions must be prompt, strong, and smart."

General Dallaire asked, "Did the ineffectiveness of the UN mission in grasping the situation and poor handling of the political, humanitarian and military response in extremis abet the genocide?" It was an alarming question. So was Dallaire's answer.

"I believe it did."

DALLAIRE'S belief was underwritten by the devastating independent report which Annan published at the end of 1999.* It found that the United Nations had failed the people of Rwanda at every level. Its "overriding failure . . . was the lack of resources and political will to stop the genocide. UNAMIR was not planned, dimensioned, deployed or instructed in a way which would have enabled the mission to stop the genocide. UNAMIR was also the victim of a lack of political will in the Security Council and on the part of Member States." The inquiry described errors of judgment on the part of officials, including Boutros-Ghali, Kofi Annan, and UNAMIR officials. And "there was a lack of will to identify the massacres in Rwanda as a genocide which was deplorable."

As if that was not enough, the failure of the international community to do anything but apply an inappropriate humanitarian poultice to the Rwandan refugee crisis in 1994, 1995 and 1996 led directly to a new and appalling refugee crisis in 1997 in which up to 200,000 people may have been killed, the war over Zaire, the replacement of a bad government there with one that sometimes appeared even worse and then the so-called Great War of Africa, which engulfed up to fourteen countries of Central Africa in 1998 and 1999.

---

* This report was published after my account was written. The report is also referred to in the Epilogue.

6

Bosnian Endgame

A T 11:10 a.m. on Monday, August 28, 1995, five 120mm mortar rounds smashed into Sarajevo near the Markale market. They killed thirty-seven people and wounded around ninety. These were the deaths which, in effect, ended the war in Bosnia.

The United Nations immediately sent crater analysis teams. Unlike in February 1994, when such a team had been unable to say categorically that the mortar which killed sixty-eight people and wounded over two hundred in the town's central market came from Serb or Bosnian lines, on this occasion the analysts were certain. All five rounds were judged to have been fired from the same location, bearing 220 to 240 degrees from the point of impact. The team concluded "beyond reasonable doubt" that the firing position was in Bosnian Serb territory, somewhere between Lukavica and Mijevica.

That morning Richard Holbrooke, who had recently been appointed the U.S. chief envoy to the Balkans, heard the news of the massacre on CNN in the U.S. ambassador's residence in Paris. The day before, in a television interview, he had warned that unless the Serbs entered serious talks "the consequences will be very adverse to the

Serbian goals." When he first heard of the Markale mortar attack he wondered if it was a deliberate response to his warnings.

What counted now, Holbrooke related later, was that the United States should act decisively and persuade its European allies to join in the sort of massive air campaign that they had often discussed but never come close to undertaking. He was called that morning from Washington by Strobe Talbott, the acting secretary of state. He, too, felt that a military response was essential, but he wanted to know what Holbrooke thought would be its effect on his attempts to negotiate an end to the war. Holbrooke felt that the Serbs had given the West a chance to do what should have been done three years before—hit them very hard. He replied that the West should not respond with "pinprick" attacks but with massive airpower. He wrote later that "this was the most important test of American leadership since the end of the Cold War." Not just that; this was part of a controversy that had gone on for thirty years about the relationship between diplomacy and airpower.

The Markale mortar attack challenged the international community, or at least Western leaders, finally to put an end to the culture of impunity with which the Bosnian Serbs and the other parties had continued to flout the United Nations. There were misgivings about this among senior UN officials, as there had always been over action that could compromise the basic peacekeeping mandates which required that the UN not overtly take the side of one party against another. Those officials, from Kofi Annan downwards, would justify their caution by pointing not only to the mandates but also to the attitude of the troop contributors who, time and time again, insisted that the lives of their men were paramount. Nonetheless, the constant, daily humiliation to which UN military and civilian officials were subjected by all sides had taken its toll and their impatience had grown.

For over a year now, the senior UN official in UNPROFOR, the secretary general's special representative, had been Yasushi Akashi of Japan, who had been, till the summer of 1993, running UNTAC in Cambodia. In Cambodia, Akashi had had a measure of success in dealing with the intransigent factions in his emollient manner. Cambodia was still seen as a UN victory. Bosnia was seen, at almost all stages, as a defeat. The praise that Akashi had enjoyed in Cambodia turned to gall in Bosnia.

When Akashi arrived at the beginning of 1994, the mission seemed on the point of collapse. UNPROFOR was riven with factional fighting—the military and civilian operations based in Zagreb often found collaboration difficult. Their disarray reflected the tensions inherent in the mission, which was far more complicated than Akashi's previous assignment. The differences between Cambodia and Bosnia are instructive.

In Cambodia the UN was deployed only after an exhaustive peacemaking process that culminated in the Paris agreement of 1991. There was a framework, and if factions tried to break out or ignore it, as the Phnom Penh regime and especially the Khmer Rouge did, that was self-evident.

In Yugoslavia, by contrast, the UN was merely responding to cataclysmic events. There was no peace plan to which all sides had signed on. The best recent hopes, the Vance-Owen plan and its successor, the Owen-Stoltenberg plan, had both been undercut by American opposition.

In Cambodia the UN had the backing of a united Security Council, whose ambassadors in Phnom Penh gave Akashi invaluable support. In Yugoslavia, by contrast, there was spectacular international disarray, which had prevented the development of any coherent policy.

In Cambodia UNTAC had supreme authority in one country. UNPROFOR, by contrast, had a much more limited mandate in several countries. In Cambodia Akashi was dealing with only one national paranoia. In Yugoslavia he faced the warring paranoias of Serbs, Bosnians, Croats and others.

In Cambodia the UN had to deal with cease-fire violations; here the UN confronted war. In Cambodia there was the overarching figure of Prince Sihanouk. He was sometimes impatient and dismissive of UNTAC, but he was a court of last resort to whom all the parties turned. Indeed, the process might have collapsed without him. In Yugoslavia there was no such unifying figure—all leaders divided and spoiled.

In Cambodia UNHCR was able to repatriate all the refugees living along the border; that crisis was solved. In Bosnia the crisis grew all the time, as thousands and thousands more people were forced from their homes. This in turn encouraged more war, as all sides, in particular the Bosnian government, strove to recover territory "ethnically cleansed."

In Cambodia Akashi had to deal with four factions, three of which were (usually) interested in making the process work. In Bosnia there was no such identity of interest. Each side constantly lied to and manipulated the UN, promising to help the effort and then finding reasons not to. In Cambodia Radio UNTAC gave the Cambodian people—for the first time ever—an objective and unbiased source of information. It diminished the evil of propaganda and was essential in convincing them that their votes really would be secret and so they could defy intimidation. In Yugoslavia the Croatian, Serbian and to a lesser extent Bosnian Muslim media poured out hate day after day.

The glaring problem was that the West had never defined a political objective for the former Yugoslavia. The history of international action had been of mixed messages from different members of the Security Council and other interested powers such as Germany. This had reinforced the different perceptions of different parties and so had escalated the conflict rather than led to resolution.

UNPROFOR now had three missions or mandates: first, an incomplete but traditional peacekeeping operation in Croatia; second, a humanitarian operation in Bosnia that had since become a peacekeeping operation; third, an observer mission in Macedonia. None was easy, but it was the second that provided the mission with the most difficulties, and it is worth reciting how it had altered and grown almost like Topsy.

Resolution 761 of June 29, 1992, had underlined the urgency of quick delivery of humanitarian assistance to Sarajevo and its environs. In September 1992, the secretary general recommended to the Security Council the expansion of UNPROFOR's mandate and strength, the better to protect UNHCR in its humanitarian relief efforts.

In October 1992, Resolution 781 imposed a no-fly zone, and UNPROFOR was requested to monitor compliance with the ban, an almost impossible task. (NATO was authorized to enforce the ban only six months later.) In November 1992, in Resolution 787, the secretary general "consider[ed] that observers should be deployed on the borders of Bosnia, to enforce compliance of the arms embargo on Bosnia and the sanctions on Serbia." The secretary general told the Security Council that this would require another ten thousand troops. None were provided, so this "mandate" was never implemented. Then in 1993 came the safe areas resolutions (824 and 836), whose fateful passage I have already described.

UNPROFOR's personality was split. At its starkest, the issue was bread versus bombs. There was a fundamental clash between UNPROFOR's two principal missions—support for humanitarian assistance and the safe area concept. To succeed in humanitarian operations, the UN had to be seen as impartial. This was made almost impossible by its parallel mandate to deter attacks against the safe areas. The safe areas resolutions were essentially anti-Serb. That may have been proper, given that the Serbs were the worst abusers of human rights inside Bosnia (with the Croats often a close second), but the new mandates of 1993 had changed UNPROFOR's role radically, in effect making the UN the apparent protector of elements of one side in the war.

Stuck in the middle was the United Nations High Commissioner for Refugees, the lead agency in the delivery of humanitarian assistance. The world's refugee agency had become the main supplier in humanitarian crises and was now cursed. UNHCR had delivered food, clothing and shelter to hundreds of thousands of people in the former Yugoslavia, but it was often unable to reach those most in need in the war zones and was hampered—and could be stopped—by the warlords at will. Even the government in Sarajevo—which increasingly saw UNHCR's mandate as an unwelcome substitute for more robust action by the international community—would block assistance when it wished to increase the political pressure on the West.

UNHCR had been forced in the former Yugoslavia to accept a new benchmark for governments that wished to co-opt humanitarian assistance for political ends. It was becoming a prisoner of its own "success" and had become a significant part of the response of the international community to the crisis in Bosnia. The political objective of some of the most influential governments—Britain, France and (though it claimed otherwise) even the United States—was to contain the conflict and reduce their own related domestic political pressures. Imposing a solution had been considered too costly, hence they had limited influence on the duration of the conflict. And so the humanitarian operation had not only to address the needs of the thousands upon thousands of victims but also to calm European and American opinion.

In short, UNPROFOR's task was virtually impossible. The UN's 1993 commander in Bosnia, General Francis Briquemont, complained about the "fantastic gap between the resolutions of the Security Council, the will to execute these resolutions, and the means available to commanders in the field." Briquemont said he had stopped reading Security Council resolutions. The pressures on Akashi and Briquemont's successor, Lieutenant General Sir Michael Rose, were considerable and often conflicting. They had important successes, but they spent much of their time in exhausting, often fruitless bargaining with Serb, Muslim or Croat leaders, who promised, prevaricated and lied in varying degrees. Akashi later summed up his quandary: "With a consensus absent in the council, lacking a strategy, UNPROFOR was forced to chart its own course. There was only limited support for a 'robust' enforcement policy by UNPROFOR. UNPROFOR thus chose to pursue a policy of relatively passive enforcement, the lowest common denominator on which all council members more or less agreed." General Rose tried throughout to resist the pressures, particularly from the United States, which he thought would force him to cross "the Mogadishu line" from peacekeeping into peace enforcement. American officials denounced him for being "soft on the Serbs." Rose rejected such charges, but he did become impatient at what he saw as dangerous deviousness by the Bosnian government.

Throughout 1994, crisis followed crisis. There was the bombing of the Sarajevo marketplace in February, which led to more calls for NATO air strikes and the imposition of a heavy weapons exclusion zone around Sarajevo; prolonged Serb sieges of the safe areas of Gorazde and then Bihac, which resulted in limited NATO air action against the Serbs; the destruction of much of the beautiful medieval town of Mostar in gratuitous shelling, principally by Croats of the Muslim areas (it is worth repeating that Croat conduct in this war was often at least as horrible as that of the Serbs); the tensions with Russia, Serbia's principal backer in the Security Council; and the worsening relationship between Europe and the United States, which posed a more serious threat to the cohesion of NATO than anything the Soviet Union had ever contrived. Through it all there were the images of the UNHCR convoys progressing slowly through burned-out and empty "ethnically cleansed" villages amid beautiful mountains; hulks of houses protected by blue UN plastic sheeting;

queues of beaten refugees waiting for handouts of food; and, as the background chorus, the endless braying propaganda of the various leaders as they strutted upon the landscape they had helped destroy.

AT the beginning of 1995, Akashi was still enduring his numbing confrontations with all the leaders, but General Rose was replaced as Bosnia force commander by another British general, Rupert Smith. Smith's approach was different. Fifty-one years old, Smith had the looks of a matinee idol and the reputation of being an "intellectual" soldier. He had been involved in Britain's Bosnia operations for the last year as assistant chief of the defense staff (operations and planning) and in peacekeeping training before that. His former British commander in the Gulf war, where Smith commanded the 1st Armoured Division, was impressed with him: "Possessed of an exceptionally logical mind and most professional to do business with, he was also refreshingly unorthodox in his ideas and liable to seek less-than-obvious solutions to the problems which confronted him."

When Smith arrived in early 1995, he knew that he was taking over at a difficult time, but then all times in Bosnia were difficult. There was now a debate over the UN mandate in Croatia. The Croatian government was threatening to expel the UN from the protected areas in Croatia. There was a new resolution before Congress to obtain the long-favored American policy of lift and strike. And the French presidential elections were coming up.

In an interview with this writer before he left for Bosnia, Smith said that in peacekeeping only four things are achievable by military force: ameliorate, contain, compel/deter and destroy. The first two can be conducted without a strategy, "but a strategy is essential if you seek to compel or deter or destroy because they require evident capability, the will to use it, the ability to find and hit appropriate targets and a readiness to escalate."

The difference between deterrence/compulsion and destruction is that the strategic objective in the former case is to change an intention, while in the latter it is to reduce capability.

Smith thought that General Aideed succeeded in Somalia because he prevented U.S. forces from finding and attacking targets at a cost or risk they were prepared to pay; he dropped below the utility of the U.S. weapons systems. In Northern Ireland, by contrast, the British army has been prepared to engage the IRA on the terms the IRA imposed. In old wars, time was the enemy; now casualties were the enemy. Human costs were more important to governments than time.

In Bosnia, Smith argued, UNPROFOR had been able to ameliorate human suffering with its humanitarian airlift and convoys. But that would not in any way lead to a solution of the conflict.

Containment was possible—as with embargoes, or with the dispatch of troops to the Macedonian border to prevent the war from spreading to neighboring countries, but it had its limits. According to Smith, the no-fly zone in Iraq had not managed to contain Saddam. He had simply dropped below the utility level of the zone—he still killed Marsh Arabs in the southern no-fly zone—but it was not on television.

According to UNPROFOR's mandates, Smith was not even charged with containment, just amelioration. And the Western powers were quite divided on what UNPROFOR should do. UK policy had always been consistent—to ameliorate and contain. The French had been willing to take more risks, he thought. The Americans had wanted much tougher action but were not prepared to pay a price for it. The real problem, Smith concluded, was, "We have no strategic aim in the Balkans except a negotiated settlement. This means that the factions are able to define strategy. They have too much power." He thought it was vital that UNPROFOR define its own strategy more precisely and then do what was necessary to carry it out. That was not easy. He did not seek to fight a war with the Serbs because, unlike some of the UN's armchair critics, he knew that would be a disaster. But he did want to try to find a way to end the humiliation of UNPROFOR and give it freedom of movement throughout Bosnia.

WHEN Smith arrived in Sarajevo in early 1995, Bosnia was enjoying relative calm thanks to a cessation of hostilities agreement negotiated by Jimmy Carter and Yasushi Akashi at the end of 1994. Humanitarian convoys were getting through and the airport was open. But it was clear that both the Croats and the Muslims were preparing for offensives when the agreement expired on May 1.

In February 1995 the United States secretly flew communications equipment into Tuzla to enable the Muslims to coordinate large-scale offensive operations. Weapons were thought to be coming in also, shipped by Islamic governments either through Croatia or into Tuzla itself. Washington had connived at such breaches of the embargo. The Bosnian army was getting stronger, and the Serbs, who had less manpower, were being stretched thinner and thinner. Smith thought that the advantage now lay with the Croats and Muslims. General Mladic, the Bosnian Serb military leader, left Smith in no doubt that the Serbs would respond to any attack as they thought necessary. To any strategist that clearly meant they would deal with the eastern enclaves, the safe areas, which now had major concentrations of Muslim troops with them, threatening Serb lines of communication and rear areas.

In Sarajevo, Smith tried to get his band of international staff officers to devise a strategy that would better meet the conflicting demands imposed on UNPROFOR, in particular that it guarantee the safe areas while also trying to guarantee UNPROFOR's own freedom of movement and security.

The basic dilemma remained as ever: Resolution 836, which set up the safe areas, was ambiguous if not deceptive. The areas would never be safe. Resolution 836 had been designed not to defend the safe areas but to "deter attacks" against them. And the Security Council never provided UNPROFOR with the number of troops needed to achieve even this lesser mission. The UN Secretariat had asked for 34,000 troops to defend the safe areas. The Security Council agreed to provide only 7,600. By March 1994 only 5,000 of these had been deployed. And many of these, like the Bangladeshi battalion in Bihac, were very poorly armed.

To supplement the handfuls of troops scattered through the safe areas, the threat of NATO airpower was used. It was not always a very effective threat. UN and NATO attempts to use force were neutralized by Bosnian Serb threats against the peacekeepers. The Bosnian Serbs used asymmetric responses such as hostage taking and disrupting the distribution of humanitarian aid. In terms of a cost-benefit perspective, this was very effective for the Serbs. They managed to paralyze the UN and NATO by exploiting the major weakness of the international operation—the vulnerability of the men on the ground. Smith knew that if the UN was to have any hope of effective action, it had to reduce that vulnerability.

In the two years since the safe areas were established, firing attacks had increased on both sides of the line. Under agreements brokered by UNPROFOR in May, Zepa and Srebrenica were supposed to be demilitarized (but they never effectively were), and the Security Council never demanded any demilitarization of Bihac, Gorazde or Sarajevo. The Bosnian army used all the safe areas for military purposes. One internal UN military memorandum of March 1995 stated that the Bosnian armed forces "have continuously used safe areas as their own tool to preserve their forces, with an ulterior motive of instigating BSA [Bosnian Serb army] targeting of the safe areas. . . . There are always two sides to any argument. . . . Although the [Bosnian Serb] blatant disregard for the safe areas cannot be condoned, neither can the BIH's [Bosnian Muslims'] motives to encourage such acts." One senior UN officer said later that in almost all the crises engendered by the safe areas there was a pattern: Muslim provocations were met by disproportionate Serb responses.

General Mladic made no secret of his hatred for the enclaves, particularly Srebrenica, from which Muslims had killed several hundred Serbs in guerrilla attacks in 1992–93 prior to its establishment as a safe area. Referring to the UN's efforts to stop him from overrunning Srebrenica in 1993, he later said, "Had there not been the involvement of the international community, they [the Muslims] would have paid dearly for everything they had done to the Serbian people. Srebrenica Turks committed some of the greatest crimes ever against the Serbian people."

In 1994 Dutch peacekeepers had relieved the Canadians in Srebrenica. The war had caused widespread outrage in Holland, the only additional Western country to answer the secretary general's June 1993 request for troops to implement the safe areas resolution.

The Dutch had endured constant shortages ever since their arrival. The Serbs limited their fuel resupply, knowing full well that that was the best way to destroy an army's effectiveness and its morale. The Dutch had to patrol Srebrenica on foot instead of in vehicles. Their generators had to be constantly switched off, so there was no power for lighting, television, deep freezes; all those modern conveniences which many young Europeans assumed to be an inalienable part of their life, even if they were soldiers, disappeared.

On November 21, 1994, after NATO planes bombed a Serb air base at Udbina, the Serbs retaliated by taking hostage seventy Dutch soldiers who were on their way out of Srebrenica to go on leave. They vanished for several days and were visited by General Mladic, who arrived in a repainted Mercedes jeep the Serbs had stolen from the Dutch. One Dutch soldier later recounted, "He was with us for five minutes. He spoke to one of our chaps and then ran his fingers across his throat." It was almost a week before the Serbs were induced by serious diplomatic pressure to release the Dutch troops unharmed.

By early 1995, there were at least three thousand Bosnian Muslim soldiers inside Srebrenica. Dutch efforts to disarm them were half-hearted and unsuccessful. Relations between the Dutch and the Muslims deteriorated; the Dutch saw Naser Oric, the Muslim leader in Srebrenica, as a murderous gangster who terrorized the refugees and profited greatly from the horror of the enclave—and from the Western aid that was delivered. After the refugees elected their own representative to help distribute food, at the insistence of the aid agencies, the man was immediately murdered, apparently by Oric's people. Oric left the enclave in April 1995 and never returned.

In the spring the Dutch battalion (Dutchbat) reported an increase in Muslim units in the safe area. The Serbs now tightened the blockade on the Dutch as well as on the local population. Conditions, already bad, became awful. Starvation and disease spread among the refugees. Drinking water became scarce. Dutchbat needed at least seven thousand liters (1,750 gallons) of fuel a day to be fully operational. By the spring they were able to use less than a thousand liters (250 gallons) a day. There was no fresh food. Access to the enclave became harder and harder. The morale of the inexperienced young peacekeepers fell even further. Many of them began to feel that their mission was pointless and that they should withdraw.

On May Day 1995 the cessation of hostilities agreement negotiated by Jimmy Carter and Yasushi Akashi expired. No side was willing to extend it. The country returned to general warfare. A Bosnian government attempt to break the siege of Sarajevo had failed and conditions in the city deteriorated. In early May, shelling between Muslims and Serbs inside the heavy weapons exclusion zone around Sarajevo killed and wounded scores of people. By now Rupert Smith was advocating a more robust response to Serb attacks on the safe areas than either Akashi or General Bernard Janvier, the overall UN-PROFOR commander, deemed prudent. After one night of heavy Serb shelling of civilians, Rupert Smith called for air strikes against the Serbs. His request went all the way to Boutros-Ghali, who turned it down. Significantly, the British foreign secretary, Douglas Hurd, wrote to the secretary general to protest his decision. Till then the British government had opposed most requests for air strikes. Attitudes were changing.

Both Smith and Janvier now felt the fighting would escalate during the summer and that UN peacekeepers were likely to be taken hostage. At a meeting in Paris on May 12, they told Boutros-Ghali that the United Nations should choose between asking for a new mandate to impose a solution by military force and drawing in the UN presence by redeploying out of the safe areas.

Boutros-Ghali preferred drawing in and drawing down the UN commitment. He asked Janvier to come to New York to brief the Security Council. On May 24, Janvier told the council that he and Smith believed that the UN must redeploy its troops out of the safe areas into central Bosnia. It would be much more effective to have just a few observers and forward air controllers in Srebrenica and the other areas; they could call in air strikes if the areas were attacked. That would enormously reduce UNPROFOR's vulnerability to hostage taking. Thus it could actually defend the safe areas better.

The idea was sensible, but it was worrying to the British and French governments and it was anathema to the United States. Janvier found himself under fierce and personal attack from Madeleine Albright. She claimed Janvier wanted to "dump the safe areas" and insisted that the U.S. would not allow it. The United Nations must not withdraw its men. This meant that the UN could not take the more robust action, in particular air strikes against the Serbs, that the U.S. was also demanding. It really was a Catch-22. U.S. rhetoric, from Albright and her superiors, condemned the UN to continue its exercise in futility—and condemned those supposed to be under its protection to insecurity, indeed to danger.

On May 22 the Bosnian Serbs had forced their way past the UN soldiers guarding a weapons collection point near Sarajevo and seized two artillery pieces. Heavy fighting erupted. The Serbs shelled Sarajevo; the Bosnian government fired back out of the city. Both sides were firing heavy weapons, the Serbs even doing so from within the collection points. Janvier, Smith and Akashi demanded that the fighting end and threatened air strikes.

The Serbs failed to comply and on May 25, NATO planes attacked an ammunition depot near Pale. UNPROFOR asked NATO not to release the nationality of the planes taking part in the attacks. "This is to protect the same nationalities of UNPF [UNPROFOR] from reprisals by the warring factions."

The Bosnian Serbs retaliated, shelling most of the safe areas, sometimes with terrible effect. In the town of Tuzla shells hit a crowd, many of them young people, enjoying coffee and drinks in the evening air. Seventy-one people died and almost two hundred were injured. Next morning a second NATO air strike took place.

Smith telephoned Mladic and said that the Bosnian Serbs' attack on Tuzla was a gross violation of the safe areas resolution. He warned Mladic to reflect very carefully on the course on which he was set and said that matters were now out of his hands. Mladic replied that he was sorry for what had happened, but he "could not forgive General Smith for his stupidity." It was Smith who was to blame for the violations of the cease-fire. He accused Smith of "crazy and unreasonable" use of NATO air strikes, which had put lives at risk. Was Smith trying to frighten him? Mladic had expected Smith to behave as a reasonable man and as a human being. He could not understand how General Smith had dared to call him. He had expected apologies, not threats. He accused Smith of being not a UN man, but rather part of NATO in its realization of "dark goals."

Later that morning Mladic ordered his men to start seizing UN soldiers throughout Bosnia. Four unarmed military observers were handcuffed to a fence outside the Pale ammunition dump, and Mladic said they would be killed if another air strike occurred. In all, three hundred UN soldiers were seized as hostages. In another telephone call, Mladic told Smith it was all the fault of his "preposterous" bombing. Smith countered that it was not the action of a professional soldier to seize unarmed men and threaten them with a televised death. Mladic replied that Smith was responsible for all the Serb soldiers and civilians killed the previous day and for the UN personnel Mladic now held.

It was a crucial moment. Nothing showed the impotence of the United Nations so vividly as the plight of its soldiers chained to potential targets. And nothing showed so graphically the need to reduce the UN's vulnerability by withdrawing its men from outlying areas.

In New York, Boutros-Ghali reminded Security Council members that he had warned them that this would happen. "Each air strike brings a new wave of hostage taking and takes us a month of negotiations with the Serbs to get the UN personnel released." He asked the council for advice: should there be a third air strike? He would make the decision, but he would value their advice. None was given. Albright was silent, according to Boutros-Ghali. "It was a unique moment. Security Council members who enjoyed micromanaging every detail of a UN operation, offering endless advice at every stage, suddenly had no counsel to offer me. . . . I was shocked at this collective abdication of responsibility. . . . The absence of U.S. leadership was appalling," Boutros-Ghali writes in his memoirs. The *New York Times* compared the Clinton administration to "a Halloween prankster who rings a doorbell and runs away." The secretary general stopped the bombing.

On May 30, Boutros-Ghali presented four options to the Security Council: withdraw all UNPROFOR troops; continue with "muddle through"; change the mandate to permit the use of greater force; reduce the mandate to purely peacekeeping functions suited to the force deployed. He thought the last option was the most realistic, but the Security Council once again ignored the reality and tried to combine muddling through with the use of greater force.

Still, there were changes. The most important was that the U.S. government was finally becoming resolved to grasp the issue. There were several reasons for this. It appears that President Clinton may only now have realized that if UNPROFOR had to withdraw, the United States was committed, through NATO, to assist. If the UN's withdrawal was not part of an overall peace settlement, it was likely to be contested and bloody. U.S. troops would be inserted and would almost inevitably and at once come under hostile fire in Bosnia. Richard Holbrooke has stated that it was he who forced Clinton to confront this unpleasant reality in the summer of 1995, but it had been the case since at least 1993.

Second, some of the commanders on the ground were growing more and more impatient. As a result of the hostage crisis, Rupert Smith formed from British and French forces two reserve battle groups intended to give more protection to other UN troops. By early June the British and French governments had agreed that these should be reinforced into two heavily armed brigades, which became known as the Rapid Reaction Force. But there were disagreements as to what it should do. On June 9, Akashi, Janvier and Smith met in the Croatian seaport of Split to discuss the crisis. Their views showed how far opinions could differ among people on the same team. Smith stated what were to him the realities: "We do not have the consent of the Serbs [to carry out existing mandates]. We have less co-operation from the [Bosnian government] than we did one week ago. To all intents and purposes we have been neutralised. . . . [T]he safe areas are under increasing threat." He said he thought the Serbs did not want a cease-fire; they wanted to continue "to squeeze us." They might well make an attack on the safe areas and UNPROFOR would find it very hard to respond, outside of airpower. At the same time the Bosnians were getting more and more impatient with the UN. There were signs that they would attack the Serbs more fiercely. The use of airpower had failed. "We have neutralised air power and further marginalised ourselves. The parties and events are moving at a speed much greater than we have proven able to keep up with." Smith was convinced that the Serbs wanted to win the war this year and would take every risk to do so.

Akashi and Janvier were still more cautious than Smith. Akashi worried that UNPROFOR was on "the edge of the Mogadishu line." If they did not cross it, they would be accused of being timid and pro-Serb; if they did cross it, they would be accused of being reckless and abandoning chances for peace. He was still in favor of talking to all parties like proper peacekeepers. Akashi wanted the name of the Rapid Reaction Force changed to Theater Reserve, so it would be less confrontational to the Serbs. Smith, by contrast, wanted a confrontation. He said that unless the force was authorized to open corridors to the safe areas, he would rather not have it at all.

Smith pointed to the danger of asking favors of the Serbs. "We need to be prepared to fight," he said. "If we are not prepared to fight, we will always be stared down by the [Serbs]. We have already crossed the Mogadishu line. The Serbs do not view us as peacekeepers."

Akashi asked, "Can we return" back over the line? Smith replied with some force, "Only by doing nothing, or by showing an absolute readiness to fight."

Janvier interrupted to say that fighting the Serbs could never provide a solution. They had to go forward by negotiating.

Beyond Bosnia, there were the wider politics. The election of President Jacques Chirac in France brought a new energy to the international community, especially to Washington. In mid-June, Chirac barnstormed Washington and conducted his own shuttle service between the White House and Congress. He tried to persuade the administration to meet the costs of the Rapid Reaction Force. Policy seemed to be out of White House hands. Clinton was embarrassed. Having long considered that muddle through was the best policy, the administration now began to believe that it was not.

Nothing focused minds so much as the horror of Srebrenica. This is what happened, in the words of a judge at the International Criminal Tribunal for the Former Yugoslavia: "After Srebrenica fell to besieging Serb forces in July 1995, a truly terrible massacre of the Muslim population appears to have taken place. The evidence tendered by the prosecutor describes scenes of unimaginable savagery: thousands of men executed and buried in mass graves, hundreds of men buried alive, men and women mutilated and slaughtered, children killed before their mothers' eyes, a grandfather forced to eat the liver of his own grandson. These are truly scenes from hell, written on the darkest pages of human history."

This catastrophe exposed more brutally and more graphically than anything else the inconsistencies and inadequacies of the way in which the world was now dealing with disorder and ethnic conflict. It was the consequence of the way in which the international community had tried to manage Bosnia, intervening to save lives but with so little decisive effect that intervention was often interference.

IN July 1995 there were some six hundred Dutch peacekeepers in Srebrenica, of whom only three hundred were infantry soldiers; the rest were in support capacities. They were lightly armed and, thanks to the Serb blockade, short of almost everything. In June, the Dutchbat commander, Colonel Ton Karremans, had complained that his forces were hostages of the Bosnian Serbs and able to do nothing.

The Serbs around Srebrenica, by contrast, were prepared for war. They had up to two thousand well-equipped soldiers from the 5th Drina Corps, armed with tanks, tracked armored vehicles, artillery and mortars. They had good logistics, good intelligence and all the supplies they needed.

On July 6, 1995, the Serbs began to shell Srebrenica and then attacked from the south. The United Nations, which had no means of monitoring Serb communications (unlike NATO, which did not always promptly share its intelligence information with the UN), judged at first that the Serbs were embarked on a limited operation to shrink the pocket from the south in order to remove the threat of Bosnian (Muslim) patrols to Serb economic assets and routes in the area.

Dutch soldiers were ordered not to return Serb fire but rather to withdraw. A Dutch outpost on the hill above the town was forced back. Others were overrun or bypassed. On July 6 and 8, Colonel Karremans requested close air support. On both days it was denied by his superiors in Zagreb. The population began to panic.

On July 8, Muslim soldiers fired on Dutch soldiers who were trying to withdraw from the oncoming Serbs; one Dutchman was killed, to the anger of his colleagues in Dutchbat.

That afternoon, Boutros-Ghali was meeting in Geneva with all the senior officials from UNPROFOR and Mrs. Ogata, the high commissioner for refugees. Srebrenica was not on the agenda, but Janvier said that the Serbs were "holding all the cards" and that the UN's nine hundred soldiers in all the enclaves were potential hostages. Mrs. Ogata said that the humanitarian situation was bleak; very few supplies were getting through to the enclaves.

By July 9 it was clear that the Serbs were embarked on a significant assault on Srebrenica. General Janvier ordered Dutchbat to establish a "blocking position"; if this was attacked, he would authorize the use of NATO close-air support against the Serbs. On July 10, the Serbs shelled the town heavily.

There was still confusion in both Zagreb and New York as to just what was happening; the Security Council was incorrectly briefed on July 10. The Serbs advanced again and the terrified inhabitants of the enclave rushed in panic toward the center, seeking protection from the Dutch. The Bosnian government ordered the Muslim defenders to fire their anti-tank weapons at the Serbs to try to halt their advance; it turned out they could not operate them.

Colonel Karremans expected massive air strikes to take place at dawn on July 11, and everyone in the enclave heard about this. They waited eagerly through the night and watched the sky all morning. No planes came. There had been a mistake in the UN chain of command.

Srebrenica fell that day. By the afternoon the Serb flag was flying over the bakery at the southern end of the town. Up until that time, at least three (possibly five) requests for air support by Dutchbat had been turned down at various levels of the chain of command. Dutchbat had not fired a single shot at the advancing Serbs.

That afternoon, airpower was finally used: NATO planes dropped two bombs on what were thought to be Serb vehicles. The Bosnian Serbs immediately radioed Dutchbat and threatened to shell the town and the Dutch compound, which was filling with refugees, and to kill Dutch soldiers being held hostage, if NATO bombed again. Karremans passed the warning to his superiors. The Dutch minister of defense called Akashi in Zagreb and Annan in New York to say that bombing was endangering Dutch troops and must be halted. It was.

Mladic drove into town and strode around, embracing his troops for the benefit of his own cameramen and ordering Muslim street signs to be taken down. He told the camera that his troops had won victory on the eve of a Serb holy day and that "the time has come for revenge on the Muslims." By evening there were massive crowds outside the UN base, as everyone sought safety. But many of the men decided to leave their families and make their way some thirty miles through the woods and hills to Bosnian government territory. A long column of about fifteen thousand men, some armed, most not, set off out of the valley.

That night Mladic summoned Colonel Karremans to two meetings. His men videotaped the encounters; they were humiliating. Mladic's arrogant self-assurance contrasted with the obvious, understandable nervousness of the Dutch officer. Mladic used most of the first session to shout at Karremans, blaming the UN for not having disarmed the Muslims and threatening to shell the Dutch and the refugees in the UN compound if there were any more air strikes. Karremans pleaded for the safety of the refugees. Mladic offered Karremans a cigarette; when the Dutchman demurred, Mladic said, "Don't worry, it won't be your last." He insisted that Karremans drink "to a long life."

He ordered Karremans to come again, after midnight, this time with representatives of the civilian population. At that meeting, Mladic said he would evacuate the wounded, but he demanded that the Muslims hand over their weapons—and again he threatened to shell the compound. At the end of this meeting Mladic dismissed those in attendance, saying, "I've finished. You're free to go." The Bosnian negotiator said he was only there by accident and could not guarantee anything. Mladic replied, "That's your problem."

Karremans reported to his superiors that there were now fifteen thousand people around his battalion "in an extremely vulnerable position: the sitting duck position." They had come in terror and in hope of protection, but they were surrounded by Serb tanks and artillery. Karremans said he could not defend either the refugees or his own battalion. He could do nothing. He begged for top-level negotiations to save them.

From Zagreb, Akashi sent Karremans's plea to New York. He reported that the Bosnian government would allow only the wounded to be evacuated from Srebrenica. They did not want the safe area abandoned. Serb shelling of the area continued, and Karremans met Mladic and his colleague General Radislav Krstic for a third time on the morning of July 12. Mladic gave a long historical monologue, complaining about Muslim attacks on the Serbs. "Mladic also insisted that he see all the men between the ages of 17 and 60 because he alleged that there were 'criminals' in the crowd gathered at Potocari and he would need to question each one of them."

Publicly, Mladic was ingratiating; propaganda—particularly on state television—was always an important part of the Serb war machine. On July 12, after Serb soldiers had surrounded the Dutch compound in Potocari, Mladic brought in a large group of Serb television cameras and journalists, and in front of them he addressed the refugees outside the Dutch compound. As his soldiers handed out bread, water and candy for the cameras, he declared, "Don't be afraid. Just take it easy. Let women and children go first. Plenty of buses will come. . . . Don't let any of the children get lost. Don't be afraid. Nobody will harm you." To a delegation of Muslims he said, "Your people need not die. Allah cannot help you, but Mladic can."

Once the cameras had gone, the deportation of about twenty thousand people outside the compound began. Serb soldiers began to divide families: women and children were allowed onto the buses; the remaining men and boys were ordered in the other direction. After the Serbs told the Dutch that the men would not be harmed and would merely be questioned as prisoners of war according to the Geneva Conventions, the Dutch dropped their objections.

By the end of the day on July 12, about five thousand women, children and elderly people had been deported. They were dropped about three and a half miles from Bosnian government lines and had to walk the rest of the way. Some of them were so badly injured that they would have had to crawl.

Janvier sent Mladic a letter in which he wrote that the humanitarian situation in the enclave "is possibly worse than at any time in this sad and unnecessary war, and will certainly become a disaster of unparalleled magnitude if urgent measures are not taken. My aim in writing to you on this subject is to enlist your support in saving lives on a grand scale." He asked Mladic to allow the UN to fly heavy-lift helicopters into Srebrenica to bring in food and take out the wounded. Mladic refused.

It seems that the Bosnian Serbs made the decision to murder thousands of men only after the fall of Srebrenica, and after they realized that the UN was scarcely reacting to the assault on the safe area. By July 12, Dutch soldiers were beginning to see random murders and scattered bodies. The largest massacres were yet to begin.

That day in New York, the Security Council was discussing a draft resolution demanding Serb withdrawal from Srebrenica. Annan sent it to Akashi for comment. Akashi felt it "raises unrealistic expectations and its failure to take into account reality on the ground will inevitably lead to further disillusionment amongst the international community and the media." He also pointed out that many of the Muslims in Srebrenica were all too eager to leave. They were refugees from elsewhere who had come into a hellish trap in which the Bosnian government forced them to stay. Akashi warned against any language in the resolution which might seem to authorize the use of force by the new Rapid Reaction Force to drive the Serbs out of Srebrenica.

Akashi also pointed out "all the inherent complexities and contradictions [of the mandate] . . . without the means to uphold that commitment, has placed this organisation in the tragic situation in which we now find ourselves." And "it is essential now for members of the Security Council to focus on humanitarian assistance, rather than suggesting, even obliquely, that the status quo ante can be re-established."

Annan knew that hypocrisy was stalking around the Security Council. He said in a cable to Akashi, "We stress [to the council] that the objectives of the draft [resolution] are in present circumstances unimplementable without Serb cooperation. . . . [T]he co-sponsors appear to appreciate these points, but have received strong instructions from the highest level of their cabinets and do not believe they will be changed."

On the morning of July 12, Annan briefed members of the council in New York; he suggested that the strong language of the draft resolution could raise unrealistic expectations and lead to further disillusionment with the United Nations. There was no real possibility of reinforcing the Dutch, who had no fuel and little food. Mladic had threatened to shell the Dutch headquarters in Potocari, including the more than ten thousand refugees around it, if the UN used force.

The French ambassador, Jean-Bernard Mérimée, recalled the original ambiguous wording of Resolution 836, which set up the safe areas. He reminded his colleagues that the co-sponsors had deliberately chosen the wording "all resources available" as opposed to "all necessary means" to deter attacks on them. If, after careful consideration, the Secretariat came to the conclusion that the objective of restoring the safe area could not be achieved with the means at hand, then the Security Council would accept and support such a conclusion. Sir David Hannay, the British ambassador, agreed, saying operative paragraph 6 was not an instruction to use force and it was for Akashi to explore which approach could achieve the results.

The ambassadors discussed whether the Bosnian Serbs might attack other safe areas as well. Annan said that with only 80 peacekeepers in Zepa and 280 in Gorazde, there was little UNPROFOR could do to prevent it. The UN just did not have the means.

That same day the council met again. Members were told that fifty-one Dutch soldiers who had been prevented by the Muslims from withdrawing into the enclave had fallen into Serb hands. The council unanimously adopted Resolution 1004. It *demanded* that the Bosnian Serbs cease their offensive and leave Srebrenica immediately. It *demanded* that all the parties respect the status of Srebrenica as a safe area. It *demanded* that they respect the safety and freedom of UNPROFOR personnel. It *demanded* that the Bosnian Serbs release immediately all UN personnel they had detained. It *demanded* immediate access to Srebrenica for the Red Cross and other humanitarian agencies. As the resolution was passed, General Mladic was still holding the Dutch peacekeepers captive and his men were preparing the massacre of thousands of Muslim men and boys. The demands and the threats of the Security Council meant nothing.

The Bosnian Serbs were entirely to blame for the massacre at Srebrenica in July 1995. But it could take place only because of the dreadfully flawed decisions made over a number of years by members of the Security Council of the United Nations.

M A N Y of the men captured by the Serbs were taken to the nearby village of Bratunac, where they were packed in a hangar. Mladic blocked access to them by UNPROFOR, UNHCR and the International Committee of the Red Cross. He told them, "Neighbors, if you have not seen me before I am Ratko Mladic. I am the commander of the Serbian army and you see we are not afraid of the NATO pact. They bombed us and we took Srebrenica. And where is your country now? What will you do? Will you stand beside Alija [Izetbegovic]? He has led you to ruin. . . ." He assured them that he was negotiating a prisoner exchange.

One witness who survived later recalled that Mladic exclaimed to his troops, "There are so many! It's going to be a feast *[mezze].* There will be blood up to your knees." And indeed, all the men were taken away to be knifed, bludgeoned or shot to death, many of them after they had been forced to dig their own graves.

As the killings began, the UN's military observers around the eastern zone began to write grim reports. Here is some of what they noted during the day of July 13:

0800 HOURS: THE NUMBER OF BIH SLDRS [Bosnian Muslim soldiers] [*sic*] POW BY THE BSA [Bosnian Serb army] IS NOT KNOWN YET BUT GEN MLADIC TOLD THE UNMO [UN military observer] TEAM AND CO DUTCHBAT THAT THE BIH HAVE SEVERAL HUNDRED DEAD SLRS IN THE AREA OF THE BANDERA TRIANGLE. HE ALSO ASKED THE CO DUTCHBAT TO CONTACT BIH SLRS AND INFORM THEM THAT IT IS NOT THE GENERAL'S INTENTION TO KILL ANY MORE SOLDIERS OF THE BIH. THEY HAVE ONLY TO SURRENDER AND HAND OVER THEIR WEAPONS.

1530 HOURS: REFUGEE SITUATION KLADANJ: 12 COACHES HAVE BEEN OBSERVED LEAVING KLADANJ FOR TUZLA. . . . UNMO VISITED THE TRANSFER POINT AND OBSERVED THE FOL:
NOT LESS THAN 5000 REFUGEES PRESENT WITH MANY MORE ARRIVING ALL THE TIME. . . . NO MEN OVER THE AGE OF 12 WERE OBSERVED

AND VERY FEW OVER 60. THE MORALE IS VERY LOW WITH A LARGE
NUMBER REFUGEES CURSING UNPROFOR. ALL THE REFUGEES HAVE
MINIMUM OF CLOTHING AND HAD BEEN STRIPPED OF ALL VALUABLES.

2300 HOURS . . . UNMO WAS ABLE TO VISIT THE TRANSFERPOINT
AND PAKBAT [Pakistani Battalion] MED POST AND WAS INFORMED
OF THE FOL:

REFUGEES HAD WITNESSED MEN BEING SEPARATED FROM OTHERS
AND SEVERELY BEATEN, STONED AND IN SOME CASES STABBED.

AT LEAST ONE BSA VEH [vehicle] DISAPPEARED EN ROUTE TO THE
DOP [dropoff point] AND PEOPLE ABOARD HAVE NOT BEEN SEEN
SINCE.

THE SEVERELY WOUNDED (APPROX 30–35 STRETCHER CASES) HAVE
BEEN TAKEN TO BRATANAK [Bratunac] BY THE BSA.

From Zagreb, Akashi issued a statement condemning "the ongoing forced relocation of thousands of civilians from Srebrenica by
the Bosnian Serb forces." He called their action abhorrent.

From Paris, President Chirac called Clinton to suggest that American helicopters carry French troops into Srebrenica to relieve it. It
was a desperate proposal which had no chance of being accepted, let
alone implemented. Richard Holbrooke said later that he recommended that NATO airpower be used against Bosnian Serb positions
in other parts of the country, but this was rejected by all the troop
contributors.

On July 13 the Serbs began to deport civilians inside the Dutch
compound. The men in particular were terrified. The devastating
report on Srebrenica published by Kofi Annan at the end of 1999
stated that the Dutch knew that Muslim men had already been
summarily executed. The men "pleaded not to be handed over to
the Serbs, but to no avail. Dutchbat then ordered them to leave
the compound and present themselves to the waiting Serbs. The
Dutchbat personnel concerned have since stated that they did not
believe they were handing these men over to certain death, and that
they believed the men would be treated by the Serbs in accordance with the Geneva Conventions. They felt that, having prepared a list of the names of those handed over, the men would
enjoy some degree of security. All 239 men on the list are still
missing."

The horror of the moment is summed up in the story of Hasan Nuhanovic, a United Nations interpreter. His mother, father and brother were with him in the Dutch compound and he begged for them to be allowed to stay. The Dutch said only he could remain. They were pushed out, and he has never seen them again. Nuhanovic said later, "Sometimes I say to myself: why didn't you grab the pistol from the major's holster and put it on his forehead and say, 'You have to keep my family on the base'? . . . But you have no brain at these moments; you are so obedient that you just do what they tell you. And nobody complained when they walked to the gate. They just walked, knowing they were going to die."

By the evening of July 13, the Annan report stated, there were now four categories of Muslim men in Srebrenica: those alive and trying to escape through the woods; those killed on that journey; those who had surrendered to the Serbs and had already been killed; and those who had surrendered and would soon be killed.

The Annan report subsequently noted that "the international community does not appear to have had any evidence at the time that executions were taking place in such staggering numbers." No one had expected or even imagined the possibility of such barbarity.

But alarm was already being expressed at various levels of the system. Dutch soldiers had seen murders. The Bosnian permanent representative to the UN wrote to the secretary general to warn that the fate of the detainees was unknown "and there are substantial grounds to fear their execution." He blamed the UN.

By July 14, Akashi was reporting to New York that Srebrenica was deserted and the Serbs were looting the town. He also passed on information from UN military observers about the mistreatment of the Bosnians by the Serbs. Rather than make an outcry, he suggested that in view of the vulnerable position of the observers, the reports be kept confidential. He also informed Annan that almost all the refugees arriving in Tuzla were old men, women and children. "We are beginning to detect a shortfall in number of persons expected to arrive in Tuzla. There is not further information on the status of approximately 4,000 draft age males. Tuzla reports four bus loads (+/−250) containing young women . . . have been missing for over 24 hours."

That same day General Rupert Smith met in Sarajevo with the Bosnian prime minister, Haris Silajdzic. The prime minister was most anxious that the UN reinforce its contingent in the safe area of Zepa to protect it from the same sort of disaster as Srebrenica. Smith replied that he had neither the capability nor the orders to do so.

Silajdzic raised the reports of atrocities in Srebrenica, including the rape of young women and the murder of a busload of refugees. Smith's note taker recorded that the Bosnian government was "worried about reports of refugees being segregated into groups and men between the ages of 16 to 60 being sent to different locations." Silajdzic asked that all convoys be escorted by UNPROFOR and that passenger lists be compiled on all buses.

Smith reckoned that the Serbs were moving fast to present a *fait accompli*. They wanted to overrun the enclaves to eliminate threats to their rear area, and to provide troops to enable them to make a decisive blow and possibly to counter the new Rapid Reaction Force. The Serbs, he wrote, were "cleansing" Srebrenica. Men of military age were being separated from the refugees, and reports of murder, unconfirmed as yet, were beginning to be heard.

Smith asked, in a memo he wrote at this time, whether the UN should "lie back," withdraw from the safe areas, bomb the Serbs or reinforce the remaining safe areas to defend them. Bombing "has not worked because we have not been prepared to escalate and the bombing does not stop attacks on this terrain. . . . Ground cannot be held: there is difficulty in finding suitable targets: air supremacy has to be achieved; the raid is not part of a coherent All Arms battle; elements of UNPROFOR remain potential hostages to capture and attack; casualties must be expected."

Smith thought that if the Serbs continued to move as fast as now, then the only option would be to "lie back." "If we have more time then we must decide whether or not we wish to fight a war. If we do, it should be for a greater aim than the defence of an enclave. Furthermore, appropriate force must be deployed and we must remove the white and vulnerable elements of UNPROFOR or we will continue to have hostages to fortune." (The UN's vehicles are always painted white, not battle camouflaged.) If the UN was not prepared to fight and escalate "then we must face the harsh and unforgiving truth" that short of a peace settlement they would have to concede or withdraw. Right now what mattered were reinforcements to deal with the refugee crisis and high-level intervention to get the Dutch soldiers freed.

Between July 14 and July 17, hundreds of Bosnian Muslim men were loaded onto buses, ordered off them, stood in fields and shot; they included many of those who had attempted to walk through the woods and had been shot at or surrendered. Some of the Serbs were wearing blue UN helmets and driving UN vehicles stolen from the Dutch. They lured some of the men into ambushes and killed them. Others were attacked with mortars and small arms.

In some cases the victims were forced to dig their own graves before they were shot. Later, in an attempt to hide their work, the Bosnian Serbs took many of the bodies from the original graves and reburied them.

Several hundred men were packed into a warehouse in Kravica and killed by small arms fire and grenades. The Annan report stated that UN personnel later "were able to see hair, blood and human tissue caked to the walls of this building."

Very few eyewitnesses to these massacres have been found. A tiny handful survived by pretending to be dead and lying still under bodies; they later escaped. One said this:

"We came near to what I saw through my right eye was a wooded area. They took us off the truck in twos and led us out into some kind of meadow. People started taking off blindfolds and yelling in fear because the meadow was littered with corpses. I was put in the front row, but I fell over to the left before the first shots were fired so that bodies fell on top of me. . . . About an hour later I looked up and saw dead bodies everywhere. They were bringing in more trucks with more people to be executed. After a bulldozer driver walked away, I crawled over the dead bodies and into the forest."

Valuable testimony was later provided by Drazen Erdemovic, a Bosnian Croat soldier who was serving in the Bosnian Serb army. He reluctantly took part in the killing under orders and later gave himself up to the tribunal in The Hague. "I wanted to testify because of my conscience," he said, "because of all that happened, because I did not want that. I was simply compelled to, forced to, and I could choose between my life and the life of those people; and had I lost my life then, that would not have changed the fate of those people. . . ."

While the massacres were under way—unseen but increasingly suspected—international officials continued to deal with President Milosevic, Radovan Karadzic and General Mladic, not least in the hope of saving people who, as it turned out, were already dead. On July 15, Rupert Smith, Akashi and others had a secret lunch meeting in Belgrade with Milosevic and Mladic. The Serb leaders agreed to give the High Commissioner for Refugees and the Red Cross full and immediate access to Srebrenica and to all "prisoners of war." Mladic reneged on this commitment.

Soon after the meeting, Akashi was informed by his staff in Zagreb that "we still have no clear idea where the Bosnian males in Srebrenica are. . . . MSF [Médecins sans Frontières] is reporting massacres on the road between Bratunac and Kladanj. . . ." Survivors who had reached Tuzla began to talk of the killings, abductions and rapes they had witnessed, but none of the survivors of mass executions had yet arrived.

Late on July 16 and early on July 17, up to six thousand of the men who had tried to walk through Serb lines stumbled into Bosnian government territory. They told UN officials that at least three thousand of the original column had been killed by the Serbs in combat as they fled and others had surrendered.

By now Zepa was under increasing Serb pressure. On July 17, Rupert Smith asked Mladic to let the civilians there go. Mladic replied that there could be no evacuation unless there was first unconditional surrender, with all Muslim weapons handed over. The Bosnian government rejected Mladic's proposal.

As Srebrenica fell, Boutros-Ghali was in Rwanda and Burundi. His journey there was chronicled by the writer Michael Ignatieff, who asked him why he did not fly back to the United Nations at once to deal with the humiliating crisis in Bosnia. Because, said Boutros-Ghali, if he did so all the African countries would complain that he was more interested in the fate of a village in Europe than in genocide in Rwanda. The UN did not have a mandate to intervene on the side of the Muslims, even if they were the victims, he told Ignatieff; nor did it have the resources to defend them. "No one realizes how long it takes for people to come to their senses," he said. One should remember how long it took for the PLO and the Israelis to sit down together.

All this was true, Ignatieff reflected, "but it does not change the fact that promises were made to people in a village in Europe that should never have been made because those who made them knew the promises could not be kept."

Boutros-Ghali pointed out in a striking phrase, "Everywhere we work, we are struggling against the culture of death." The UN might not have succeeded completely in Bosnia, but look at the countries where it had been able to do even less to counter that culture— Afghanistan, Chechnya, Sri Lanka, Sierra Leone, Liberia. Boutros-Ghali saw these as "orphaned conflicts," in which the West had no interest, for whatever reason.

In Rwanda, the Patriotic Front government took Boutros-Ghali on a tour of some of the "memorials" to the victims of the genocide conducted by the Hutus, where the bodies of Tutsi victims had been left in the open as a reminder of the horror which the "culture of death" had visited upon that country. In Burundi, which was experiencing a sort of slow-motion genocide, a hundred people here, a dozen there, Boutros-Ghali watched and listened as the Hutu and Tutsi politicians he had summoned denounced each other. He then told them that they made him ashamed to call himself an African. The international community would not save them from themselves. It had not saved Beirut. "God helps those who help themselves," Boutros-Ghali said. "Your enemy is not each other but fear and cowardice. You must have the courage to accept compromises. That is what a political class is for. You must assume your responsibilities. If you don't, no one will save you."

That night, on CNN, there were stories that Serb soldiers, wearing the UN's blue helmets, were luring Muslim civilians out of the safe haven of Zepa and shooting them dead. Ignatieff thought he had witnessed "the moment when liberal internationalism reached the end of its tether."

ON July 19, Rupert Smith met with Mladic at a restaurant in Serb-held territory outside Sarajevo. The Serb general, fresh from the killing fields of Srebrenica, was in a "chipper mood" according to Smith's note taker. Smith asked for access to Srebrenica for the Red Cross and UNHCR. Mladic agreed but said convoys would have to drive via Belgrade. Smith asked him for an account of the activities of his troops in Srebrenica. According to Smith's note taker, "General Mladic was at pains to point out that Srebrenica was 'finished in a correct way.' . . . He said he engaged personally in this operation and organised as much food and water for the refugees as possible."

Smith said he had information that not all wounded Muslims had been able to leave Srebrenica. "Mladic appeared to have no knowledge of this but agreed to find out and resolve the matter," Smith related. Mladic claimed that he had opened a corridor to allow men to escape to Tuzla (in fact he had opened a trap in which they were slaughtered). All he would acknowledge was that some skirmishes had taken place with casualties on both sides and some "unfortunate small incidents" had occurred.

By now the scale of the massacre was still unknown, but stories of the atrocities were beginning to emerge. According to Boutros-Ghali, it was not until July 21, as the last Dutchbat soldiers were released from Srebrenica, that "UN civilian officials were told about the horrors perpetrated by Mladic's men." This is not quite accurate. Refugees arriving in Tuzla and elsewhere had sounded the alarm as early as July 13. In the following days it became clearer that something truly terrible was happening. The military had had a pretty good idea for days. U.S. satellites had filmed mass graves being dug, but it is not clear when these pictures became available to senior U.S. officials. Madeleine Albright revealed them only on August 10.

On July 21 the foreign and defense ministers of NATO, together with the Russians, met in London to discuss how to respond to the disaster. The London conference made crucial decisions. The ministers—though not the Russians—decided that any new Serb attack on Gorazde or any other safe area, like Sarajevo, would be met with a "disproportionate" or overwhelming response including NATO airpower and the Rapid Reaction Force, which had been deployed around Sarajevo. They also decided to change the mechanics of the dual key to unlock NATO bombing strikes. From now on the two air strike launch "keys" would be held by military men—one would be with the commander of UN forces, General Janvier, rather than with Yasushi Akashi; the other key remained in the hands of Admiral Leighton Smith, NATO's Southern Region commander. From now on, bombing could begin if the two commanders agreed that a safe area was under serious threat. It could be suspended temporarily by either NATO or the UN if necessary for the safety of UN troops.

Once the dual keys were turned, the UN's force commander would be required to continue the bombing until he and the NATO command agreed that attacks on or threats to a safe area had ceased. The London meeting in effect abandoned the international community's previous policy of containment.

That was not all. At last—and crucially—the United States embraced a plan for a "comprehensive settlement" which included the division of Bosnia into two entitities, 49 percent Serb and 51 percent Muslim-Croat. On July 22, Presidents Tudjman and Izetbegovic adopted the Split declaration, which provided for a joint defense of Bosnia. It legalized the presence of Croatian troops in Bosnia and strengthened the overall military capacity of the Muslim-Croat federation.

By this time the Serbs, emboldened by Srebrenica, were becoming more aggressive elsewhere. They began an attack on the Bihac enclave and increased their shelling of Sarajevo. On July 22, two French UNPROFOR officers were killed in Sarajevo and four other UNPROFOR members were injured. UNPROFOR fired ninety mortar rounds at Serb targets around Sarajevo to try to suppress the fire. But the Bosnian ministry reported that twenty-five Bosnians were killed in Sarajevo that week and seventy-five more injured.

On July 26, General Smith met Mladic again. Mladic arrived by helicopter, in yet another breach of the UN's no-fly rules. He was "in a serious and purposeful mood," according to Smith's note taker. He was dismissive of the ultimatum from the London conference. "People have no right to tell Serbs how to conduct themselves in their own country," he said. "We did not start the war, we did not endanger the countries who delivered the ultimatum, all we require is equal treatment, the lifting of sanctions and the right to live on our own land."

Zepa, which, bizarrely, had not been discussed at the London conference, was the main item on the generals' agenda. The Bosnian government still did not wish to accept its surrender. In frustration and terror, three members of the Zepa war presidency had signed their own surrender agreement with Mladic. He told Smith to tell the Bosnian government that those men who refused to hand over their weapons "would be liquidated."

Smith went to Zepa itself and talked to the three men who had signed the agreement. They told him they were in an impossible position; they were upset that their government had failed over four-teen days to conclude an agreement for the exchange of prisoners of war. Smith was in a quandary over whether or not to withdraw UNPROFOR from Zepa altogether. The Serbs were still insisting that all Muslim fighters must surrender to them. They were not planning to attack and drive the Muslims out. "It is clearly in BSA interest to keep UNPROFOR troops in the pocket especially French troops, as potential hostages," wrote Smith. There were about 2,800 civilians and 1,500 fighters in Zepa; they would be very difficult to separate. The Bosnian government was insisting that the UN peacekeepers—less than two hundred—stay.

Smith reported, "I consider UNPROFOR has a duty, both moral, mandated and stated in the recent [Security Council] presidential statement, to remain in the pocket as long as civilians are unaccounted for. To withdraw will mean the abandonment of these people with further loss of UN credibility." But he knew that "To stay will run the risk of hostage taking which may foreclose on other actions elsewhere in the theatre." That, as always, was the problem. It was one with which Smith was dealing—by gradually withdrawing peacekeepers from the areas in which they were most vulnerable.

The Bosnian government remained opposed to the surrender of Zepa and Mladic remained obdurate. He ordered the murder of the local leaders from Zepa with whom he had been negotiating. By July 28, Smith feared an all-out Serb attack on the enclave. But just before that happened, Croat forces seized two Serb-held towns in southwest Bosnia, creating ten thousand Serb refugees and exposing Knin, the capital of the Serb-held Krajina region of Croatia. Mladic immediately turned his attention toward the new threat from Croatia. He withdrew most of his regular forces from around Zepa; many of the Bosnians in Zepa were able to escape the dreadful fate of those in Srebrenica.

At Srebrenica an estimated 7,414 men and boys were murdered. It was the greatest war crime committed in Europe since the Second World War. The agonized debate over responsibility for it continues to this day.

As Kofi Annan's remarkably detailed and painful report to the General Assembly on Srebrenica (1999) made clear, there is blame enough to go around. Colonel Karremans believed that, given the weakness of the Dutch defenses, air support was essential, but his requests for it went unheeded or were denied. Why? Because all senior UN and UNPROFOR officials believed that this would bring the UN into the war against the Serbs, which was not authorized by the council and would be fatal to a peacekeeping mission. It would endanger UN troops; it would disrupt what was still seen as UNPROFOR's primary mission—to deliver humanitarian aid. These were all powerful reasons, but as Annan's report acknowledged, "We were with hindsight wrong to declare repeatedly and publicly that we did not want to use air power against the Serbs except as a last resort."

Once Karremans was told (by the Dutch Defense Ministry as well as the UN Secretariat) that the security of his troops took precedence over "deterring attacks" on the safe area, the Dutch battalion withdrew to its compound. Dutch troops were ordered never to fire on the attacking Serbs. Had they done so, events might have unfolded differently.

The Dutch did not know that the Serbs were bent on massacring thousands of men and boys, but they were aware that something sinister was happening and they did not report it fully. This failure of intelligence sharing was an endemic weakness of UNPROFOR.

Despite the evidence of random murders, the Dutch obeyed Mladic and handed over the refugees. "Perhaps they should have allowed everyone into the compound and then offered themselves as human shields to protect them," said the Annan report. "This may have slowed down the Serbs and bought time for negotiations to take effect."

The background to all these failures, as I have tried to show, was the way in which the Security Council year after year commanded the UN Secretariat, and through it UNPROFOR, to keep peace where there was only war. The council may have originally expected that the "warring parties" on the ground would respect the authority of the UN. If so, it should soon have been disabused of this notion. It was not. Nor did the council understand that the Serbs and Croats would view the UN's humanitarian operation not as an obstacle to the systematic and ruthless campaigns they were conducting but as an instrument of their aims.

Annan's 1999 report acknowledged that the Secretariat of which he was a prominent member had been wrong. It "had convinced itself early on that the broader use of force by the international community was beyond our mandate and anyway undesirable. Knowing that any other course of action would jeopardize the lives of the troops, we tried to create—or imagine—an environment in which the tenets of peacekeeping—agreement between the parties, deployment by consent, and impartiality—could be upheld."

Annan wrote, "It is with the deepest regret and remorse that we have reviewed our own actions and decisions in the face of the assault on Srebrenica. Through error, misjudgment and an inability to recognize the scope of the evil confronting us, we failed to do our part to help save the people of Srebrenica from the Serb campaign of mass murder. . . . The tragedy of Srebrenica will haunt our history for ever."

A brutal and crucial new force on the ground now came into play. In early August the Croatian army, which had been retrained by retired U.S. officers acting in a mercenary role, stormed through Krajina and drove about 250,000 Serbs out of homes they had occupied, in some cases, for centuries. The spectacle of these refugees, poor peasants in the main, on their tractors and carts, winding east toward Serbia, was appalling. This was probably the biggest single example of "ethnic cleansing" during the entire war and was conducted harshly. Hundreds of Serbs were murdered by the Croats, who abused human rights as viciously as the Serbs had elsewhere. But because the victims were Serbs, they invoked almost no international attention, still less sympathy. Indeed, the Croatian blitzkrieg had the support of the United States.

The offensive suited the U.S. aim to roll back the advances made by the Serbs in the last three years. In his book *To End a War*, Holbrooke quotes a note written to him by Bob Frasure, a senior State Department official, at a meeting with Tudjman in Zagreb: "Dick: We 'hired' these guys to be our junkyard dogs because we were desperate. We need to try to 'control' them. But this is no time to get squeamish about things. This is the first time the Serb wave has been reversed. That is essential for us to get stability, so we can get out." This view was not shared by all in the Clinton administration, but it was the view that prevailed. It was helped by the fact that, despite previous warnings, Milosevic did nothing to help the Krajina Serbs. During August and September the Bosnian Serbs lost some 30 percent of the ground they had controlled to Croat and Bosnian attacks.

Two days after he wrote this note, Frasure and two other senior

U.S. officials, Joe Kruzel and Nelson Drew, working with Holbrooke to secure a peace agreement, were killed. On August 19 the armored car in which they were riding to Sarajevo fell off the Mount Igman road and crashed down the hillside. These were the first deaths of American officials in the Yugoslav wars, and they added a personal, emotional incentive for Holbrooke and their other colleagues to see the defeat of the Serbs.

Peacekeeping is filled with bizarre compromises. On August 22, Rupert Smith had lunch with Mladic in a villa near Zepa. The meeting was requested by Mladic. He wanted to discuss UN support for the tens of thousands of new Serb refugees from Krajina. Smith felt this gave him something to bargain with in discussing his most important concern: the planned withdrawal of British and Ukrainian troops from Gorazde, the last of the remote eastern safe areas in which peacekeepers were still based. Smith wanted the last potential UN hostages out of the Serbs' reach.

Mladic provided a barbecue of mutton. Just over a month after the massacre at Srebrenica, he appeared to Smith's note taker to be "fit and rested. He was very cheerful but as open, balanced, and as attentive as we can remember." His bodyguards explained that he had been on ten days' leave. He offered to help with the withdrawal of UN troops from Gorazde.

When Smith explained the outlines of the Holbrooke peace initiative, Mladic said the Bosnian Serbs could not and would not accept federation or a union with the Croats or Muslims: "Our children drew the map with their blood. We can only be one nation in one state." Smith stressed the outrage that had been aroused in the world by Srebrenica and said that Bosnian Serb actions had undermined whatever support they might have enjoyed in the international community. In an emotional outburst Mladic declared, "I am a war criminal, but you have to talk to me as I am the only one who can allow you to leave Gorazde."

EVERY day through August the Rapid Reaction Force of British and French troops was more fully deployed in Bosnia. Meanwhile, NATO and the UN staff drew up a NATO secret planning document which compiled target lists for NATO aircraft in each of the safe areas. There were three sets of targets. The Option 1 list included heavy weapons violating the exclusion zones established around the safe areas, in particular Sarajevo. The Option 2 list included Serb military interdict targets and installations in and near the exclusion zones. Option 3 targets were more clearly civilian; bombing them would present more obvious political problems.

By the end of August all that the international community needed was an immediate excuse to bomb. It was provided by the mortaring of Sarajevo's Markale marketplace on the morning of August 28.

General Janvier was away in France, and so the UN's air strike key was in the hands of Rupert Smith. At 5:30 p.m. local time, after he had received the first of the crater analysis reports confirming that the mortars had come from Serb territory, Smith spoke to Admiral Leighton Smith, who held NATO's key, in Naples. The two men discussed the different responses they could make. The admiral did not think that artillery fire from the Rapid Reaction Force would be adequate. He was clearly expecting air strikes and he told the general that his key was already turned. He also said that it would take about twenty-four hours to put together the aircraft packages required for a sustained air assault.

Rupert Smith was also expecting air strikes. He had quietly been moving UN troops out of reach of the Serbs for weeks. His last vulnerable troops—the British in Gorazde—were, as it happened, due to leave Gorazde that evening. The night was stormy and communications with the British units were poor. When he heard the last British convoy was safe at 10:30 p.m., Rupert Smith turned his key. He was still concerned to make arrangements to protect UN troops against retaliatory fire which might inflict serious casualties on them.

Next morning, August 29, Smith talked on the telephone with Mladic. The Serb general specifically denied that Serb mortars had struck the market. Smith was careful not to let his voice betray his views or the fact that he had already turned the key. He had insisted that the UN's public statements be noncommittal so as not to forewarn the Serbs. He convinced Mladic that he was still "investigating" the market massacre.

When Janvier returned from France he said, *"J'ai trouvé la clef tournée"* (I found the key turned). He had classic peacekeeping concerns. He wrote in one memorandum that the bombing "will lead to the perception by the party affected that NATO and the UN have declared war on it. . . . UN troops will have become a party to the conflict . . . hostages will be taken. . . . The delivery of humanitarian aid into the territory of the party concerned will come to a halt and deterrence will have failed. . . . UNPROFOR's mission will come to an end under its present mandate."

In New York, Annan had to explain the sequence of events to the Security Council, especially to the Russians, and he was worried that he was inadequately informed about events of the day after the mortars struck. As far as the United States was concerned, Annan's role was crucial and invaluable. Holbrooke describes him as Boutros-Ghali's "best deputy." On that morning, August 29, Annan told Albright that he had instructed UN civilian officials to relinquish for a time their authority to veto air strikes. This meant, in effect, that the decision on air strikes was now in the hands of NATO and the UN military. Holbrooke wrote later that Annan's "gutsy performance" played a central role in Washington's subsequent decision to replace Boutros-Ghali with him as secretary general. "Indeed, in a sense Annan won the job on that day."

Operation Deliberate Force began at 2 a.m. Bosnian time on Wednesday, August 30. It was the largest NATO military operation ever to date. On the first day more than sixty planes attacked Bosnian Serb positions around Sarajevo. The first attacks were hampered by fog, which restricted targeting. They were against the Serbs' air defenses and other fixed military targets, including munitions factories, ammunition depots and military storage depots. At the same time the French and British artillery from the Rapid Reaction Force on Mount Igman fired some six hundred rounds at Bosnian Serb artillery, mortar and air defense positions around Sarajevo.

Janvier wrote to Mladic saying the Bosnian Serbs must end all attacks against all the safe areas, withdraw all heavy weapons from the twelve-mile exclusion zone around Sarajevo and end all hostilities throughout Bosnia. When the Serbs complied, Janvier would recommend to NATO that the air attacks be halted.

From New York, Annan asked Akashi, "How long can we persist with our present course, in the event that Mladic does not accept your demands?" What would happen when all the targets listed were hit and the Serbs were still not in compliance? "Are we now committed to continuing the air action until such an agreement is obtained? It is imperative our action should not go beyond a zone of reasonableness that is circumscribed by our mandate, by our basic and indispensable impartiality, and by our need to continue to work with all parties to achieve a durable settlement of the crisis."

On August 31 bad weather stopped all air strikes. Russian ambassador Sergei Lavrov wrote to Boutros-Ghali demanding an immediate end to the use of force by NATO, "an operation which we are convinced goes beyond the limits established in the relevant resolutions of the Security Council." Radovan Karadzic wrote a furious letter to Akashi complaining that NATO "has involved itself in this civil war on the side of our enemies." The NATO attacks, he said, had nothing to do with the Markale mortars; their goal "is to weaken our military strength in order to soften us up before the continuation of negotiations."

Yugoslav president Slobodan Milosevic asked that Janvier meet Mladic in Belgrade. Willy Claes, the new secretary general of NATO, called Annan from NATO headquarters to say that he did not want Janvier to give too much away to Mladic; he wanted to find out who would evaluate the meeting between the two men and decide whether Mladic had conceded enough for the bombing to be ended. Annan replied that if Mladic undertook not to attack the safe areas anymore, Janvier would recommend that air strikes be suspended.

Annan pointed out in a memo to Boutros-Ghali that Leighton Smith might disagree with Janvier about the adequacy of any undertaking from Mladic. In that case the dispute would be referred up the chain of command. But the UN secretary general would be on a long flight to Beijing. "I wonder, therefore," Annan wrote to him, "whether you would wish to delegate to me the responsibility for resolving such a problem should it arise at a time when you are out of contact with this headquarters." Boutros-Ghali did so. Annan was right: Janvier and Admiral Smith disagreed on suspending the bombing. Annan had several discussions about it with Willy Claes. These were inconclusive, and so Annan decided to deal directly with Washington. In the end he and Sandy Berger, Clinton's acting national security adviser, and Strobe Talbott agreed on a seventy-two-hour pause.

At 5 a.m. on Friday, September 1, air operations were suspended in order to allow for Janvier's meeting with Mladic. The meeting was set for 9 a.m. at Mali Zvornik on the Bosnian border with Yugoslavia. But when Janvier was already in the air en route, Mladic canceled it.

Janvier had to turn around and fly back to Zagreb. Later that day Mladic changed his mind, and Janvier set off again.

It was a tense and angry encounter which lasted thirteen hours. Mladic was shouting and ranting much of the time; he was apparently both furious and nonplussed that his long bluff of the United Nations had finally been called. NATO had provided the airpower which, together with the UN's Rapid Reaction Force, made this possible. Mladic eventually promised Janvier not to attack the safe areas and agreed in principle to withdraw his heavy weapons. But he made other conditions which in the end were not acceptable to NATO. Janvier then wrote to Mladic setting out his demands for Serb withdrawal again, demands which had to be met by 11 p.m. on Monday, September 4, or the bombing would resume.

There was a flurry of calls around Europe and across the Atlantic. Willy Claes told Annan, "We must not let Mladic be in control. He is using typical communist tactics, refusing to meet, imposing new conditions, accusing us of lying." Claes said he could accept an extended pause in the bombing. Richard Holbrooke was against even that. He and other U.S. officials felt that Mladic had not conceded enough. Sandy Berger called Annan to say that Mladic should remove heavy weapons from around Sarajevo and make a unilateral commitment to end the shelling.

On September 4, Janvier wrote to Mladic telling him to withdraw his heavy weapons at once. The United Nations wanted to see evidence that this had begun before 11 p.m. that same day. The operation must be completed by September 7. "If either or one or both of these conditions are not met," Janvier warned Mladic, "air and military attacks will be resumed."

Rupert Smith sent Mladic a letter of instructions. He said that "proof of your intention to move your heavy weapons by 2300 local time 4 September 1995 will be required." Smith wanted "clear evidence of a continuous movement of your heavy weapons systems out of the EZ [exclusion zone], on the designated route" by that time. If all heavy weapons were not out by 11 p.m. on September 7, bombing would resume. At the same time all UN weapons and vehicles stolen by the Bosnian Serb forces must be returned. Akashi asked the UN's man in Belgrade, Yuri Miakotnykh, to pass these demands on to Milosevic.

Also on September 4, Mladic wrote Janvier a four-page letter rejecting the UN/NATO demands. He denounced the United Nations and called NATO worse than Hitler. He declared that by demanding the withdrawal of heavy weapons from around Sarajevo, the UN was violating the Geneva Conventions on the status of safe areas. He would not leave Serb civilians under threat from armed Muslims in Sarajevo.

That night Holbrooke was dismayed to learn that there was debate over whether to resume the bombing. He called Washington to try to persuade his colleagues that the bombing must begin again if NATO was not to look like a paper tiger. "History could well hang in the balance," he declared. "Give us bombs for peace."

He had his way. On September 5, ninety NATO aircraft attacked a military storage facility near Sarajevo and other military targets in Bosnia, including an ammunition depot and a military repair facility in Hadzici, and a radar tracking facility in Jahorina. In the early hours of September 6 planes attacked a military repair and storage site at Brod. In parallel, the Rapid Reaction Force was constantly firing on Serb mortar and artillery positions around Sarajevo.

The weather made both more sorties and proper bomb damage assessments difficult. On September 6 some of the planned air strikes had to be abandoned. It was also difficult to tell whether the Serbs really were withdrawing their weapons. That day Akashi wrote to Karadzic urging that Mladic keep in frequent contact with Rupert Smith. Akashi praised Karadzic for recent initiatives: "They are important and courageous steps towards an end to this tragic conflict." There was now, wrote Akashi, "an enhanced opportunity" for peace, as well as the "unspeakable dangers of further escalation."

That day Annan briefed the Security Council at length on the bombing. Only one person responded—Sergei Lavrov held forth for thirty-five minutes on the UN's sins of omission and commission. He insisted that the air strikes must stop; they were undermining a peaceful solution. The council had not been adequately consulted on the bombing; the United Nations had become a "bystander" to a NATO operation—and much more.

The next day, September 7, Akashi reported that there was still no sign that the Serbs were withdrawing their heavy weapons. There were reports of rows between the Bosnian Serb politicians and the military.

Professor Nikola Koljevic, a colleague of Karadzic in the Bosnian Serb leadership, called Akashi from Belgrade, just before meeting with Richard Holbrooke. He said the withdrawal of heavy weapons from around Sarajevo was proving difficult for three reasons. First, it was being hampered by civilian protests that "almost culminated in rebellion" that morning. Second, the Bosnians had attacked some heavy Serb weapons that were about to be withdrawn. Third, communications had been disrupted by the air strikes. So Karadzic had decided to continue the withdrawal during darkness when the chances of interference by Serb civilians "who we cannot shoot" and by the Bosnian military would be reduced. Koljevic also said they "have had problems with their general [Mladic], who's been put under control."

Akashi replied that two things were essential—a clear written statement signed by Mladic, indicating his agreement, and immediate movement on the ground despite the difficulties. Koljevic called back later saying it was still difficult for him to get hold of Mladic. He suggested that Rupert Smith try to reach him at Lukavica barracks.

O N September 10, Janvier flew to Belgrade to meet again with Mladic. He told him that the air strikes would not end until Mladic accepted the three conditions laid down in his letter of September 4 and, in particular, start the withdrawal of heavy weapons from around Sarajevo.

Mladic was less emotional than at their previous encounter in Mali Zvornik, but he spent the entire four-hour meeting demanding an end to the bombing before he would discuss Janvier's letter. The meeting degenerated into personal accusations by Mladic. He said if Janvier did not have the authority to stop the bombing he wanted to meet with the NATO commander, who did. Janvier tried to calm him down to no avail. Mladic said three times that if the bombing did not stop he would attack UN forces.

At the United Nations, the Russians complained again about the continued bombing. Annan wrote to Boutros-Ghali to say that Mladic had still not complied with NATO/UN demands. The bombing was continuing, but the problem was that Option 1 and 2 targets were almost exhausted, and he was concerned that with its strikes on bridges and communications centers well beyond the safe areas,

NATO had actually expanded into hitting Option 3 targets without saying so. Annan's view was that after eleven days of bombing (minus the three-day pause) NATO and the UN should assess how effective their actions were. Air strikes were supposed to continue until "in the common judgment" of the UN and NATO commanders, they had achieved their objective. "But with General Mladic dug in," Annan wrote, Janvier now doubted whether that was possible. NATO had no plans except for more strikes. Annan thought that NATO should also be made aware of UN unhappiness with its reporting, "particularly the lack of information on the damage inflicted by the strikes, which has embarrassed us vis-à-vis the Security Council. After all, the current NATO operation is formally conducted under the Security Council's authority; the lack of adequate reporting undermines this authority and thus the legitimacy of the operation itself. We cannot be sleeping partners, taken for granted by NATO."

On September 14, under pressure from Holbrooke, the Bosnian Serbs agreed to UNPROFOR's conditions. The bombing ended. Serb heavy weapons were pulled out of the Sarajevo exclusion zone, the siege of Sarajevo was lifted, and humanitarian relief began to be airlifted in again. Plans for a peace conference began to take shape.

At the end of September, Rupert Smith pointed out to his senior UN colleagues that recent advances had been made "by the deliberate, disproportionate and extensive use of force." He spelled out just what had happened to the United Nations in the last month. "As a consequence of our enforcement action UNPROFOR abandoned its peacekeeping mission at least in the Sarajevo area. We remain, for the time being, in the position of combatants, coercing and enforcing our demands on the BSA. . . . We cannot put the clock back. . . ."

Fortunately, they did not need to try. On October 5, President Clinton announced that a cease-fire, negotiated by Richard Holbrooke, would take place throughout Bosnia in five days. It would be followed by a peace conference to take place in the United States. Holbrooke was in Zagreb at that moment, urging Tudjman to press ahead with his offensive against the Serbs in Bosnia. "You have five days left, that's all," he told the Croatian leader. "What you don't win on the battlefield will be hard to gain at the peace talks. Don't waste these last days."

Afterwards Holbrooke and other American officials asserted that the cease-fire in Bosnia had been achieved by the bombing. "Airpower works" became their refrain.

In fact, the bombing was only partially successful. It was hampered by bad weather. NATO ran out of suitable targets and had to bomb some of them several times in order to keep up any air campaign at all. Bombing alone did not break the will of the Bosnian Serbs. The bombing was accompanied by other pressures which were equally vital, in particular the aggressive use of the artillery of the Rapid Reaction Force. Also absolutely vital was the Croat offensive through Krajina and into Bosnia, which cost the Bosnian Serbs large swaths of land which they had hoped to retain. The Bosnian Serbs were also being given political inducements. The Holbrooke plan included a Bosnian Serb entity in Bosnia, which meant that they were no longer compelled to surrender their independence to the government in Sarajevo. Karadzic had said several times, before the bombing began, that this peace plan was acceptable to them.

At the same time Milosevic himself was tiring of the Bosnian Serbs and had informed them, before the bombing began, that he would negotiate for them with Holbrooke. He had presented Holbrooke with their signed acquiescence to his new role just a few hours before the bombing began.

THE administration chose Wright-Patterson Air Force Base in Dayton, Ohio, for the peace talks, which they proposed should be hosted by the United States, the European Union and Russia. The U.S. government decided to cut the United Nations, which had carried the water so long for both the Europeans and the Americans, out of the peace process entirely. The United Nations was also excluded from the agreement that came out of Dayton, which was to be enforced by NATO troops. The only things left to the UN were the organization of the civilian police force and the return home of the refugees and displaced.

On November 21, the Dayton peace plan was agreed to by the leaders of the combatant nations of the former Yugoslavia. It ended the war in Bosnia and, in theory, established a single multi-ethnic country. A unitary government was maintained (or created), but

Bosnia was divided, 49 percent to the Bosnian Serbs and 51 percent to the Croat-Muslim Federation. The agreement called for Sarajevo to be reunified, with the Serbs of the city living under federation control. The agreement was to be enforced by a fully armed NATO force of sixty thousand troops, called the International Implementation Force (IFOR).

Dayton was a triumph of American will, but it was inevitably an agreement with serious flaws. Despite the denials of U.S. officials, it did legitimize ethnic cleansing; there was no alternative. But in some ways Dayton legitimized more Serb gains than previous peace efforts which the United States had undercut. Earlier UN and EU plans had not given them contiguous territory as Dayton did. Earlier plans gave the Muslims and Croats more and better land. Other aspects of Dayton undoubtedly favored the Muslims more, but the key fact was that the U.S. was now pressing for acceptance rather than attempting to undermine agreement. A bitter joke began to circulate: "What is the difference between the Vance-Owen plan [which the U.S. had undermined in 1993] and the Dayton agreement?" "Nothing except the number of bodies in the graveyard."

BOUTROS-GHALI asked Kofi Annan to go to Zagreb after Dayton to replace Akashi, wind up UNPROFOR and hand over to NATO. Akashi was a sad figure; he had been praised for running the UN mission in Cambodia, but had been badly damaged by his time in Bosnia. He was seen, particularly in Washington, as impotent and ineffective in the face of Serb bullying. Richard Holbrooke thought his treatment had been unduly harsh and wrote that his apparent weakness "was not entirely his fault: he was operating under tight constraints imposed by Boutros-Ghali. . . . I felt sorry for Akashi. He was leaving Zagreb with his previously distinguished record blemished, but his mission had been doomed from the start because of limits imposed from New York."

That was true perhaps, but those limits were set by the Security Council rather than by Boutros-Ghali. The United Nations as a whole was to be branded for its apparent failure in Bosnia, when the failure was, in fact, that of the Security Council and its permanent members in particular.

Now Boutros-Ghali told Annan that he was the only senior UN official who had the confidence of NATO and other governments. Washington was indeed pleased. Holbrooke said that since the August bombing, "Annan was the U.N. official in whom we had the greatest confidence, and his arrival was good news." (There were those who suspected that Boutros-Ghali had also identified Annan as a potential rival and successor, and wanted to hand him the same Balkan chalice that had poisoned Akashi and many others.)

On a rainy evening a few weeks after his arrival, I accompanied Annan as he crossed the bridge in Sarajevo which divided the Muslim and Serb sections of the city. He was due to meet officials of the Serbian suburb of Grbavica. The mayor, Milorad Katic, met him at the bridge and led him in the rain through unlit streets to his office where, over coffee, he said that the Dayton peace plan was unacceptable to the Serbs of Sarajevo, who claimed to number over 100,000.

It was easy to say that after their appalling abuses of human rights, and their brutal shelling and sniping into Muslim-dominated Sarajevo, the Serbs deserved what they had got. The fact remained that without the acceptance of most ordinary Serbs, the Dayton agreement could not work as intended.

The reunification of Sarajevo was emerging as one of the most difficult aspects of Dayton. Tens of thousands of Serbs who lived there claimed they were horrified that the Dayton agreement, signed by President Milosevic of Serbia on their behalf, reunited the city under the rule of the Muslim-dominated government.

Many of them now saw President Milosevic as a traitor. With their own leader, Radovan Karadzic, indicted as a war criminal by the international tribunal in The Hague and thus denied office by Dayton, they were now in a state of apprehension which, if it tipped into panic, could destroy the hopes of peace.

The International Implementation Force was intended to be far tougher than the UN force it was replacing. Yet it would face many of the same dilemmas. The United States had a swift and essentially military perspective; the Europeans saw Dayton as a long-term process in which political, economic and humanitarian efforts—and acceptance— were paramount. Annan tended to the European view.

As he crossed the Grbavica bridge, Annan had just heard grim warning of what could come. Bosnian Croats had begun to burn the area of Mrkonjic Grad in central Bosnia, which Dayton had ordered them to give up to the Serbs. They were leaving only a charred wasteland behind. One fear was that the Serbs could do the same to their parts of Sarajevo. Karadzic had threatened to turn Sarajevo into another Beirut. And Bosnian government troops had just invaded the UN offices at Velika Kladusa at midnight, held UN officials at gunpoint and stolen every vehicle they could lay their hands on.

In the mayor's office, Katic and his colleagues asked that the Sarajevo section of Dayton be renegotiated before or during the Paris peace conference. "We want to stay here. We want special status for Sarajevo and UN protection," they said.

Annan courteously but firmly replied, "I have to be frank with you. Dayton was a compromise. But it was signed by the heads of state and it is not negotiable either here or in Paris. What is important is that it should be implemented fairly. Don't try to reopen Dayton but work for its implementation. You should let the world hear you—that you want to live in peace."

The head of the Grbavica Executive Council, Mirko Sarivic, warned Annan that if the Serbs remained unsatisfied there would be a massive exodus from the Sarajevo area: "It will be a very big ethnic cleansing." Annan said that IFOR would be here for one year to put in place democratic processes; an international police force would protect human rights. "I know about your anxieties," he told them, "but try to work with the international community. It's a new period. You should let IFOR into your territory. It will be evenhanded."

Annan urged the Bosnian president, Alija Izetbegovic, to be magnanimous toward the Serbs. Izetbegovic replied that Serb civilians were welcome, but not the soldiers who had shelled the city. Almost every Serb family contained a militiaman if not a soldier. But, given what the Bosnian Muslims had suffered at Serb hands, it was politically impossible at this stage for Izetbegovic to be more generous. The divisions in his own government were manifest at Dayton.

It was clear that the faster the IFOR deployed, the better its chances of success. The French and the British troops, who had been serving in UNPROFOR, were already in place. The French were charged with reuniting Sarajevo over Serb objections. The Pentagon was still reluctant to send Americans into Bosnian Serb territory.

Before leaving Sarajevo, Annan visited the French military headquarters and the British artillery battalion, dug into frozen underground bunkers on Mount Igman. He told them that despite media and politicians' attacks, the United Nations had done a good job in Bosnia, according to its mandates if not newspaper and political rhetoric. He said that victories always go to governments. Defeats stay with UN peacekeepers.

As Annan drove down Mount Igman we passed both Bosnian government and Serb soldiers dug into bunkers at different heights of the mountain; IFOR would have to separate them farther. At the bottom, near the airport, in the suburb of Ilidza thousands of Serbs were demonstrating against Dayton. It seemed to me that IFOR would have to reassure them if it was to be able to help rebuild Sarajevo at all. And it would have to provide the conditions in which Serbs, Bosnians and Croats could all vote freely for a new generation of leaders, ones unsullied by the past. Did those leaders exist? Could they be found, let alone be persuaded to run for office?

The tasks of the next few months were vast. And there was an obvious irony. Peacekeepers had been sent into Bosnia when there was no peace to keep. Now a much larger force of warriors had been sent in when there was supposed to be no war to fight. Of such contradictions was policy made by the international community.

It seemed to me that with an overwhelming force such as IFOR vengeance could be put to sleep for a while, but it would linger and could be resurrected easily. A bad peace was better than a war, but it was hard to see Bosnia survive as a state divided like this.

There was a conspicuous item missing from the agenda at Dayton. No one paid any attention to Kosovo. True, the conference was designed to settle only the Bosnian problem. But it was by promising to defend Serbs in Kosovo against the Albanian majority that Milosevic had begun his rise to power at the end of the eighties. He had repressed the Albanians since. Under the moderate leadership of Ibrahim Rugova, they had been remarkably patient. As a result their problems and their rights had been ignored. Rugova was not invited to Dayton. Serb repression continued. Radical Albanians began to grow in strength, and started to kill Serb policemen and others. Kosovo remained a disaster in waiting.

In 1914, just after the First World War began in Sarajevo, the historian R. W. Seton-Watson wrote to the British Foreign Office saying that unless "the Southern Slav question" was solved, trouble was bound to be caused between at least Britain and Russia. "Only by treating the problem as an organistic whole, by avoiding patchwork remedies can we hope to remove one of the chief danger centres in Europe." Eighty years later that danger center remained.

7

Cultures of Impunity

I N February 1996 hundreds of Sierra Leoneans had their fingers, hands, arms, noses or lips chopped off with machetes in the cause of democracy. They were being punished either for voting in, or for the mere fact of, the first round of the country's first multi-party elections in more than twenty-five years. The assaults were carried out by men in uniform, often very young men at that. They were teenagers or younger, members of the world's fastest-growing army—children.

Among those whom I met in Bo, a little diamond-trading town deep in the interior, was a man who had had his right ear and his lips slashed off. Someone had carved with a knife the word TERROR on his chest and on his back AGAINST THE ELECTION FEBRUARY 26. Some men and women had had their arms hacked off above the elbow; some had lost their hands at the wrist.

Yet, despite such atrocities, it seemed that the elections could be an important step toward normality for this impoverished West African country which had suffered twenty-nine years of dictatorship. On February 26, hundreds of thousands lined up to vote at election offices. Their enthusiasm gave hope that Sierra Leone could pull out of the terrible spiral of war, militarism and poverty through which it had been falling for years. People said they saw elections as their only possible path out of the horror.

Just before the second round of the election in February, I went to Sierra Leone as a member of the International Crisis Group, the watchdog organization set up in good part through the passions of my friend Fred Cuny, the engineer and humanitarian who had been killed in Chechnya in unknown circumstances the year before. The first director of ICG was the former head of Save the Children in Britain, Nicholas Hinton. He had decided that Sierra Leone was a place where ICG could make a difference and we had established a group there to help the restoration of civil society. He asked me to pay a visit.

I thought of Fred Cuny as I flew via Amsterdam to Sierra Leone; he was one of those people whose presence remains with you long after they are gone, and I knew he would have had some unusual way of looking at the horror of Sierra Leone. On the flight were several diamond dealers on their way to try to harvest what had become one curse of Sierra Leone, its open-cast diamond mines, coveted by all the neighbors and a source of finance for the rebels. As we flew across the Sahara, I read about the country's calamitous recent descent into horror.

Under British colonial rule the country was one of the most successful in West Africa partly because of its richness in diamonds and rutile, or titanium dioxide. It had the oldest university in West Africa. Lebanese diamond traders arrived at the end of the nineteenth century and formed the core of a new mercantile class.

After independence in the winds of change in 1961 its first president, Milton Margai, much loved, changed almost nothing. But after his death three years later, his brother Albert took over, and the country began to disintegrate into corruption and autocracy. He tried to turn Sierra Leone into a one-party state—that of the Sierra Leone People's Party (SLPP), of the southern Mende tribe. That, of course, led to the creation of a rival party to represent the northerners, the All People's Congress (APC), led by Siaka Stevens, who was placed in power in 1968 after a series of coups. Stevens held power until 1985; a seventeen-year plague of locusts, his rule was called. He did not kill, but he corrupted. Throughout his rule the country was mismanaged and robbed.

In 1980 the government hosted a meeting of the Organization of African Unity with all the pomp and circumstance that such organizations deploy, and more. A separate villa was built for each head of state who attended—for all of a couple of days. Fleets of expensive cars were imported. The shindig cost the country $100 million and exhausted all of Sierra Leone's foreign exchange reserves; it had to borrow millions more.

Lebanese traders and merchants seduced, corrupted and controlled almost all commerce in the country, from shops to national enteprises. Stevens was closely involved with one group of very rich Lebanese businessmen who were widely believed to be organizing the theft of Sierra Leone's resources. Despite its diamonds, rutile and bauxite, the country was wrecked by the mid-1980s. Apathy, if not despair, was widespread among the population and led to violence.

In 1985, after army units turned upon Stevens's praetorian guard, he decided he could not safely stay in office, and so he backed his undistinguished force commander, Joseph Momoh, for president. Momoh's first cabinet was filled with Stevens's corrupt ministers. People said, "Same taxi, different driver," but by 1987 Momoh had thrown off Stevens's control and buckled the country to a structural reform program developed by the World Bank and the International Monetary Fund. There was fantastic inflation. Electricity in the capital, Freetown, disappeared down the line. Oil dried up; rice, which the country used to export, vanished. The government stopped paying all civil service salaries. The country fell apart. It could no longer afford to pay even the paramount chiefs. One senior broadcasting official was reported to have sold the broadcasting tower and bought a Mercedes, so there was no radio beyond the capital. The statehouse was surrounded by desperate beggars. It was, I was told, like Port-au-Prince, in Graham Greene's *The Comedians*. (Greene's book *The Heart of the Matter* is set in Freetown.)

Next door, at the end of the eighties, Liberia exploded in an orgy of uncontrolled and undirected factional violence where drugged young men in carnival masks killed each other. Charles Taylor, the leader of one of the nihilistic gangs or factions there, who was eventually victorious, sent his young killers across the border to attack Sierra Leone and grab diamonds.

In March 1991, at around the same time as the disintegration of Yugoslavia began, a group of about one hundred fighters, including Liberian guerrillas and dissidents from Sierra Leone, invaded eastern Sierra Leone from Liberia. Foday Sankoh, an embittered former corporal in the Sierra Leone army, claimed that this was the Revolutionary United Front (RUF) and he was its leader. There was certainly much to complain about in the kleptocracy in Freetown. But ever since, employing what passed for populist rhetoric, the RUF had waged war against the farmers, villagers and miners of Sierra Leone by using mutilation and terror to show that the government was unable to protect its citizens.

The RUF was part of a post–Cold War phenomenon—a nonideological guerrilla movement. As elsewhere in Africa, AK-47s gave dispossessed young men more money and more raison d'être—even if it was only senseless violence—than peace. In the words of the International Crisis Group, the RUF "serves as an umbrella group for disparate gangs of disaffected youths suffering the effects of poverty, unemployment, malnutrition and poor education and health services."

On one level the RUF advance could be seen as a rural revolt against the cities, not unlike that originally launched by the Khmer Rouge in Cambodia in the 1960s. But at the same time most of the victims of RUF attacks were the rural poor, whom they mutilated and murdered in horrific ways. In its attempt to control and cow the countryside, the RUF burned villages, forced farmers to become indentured laborers and treated peasants like pack animals on long foot campaigns.

Sankoh himself remained in the shadows; no one outside his cruel movement met him until the mid-nineties. He was nothing more than an occasional disembodied voice on an International Committee of the Red Cross radio network. He evidently had charisma for his followers, but when he later started to give occasional interviews he seemed driven by personal anger at his own lack of success within Sierra Leonean society rather than by ideology. He was completely indifferent to the horror that he was inflicting upon ordinary people. "When two lions or elephants are fighting, who is going to suffer?" he said, when Howard French of the *New York Times* asked him about atrocities. "The grass, of course. I cannot deny it."

Momoh asked Britain for military advisers and communications and intelligence capacity to fight the RUF. He was turned down. So the government went on a wild recruitment drive, press-ganging orphans, other children and vagabonds into the army. Thousands and thousands of people with no jobs were given guns and rushed off to fight. But it became ever clearer that both the soldiers and the RUF were much more interested in killing civilians than fighting each other. To ordinary Sierra Leoneans, soldiers and rebels were often indistinguishable, so much so that they became known as "sobels."

In April 1992 a coup occurred by accident. A group of army officers led by Captain Valentine Strasser delivered a letter to Momoh, complaining that his leadership was leading to a collapse of army morale. Momoh was terrified that he was about to be overthrown and rushed out the back door. Surprised, Strasser and his men seized the presidential office and then the radio station. They announced the formation of the National Provisional Ruling Council and chose a colonel admired for his fighting qualities to lead them. But when he gave a radio interview they did not like, they killed him. Valentine Strasser spoke good English; he was made president in Momoh's place.

Strasser brought civilians into the government, but not much changed. At the end of 1992 he launched a major offensive against the RUF. They were driven out of the diamond areas in the southeast of the country, back into Liberia, where they found succor with Charles Taylor's guerrillas, regrouped and counterattacked in early 1993. To support Strasser, Nigeria led a West African peacekeeping force and sent two battalions of troops and some jet fighters. It was not enough. By early 1995 the RUF was on the edges of Freetown. Boutros-Ghali appointed Berhanu Dinka, an Ethiopian diplomat, as a special envoy to try to negotiate a settlement.

When the RUF was just twenty miles from Freetown and closing, Strasser turned in desperation to Executive Outcomes, a private South African security force—mercenaries, in other words—for help. Run by a former member of South African Special Forces, EO had been active in covert operations in Mozambique and Angola. Strasser agreed to pay them with income from the diamond fields, once Executive Outcomes had liberated them.

EO's men were South African Defence Force veterans—black troops with white officers. Its mission, according to its corporate statement, was to "create a climate for peace and stability for foreign investment, focussing on military training, including a particular emphasis on special forces and clandestine warfare."

When EO arrived in Sierra Leone, the rebels were only about twelve miles from Freetown; most foreigners had left the country. The government had also lost control of the country's diamond, titanium dioxide and bauxite mines, which had between them produced most of the country's export earnings. EO's objectives were to secure Freetown, to regain control of the mines, to destroy the RUF headquarters and to clear the remaining areas of RUF occupation. EO began to train Sierra Leonean troops and within three months had mounted successful offensives.

Together with Nigerian and Ghanaian troops in the West African peacekeeping force, EO drove the rebels back from Freetown in May 1995. Then they retook the Kono diamond mining area and the Sierra Rutile titanium dioxide mine. They swept out of Freetown with armored vehicles and helicopters up roads which the rebels had till now controlled, killing rebels or soldiers who stood in their way. They claimed that no civilians died in the operation. With EO helicopters on patrol, the diamond mines were reopened, providing income for the Lebanese traders, and for EO itself.

That August the military regime, under pressure from the small but growing number of civic groups in Freetown, and from some foreign governments, particularly Britain and the United States, agreed to hold elections in February 1996. Without the success of Executive Outcomes, this would not have been possible.

In January 1996, Valentine Strasser was overthrown. Many thought that his usurper, Julius Maada Bio, might cancel the elections—after all, his sister was a prominent member of the RUF. But Freetown's market women, apparently fearing just this, marched through the town and threatened to expose politicians receiving bribes from the military to halt the election process. Another conference of party and civic leaders, tribal chiefs and other movements, including the women's groups, demanded that the elections not be canceled. Bio agreed to let them go ahead.

Military motives were mixed and unclear. The leaders were all young and, having made enough out of their misrule, were said to

want to move on, preferably by international flight. They also knew
how widely they were hated. Bio was said to have remarked to one
Western ambassador, "It's like when you have a girlfriend and she
says no, she doesn't want you anymore. You try and try but eventually you have to give up."

Like the Khmer Rouge in Cambodia, the RUF, or the sobels, did
everything to terrify the population into boycotting the election.
Thousands of people across the country had their hands chopped off
or were otherwise mutilated in the weeks leading up to the first vote
on February 26. In the face of such awful brutality it seemed obscene
to say that in most other senses the elections were a success, certainly
much greater than anyone had dared to hope.

The election commmission, INEC, was run by a former under secretary general of the UN, James Jonah. Despite few resources, and
despite the atrocious violence in places, he managed to conduct the
election in a way which Commonwealth and other observers
thought largely fair. About 1.4 million of the 4.5 million population
had been registered. On election day over 60 percent of them voted.
It was extraordinarily moving to see people standing in line for hours
to exercise their franchise. There was the same sort of excitement
and pleasure that I had seen in the elections in Cambodia.

In Freetown there was shooting from the army barracks in town.
People continued to stand outside the polling stations. They said
things like "They can kill some of us but not all." As night fell, thousands of young people took to the streets and shouted "Foday
Sankoh doesn't exist. Bio is a rebel." The military slapped on a cur-
few for a week.

In some places, particularly provincial towns like Bo and Kenema
farther to the east, voters were in grave danger as mobs of men in
uniform—soldiers or rebels—rampaged through towns. Allister
Sparks, the veteran anti-apartheid editor of the *Rand Daily Mail* in
South Africa, was an observer in Kenema. He said, "The rebels ran
down the street shooting and shouting 'No election.' But people
came pouring into the streets saying, 'We want to vote.'" The
van played the electoral song on its loudspeaker and said, "The election commission is on." It seemed to mark a new moment.
Sparks said, "The voting showed a new assertiveness by the people—
that they have had enough of the military and the war." Unfortunately, no one party won the required 55 percent of the vote needed

under the electoral law to win the presidency. Another round between the two front-runners was scheduled for March 16.

WE landed at Freetown's ramshackle Lungi airport late at night. Eventually, I fought my way through the crowds of people in the decrepit terminals. Rather than take what I expected to be an alarming Russian helicopter into Freetown, I chose the ancient airport bus. It waited an age until the ground crew had seen off the plane and closed up shop for the night. Finally we trundled down unkept roads and onto a car ferry which crossed the dark bay to Freetown; then the bus made a long tour up and down hills, through various dilapidated, unpainted districts of Freetown, dropping off passengers one by one, until only I was left; I arrived at my hotel in the early hours of the morning.

I then flew, with two colleagues from the International Crisis Group, David Shearer and Alice Jay, in a small plane piloted by a Russian, to the diamond-trading town of Bo. There I saw and talked to some of those wretched people who had been mutilated.

We went to the Bo town hospital late in the afternoon. In the emergency ward there were dark green walls, brown blankets on the beds, with people lying motionless and quiet. The bright white bandages on the victims' stumps shone in the dark wards.

Martine Hannaux, from the international humanitarian group Médecins sans Frontières (MSF), was the only surgeon in the town. Without her these people would all have died. In the week of the election Hannaux conducted thirty operations. "I am not an orthopedic surgeon—just general. I have never had to do anything like this." The lucky ones had their hands cut across the back of the wrists rather than completely amputated. "When the tendons are cut, it's like fishing. I reach up into the arm to find the tendons and try to clamp them together again." She showed us X rays of hands with long, thin pins inserted to help them bind and heal. "Maybe they'll never play the piano, but . . ." She shrugged.

One young man had come in with "an incomplete traumatic amputation," Dr. Hannaux said. In other words, his left arm was still hanging partly attached to his body. She took it off. The sobels had attacked his right hand, too. She managed to save most of that. Another patient had had a fierce machete blow across his face. "I had to remove an eye; I had never done that before," she related. In another emergency ward, a tent, there was a young man whose nose had been slashed and who had a huge wound in his thigh. An old man with no hands asked a young boy, perhaps his son, to put on his shirt. He could not do it alone. In bed after bed after bed, the gleaming white bandages told of missing legs, arms, hands, fingers, ears or noses.

Walking around the wards, I was struck by the silence. All of these atrocities had happened in the last few days. The victims were in shock. The thought of their lives ahead was terrible. With one savage blow, or with many awful sawing cuts, they had been deprived of any livelihood, if not of their lives.

In Bo a soft-spoken humanitarian official said, "When they expanded the army they filled it with pickpockets and other criminals. In this country if you give a man a gun and a uniform you don't have to pay him—he makes money out of the people. We were shy to blame the attacks on our army, but we cannot hide it anymore. The 'rebels' always come into town from just one direction—the brigade headquarters."

The townspeople of Bo had organized a local civil defense force, a band of local hunters, to defend the town against these marauders. On election day, when rebels invaded the town center, the defense force caught at least five of them and beheaded them. Some say as many as ten of these men lost their heads. "Jungle justice," said one relief official. They were soldiers, he believed, or sobels.

There were over 210,000 displaced people in and around Bo—refugees from the countryside and the low-level but vicious fighting between the government and the rebels, the RUF. After the week's attacks there would be many more. "If you see someone in a village who has no arms, you leave at once," the relief official said.

Amputees who could speak said the rebels who assaulted them asked for whom they had voted. If they gave the "wrong" names, they had their hands cut off. In Hima district lips and noses were cut and people had anti-election slogans carved into their backs.

From the hospital I went to the MSF camp where those who had had amputations several weeks ago were living. I talked to S. Mannah, a fifty-nine-year-old carpenter from Bo who said that in July last year he went out to a village to collect oil. "The rebels came in. They were in combat dress. They started killing people and hacking at them. They were young, about fifteen years old. They didn't say anything."

James Eissah, a sturdy man who had been a telecommunications technician, held the stump of his right arm protectively, as he said what had happened to him. "I was captured in the countryside when I was searching for food. I met them in an ambush. There were about fifteen of them and they stopped six of us. They said they were going to send me back to the camp to tell them that they were in the area now. And to prove it they were going to cut off my arm with a machete."

Who were the people who did this to him? I asked. "I don't know. Some were in combat uniform. Some were in jeans, some were half and half."

An old woman, Sallay Goba, was set upon in her village just three miles from Bo. What did they say to you? I asked her. "They said they would give me a letter to tell the people in Bo that they were here. This was the letter." They had cut off both of her hands. She stood motionless, her stumps by her side. When Myriam, the MSF nurse, hugged her, she smiled.

Now, after the first round, the two front-runners for the presidency, who were supposed to have a runoff next week, were John Karefa-Smart of the United National People's Party and Ahmad Tejan Kabbah of the Sierra Leone People's Party. They won 22 percent and 36 percent of the vote, respectively. Each had been in exile for years; Karefa-Smart was in his eighties. Many Sierra Leoneans hoped they would form a coalition. In towns like Bo, people were terrified of the prospect of voting again. I met there an elegant woman who worked for Catholic Relief Services. She was almost in tears as she said, "Of course I voted. But I'm really frightened of the second vote."

Although the military government accepted the elections and said that it would step down when a government was appointed, many officers and soldiers feared the ballot box because a civilian regime would have to demobilize large parts of the lawless army which had been expanded from three thousand to fifteen thousand in four years, in theory to fight the RUF.

* * *

IN some areas people still had their arms; they were safe as they went to vote not because of the government but because of the efficient firepower of Executive Outcomes. Nowhere was the election conducted so peacefully as where the South Africans were deployed.

The soldiers of Executive Outcomes might well fit the traditional image of "dogs of war," in some senses. They were obsessed with secrecy and discouraged almost all attempts to get close to them. It seemed to me that they might have been doing themselves a disservice. They were far from a humanitarian agency, but they appeared to be immensely popular in the areas they policed because they protected the people from the sobels.

In Kono people spoke only well of them. By defending the area they had enabled about 300,000 people to get on with their lives, mostly farming. They had also created a consultative committee to be involved with local problems in schools and hospitals. Had Executive Outcomes been more widely deployed during the first round of the elections, they could undoubtedly have saved dozens of people around Bo from having their hands, noses and lips chopped off with machetes. At a time when Western governments were more and more reluctant to commit their own troops, especially in Africa, it seemed to me that, under proper control, private armies such as Executive Outcomes could play an increasingly useful role.

ON March 15 the second round of the elections took place and Ahmad Tejan Kabbah was declared the winner with 59.9 percent of the votes cast. John Karefa-Smart complained of widespread fraud, but that was not the impression of international observers. Kabbah took office on March 31 and said that he planned to retain the services of Executive Outcomes. The Paris club of creditor nations agreed to provide debt relief of up to 67 percent for Sierra Leone.

In April, Kabbah met in the Ivory Coast for peace talks with Foday Sankoh, the leader of the RUF. Until the success of Executive Outcomes against his forces, Sankoh had refused all negotiations with the government. Now he demanded that Executive Outcomes, the only force that kept the RUF at bay, be expelled from Sierra Leone and its contract with the government be revealed. Understandably, Kabbah wanted to keep them. Talks were suspended over this issue, but a cease-fire agreement was signed.

The atrocities of the RUF continued nonetheless—indeed they appeared to become even more vile. In the town of Magburaka, east of Freetown, the sobels assaulted women, sewing up the vaginas of some with fishing line. They sewed up the rectums of men. They also clamped padlocks on the mouths of some men and on the vagina of at least one woman.

By the summer of 1996, hundreds of thousands of people who had expected a civilian government to end the miseries of war, inflation, unemployment and poverty as if by magic were disappointed. Disaffection increased when Kabbah raised the price of fuel by 28 percent. He became ever more unpopular with the army when he announced he would reduce its size and start extensive retraining. There was then something of an outcry when it was revealed that Executive Outcomes was charging the government almost $2 million a month. The International Monetary Fund demanded that this be reduced. Kabbah renegotiated the fee to $1.2 million a month. But reports of covert fees and illegal activities in the mining fields persisted.

Altogether, EO's operation in Sierra Leone is thought to have cost some $35 million. This was a lot for a bankrupt little country to pay. But it represented only one third of the cost of the government's war and, by comparison, the UN observer force, which would spend only eight months in the country after the peace agreement was signed, was to cost $47 million. In the end the rebels refused to allow the UN to be deployed.

In many ways, EO's achievement was cheap. Foday Sankoh acknowledged that had EO not intervened, the RUF would have captured Freetown in 1995 and won the war. According to David Shearer, EO had "bolstered the strategic position of the government significantly. There was a clear link between the outcome of EO's military operations and the RUF's willingness to negotiate. Military successes against the RUF made elections possible; most of the one million people displaced by the fighting were able to return to their homes."

On November 30, 1996, after Kabbah had authorized another EO attack on the rebels, he and Sankoh signed the Abidjan peace accord to end more than five years of fighting. Kabbah had to agree that Executive Outcomes would leave. Once the South Africans pulled out, Sierra Leone began to fall apart again. It happened at the same time that Zaire collapsed into new wars around the Great Lakes, which meant new disasters for the peoples of those countries and new challenges, to put it mildly, for those hoping to control the warlords.

KABBAH tried to create a power-sharing multi-party cabinet in which the RUF was supposed to participate. But the government moved slowly, and the military, threatened with extensive reduction, became more and more discontented. Rumors of coups and evidence of attempted coups were rife. UN military advisers, charged with disarming and demobilizing the RUF, began to arrive. Foday Sankoh flew to Nigeria on what was thought to be an official mission; he, and everyone else, was quite surprised when he was arrested by the regime of Sani Abacha and held in the Abuja Sheraton.

The promise of the election was destroyed in May 1997 when a group of junior officers, furious at the army cutbacks, led by Johnny Paul Koromah, staged a successful coup. President Kabbah fled to Guinea and Koromah declared himself leader of a military junta. Soldiers stole cars and looted Freetown. The Ministry of Finance was burned down. A Nigerian attempt to remove the new junta failed abysmally.

Koromah declared that Sankoh was his spiritual leader. While the United States and France evacuated hundreds of people by sea, Koromah invited the RUF to join his junta. They did so. But the regime and therefore the country was completely isolated. It was challenged militarily by the Nigerians (themselves virtually outlawed under the Abacha regime at this stage), who increased their troops in Sierra Leone, and by the Kamajors, the tribal leaders in the interior.

The coup leaders realized perhaps that they were incapable of following through. They asked for $46 million to return President Kabbah to power; they did not get it.

In exile in Conakry, Guinea, Kabbah accepted the services of another mercenary group, Sandline, run by a British officer, Tim Spicer, who had served in the command of the United Nations in Bosnia. ECOWAS (Economic Community of West African States) formed a four-nation committee (Nigeria, Ivory Coast, Guinea and Ghana) to try to negotiate with the junta the return of Kabbah. The

UN Security Council in Resolution 1132 imposed an arms ban on Sierra Leone, though there was subsequently some dispute as to whether this applied just to the junta or to the supporters of the legal government as well.

Kabbah's rights as legitimate head of state were recognized by both the Commonwealth and the United Nations. But Charles Taylor, the president of Liberia, made no secret of his support for the junta.

In January 1998 the Nigerians backed an offensive by the Kamajors, with logistical and intelligence support from Sandline, against the junta. Its leaders fled Freetown, and in March, President Kabbah returned and was reinstated as president. In one of those odd quirks of foreign relations, he was brought back by Sani Abacha, the Nigerian leader, whose misrule at home had brought the obloquy of much of the world down on his head.

With Kabbah back, Sierra Leone was embraced again by the international community: the World Bank announced $100 million in emergency aid; the Security Council approved Resolution 1156, terminating the oil embargo on Sierra Leone; the Commonwealth agreed to send judges to try members of the junta; and a row took place in Britain over the role of Sandline and whether the Foreign Office was involved.

In June 1998 the Security Council approved Resolution 1181, which set up UNOMSIL, with seventy military observers for an initial period of six months, and an amnesty was announced for child soldiers. Foday Sankoh was transferred from Nigeria to prison in Sierra Leone.

In October a jury found him guilty on seven counts of treason. He was condemned to death but not executed. The war continued and, as I have mentioned in Chapter One, just as Kosovo began to implode at the end of 1998, so Sierra Leone dissolved into bloodshed again; it was as bad as anything in the Balkans.

Yet, because the permanent five members of the Security Council had no such interest in Sierra Leone as they had in the former Yugoslavia, the only solution that any outsider, Kofi Annan included, could envisage, was that the elected president, Kabbah, would have to share power with the murderers of the Revolutionary United Front. As we shall see, in 1999, to the horror of many human rights groups, Kabbah signed another peace accord with Foday Sankoh;

this time the rebels were invited into the government and Sankoh himself was given control of the diamond fields. A blanket amnesty was extended. President Kabbah signed the agreement accompanied by a little girl with an amputated arm.

Impunity ruled.

o

AROUND 10:30 a.m. on Saturday, May 18, 1996, Thun Bun Ly, a Cambodian newspaper editor who was highly critical of the Cambodian government, left his house in Phnom Penh on a motorbike taxi. As the bike drove down Street 95 another bike sped up. The passenger on the second bike fired a K-59 pistol at Thun Bun Ly and the bike then sped away. Most of the eyewitnesses believed that the driver of the second bike wore a uniform and the gunman was in civilian clothes.

Thun Bun Ly was hit by two bullets in the chest and a third in his left arm. He died in the street and his body was then taken by neighbors to a temple. Later that day, according to reports received by Amnesty International, policemen came to the temple and, using sticks, dug the bullets out of his body, thereby removing the evidence.

Thun Bun Ly had known he was in danger. He had been an outspoken critic of the growing violence perpetrated by the coalition government that the United Nations had left behind in 1993. The superbly staged UN election of May that year had resulted in a victory for the noncommunist party of Prince Norodom Ranariddh. But when the former communist People's Party brutally refused to give up power, the UN had been compelled to bless an unholy coalition between the two, with the newly restored King Sihanouk presiding as a constitutional monarch.

It quickly became clear after the UN had left in September 1993 that Hun Sen, the former communist who still ruled by party methods, was determined to dominate the government. He was easily able to do so: Ranariddh and Funcinpec were weak, and communist (or former communist) officials still controlled almost every level of the administration, down to the villages.

Critics of the regime, whether politicians or journalists, had been under threat ever since. In September 1994, Nuon Chan, the editor of the *Voice of Khmer Youth,* was shot dead in the street. In August 1995 a hand grenade was thrown into the house of the publisher of *Morning News* after he published reports about military complicity in the heroin trade. *New Liberty News* was ransacked that October; among the gang of looters were bodyguards of Prime Minister Hun Sen. The printers for other opposition papers stopped printing them out of fear.

Thun Bun Ly had stood trial for attacking the government in his paper. He told the judge, "If the press has to coddle the testicles [of the co–prime ministers] then the country will be completely ruined." This remark and others prompted loud cheers from the court. Thun Bun Ly's murder was condemned by Ranariddh but not by Hun Sen. The U.S. embassy put out a rather mild condemnation of the murder. Other embassies said nothing at all. Human rights in Cambodia used to be an international issue. Not now.

Soon after my trip to Sierra Leone, I returned to Phnom Penh. It was almost three years since UNTAC's triumphant elections, and Cambodia's recent past seemed to have happened in another country. The imperial presence of the United Nations—its thousands of vehicles, twenty thousand men and women and hundreds of offices—had been reduced to one senior official who worked out of a tiny office in the basement of a hotel. But the UN had retained the field office of the Human Rights Commission. This presence was important: the office continued to train human rights workers and tried to protect individuals whose rights were abused.

My first morning back in Phnom Penh I had tea with a friend. He saw Cambodia now being dominated by a casino culture: This was now a state of two hundred very rich families and nine million poor people. Only the fastest bucks mattered. The glorious forests were being trucked away at full speed to make cheap furniture in Japan and elsewhere. The waters of the Great Lake were being poisoned or silted up because of deforestation; fish were disappearing. The unspoiled majesty of Angkor, the country's most important artifact and tourist attraction, was threatened by unchecked theft of the carvings for sale on the ruthless international art market.

There was new building all over Phnom Penh, and some of the most obvious new structures were banks. Many were said to be fronts for laundering money corruptly acquired by leading politicians, generals and businessmen. Cambodia had been named by President Clinton as a conduit for drug trafficking. One of the country's richest businessmen was reported to be a major trafficker; he was also very close to both prime ministers.

The two prime ministers had become rich men. King Sihanouk said to me, with a wry laugh, "Since the 1993 election Hun Sen and Ranariddh have chosen to share everything. I speak carefully. They've found a miraculous formula or recipe. It's delicious." I spent two hours with the king in his palace on the banks of the Mekong. He was his usual charming and voluble self, serving Taittinger and chocolates. But he seemed a saddened man. He said he saw Cambodia as lurching from crisis to crisis, over which he had little or no control. He was once accustomed to absolute power, and then to being the linchpin in all arrangements; now both his prime ministers tried to ignore him.

"I am like a piece of ham in a sandwich but not delicious sandwich like those created by Lord Sandwich," Sihanouk explained. "I'm stuck instead between the government and the opposition. I am very miserable. Very, very miserable. I would like to conciliate. I cannot. I cannot reunite the two sides. My hope for Cambodia to become one of the world's most advanced liberal democracies is finished."

The United Nations had inevitably created unrealistic expectations—of utopia coming to Cambodia in white vehicles. I remembered one optimistic UNTAC official telling me in 1993 that UNTAC would completely transform Cambodian life. It could do nothing of the sort in a country whose only tradition was authoritarianism, which had emerged from twenty-one years of civil war, and where the insane mass murder of the Khmer Rouge had been followed by a more orthodox but fairly brutal communist regime. As soon as the UN left, the country's brutal traditions reasserted themselves. Steven Heder, the American scholar of the Khmer Rouge, described the UN process as "Cambodia's democratic transition to Neoauthoritarianism."

UNTAC's experience suggests that a fleeting UN presence, however well organized and well intentioned, cannot ever do much more than skim the surface of any pond, whether in the Balkans, Indochina or Africa. It cannot dredge the monsters which lurk below. It cannot stop political or ethnic groups from using the political or military forces at their disposal.

Dissent was now characterized by the government as support for the Khmer Rouge and destructive of the course of "nation building" on which Ranariddh and Hun Sen claimed to be embarked. Officials opposed to Hun Sen had been jailed for long terms on charges of inspiring coups. Ranariddh had sacked Sam Rainsy, the minister of finance, one of the most successful ministers; Rainsy was also an outspoken and diligent enthusiast for fiscal reform, which posed a serious threat to the deeply vested and lucrative commercial interests of political leaders.

Amnesty International reported in May 1996 that there had been "a steady deterioration in respect for human rights" in Cambodia. Rights of expression, association and assembly had been undermined in the last three years, while policemen and soldiers had not been punished for violent attacks on people critical of the regime.

One of his government's actions at which King Sihanouk was most horrified was the amnesty it gave to leaders of the Khmer Rouge in August 1996. While Hun Sen tried to quell opposition within Phnom Penh itself, he and Ranariddh competed to secure the defection of Ieng Sary, Pol Pot's longtime political partner, who was now a warlord with a fortune based around the gem mines of Pailin on the Thai-Cambodian border. Ieng Sary publicly denied that he had had anything to do with the massacres committed by the Khmer Rouge in the 1970s; they were all the fault of Pol Pot, he said. Pol Pot's redoubt was now farther north on the Thai-Cambodian border.

The two prime ministers rushed through an amnesty for Ieng Sary. King Sihanouk acted, as he often did, more honorably than his officials. He wanted Ieng Sary's crimes to be investigated, as did Amnesty International, which wrote to him, "Amnesties which have the effect of preventing the emergence of the truth and subsequent accountability before the law should not be acceptable." The king replied that he agreed, but as a constitutional monarch he had no choice but to do as his prime ministers and parliament requested. But he stressed that he hoped nothing would prevent an international tribunal from pursuing the Khmer Rouge leaders. Apart from Amnesty's intervention, the entire affair of the pardon was greeted with silence around the world. A leader of what had long been acknowledged as one of the most odious regimes of modern times had been pardoned for reasons of local expedience.

In the next two years Hun Sen consolidated his power by force and by guile, in a concerted attempt to nullify the results of the 1993 election. The electorate had then rejected and discredited the forces of extremism, but UNTAC's inability to remove the authoritarian structures of government allowed Hun Sen to imprison, exile or cow the leaders of Funcinpec and other opponents. When Sam Rainsy set up the Khmer Nation Party and denounced corruption and human rights abuses, he won wide support—and therefore came under serious threat from Hun Sen. In March 1997, a peaceful rally of Khmer Nation followers that was being addressed by Rainsy ended in the deaths of over a hundred people when grenades were thrown into its midst. Agents of Hun Sen were widely suspected, but no one was arrested.

All of this was depressing. Nonetheless, I had no doubt that Cambodia and Cambodians had benefited from the Paris peace agreement and the UN's mission; Cambodia was better off than it would have been without the UN. Hundreds of thousands of refugees had returned; for the most part their lives were very hard, but they were out of the camps. UNTAC created and left important benchmarks. More and more Cambodians had became aware that they were entitled to freedoms that were being denied them. The country was now a signatory of the UN Covenants on Human Rights. These provide standards of international law to which the Cambodian government can and should be held accountable.

UNTAC established the roots of civil society in a country where no such concepts had ever existed. For the first time Cambodian human rights groups were allowed to form and a free press began to flourish. The unheard-of happened: people began to feel confident enough to criticize their leaders, often in abusive terms—to the fury of those same leaders.

Despite constraints on the press, Cambodia's own human rights groups, set up during the UN's time, have survived and even, in some cases, flourished. They were stronger in the provinces than any comparable groups in, say, Indonesia or Malaysia, let alone Vietnam or China. But they still need outside support. In 1995 the two prime ministers asked Boutros Boutros-Ghali to shut the Phnom Penh office of the UN Office of Human Rights. The proposal raised a firestorm and the government eventually backed down.

That kind of international commitment to the institutions the international community had spent so much on building in Cambodia was still essential. The world's attention had passed on to other firestorms. This was understandable: Rwanda, Burundi, Bosnia,

Zaire and many other places had had crises of governance since the Cambodian elections. But the lesson of UNTAC is that continual attention is essential. Countries like Cambodia need more than fifteen minutes of fame if their civil institutions are to grow. The real threat to Cambodia now did not come from the disintegrating Khmer Rouge, which was crippled by the Paris agreement and the UN mission. The danger came from the complicity of leading politicians in tolerating the worst crimes of the past as well as those of recent years. As Amnesty International pointed out in its letter to the king, "Impunity is one of the main contributing factors to continuing cycles of human rights violations worldwide."

Impunity is still the cloak of warlords and killers everywhere, whether it be in Sierra Leone, Bosnia, Rwanda, Chechnya, Somalia or Cambodia. But that is beginning to change. Tentatively, a new global legal architecture is being created.

In 1993 the Security Council established an international war crimes tribunal to judge war crimes committed in the former Yugoslavia. This was the first time that such a tribunal had been set up not by the victors, as at Nuremberg and Tokyo after World War II, but by the international community, acting through the United Nations. After the genocide in Rwanda, a similar tribunal, acting under the same authority, was created in Arusha, Tanzania, to deal with some of the killers of the hundreds of thousands of Tutsis murdered in 1994.

The Yugoslav tribunal was created not as a consequence of peace but as a mechanism to try to achieve peace, on the grounds that peace and justice are, if not indivisible, at least close associates. The relationship is a matter of fierce debate. There were those who feared that the creation of the tribunal would inhibit rather than assist the search for peace in Bosnia. As one anonymous writer put it in *Human Rights Quarterly,* "The quest for justice for yesterday's victims of atrocities should not be pursued in such a manner that it makes today's living the dead of tomorrow." That was a risk, but it is arguable that the indictment of Radovan Karadzic and Ratko Mladic, the Bosnian Serb leaders, in fact made it easier to reach a peace agreement in Dayton, Ohio, in November 1995. As indicted men, they were excluded from Dayton and the Bosnian Serbs were represented there by Slobodan Milosevic. Leaders of the Bosnian government said they would not have agreed to negotiate with Karadzic himself so soon after the massacre at Srebrenica.

Building on the precedents of the Yugoslav and Rwandan tribunals, in July 1998 the international community finally created one of the last great institutions of the twentieth century, a permanent international court with the power to try war crimes, crimes against humanity and genocide. Such a court had been proposed after Nuremberg but delayed for almost fifty years by the Cold War and the opposition of the Soviet Union.

During that time the United States had been one of the great proponents of such a court, but in 1998, Washington fought the creation of the new tribunal, arguing that it could lead to politically motivated prosecutions of American soldiers serving abroad. The U.S. delegation to the treaty talks in Rome tried and failed to have Americans exempted from trial by the court. Such exemptions would, of course, have undercut the whole process. The underlying reason for U.S. opposition was apparently that Senator Jesse Helms had warned that any treaty exposing Americans even theoretically to such a court would be "dead on arrival" in the Senate.

The treaty was agreed to in Rome, 120–7. In voting against, the United States was in the company of Iraq, Libya, Qatar, Yemen, China and Israel.

8

Uniting Nations

In February 1996, as the United Nations and in particular Boutros-Ghali became an issue in the presidential primary elections in the United States, Kofi Annan was completing his assignment to hand over the UN mission in Bosnia to NATO. After he visited NATO headquarters in Brussels, I flew with him to Zagreb on a small Russian jet provided to the UN. Sad news awaited our arrival. The Russian diplomat Yuri Miakotnykh had just been been killed. It was a personal tragedy which encapsulated the crisis of the United Nations.

A rotund and jovial man, Miakotnykh was one of the most gifted senior UN officials in the Balkans. Before that he had been one of Moscow's top Indochina experts. In the early nineties he was the Russian ambassador in Cambodia. I had known him there. His diplomatic skills, knowledge and good humor had been important in securing the UN peace process in Cambodia. He had persuaded Hun Sen and other former communist leaders close to Vietnam and to Moscow that they must cooperate with the UN plan.

That afternoon he had set out by car from his office in Belgrade to meet Annan in Zagreb. He was exhausted, said his staff, by months of cajoling the Serbs to abide by the terms of the Dayton agreement.

Just as he was nearing the Croatian capital he fell asleep at the wheel. His car drove off the road and he died instantly. His colleagues were furious that the UN had not provided him with an international driver. (The Serb UN drivers in Belgrade were afraid to drive into Croatia.) The UN's financial crisis was the reason, they said. He left a wife in the hospital in Belgrade recovering from open heart surgery and a daughter who was also unwell. Now the question was whether the straitened UN would be able to find money to give her and her daughter decent compensation.

Two hundred ten UN soldiers and officials had died or been killed in the course of the hazardous and often vilified peacekeeping operation in the former Yugoslavia, which began in 1991 and ended with the takeover by NATO's Implementation Force, IFOR, after the Dayton peace agreement was signed in mid-December.

Whatever effect IFOR's promises had upon ordinary Bosnian Serbs, their leadership was determined to resist. Hard-line Muslims in the ruling SDA Party also wanted to see Serb citizens leave and formed an unholy alliance with extremist Serbs to force them out. In early 1996 the Serbs began digging up the graves of their dead and burning their apartments as they left them. Hundreds of thousands fled the city. NATO troops stood by and did nothing.

Annan visited the IFOR commander in Sarajevo, Admiral Leighton Smith, who was also NATO's southern commander. He asked Smith if he could not put NATO patrols onto the streets of the Serb suburbs to stop the arson and bring calm. The admiral declined.

ANNAN flew to Prevlaka, an exquisite spit of land which runs into the Adriatic just south of the medieval town of Dubrovnik, where Croatia borders Montenegro. There were snowcapped mountains in the background, with forests on the hills below, and little fishing villages along the coast road. Before the breakup of Yugoslavia, Prevlaka was a base of the Yugoslav National Army, so the promontory had never been developed. Now it was a lonely UN outpost. Twenty-eight UN military observers lived there—British, Irish, Ghanaian, Portuguese, Pakistani, Swiss, Swedish soldiers—twenty-seven different nationalities among the twenty-eight.

This team lived in rather primitive quarters and constantly patrolled the peninsula and its hinterland which were supposed, under a 1992 agreement, to be demilitarized. That was honored more in the breach. We were driven up a hill to see a Croat special police bunker, a spectacular view—and a bolted cabinet into which the Croat policeman would not allow us to look. They also showed us how the Croats had laid small anti-personnel mines on the road within yards of one of the UN military observation posts, where they invited us for tea. Without the UN, the probes by both sides would probably escalate at least into small skirmishes.

We flew on to Belgrade. Annan had brought with him a check for $1 million and an agreement worked out between UN lawyers and the Yugoslav government that this was to be in full and final compensation for damage to an army barracks allegedly caused by French troops with the UN. He was to hand it over to the prime minister. But outside the prime minister's office Annan was told that the army wanted another $300,000. This would mean reopening the whole saga.

The prime minister began by speaking of Yuri Miakotnykh; he said that the UN had lost a hardworking official and Yugoslavia had lost a very good friend. Annan told the prime minister that he hoped he could leave the check and settle the whole matter before he left that day. One official, smiling, said something to the prime minister. Annan said, "I know why you are smiling. You have an objection." He said it had not been easy to get even $1 million compensation; he hoped that the Yugoslav side would not reopen the whole matter.

The prime minister would not take the check himself. In the end he ordered the minister of defense to sign for it.

Annan brought up the plight of the 250,000 or more Serb refugees who had been forced out of their homes in the Krajina area of Croatia in summer 1995 and were now living in difficult, sometimes awful conditions inside Serbia. Under Dayton they should be allowed to return to their homes, but Croatia was not making that easy.

Half an hour later, Annan saw President Milosevic, who began by saying how much he loved New York City. He said that normalization of Serb-Croat relations would make a radical change in the Balkans—and the only unresolved problem now was over Prevlaka. (He showed no interest in Krajina or the fate of the Serb refugees from there.) Annan asked if he was now optimistic about Bosnia, and Milosevic stated firmly, "Oh yes. The war is over. No doubt."

On the flight of Serbs from the suburbs in Sarajevo, Milosevic was scornful of Dr. Karadzic and the Bosnian Serb leadership, who had encouraged people to leave. "They were totally crazy," he said. But the Bosnian government was also responsible, and if international sanctions on the Bosnian Serb Republic had been lifted a month before, confidence would have grown and the exodus might have been prevented. Milosevic went on to talk about his relationship with both Tudjman and Izetbegovic, and was optimistic about almost everything. He insisted there was no need for the international war crimes tribunal in The Hague; suspected Serb war criminals were already being tried in Belgrade. He said that complete normalization of relations in the Balkans would happen only when all international relations were normalized, and this included full participation in the UN. It was ironic, he said, that Serbia, now the most multi-ethnic state in the Balkans, was the most ostracized.

What about Kosovo? asked Annan. Milosevic replied that it was an internal issue. Decades ago it had been a problem. The issue had been one of Albanian separatism, though not all the Albanians were separatists. They were equal citizens of Yugoslavia, he said. Around six hundred of them were in the police force in Kosovo. Separatism in the area was on the decline. Many exiled Albanians had been financing the movement, but they had been duped by separatist leaders who had made a lot of money out of them. He blamed the separatists for attempting to internationalize the problem and recalled telling David Owen, who had once asked to attend a meeting between Milosevic and the Kosovo Albanians, that it was an internal matter and not his business. "Kosovo is not simply another area," he said. "It is the heart of Serbia."

o

THE man dealing with the Balkan warlord was a West African chief. The more I traveled with Annan and talked to him in the early nineties, the more remarkable he seemed—an international civil servant who had not become a bureaucrat. He dealt with people in a familiar yet persuasive way and managed to retain both dignity and authority. He is not a tall man, but he has an unusual presence that seems to come from an innate sense of calm and politeness. He speaks softly and rarely appears angry or even flustered. He also has a very lively, indeed sometimes even mischievous, sense of fun. He is quite different from anyone else I have met at the United Nations or in most other places. One senior official told the *New York Times:* "He has this uncanny ability to get people to shift their position without feeling threatened or without any tension."

Annan was born in Ghana in 1938. His mother was a Fante, from the Cape Coast of Ghana; his father was half Fante and half Ashanti, from the interior. Annan could have been a chief from either side of his family. Indeed, in the early nineties, the paramount chief of the Akwamu region died and Annan was asked if he would allow himself to be considered. He declined.

Annan's father had worked as a manager for the United African Company, part of Lever Brothers, dealing in cocoa exports and various imports. He was also a leading Freemason in Ghana. During Kofi's childhood they lived wherever in Ghana the company sent him. On retirement he became the governor of the Ashanti region. Annan was brought up in Christian boarding schools established under British rule. "I was not particularly religious," he said to me once. "I'm still a believer, but I'm not the sort of person you will see quoting the Bible. But it's there to fall back on when you need it. And the sense that you are not alone in whatever situation."

The winds of change were blowing through Africa in the 1950s—independence was in the air. It was a time, Annan often said later, "when you believed anything was possible. Everything could be done."

After boarding school, he studied economics at the College of Science and Technology in Ghana, in Kumasi. Then he won a Ford Foundation scholarship to Macalester College in St. Paul, Minnesota, at the end of the fifties, where he discovered snow. He quickly adapted to wearing heavy clothes, but drew the line at earmuffs until one particularly cold day, when he appreciated their value. It helped teach him, he used to say later, that it was sometimes unwise to second-guess the locals.

At Macalester, Annan did some work for Pillsbury, the flour merchants. They were thinking of setting up a mill in Ghana, but the Ghanaian president, Kwame Nkrumah, embraced socialism and therefore chose Bulgaria. The mill was never built. Instead, Annan went to Geneva to do post-graduate work.

He had begun working for the United Nations low on the ladder as an administrative officer and budget officer, in Geneva in 1962. He spent three years with the World Health Organization (WHO) in Geneva and then applied for field assignments in Congo-Brazzaville and Alexandria, where WHO had regional offices. Instead, the head of personnel, a Frenchman, talked about India and Manila and finally offered him Copenhagen. "But I really wanted to work in the developing world, preferably in Africa. So I resigned from WHO and joined the Economic Commission for Africa in Addis [Ababa]."

Ethiopia during the last days of Emperor Haile Selassie gave him a feel for the fragility of much of post-colonial Africa. "I used to say in Addis that after a while I could tell where the next political problem was going to be," Annan recalled. "When you get a job application from the governor of a central bank, you know there's going to be a problem in his country. Invariably it followed."

After five years he was ready to move on. "I called it my midlife crisis," Annan said. "But I had it in my early thirties. I wasn't sure whether to stay in the UN or go back to Ghana."

From Addis Ababa he went to the Massachusetts Institute of Technology (MIT) to study management. In the mid-seventies he went home to Ghana to run the Ghana Tourist Development Company. "I wanted to make a contribution to Ghana," he explained, "but I found myself constantly fighting the military, so I went back to the UN." He later told the newspaper of his alma mater, Macalester College, that his life had not turned out as he had expected: "I figured that after my schooling I would make some money in the business world, then I would—at, say 45—enter politics in Ghana and help develop the country. At 60 I would retire and become a farmer. And I would die at 80 in bed. But it's one of those things God does. Our most intricate plans don't always turn out as we expected."

He was at the High Commissioner for Refugees in Geneva in the early eighties, at the height of the boat people exodus, and the crises of refugees from Afghanistan and Central America.

He and his wife, Titi Alakija, separated after their return to Geneva and later divorced; she went back home to Lagos. They agreed that their children, Ama, eleven, and Kojo, six, should remain with their father until they were old enough to go to boarding school. In 1981 he met Nane Cronstedt, a Swedish lawyer who was working for UNHCR. They married in 1984. Her father, Judge Lagergren, was a distinguished jurist and her mother was the sister of Raoul Wallenberg, the Swedish diplomat who rescued tens of thousands from the Nazis in the closing days of World War II. Arrested by the Russians, he disappeared in the gulag.

Annan moved to New York in the mid-eighties; he became director of the budget, then assistant secretary general for personnel and later controller and head of planning, programming and finance. In 1990, after the Iraqi invasion of Kuwait, he was sent to Baghdad to negotiate the repatriation of nine hundred UN staff and help resolve the fate of 500,000 Asians stranded in Kuwait and Iraq.

In 1992 he moved closer to the center of the frame when Boutros-Ghali made him first deputy and then head of the peacekeeping department. It was a surprising appointment; within the UN he was seen as an economist and financial manager. This was the time of explosion in peacekeeping. "We all had high hopes," Annan remembered. "The Cold War was over. The new consensus in the council permitted agreement on operations that had not been possible."

Somalia, Bosnia and Rwanda all helped destroy that optimism. Annan said that when UNPROFOR was thrown into the former Yugoslavia, the whole world saw it as a fight between good and evil. The problem was that peacekeeping was supposed to be neutral.

He recognized that the nature of the whole business had changed. The UN was no longer keeping regular armies apart but was dealing with, in his words, "myriad paramilitary groups, militias and uncontrolled elements" which would constantly disregard whatever their nominal leaders might agree to.

The other great difference, as Annan once told the *New York Times,* was that today "political tolerance of casualties is very low—sometimes just four or five"—among nations prepared and able to contribute effective troops. (It is startling to recall that as late as the early seventies, the United States was enduring several hundred casualties in Vietnam every week.)

Annan was fiercely critical of the speed with which the Clinton administration withdrew its troops from Somalia after the deaths of eighteen American soldiers there in 1993. He said that "the impression has been created that the easiest way to disrupt a peacekeeping operation is to kill Americans." He was equally critical of the way in which the USS *Harlan County* had turned and fled from Haiti because of a hostile demonstration on the dockside. He upset African ambassadors in 1994 when he told the French newspaper *Le Monde* that it was difficult to recruit African troops for peacekeeping missions because their governments "probably need their armies to intimidate their own populations."

In summer 1994 he bemoaned the fact that no governments would provide the UN with a quick reaction force of a type that could have saved hundreds of thousands of lives in Rwanda. Those African troops available had no equipment. Marrying them with equipment from the United States or Europe just took far too long. Back in 1960, when communications were far less sophisticated, the UN was able to move three thousand troops in three days into the Congo. In Rwanda in 1994 a response took months. In one case the political will existed; in the other there was none.

Annan had overseen the end of the tragic Somali operation in spring 1995. It was by no means all a disaster; before George Bush sent the first American troops, about 350,000 Somalis were thought to have died from famine. The U.S. and UN missions between them may have saved at least a quarter of a million others. But more than 130 peacekeepers (including Pakistanis, Moroccans and others from developing countries) and thousands of Somalis had died as a result of the $1.6 billion operation which at its height had involved some thirty-seven thousand troops from twenty-eight countries. No one now remembered the optimism with which the U.S. Marines had waded ashore in a television spectacle that was meant to symbolize the new humanitarian world order. Since the operation was diverted from a relief effort to the manhunt for Mohammed Farah Aideed, which resulted in the deaths of the eighteen American soldiers and hundreds of Somalis, the mission had been covered in shame.

After the UN's ignominious departure, from a beach close to the one on which they had landed with such fanfare two years before, anarchy reinherited Somalia. Young clansmen in "technicals"—vehicles with machine guns mounted on them—roared around the streets; they stole so much fuel from Mogadishu's water pumping station that it closed down; malnutrition became visible again. The world had gone away.

Reflecting on the operation one year later in Zagreb, Annan said to me, "The council made an abominable mistake to go after Aideed. They were very angry. Pakistanis had been killed and Pakistan was on the council then. And with the Americans it was like having a judge whose son has been killed. The Americans were determined to teach the clan leaders a lesson."

He thought that if the UN had not deviated and gone into an aggressive policing operation, "we might have stood a chance. We would have left the situation in a better way, left a better record behind."

In Bosnia the record was also moot. Now, after several months closing down the UN mission in the former Yugoslavia, Annan was far from certain that the Dayton blueprint of a multi-ethnic Bosnia would work. Why should it if a multi-ethnic Yugoslavia could not?

He talked also of the difficulty of finding peacekeeping troops. He had been searching for forces to keep the peace in eastern Slavonia, which Boutros-Ghali had hoped would be covered by IFOR but which the United States insisted must remain a UN responsibility.

The U.S. accused Boutros-Ghali of having a "misguided and counterproductive" position and of trying "to shy away from legitimate operations." The UN then asked for twelve thousand troops for the job, but Secretary Albright said that five thousand would do. They had an intemperate exchange and Boutros-Ghali complained later, "There is, sadly, a history of tasking the UN to undertake peacekeeping missions without providing it with the requisite mandates, troops and equipment."

Eventually Annan persuaded Pakistan, Belgium, Russia and Jordan to send one battalion each—altogether around five thousand men. It was clear, he said, that there were now different models for peacekeeping. The United States would have insisted on sending fifteen thousand Americans so that the force would be overwhelming and therefore in theory safer. In Somalia the United States had deployed twenty-eight thousand men in only 40 percent of the country, whereas the UN had to make do with twenty-two thousand troops in the whole country. Many Third World countries had begun to realize that the United States had far higher standards of safety for its own forces than for those of other peacekeeping nations. It was a crucial and growing problem.

AT supper one evening on this trip in February 1996, I talked to Annan about the rumors that Boutros-Ghali had seen him as a potential rival and had expected him to be damaged by this assignment in the former Yugoslavia. The Balkan chalice had already poisoned his predecessor, Yasushi Akashi. Annan smiled and shrugged. No such damage had been inflicted on him yet. His style, more direct than Akashi's, though not confrontational, had won him praise, even among the warring parties in the Balkans, as well as within the NATO community. Of course, his job was also easier than Akashi's; he was winding down the UN commitment with the consent of all involved, not trying to use moral suasion to impose a peace on intransigent fighters. Unlike Akashi, Annan did not have to placate and persuade men like Radovan Karadzic on a daily basis.

By this time in early 1996 there was already talk of Annan taking over the UN. He discouraged it, even privately. But Boutros-Ghali was clearly in trouble. He was under fierce attack from American conservatives, and there was reason to suppose that the Clinton administration would not support him for the second term which he might think would become his due at the end of 1996.

I asked Annan if he really wanted to be secretary general. He said he was not at all sure. It would mean an enormous change of life. He and his wife lived in a modest apartment on Roosevelt Island in New York. Nane was a painter and had a studio in Brooklyn. If he became secretary general, he would have security guards with him at all times. All personal freedom would be lost.

And, of course, no one really knew what the job was meant to be. No one ever had known, and the end of the Cold War seemed to make the task more difficult than ever. The UN Charter is almost silent on the task of the secretary general. He is described as "the chief administrative officer of the Organization," but Article 99 states that he "may bring to the attention of the Security Council any matter which in his opinion may threaten the maintenance of international peace and security." It is in those few words that the drama and the temptation of the job are embodied. The old conceit was that the holder of the job could try to be either a secretary or a general, but would hardly be able to combine both tasks. The question asked of every incumbent was whether he (it had always been a he) would be more a secretary or a general.

The only secretary general really to have measured up to the great potential of the job was Dag Hammarskjöld, the Swedish diplomat who became the organization's second leader, after Trygve Lie, in 1953. Hammarskjöld had seemed, before his appointment, likely to be far more secretary than general, but in fact he became an activist moral leader, and his death in a plane crash while on a peacekeeping mission in the Congo in 1961 meant that he became the martyr of the organization.

His successors never came near to his stature. One historian of the United Nations, Rosemary Righter, has tartly observed: "U Thant was invisible; [Kurt] Waldheim was a liar; Perez de Cuellar was a man of whom U.S. general and ambassador to the UN Vernon Walters once said, 'He couldn't make waves if he fell out of a boat.' " And now Boutros-Ghali had turned out to be somehow too difficult, perhaps too politically and intellectually cantankerous, for the job.

By early 1996 the UN was, in a real sense, fighting for its political and economic life. It was an organization with a split public profile—one in which hundreds of millions of people reposed inordinate hopes, but also one which many governments either exploited or treated with cynicism. Its central secretariat had around ten thousand employees, many of them placed by their governments on the basis of favor rather than merit. Its fiftieth anniversary celebrations in October 1995 had been much more a moment of self-congratulation and platitude than analysis.

Of course, disillusion with the UN was always inevitable. Richard Gardner, the U.S. ambassador to Spain in the mid-nineties, recalled that at the founding of the UN an American banker, Beardsley Ruml, had prophesied: "At the end of five years you will consider the United Nations is the greatest vision ever realized by man. At the end of ten years you will find doubts within yourself and all through the world. At the end of fifty years you will believe the United Nations cannot succeed. You will be certain that all the odds are against its ultimate life and success. It will only be when the United Nations is 100 years old that we will know that the United Nations is the only alternative to the demolition of the world."

Now, after half a century, some congratulation was due. The UN had survived already twice as long as the League of Nations. If the faults of the league and the UN were similar, that was perhaps because they were both based upon a utopian ideal which could never be realized. Woodrow Wilson had believed that if only "power politics" were abolished, "peoples, not governments, would run things"—and run them much better, in the interests of cooperation and peace. That is not the way of the world.

The paradox, considering the current chill between the two, was that America had always been crucial to the development of the UN. Franklin Delano Roosevelt had not only been present at its creation, he was also in a real sense its creator. Having served under Woodrow Wilson, Roosevelt knew how the failed peace after World War I contributed to the Great Depression and the age of the tyrants. With great skill, during World War II he had constructed a consensus among the Allies that another attempt at international security should be made. Without Roosevelt there would have been no UN, no Bretton Woods institutions, no General Agreement on Tariffs and Trade, no World Health Organization, Food and Agriculture Organization, UN Educational, Scientific and Cultural Organization, or any of the other permanent international organizations. When the UN Charter was adopted by unanimous vote at the San Francisco Conference in June 1945, the new president, Harry Truman, exulted: "Between the victory in Europe and the final victory in Japan, in this most destructive of all wars, you have won a victory against war itself."

Would that it had been so. As the *New York Times* put it a half century later, the UN has all too often been oversold and has therefore disappointed. The General Assembly is not a global parliament; the Security Council (like the pope) has no divisions to call its own; UN peacekeepers are usually vulnerable monitors; and the secretary general is the servant of his masters. There is often absurd pomp, self-righteousness and cronyism—national, political and financial—above all because the bureaucracy is still too much governed by national quotas which no nation will even modify, let alone relinquish. Its debts and the disdain in which some hold the UN discolor its reputation and its real successes. There has never before been a world body to which almost all the nations of the world have had uninterrupted access to air grievances for over fifty years. It began with 50 members; now it has close to 190.

The UN Charter commits nations for the first time in history to collective action in the fields of peace and security, economic and social development, and human rights. In the early years, the UN oversaw the process of decolonization with some success. The Cold War paralyzed the organization in a real sense, but at the same time the organization helped paralyze the Cold War. During such critical moments as the Cuban missile crisis, it had been an essential talking shop, helping defuse the strains. It helped liberalize world trade; it provided technical and financial assistance for economic development and recently for the transformation of communist economies into market economies. Beyond politics, the UN has done an enormous amount in helping eradicate diseases like smallpox, taken care of thirty million refugees (at least), immunized children, provided for the victims of both man-made and natural disasters, pushed for development (not always with clear success), reduced global illiteracy, helped save millions of lives. Now one of its greatest tasks is probably to confront the reality of globalization and the dash into the marketplace of three billion more people, including those of China and the states of the former Soviet Union.

Human rights had been a revolutionary concept when the Universal Declaration of Human Rights was launched in 1948. The declaration expresses better than any other document the universal rights of man. Frequently (perhaps usually) ignored or flouted, it provides everyone with a benchmark against which both progress and tyranny can be measured. It has since led to such extraordinary developments of international law that by the mid-nineties the way in which governments treat their own citizens is often no longer regarded merely as an internal matter. By now human rights has become an integral part of international politics and the foreign policy of the United States, ahead of most other nations.

The UN, the American writer William Pfaff argued, is a human institution embodied in contemporary political history, sometimes useful, sometimes not. Its failures are human failures. It failed in Bosnia because its members were unwilling to make it succeed. It succeeded, up to a point, in Cambodia because they mostly agreed and conditions were favorable.

Annan thought it was all very well for governments like the United States to talk about reform, but to be significant it must include reform of governments' attitudes—like paying bills on time, not using the UN as a scapegoat, not writing absurd mandates, not sending troops into danger where governments would not send their own men under their own command. He thought that a lot of time had been lost in the last decade. In the eighties, the West had become interested in such issues as drugs, terrorism, the environment and human rights. All of these are important, but necessary debates over how to combat poverty and create sustainable development have gone by the board.

There are several United Nations. There is the international body of nations which does so many tasks—from vaccinating children to distributing food—with considerable success. It is less happily engaged when it sends lightly armed men to try to keep a nonexistent peace between ferocious warlords, or (at the opposite extreme) when it sends myriad delegates to interminable international conferences where too many words are rehearsed and too much money is spent.

Another United Nations, perhaps the most intractable, was made up of the vast and largely autonomous baronies constituted by the various agencies which carry out the UN's development and relief work. Among them were the Food and Agriculture Program, the World Food Program, the High Commissioner for Refugees, the UN Development Program, UNICEF and the World Health Organization. Undoubtedly they contained time-servers, like the central secretariat itself—perhaps more than did nongovernmental organizations working in the same areas—because of the quotas insisted upon by governments. Moreover, the agencies guarded their sovereignty as fiercely as any member state and fought any attempts to diminish their autonomy through coordination. Directors would not hesitate to call upon their own national governments to fight any attempt by the secretary general to dismiss incompetent senior staff or to rationalize missions, as both Boutros-Ghali and later Kofi Annan found to their cost. Thus UNHCR, for example, strenuously resisted the attempt by Boutros-Ghali to place much of its work under the umbrella of the newly created department of humanitarian affairs, which was established after the Persian Gulf crisis in order to improve UN coordination.

Then, lurking behind the bureaucracies, was what the *Washington Post* called the "demonic United Nations," much beloved of conspiracy theorists on the further marches of the right. This is the grimly efficient international plot known as the UN, which has slipped control of its members and is bent on taking over the United States, secretly training forces equipped with black helicopters deep in the American desert in anticipation of that day. Conspiracy theorists denounced Boutros-Ghali, whose nonexistent helicopter was the biggest and blackest of them all, as the head of an organization secretly dedicated to world domination.

By the mid-nineties, the mutterings of the paranoid dark were echoed in the light. Senator Jesse Helms called the UN "the nemesis of millions of Americans." Bob Dole, the Republican candidate for president in 1996, made UN bashing into a favored pastime. In speech after speech he declared that if he were ever to send American troops abroad, "I will be in charge of that decision, not Booooutros Booooutros-Ghali." He almost always got a laugh. But how far the American people actually saw the UN as an important issue was moot; indeed, many polls showed that Americans viewed the UN much more favorably than the rhetoric of its populist critics would suggest.

Both sides of Congress constantly depicted Boutros-Ghali now as a man who had failed to reform the world organization. He had actually done some things. He had already proposed to cut a thousand from the ten thousand staff posts of the central secretariat; to undertake further economies to save some $140 million a year; and, under U.S. pressure, to create a new UN "watchdog" post, under secretary general for internal oversight services.

But White House and State Department officials insisted that along with almost every other large institution facing the challenge of globalization, the UN had to embark on real downsizing. The problem, often pointed out, was that the stockholders of the UN were the nearly 190 member countries, and to many if not most of them downsizing meant the loss of cherished positions.

By the spring of 1996, administrative officials were arguing that whatever the strength of feeling in the country, the feeling in the Congress was such that if Boutros-Ghali stayed for a second term, the Republicans would never agree to fund the UN. Therefore even for those who supported the UN (or perhaps especially for them) his removal was essential.

The U.S. refusal to pay its contributions was the most important cause of the financial crisis. Half the UN's total expenses were now being paid by European Union members, and Japan had become the largest single contributor. The accumulated arrears were now standing at $2.3 billion, and the Secretariat only just managed to keep functioning by skillful financial subterfuge: it stole from the peacekeeping account to finance its general budget. This was possible only because the UN was always so far in arrears in its payments to troop-contributing countries. In the case of poor Third World countries such delays really could hurt—and usually meant that the soldiers who had served in Bosnia or Somalia were not getting paid at all.

With less cash expected in peacekeeping in 1996 the financial straits were likely to become more desperate.

By international standards the sums were pretty tiny. The General Assembly's Portuguese president pointed out that the Secretariat's budget, at $1.3 billion, was only about one fifth of his own country's education budget. But if the organization as a whole was relatively cheap, its organization was not always wise. Some parts were ludicrously overmanned; others, like peacekeeping, were inadequately staffed. The peacekeeping staff of some three hundred people had found it impossible to supervise some seventy thousand soldiers properly in up to twenty operations at a time. Yet other, near-moribund agencies such as the Committee on Missing Persons in Cyprus continued, thanks to Greece's friends in the U.S. Congress. (It had not found a missing Cypriot in twenty-two years.) The Committee on Decolonization remained even though almost no colonies exist. In summer 1996, twenty-four members of this committee made a trip to Papua New Guinea at a cost to the UN of $150,000. Equally ludicrous was the Committee on the Effects of Atomic Radiation, originally set up for just one year, 1955. It was easy but not quite fair to blame the Secretariat for such anachronisms. The General Assembly was responsible and so, in fact, was the United States itself, if only because in the 1980s the U.S. had insisted that the budget must be adopted by consensus, which gave every member state a veto on deletions as well as additions. Thus, in 1996 the U.S. supported the voting of new mandates for a UN political presence in Guatemala and for human rights monitoring in Haiti. Boutros-Ghali said he would need more money for these activities, but the U.S. had insisted that they be financed within the agreed budget and that old or out-of-date activities be scrapped to make room for them.

By early 1996, Boutros-Ghali had announced that he would seek a second term, though when first elected he had promised he would not. He explained, "Only stupid people don't change their minds." He could—and his personal staff did—put forward a reasonable account of his five-year tenure. The strategic analyst Mats Berdal suggested that in the end Boutros-Ghali's period as secretary general "will look rather less flawed than the domestically driven and, far too often, purposeless foreign policy of the Clinton administration during its first term of office." But Boutros-Ghali's record did not sway his critics.

He was a brilliant man, but his imperious manner was resented. His style of diplomacy, learned from Anwar Sadat and Hosni Mubarak, was to conduct all-important negotiations with foreign leaders tête-à-tête—and then never tell any of his colleagues what had been agreed. He had also made enemies by the management technique he himself called "stealth and sudden violence." The *Financial Times* went so far as to say that he was "an appalling manager" who was "detested by his staff." One historian of the office of the secretary general, Edward Newman, wrote that Boutros-Ghali came to be seen by many of his staff as "high-handed, distant, aristocratic and arrogant." They did not like being "chained to their desks" and told only at the last minute whether or not their contracts (which he had reduced from three years to one year) would be renewed. It was a commentary on the atmosphere of fear at the UN under Boutros-Ghali that some officials even began to refer to his efficient Haitian chief of staff as his "Tonton Macoute of the thirty-eighth floor."

More important was his relationship with member states, especially the United States. He was proud and prickly, and showed he had little patience with protocol, sensitivities and tradition. He found Madeleine Albright an intellectual disappointment as U.S. ambassador to the UN. He was perfectly prepared to make his feelings known. On one memorable occasion he had accused Albright, in front of the council, of "vulgarité." (In his memoir he also writes that he was told that Albright had said she would "make Boutros think I am his friend, then I will break his legs.") No secretary general had fought so fiercely with members since Dag Hammarskjöld tangled with the British, French and Russians over the Congo peacekeeping mission in 1960.

Boutros-Ghali had accused the Security Council of ignoring the famine in Somalia and concentrating on what he called the "rich man's war" in Bosnia. More remarkable, he told citizens of Sarajevo, at a press conference punctuated by sounds of distant sniper fire and the burst of artillery shells, "You have a situation that is better than ten other places in the world. . . . I can give you a list." Such remarks were neither necessary nor welcome.

He had been much more prepared than his predecessors to confront member states with the consequences of their own "fragmented and self-deceptive responses" to crises. He would also offer the council analytical reports that proposed specific "options" and, by giving his own opinion, would try to limit the council's freedom to make choices that might be politically expedient but were in his view inadequate or inappropriate for the United Nations.

Needless to say, this self-confident behavior often highlighted the tension that exists between the role of secretary general as "chief administrative officer" and his duty to warn of matters "which in his opinion may threaten the maintenance of international peace and security."

He pointed out time and again that attacking the UN for its failures to deal with wars was all very well, but it was the United States that really mattered. "To put it bluntly, I have no power, no independence. You are free to send the troops or not to send the troops. You are free to pay the money or not to pay the money. So unless I obtain your goodwill, I will not be able to do the work."

Washington was infuriated by his criticisms of Israel, by his assertions that the United States would have no credibility unless it paid its debts and by his insistence on controlling air strikes in Bosnia. For his part Boutros-Ghali had been astonished (understandably so) when Clinton, in his first speech to the United Nations in September 1993, had blamed the UN for assigning itself new tasks and had insisted that the UN had to "learn to say no." "It is not I or the United Nations that says Yes or No," said Boutros-Ghali to the *New York Times*. "It is the member states. . . . I only receive the mandate and then I have to try to find the troops."

In May 1996, U.S. Secretary of State Warren Christopher traveled to New York to call at his residence on Sutton Place to tell him that the United States wanted him to step down at the end of the year. In a sense the U.S. was "dropping the pilot" of the course of "assertive multilateralism" on which it had embarked in 1993. This was the first time that any secretary general had been refused a second term.

"When I asked him the reason why, he declined to give one," Boutros-Ghali said later. He said that Madeleine Albright also refused to give him a reason and that he had no idea what had prompted America's attitude. He said that it was probably because "I was too independent as secretary general. Clearly, I was not successful in my relationship with the principal actor." A principal reason, beyond his control, was that by 1996 the Clinton administration wanted to prevent the Republicans from exploiting the charge—which was as

populist as it was absurd—that U.S. foreign policy had been "subcon-
tracted" to the UN. Dumping Boutros-Ghali was an easy way of asserting U.S. power over the organization.

The United States had every right to oppose Boutros-Ghali, but
there were those who felt that this right could have been exercised
with more care. It might have been wiser to consult the other permanent members of the Security Council rather than first leak U.S.
intentions to the press. It was inevitable that this would be seen as
an attempt by the only superpower to control the United Nations
absolutely.

In mid-June, Washington went public and announced that it
would vote against Boutros-Ghali's receiving a second term. It would
use its Security Council veto if necessary, officials said. Madeleine Albright declared, "He has lost the confidence of the United States. It is
important, when the most powerful country in the world looks at an
international organization, that we have somebody at the head of it
who, we think, is suitable to take it to a dynamic new age." Boutros-
Ghali said, "I hope they will change their minds." The administration
stated there was no possibility of that.

The blunt dismissal of the seventy-three-year-old Egyptian infuriated many Third World countries and their diplomats. But American
officials were sanguine in the belief that the UN's supporters in the
Third World would realize in the end that the organization had to
have the support of the world's most powerful country if it was to
survive, let alone prosper—and that protests would fade.

The United States now began to use the fact that it owed the
United Nations more than $1 billion in back dues as a kind of black-
mail. There was no hope of getting this paid, the mantra went, unless Congress believed it had a man it trusted at the head of the UN.
The administration could not force Congress to trust Boutros-Ghali,
so it was doing the UN and its supporters a favor by dumping him.

Boutros-Ghali began to campaign to have the world resist the
United States. In Germany he played the racial card, saying, "Every
UN secretary general has received two terms. Should I—the first
African—not get a second?"

Africa's endorsement was not automatic; many Africans considered that an African secretary general should have done better with
Somalia, Rwanda, Angola, Liberia and Burundi, to name but a few re-

cent scenes of horror. But at the summit of the Organization of African Unity in Cameroon, he won wide support. Washington sent Assistant Secretary of State for African Affairs George Moose to the meeting to affirm that if Clinton was reelected he would not reverse his opposition to Boutros-Ghali. The United States also complained about Boutros-Ghali's use of UN staff to lobby for his reappointment.

He kept the support of China; the Communist Party paper, *People's Daily,* said (not entirely wrongly) that his future was being sacrificed on the altar of Republican and Democratic presidential politics and that the U.S. was dumping him because he did not do its bidding adequately. The UN would lose all credibility if it became the tool of Washington, the paper warned.

In early July the UN's record on Bosnia lost Boutros-Ghali the vote of Malaysia, but he had the support of President Jacques Chirac of France, who said that the secretary general should indeed win the "traditional" second term. The French were determined to resist the Americans, and they considered Boutros-Ghali, who speaks beautiful French, a fine secretary general.

One problem was that the lack of an open process in choosing the secretary general made it virtually impossible for any other candidate to declare him- or herself while Boutros-Ghali was in the picture. There was no date for nominations to be submitted; no short list; no interviews; no need for any candidate to submit even a résumé, let alone references or a manifesto.

The principal alternatives now spoken of as possible successors included Mary Robinson, the Irish president; Gro Harlem Brundtland, the Norwegian prime minister; Kofi Annan; Sadako Ogata; Amara Essy, a former president of the UN General Assembly and foreign minister of the Ivory Coast; and Olara Otunnu, a former Ugandan diplomat who now ran the International Peace Academy in New York with panache.

Through the autumn of 1996 the United States continued to state that its decision was irrevocable; U.S. officials also began to say that Washington would support an African, so that Africa would have a full ten years, but were careful not to name anyone, realizing that the touch, let alone the embrace, of the U.S. would spell the end of any candidate. Boutros-Ghali remained adamant. So did the United States.

* * *

THERE were other crises. Chief among them at the moment was the horror of the Rwandan refugee camps in eastern Zaire and Tanzania. This was a crisis in which French-American tensions played an important part.

By now the humanitarian fiasco on the borders of Rwanda had become intolerable. Nominally under the care of UNHCR, the 1.2 million refugees were still controlled by the Hutu extremists who had butchered the Tutsis in the genocide of 1994 and then fled across the borders, dragging local populations with them. The camps were awash with weapons and the Hutus were still mounting vicious attacks across the border into Rwanda.

Despite its inability to separate genuine refugees from the armed killers, UNHCR had stayed in the camps, subcontracting much of the assistance work to nongovernmental organizations. Mrs. Ogata, the high commissioner for refugees, felt she had no choice. Her staff was increasingly worried. Her chief troubleshooter, Sérgio Vieira de Mello (a veteran of Cambodia and Bosnia), reported in September 1996 that he had never seen UNHCR "at the center of such an intricate and explosive combination of ominous interests."

Protection was impossible, he said; everyone was controlled by the Hutu extremists. "The genuine refugee population is hostage of forces of doom, and so are we. Massive care and maintenance assistance being provided by a heavy and costly international machinery, with no solution in sight, reflects humanitarianism at its worst."

The whole region was collapsing into a new, wider war, he warned. Though the Zairean government of Marshal Mobutu was supporting the Hutu refugees' attacks into Rwanda, the eastern region of Zaire was being destabilized by their activities. By October 1996, fighting between Zairean army and armed Banyamulenge (Zairean Tutsis) was spreading. De Mello urged that UNHCR not continue with "business as usual" but promote the return of the bulk of the refugees in the camps to Rwanda. Reports of killings on all sides spread. Chaos beckoned.

At a meeting with his senior staff and Mrs. Ogata on October 23, Boutros-Ghali complained about the "primitive" nature of the conflict and the environment of vengeance, saying that "such people don't mind killing women and children." Mrs. Ogata said she felt "very alone in the Great Lakes." Two days later she told the Security Council that rarely had UNHCR found itself in "such a quandary of humanitarian, political and security challenges." There was fighting in and around many of the camps, refugees were fleeing in large numbers and she was concerned that a new "humanitarian disaster" might be imminent.

Mrs. Ogata also took the opportunity to tell the council of the serious problems UNHCR was having elsewhere. Despite the provisions of Dayton, it was proving almost impossible to persuade Bosnian refugees to return home to areas where they would now be in an ethnic minority. No Croat refugees wanted to live among Muslims, no Muslims close to Serbs and so on. New fighting in northern Iraq had forced some sixteen thousand more Kurdish refugees into Iran in recent days. The war in Afghanistan appeared to be inducing a flow of more refugees and the Taliban's oppression of women seriously hindered UNHCR's work there. On behalf of the twenty-six million refugees for whom UNHCR was responsible, Mrs. Ogata said, "I count on the continuing support of the Security Council to solve humanitarian crises."

At the end of 1996, two years after the emergency began, the Security Council finally took up the crisis of eastern Zaire. Under the leadership of Canada, and with the enthusiastic backing of France, which wanted to save the Mobutu regime from what some officials saw as "the Anglo-Saxon conspiracy" to destroy Francophonie, a multinational force composed of a "coalition of the willing" was devised. It was to have between ten thousand and fifteen thousand men, but its proposed mandate was restricted. As Kofi Annan put it in a note to Boutros-Ghali, "the force would not disarm former Rwandan government forces; would not interpose itself between opposing forces; and would not separate former Rwandan government forces personnel and militia members from the civilian refugees. However it will, albeit reluctantly, assist in the voluntary repatriation of refugees." In short, the force would not take the vital actions urged by UNHCR over the last two years.

Annan was concerned that the plan left much unresolved. How was food to be brought to the refugees, how would they cross lines of confrontation, what would be the relationship between the multinational force and the United Nations, what would the force do if fighting broke out and/or refugees were attacked in its vicinity?

Despite such concerns, on November 15, 1996, the Security Council approved Resolution 1080. This mandated a multinational force that would use "all necessary means" to mount a humanitarian operation in Zaire. Its tasks included locating refugees by aerial reconnaissance, mounting airdrops of food to them and facilitating their repatriation.

That very same day the Rwandan government, in alliance with Uganda, attacked the camps to drive the refugees home and forestall the multinational force. They did so under the banner of a new Alliance for the Liberation of Congo-Zaire (AFDL). Its nominal leader was Laurent Kabila, a Congolese former nightclub owner and so-called Marxist. Kabila was controlled by Rwanda and Uganda.

Vice President Paul Kagame of Rwanda, the dominant person in the RPF government, later said that its strategy was simple: under cover of an uprising against Marshal Mobutu, it would destroy the structure of the Hutu army and militia based in the camps by bringing the Hutu combatants back to Rwanda and "dealing with them here or scattering them."

The bulk of Rwandan refugees immediately began to stream back home, but several hundred thousand others, many but not all under the control of the Hutu killers, were driven into the jungles of eastern Zaire. Fighting spread.

Suddenly the need for the multinational force was questioned by Western governments, almost immediately after they had authorized it. The Rwandan government made its opposition to any operation clear, and the U.S., which supported many of Rwanda's ambitions, began to withdraw support. France wanted the operation to continue, in the hope that it could contain the rebel advance through Zaire.

By now about 700,000 of the refugees known to be in the camps had gone home, but UNHCR believed that there were about 500,000 still unaccounted for in Zaire. Indeed, some deliberately turned a blind eye to their fate—or even sought to deny the existence of the several hundred thousand refugees who had fled or been driven toward the interior of Zaire rather than home. Many of them met a terrible fate in the months ahead, but, under the canopy of the remote jungles of eastern Zaire, it was unseen and was deliberately ignored by most Western governments.

The U.S. military claimed that its satellite photographs showed almost no refugees in eastern Zaire. Rwandan officials endorsed the U.S. position and poured scorn on UNHCR's concerns. A senior Oxfam official, by contrast, said that the refugees had been "airbrushed from history." Troops of the Rwandan-Ugandan alliance under Kabila continued to march through Mobutu's ramshackle and impoverished territories toward Kinshasa, the capital. As the fall of Mobutu became more likely, French official fury with *"les anglo-saxons"* grew.

ON Tuesday, November 19, 1996, the United States, as it had warned, vetoed the reappointment of Boutros-Ghali. The vote was 14–1—even the British supported Boutros-Ghali, though the British vote was certainly predicated on a U.S. veto. Boutros-Ghali vowed to fight on, despite the difficulties. He asked with a touch of the sarcasm which had made him both famous and feared at the UN, "Do I present a danger to the security of the United States? No. Did I smuggle something? Am I Noriega or Saddam Hussein?"

Boutros-Ghali's backers now pursued a high-risk strategy—not to seek a further ballot lest that show an inevitable erosion of his support. His majority would almost certainly fall first to ten and then below the magic number of nine, which he needed to be reelected. Instead, the strategy was to ask the Organization of African Unity to come back with further instructions as to what its members wanted. The French in particular had urged the OAU to say that they had no new instructions, that Boutros-Ghali remained their candidate and that they would like the United States to change its mind.

This plan was intended to maintain the viability of Boutros-Ghali and make it impossible for any other African to come forward, thereby, France hoped, forcing the U.S. to give in. If the U.S. did not, and put forward other names, the presumption was that the French or others would veto them and the resulting deadlock would throw the election into the General Assembly, where Boutros-Ghali would be reelected by a resounding majority determined to resist U.S. "hegemony." American diplomats were quick to warn that they would consider any secretary general elected in this way as illegal and that Washington would not cooperate with him.

The subtext of the row over Boutros-Ghali was the long-simmering and sometimes flaming distrust and rivalry between the

United States and France. UN officials recounted that when President Chirac visited New York in the summer of 1995 he astonished them by saying, "If you want to find idiotic behavior you can always count on the Americans." In the year since then U.S.-French relations had worsened, especially because of a row over NATO. The French had said that they would once again become full members of the alliance, but only if the U.S. agreed to allow a French admiral to take over NATO's southern command in the Mediterranean. President Chirac had even sent a handwritten note to Clinton saying, "This is of capital importance to me."

With or without such a personal presidential appeal, there was no way in which Washington was going to allow its Sixth Fleet, in the American lake known as the Mediterranean, to be placed in the hands of the French, and it was foolish of Chirac to attach his own personal prestige to such a request. Nonetheless, he told a French TV interviewer in early December that European union was essential to counter "American hegemony."

French pique with the United States was sometimes very obvious. When departing Secretary of State Warren Christopher made his farewell appearance at a gathering of NATO foreign ministers in Brussels, and a toast was raised in his honor, the French foreign minister, Hervé de Charette, turned and walked away. France's ambassador to NATO, Gérard Errara, then took his place, but he, too, refused to join the toast. Instead, he turned his back and talked with an aide while NATO's new secretary general, Javier Solana, did his best with his words about Christopher.

French sensitivities were transferred to the battle for the United Nations. In early December, Chirac met in Burkina Faso with leaders of the former French Africa. They were by now under pressure to come up with another African name. Few of those they suggested were very impressive. The danger was that out of spite the French would veto anyone with merit whom the Americans proposed.

In New York, Annan's name was by now being widely whispered. He was, as James Traub of the *New York Times* later put it, "the living opposite of Boutros-Ghali" and was known for "his efficiency, his exquisite tact and his slightly mysterious powers of persuasion." The NATO countries had been impressed with the way he had handled the transition from UNPROFOR to IFOR in Bosnia. The only question raised about him was whether he was too nice to be tough and whether he was, as one diplomat put it, so "conflict-averse" that he would be unable to confront, let alone impose, difficult decisions. Annan himself believed that this was a question of manner, if not manners. "Screaming and getting bitter and being angry is negative energy, and takes a lot out of you, and doesn't help any."

There were those who thought he would not be acceptable to other nations because he was perceived as being the U.S. choice. His supporters were quick to point out that he had often been critical of American policies. They argued that he had real skills as a manager, which were desperately needed; that he had a proven track record in reconciling countries and crises, as Somalia and Bosnia had shown; and that no one else was so well placed to repair bridges with Washington.

Annan could not be seen to be campaigning against the man for whom he worked, whose office was exactly one floor above his own on the northeast corner of the building. Indeed, he made a virtue of not campaigning. He was not like a politician whose career had been directed to high office; until very recently, the idea that a lifetime UN official could become secretary general would have seemed fanciful. He explained his refusal to push for the job in characteristic terms: "If it's to come to me, it will; if not, it won't." Privately he doubted the job was doable, unless the major powers could agree on what they wanted from the UN.

Straw polls for the new secretary general took place in the Security Council through the week of December 7–14. On each occasion the French vetoed Annan, and on each occasion the Americans and the British vetoed France's preferred candidate, Amara Essy, foreign minister of the Ivory Coast.

To the dismay of the French, they won no support from other members of the permanent five. Neither the Russians nor the Chinese seemed eager to confront Clinton and Madeleine Albright, who had just been named his new secretary of state, on this issue. They realized, perhaps better than the French, that a United Nations from which the United States was alienated would be of little use to them or anyone else. That was the reality of a one-superpower world.

That reality was spelled out by the chairman of the Joint Chiefs, General John Shalikashvili, who explained to Martin Walker of *The Guardian,* "This is no longer a world where you limit yourself to vital interests. Today, we protect our interests when they are threatened in order to shape the environment to ensure that what develops is in accord with our goals, using American military forces in situations when lesser interests are threatened so they don't grow.

"When I was Supreme Commander of Allied Forces in Europe, I thought the day would come when the NATO horizon would stretch beyond Europe. I can envisage when member nations see it useful to deal with humanitarian and other operations in Africa or the Middle East, utilizing NATO command and control." He made no mention of the United Nations.

Ghana formally nominated Annan on December 10. The French continued tilting at the U.S. windmill until finally, on Friday, December 13, they stopped blackballing Annan. The Security Council unanimously agreed that he should become the UN's seventh leader, and the following Tuesday the General Assembly ratified that choice.

The assembly gave a standing ovation to Boutros-Ghali. He was pointed in his farewell remarks, saying that the UN's financial crisis was not the result of mismanagement but "the refusal [of the United States] to fulfill a treaty obligation." In a thinly veiled warning to Annan he also said that nothing was more precious to the UN than its impartiality and equity. "If one word is to characterize the role of the secretary-general, it is independence. The holder of this office must never be seen as acting out of fear of, or in an attempt to curry favor with, one state or group of states. Should that happen, all prospects for the United Nations would be lost."

Annan said, "This is an honor not just for my own country, Ghana, but also for Africa as a whole." He promised that he would try to create "a more open" UN, "closer to the people and non-governmental organizations." He said that he would go to Washington to try to persuade Congress to pay its $1.4 billion debt to the UN. He embarked on change.

In July 1997, Annan published plans designed to reform the organization to create "greater agility in responding to an increasingly dynamic and complex world." He insisted that the UN's highest priority must be "alleviating poverty and enhancing the prospect of the developing countries." Thus he pledged to earmark some of the funds won back in cost cutting, which many Third World countries disliked because it meant fewer jobs, for a "development dividend."

Given the bureaucratic, geographic and political resistance to change within the UN, the reforms were a good start. He was forced by opposition from the barons and baronesses who run the specialized agencies like UNICEF to retreat from one proposal to coordinate all UN humanitarian activities under the umbrella of UNHCR. But he created a new management structure, which included the appointment of a deputy secretary general and a more cabinet system of administration in which he divided responsibilities into four primary areas: peace and security, economic and social affairs, development, and humanitarian affairs, including human rights. Even more important was his inclusive style. Unlike Boutros-Ghali, he was accessible to his senior officials and consulted widely. This was a welcome change.

The Clinton administration stated that it welcomed the reforms. Conservative members of Congress were less enthusiastic. The change from Boutros-Ghali to Annan meant little to them. In a way, the administration had only itself to blame. It had exaggerated the power of the UN bureaucracy in order to be able to blame it for such tragedies as Bosnia or Somalia, where blame more properly lay with member states. "The UN" had been roundly abused for years, so now it was hardly surprising that Congress found it so easy to deny it the funds the United States owed. Clinton was apparently unwilling to expend political capital fighting the Republican-dominated Congress on behalf of the United Nations. The legislators remained obdurate. Despite the implicit promise of the Clinton administration that the U.S. would meet its financial commitments if Boutros-Ghali were replaced, it did not. Annan made many trips to Washington, the UN's cap in his hand, and discussed the financial crisis not only with Clinton but also with Senator Jesse Helms, chairman of the Senate Foreign Relations Committee and the UN's most hostile critic in Congress. But by the fall of 1999, the U.S. was still in massive default. The United Nations was still broke. The emollience of Kofi Annan seemed at first little more successful than the irritation of Boutros-Ghali in persuading any branch of the U.S. government that it was inappropriate to demand reform of the UN and certain specific policies and yet continually refuse to meet U.S. responsibilities. The impatience in Congress with the UN for not reflecting America's unique power in the world may have been understandable but it was not wise, and it did not reflect a sensible way of demonstrating American hegemony.

***

ONE of Annan's first crises was how to deal with the dark stain of atrocity spreading, largely hidden beneath the jungle canopy, across eastern Zaire.

It was a story as macabre as any other, involving genocidal attacks against refugees some of whom were guilty of genocide themselves; mercenaries of the traditional "dogs of war" variety; the smashing of refugee encampments and the perversion of humanitarian assistance; Western businessmen with mobile telephones and an intense desire to follow the victors and fix new contracts for exploiting Zaire's diamond and copper mines; and the defeat of a dying old dictator.

All these and more were involved in a vicious game of pursuit through the steaming jungles of eastern Zaire.

"Warlords, rebel leaders and imploding governments from Bosnia to Brazzaville now manipulate aid agencies as never before," wrote John Pomfret of the *Washington Post*. They also targeted aid workers. In the old days humanitarian workers used to be relatively safe. No longer. Lionel Rosenblatt of Refugees International said that since Western powers were not prepared to send troops to conflicts which did not directly affect their national interests, "the only pieces that will be free to move on the chessboard will be the aid agency pieces." That put them at the front line—and in more danger than ever.

The first time the International Committee of the Red Cross had ever abandoned its hundred-year-old policy of never carrying arms was in Somalia, where aid workers had to hire gunslingers to protect themselves from the marauding kids on "technicals," their heavily armed trucks. In 1996, eight Red Cross workers were murdered in Chechnya. Others had been killed in Burundi so that the Red Cross would not be witness to the slow genocide there. In the Great Lakes area, twenty-six staff members from UNHCR alone were killed or had died or disappeared by 1997.

By early 1997 Laurent Kabila, the nominal leader of the rebel alliance, was marching quickly westward across Zaire at the head of what was basically a Tutsi army provided by Rwanda and Uganda and reinforced by Tutsis from eastern Zaire.

The alliance enjoyed at least the diplomatic support of the United States and other Western powers—with the notable exception of

France, which still clung to the increasingly frail person and state of Marshal Mobutu, who was in the advanced stages of cancer.

The alliance's nominal aim was to topple Mobutu's "kleptocracy." But there was a hidden agenda. One UNHCR official expressed the fear of many, that Kabila had "made a pact with the devil." In exchange for Rwandan military assistance, Kabila's alliance was cooperating with a Rwandan policy of systematic extermination of Hutu refugees, including women and children.

The refugees in question were from the Hutu camps that had been broken up by the Rwandan army at the end of 1996. They were "airbrushed from history" when the U.S. government claimed, on the basis of aerial survey, that they did not exist. Many of them may have been guilty of terrible crimes against the Tutsis during the Rwandan genocide of 1994. But many were innocent, and summary justice was now being meted out—with impunity.

In his desperate effort to halt the rebel attacks, Mobutu hired the worst kind of mercenary; in the defense of Kisangani in northeastern Zaire, Ukrainian pilots roared into the sky in Yugoslav jets, bombing whatever they could see moving. On the ground, Serbian trainers with tattoos and shaven heads and perhaps guilty of war crimes themselves, trained Zairean troops in the use of new machine guns and rocket launchers that Serbia (itself under an arms embargo) had supplied to Zaire despite the embargo on that country. Kisangani still fell. Scores of thousands of refugees were cut off, and the hunt for them began in earnest.

Obscure names like Tingi-Tingi became famous for five minutes. This was a landing strip where tens of thousands of Hutu refugees gathered in February 1997. The stench of disease, human waste, death and wood smoke mingled here as in all other such encampments. The earth was slick. Families lay helpless; heavily armed men prowled.

UNHCR flew in food and water, medical supplies and tents, but then the Zairean army co-opted humanitarian plane after humanitarian plane and sent them filled with cheap guns into Tingi-Tingi for the fleeing Hutus to use against the approaching rebel alliance.

It is impossible to exaggerate the importance of light weapons in the wars of today. They are far more deadly than tanks, warplanes and warships. Of the forty-nine conflicts which broke out between

1990 and 1997, light weapons were the only weapons used in forty-six. (The Gulf war against Saddam Hussein was the only conflict dominated by heavy weapons.)

Many of these weapons flood across the world from armaments factories in Eastern Europe, now deprived of their traditional Cold War markets. Others are detritus from the Afghanistan war, into which the CIA piled some three million AK-47 assault rifles to enable the mujahideen to resist Soviet occupation. Now the surplus killing power of these weapons has spread through Africa.

Kofi Annan called upon the Zairean army to end the militarization of Tingi-Tingi, which, he said, "is endangering the lives of innocent refugees and humanitarian workers." Zaire took no notice. But the arms flung to the Hutu refugees by Zairean troops did not stop the rebels. When the alliance soldiers arrived, they smashed Tingi-Tingi, drove the refugees, armed and unarmed, into the bush and hunted them down.

Kilian Kleinschmidt of UNHCR was searching in the jungle for refugees. He wrote later, "The dark misty forest: living zombies with big eyes and no reaction. A woman fallen into a swamp three days ago, still alive. Crying children. The dead and dying in the mud. There were some strong men and they made us feel uncomfortable; they had perhaps hunted the others [in Rwanda], but had now become the hunted themselves. Should we ask questions when assisting the dying?"

There was another way the rebels used the aid agencies: as bait. The agencies would find refugees, encourage them to emerge from the jungle—for food or repatriation—and then the rebels would either drive the foreign officials out or make conditions so unsafe that they left. They then killed the refugees.

Dianne Stewart of the UNHCR emergency team was in another jungle slum called Biaro, where refugees were huddled under makeshift shelters in the mud, desperate with starvation and fear. They begged Western aid officials to get them out. UNHCR commandeered an ancient train made up of cattle wagons tied together with rusty wire.

On one ghastly ride a hundred refugees suffocated to death in the wagons; barely living refugees stood on piles of corpses a yard high. On another occasion, as Stewart patched up the face of a young boy, "he tugged constantly on a thin cord attached to his wrist and his only remaining possession—a neatly wrapped Bible. I was amazed anyone who had lived through such an experience could still believe in anything."

Stewart helped evacuate seventeen thousand refugees on this train. Sometimes they sang and "that was really bizarre—a train of misery chugging through the forests with the most beautiful harmonized songs floating from the wagons."

Aid officials constantly had to ask themselves whether they were doing more harm than good—whether their assistance was killing more refugees than it saved. When the rebels needed to airlift troops to attack the town of Lumumbashi, they stole the fuel they required from a UNHCR depot near Goma. Kilian Kleinschmidt wrote, "The whole of eastern Zaire was an impossible mission. There were many mistakes, but I still don't know what we should have done differently, as humanitarians or human beings."

At the end of March the rebels started killing even more ferociously after a so-called ideological seminar in Shabunda. All community chiefs in the region had to take part in "cleaning the road"—sweeping away evidence of killings. "We're catching the refugees and killing them," a rebel soldier calmly told Nicholas Kristof of the *New York Times*. "Every day we kill them. They fled, so they must be bad people. So we catch them and take them back to our commander and then we kill them."

By now it was also becoming clear that among the most dedicated killers were Rwandan soldiers under the command of the Tutsi-led government of Rwanda. Those to whom genocide had been done were doing genocide in their turn.

The massacres gave aid workers another agonizing choice—how frank should they be in public? The risk of revealing what had been happening would imperil not only aid workers themselves but also their efforts to save whom they could. Filippo Grandi, who was with UNHCR in Kisangani, said, "It was my very worst moment. We were cautious with the truth. Perhaps in retrospect we could have spoken out a little more. But it was truly an impossible dilemma."

In April UNHCR went more public than before. The agency asserted that there were some 300,000 refugees missing and being hunted through Zaire; a spokesman talked of "increasingly shocking reports of atrocities."

Kofi Annan knew that it was a mistake that the multinational force led by Canada had been disbanded at the end of 1996; instead it should have been suspended and then reactivated. Now it would be very difficult to reassemble. "In the absence of the willing and the will, there is very little the UN can do in terms of putting in a force," he said.

There was no will at all. In April, Mike McCurry, the White House spokesman, declared that "Mobutuism is about to become a creature of history," thus nailing U.S. colors more publicly than ever to Kabila's alliance. Emboldened, Kabila and the Rwanda government both made personal attacks on Annan for his expressions of concern over the plight of the refugees.

In April the UN Commission on Human Rights requested an investigation into the allegations of mass killings and other gross violations of human rights. This followed a report from the UN special rapporteur on Zaire, Roberto Garreton, that the alliance had "undoubtedly" committed massacres. He named forty sites.

The commission was set up, but Kabila made it clear that he did not intend to cooperate with it. Mrs. Ogata, the high commissioner, wrote to Annan to say that representations "do not appear to have had any effect. The Alliance leadership continues to deny such gross abuses are occurring. . . . I realise that with the innocent vicims there are those not deserving of international protection. But such considerations must not be allowed to excuse inaction, still less to indirectly sanction summary killings."

The atrocities continued. Early one morning in late April about twenty Rwandan or alliance troops entered Lwiro Hospital north of Bukavu in Zaire. They seized about fifty children who were there for therapeutic feeding and flung them brutally into the back of a truck. They also took away about sixty adults, including members of the children's families and caregivers.

At Kasese at the end of April, 80,000 people were waiting for planes. None came. Every night another 200 or so people died. The rebels deliberately drove the aid workers away for a week. When they were able to return the place was empty. "Nobody. All gone," said Kleinschmidt. "The once full cholera station abandoned. Stretchers, but nobody on them. Even the smell of death had gone, the smell we had worked with all those weeks. A feeling of being manipulated as part of a buildup to something evil."

The refugees had been killed or were now being hunted through the forests, "and the best game were the women and children who had no chance to defend their lives."

Under pressure from the UN, from the EU's special envoy, Aldo Ajello, and from Bill Richardson, the U.S. ambassador to the UN, who was acting as a special envoy, Kabila gave UNHCR sixty days from May 1 to repatriate the estimated 80,000 refugees who had recently disappeared from encampments south of Kisangani. Mrs. Ogata pointed out that this was "daunting"—it meant sending home 1,200 people a day.

UNHCR worked frantically. There was no time to interview any individual—everyone was crammed into trucks and planes. In the end UNHCR and other agencies managed to save around 185,000 of the missing refugees, and about 62,000 of these were airlifted home to Rwanda in the biggest air bridge Africa has ever known. It was not a repatriation, it was an evacuation. UNHCR's normal standards of protection had to be set aside.

In early May Mobutu left Zaire for the last time, and on May 19 the rebel forces captured Kinshasa. Mobutu was now indeed a "creature of history"—but there was little reason to suppose that the creature who replaced him would be wiser.

On June 3 Annan met the new president of the Democratic Republic of the Congo, as Kabila had renamed Zaire, at an OAU meeting in Zimbabwe and tried to persuade him that it was vital for the credibility of his new regime to cooperate with the UN investigation, because both the U.S. and the European Union had conditioned aid to Congo on the success of the inquiry.

Kabila promised to do so. He then agreed with Ambassador Richardson that the UN team could start its work on July 7. The UN team of forensic scientists and others arrived in the middle of June.

But they found themselves confined to their hotel in Kinshasa, as the government threw up obstacle after obstacle to their work. First it demanded that Roberto Garreton, who had already criticized the alliance's human rights record, be removed from the team. In hopes of moving forward, Annan reluctantly did so. Annan was criticized by some human rights activists for this concession. He said later to me, "I felt the issue was not Garreton but getting to the facts and not allowing impunity to stand." His gesture did not have the desired effect. Kabila's people next insisted that whatever had happened in the last six months in Zaire could not be separated from what had happened during and since the genocide in Rwanda in 1994; that too must be investigated. There was some logic in this claim, though its intention was clearly to make sure that blame would be cast widely enough to embrace Mobutu, the French, UNHCR and the aid agencies—removing the spotlight from the behavior of the Kabila forces. This too was eventually conceded.

And so it went on all year; one reason after another was found to block the team's access to alleged massacre sites. Emma Bonino, the European Union's humanitarian affairs commissioner, said, "If nothing has been hidden you do not set up obstacles. . . . I find it intolerable the way the international community puts up with this contempt." Apart from France, it did.

Month after month went by, and it became clearer that most governments just did not want to know what had really happened in the jungles of eastern Zaire in the first half of 1997. UNHCR might say that 230,000 Hutu refugees were still unaccounted for, but the U.S. had always disputed these numbers. Now it seemed more urgent to deliver aid and forge relationships with the new regime than to examine the past, even the very recent past. There was a clear logic to this and it was certainly true that the people of Zaire needed all the assistance they could get.

Pragmatism prevailed and eventually Annan was compelled to withdraw the UN team of investigators. They had been able to do virtually nothing. It was difficult to avoid the conclusion that humanitarianism had reached its own heart of darkness in the very same jungles of which Joseph Conrad had written ninety-five years before.

9

Sunday in Baghdad

A n hour into the meeting between Kofi Annan and Saddam Hussein on Sunday, February 22, 1998, the Iraqi president stood up and said to the UN secretary general, "I think you can work out the details with Tariq."

"This was my nightmare," Annan said. Tariq was Tariq Aziz, the Iraqi deputy prime minister with whom Annan had already spent hours of negotiations. Aziz did not have the authority to make crucial decisions; only Saddam Hussein had that. Annan believed it vital that he have a one-on-one meeting with Saddam if he was to reach an agreement; now it looked as if that would not happen.

In the last hour he and Saddam had smoked cigars as they and their officials had discussed, among other matters, the relative merits of Iraqi and Algerian dates. Annan had congratulated Saddam on the reconstruction of Iraq since the Gulf war. Saddam had told him that, a few days before, he had gone out on one of his palace's balconies in order to speak to it. "You are so beautiful, palace," he said, "it would really be a great pity if you were destroyed. But if it has to happen we won't really care."

Annan said that during his stopover in Paris on the way to Baghdad he had met with President Chirac, who had sent his greetings to President Hussein and expressed great esteem for Iraq. Saddam said he admired Chirac for his insight and knowledge.

Saddam had taken Annan through a litany of complaints about the way in which the world had treated Iraq. He spoke of the humanitarian problems created by the economic sanctions imposed by the UN and still in force because Iraq was not deemed to have disarmed as required after the Gulf war. He complained of the intrusion of the UN inspectors' pursuit of banned weapons. Iraq's dignity and sovereignty had to be respected, he said. He had been mild if not affable. But he had come nowhere near to agreeing to the continued inspections that Annan had come to Iraq to seek. To have any hope of getting such an agreement, Annan knew he had to see him alone. Otherwise, he would leave Baghdad empty-handed, his own authority and that of the UN diminished if not destroyed. With the failure of diplomacy, the United States and Britain would start bombing Iraq, with consequences unknown.

Everyone stood: Tariq Aziz, the other Iraqi officials, the Iraqi interpreter and the senior UN officials accompanying Annan.

"I was a bit baffled," he said later. "I was about to ask Tariq, 'What's happening?' " But then the interpreter said to Annan, "You are to stay." Much relieved, he sat down while the others filed out of the room. He was at last left alone with Saddam and the interpreter. Saddam offered Annan another cigar. The wrapping was coming off the one Annan picked. Saddam said: "Why don't you take a fresh one." Annan did. The most important and difficult moment of his career had now arrived.

It was an extraordinary encounter. On the one side Kofi Annan, a career international civil servant who was one year into his term as secretary general of the United Nations. A Ghanaian Christian who, in a few short months, had captured international attention with his mild yet dignified manner. Annan was the world's secular pope, the repository of hope and the representative of such civilized standards of international behavior as we have been able to devise.

On the other Saddam, almost a comic book dictator who had forced his way into power by murder and maintained himself there by murder, who ran a regime of terror at home and as far abroad as he was able, who had invaded his neighbors and used poison gas against Iraq's own citizens. For the past seven years he had attempted to manufacture and conceal outlawed weapons of mass destruction—nuclear, chemical, biological—and the missiles to deliver them, in defiance of international law and innumerable United Nations resolutions. After his daughters' husbands defected to Jordan and revealed details of these programs, he lured them back to Iraq and had them murdered.

The issues which Annan and Saddam had to discuss lay at almost every level of understanding, of law, of politics and of morality. They touched on sovereignty, on the threat of U.S. "hegemony" and on the ability of the world, or at least the international community, to protect itself by force against those who openly flouted its rules and threatened its safety. The story of the United Nations and Iraq is the story of the most extreme intrusion in the affairs of a member state that the UN is ever likely to make. It shows both the successes and the limits of intervention.

IRAQ began to try to create a biological weapons program back in the 1970s—after it had signed the 1972 international convention banning the development and production of such weapons. Biological weapons are often called the poor man's atomic bomb; they provide a way of killing millions of people far more easily and cheaply than nuclear weapons, and in the most repulsive manner. Anthrax, which Iraq now admits to having developed and produced on a massive scale (more than eight tons), is fatal in only a tiny dose. When it enters the body it virtually dissolves the kidneys, liver and lungs, and victims die over days in agony.

Throughout the eighties Iraq developed its biological and chemical stockpiles. The original intention was to use them perhaps against Israel and certainly against Iran, with whom it fought a vicious war through much of the eighties, and the Kurds of northern Iraq, always attempting to push for autonomy.

Iraq later acknowledged that it had used 101,000 chemical warfare munitions in the course of the war with Iran. In March 1988 Saddam Hussein's troops attacked the Kurdish town of Halabja in revenge for what he considered Kurdish collaboration with his Iranian enemy. After Iraqi troops had withdrawn, Iranian Revolutionary Guards entered Halabja and found the streets filled with corpses. Whole families still lay where they had fallen; they had been gassed with hydrogen cyanide. At least five thousand people were killed and another seven thousand were dreadfully injured. Saddam made no attempt to hide his culpability. Halabja will live as the name of the first place where a government gassed its own people.

The UN Special Commission, UNSCOM, was set up by Security Council Resolution 687 just weeks after Iraq was defeated in the Gulf war in February 1991. The resolution was intended both to punish Iraq for its invasion of Kuwait and to deprive it of the power to threaten its neighbors and the world again. It decreed that Iraq must unconditionally accept, under international supervision, the destruction, removal or rendering harmless of its weapons of mass destruction and of ballistic missiles with a range of over 150 kilometers (approximately 100 miles), as well as their production facilities. The resolution also specified a monitoring system within Iraq, to see that the country did not just reacquire such weapons. Until this was certifiably done, and until UNSCOM declared that it had been done, an oil embargo against the country would remain in place.

UNSCOM was an unprecedented agency with an extraordinary, powerful mandate. Disarmament had long been a ritual (and largely ineffective) call sign of the UN, but never before had there been a UN body which was *empowered* to disarm. After the Second World War, Germany was disarmed by the occupying powers.

In the jaws of defeat, Iraq went through the motions of compliance. It formally accepted Resolution 687, and in an exchange of letters agreed that the UNSCOM inspectors would have total freedom of entry and access in Iraq. The inspectors were a mix of Sherlock Holmes and Indiana Jones, men and women from forty different countries around the world—biologists, diplomats, physicists, chemists—who through most of the nineties showed themselves capable of analysis, courage, luck and sheer persistence.

Their story involved truck and helicopter chases across the deserts, searches in riverbeds and in tunnels for warheads fitted with deadly germs, in ministries and universities for missing files or even just stray documents that could give clues to the production of weapons; trawls through the archives of cooperating companies around the world that had sold goods to Iraq when it was still legal, before Saddam Hussein invaded Kuwait in 1990.

At first the Iraqis threw UNSCOM a few bones. They declared that they had about fifty Scud missiles, twelve mobile launchers and some eleven thousand chemical munitions. They also admitted to a chemical factory that had been bombed during the war. But the munitions they produced were mostly at the end of their shelf life and the rocket motors surrendered were too dangerous to be fired. In effect, they offered up defunct stock.

More important, they promised that they had no biological weapons program whatsoever, nor any nuclear weapons program. Since then UNSCOM and the International Atomic Energy Agency (IAEA) had discovered that both these assertions were untrue and that Iraq's chemical weapons and missiles were far more numerous and technologically advanced than the regime declared.

The Iraqis, or some of them, appear to have believed that UNSCOM would be a typical UN paper tiger, rather like the IAEA itself, which, on its routine inspections before the war, had failed to discover Iraq's nuclear weapons program. The Iraqis, said Tim Trevan, a former British political adviser to UNSCOM, "had expected a cup of tea and a naive chat. They thought it would all be over in forty days. As for the West, we saw them as a defeated nation so desperate to sell their oil and rebuild that they would hand over everything as fast as they could." Both sides were wrong.

Saddam Hussein has said, "Victory is ensuring your enemy does not get what he wants." Saddam's view of the outcome of the Gulf war was very different from that of the allies ranged against him. He had been defeated on the battlefield, but he was still in power—one victory. The enemy now wanted all his weapons of mass destruction—hide them, deny them, and that would be another victory.

The Iraqis certainly did not anticipate the kind of interrogation and skepticism to which UNSCOM inspectors subjected them. They did not expect the searches to go beyond weapons to production facilities, let alone to documents. But that was what happened. And because of Iraqi intransigence, it did not end.

UNSCOM's first executive chairman was Rolf Ekeus, a quiet but persistent Swedish diplomat. Most of his polyglot staff worked out of cramped offices, piled high with padlocked filing cabinets, on the thirtieth floor of the United Nations building. Here a team of about forty analysts, some of them with backgrounds in their own national intelligence agencies, some of them scientists, pored over documents seized by their colleagues in Iraq and tried to follow the paper trails around the world and through Iraq itself. Analysis, inspection, analysis, inspection was the pattern of UNSCOM's work throughout the mid-nineties.

In Iraq, the inspectors encountered an unpredictable mix of businesslike efficiency and obstruction. In June 1991 the nuclear inspectors tried to intercept Iraqi vehicles carrying calutrons, vital parts of nuclear weapon production. Iraqi soldiers fired warning shots to deter the inspectors. But the calutrons were later seized and destroyed. This first standoff led to Security Council Resolution 707, which explicitly allowed the use of high-altitude reconnaissance aircraft, American U-2s. Together, resolutions and exchanges of letters gave UNSCOM almost total rights of access, surveillance and investigation throughout Iraq. And Iraq had no right of possession over anything related to weapons systems, or documents about them.

After Resolution 707 the inspectors demanded to be able to use their own helicopters. The Iraqis resisted, but eventually Ekeus got what he wanted. This gave UNSCOM more advantage of surprise, though the area of operation had to be fixed in advance. The inspectors would swoop out of the desert sky into sites suspected of producing prohibited weapons, giving officials less time to conceal or destroy evidence. On one of the first helicopter flights across the desert into the western zone, UNSCOM found fifty Scud launch sites in various stages of construction. None had been declared. All were destroyed.

In September 1991 the inspectors found a large cache of documents which described Iraqi attempts to acquire nuclear weapons. There was one document in particular, a progress report, which the Iraqis seized back. The inspectors, led by an American, David Kay, refused to give up the rest. After four days in the parking lot, where the Iraqis detained them, they were allowed to leave, but the crucial progress report was not returned.

And so it went on.

Despite Iraqi obstruction, UNSCOM had considerable success. In the next six years it destroyed (or verified the destruction of), removed or rendered harmless a formidable array of weapons. These included:

- An assembled supergun, components for four other such guns and one ton of propellant;

- Over 133 Scud missiles, 6 mobile Scud launchers, 30 chemical warheads for Scud variants, 28 Al-Hussein Scud fixed launch pads, 32 other launch pads, a variety of long-range missile production equipment including decoy missiles, decoy vehicles, SS-21 guidance and control sets, and more than 200 imported guidance and control components.

In chemical weaponry UNSCOM inspectors found and destroyed some 38,000 filled and empty chemical munitions, which included eight types of munitions from rockets to artillery shells, bombs and ballistic missile warheads; 690 tons of chemical weapons agents; more than 3,000 tons of precursor chemicals for the production of chemical warfare agents; 426 pieces of chemical weapons production equipment and 90 pieces of related analytical instruments.

Thus UNSCOM destroyed more Iraqi weapons than the alliance managed to eliminate by bombing in the Gulf war. But it was not enough. Their mandate was to eliminate all Iraq's proscribed weapons of mass destruction. Their least successful program had been in tracing arguably the most dangerous weapons—biological.

In July 1995, the Iraqis finally admitted to a biological weapons program. But it was tiny and, they claimed, never weaponized. They also warned the Security Council that unless sanctions and the oil embargo were lifted, they would end all cooperation with UNSCOM. Less than three weeks later an astonishing thing happened: General Hussein Kamel, Saddam's son-in-law and the minister of industry and the former director of Iraq's Military Industrialization Corporation, arrived in Jordan and said he wanted to defect. He began to tell Western intelligence officials and UNSCOM inspectors what he knew.

In Baghdad, Iraqi officials immediately changed their tune. They withdrew the third "Full, Final and Complete Disclosure" they had made of their biological weapons program, and admitted they had done far more than they had claimed. They did weaponize some 166 biological bombs and 25 missile warheads after all, they said.

How did they explain this about-face? They said that they had been in ignorance of it themselves because Hussein Kamel had concealed it. When Ekeus next went to Baghdad, officials took him to a chicken farm outside the city. The farm belonged to Hussein, they said, and they had just found hidden on it a huge cache of documents they had thought destroyed. They handed over 680,000 pages of printed documents, as well as computer discs, videotapes, microfilms and microfiches which, printed out, amounted to another million pages.

Subsequently, Tariq Aziz told Richard Butler that Hussein Kamel was an "idiot," which may in one sense be correct—Kamel subsequently returned to Iraq, where he and his brother-in-law were promptly murdered on Saddam's orders. Thereafter, the cat-and-mouse game between the inspectors and the regime continued ever more fiercely, with the Iraqis raising the ante and continually exploiting French and Russian desires for an end to the stalemate.

In May 1996, UNSCOM destroyed the Al-Hakam biological warfare center. The next month, Iraq began to bite back. It denied UNSCOM access to certain sites, claiming that they were "sensitive," for reasons of sovereignty or security. As a result the Security Council adopted Resolution 1060 condemning Iraq's actions as a clear violation of the council's provisions and demanding full access. Ekeus then visited Baghdad, at the behest of the Security Council, to resolve the problem of access to all sites. He did so, but he also agreed to new modalities for the inspection of so-called sensitive sites in order to take account of Iraq's "legitimate security concerns." The new modalities included limits on the number of inspectors, on the taking of photographs and on helicopter overflights of the so-called sensitive site under inspection. Ekeus argued that limited access was better than nothing, but some of his inspectors felt that he was ill advised to give away rights that the Security Council had invested in UNSCOM. If he had expected the agreement to be kept secret, he was disappointed; the Iraqis immediately informed the French, the Chinese and the Russians, their principal supporters on the council. Allowing the notion of "sensitive sites" was a crucial concession that Iraq frequently exploited thereafter.

That month Iraq presented more reports purporting to be "Full, Final and Complete Disclosure" of its prohibited biological, chemical and missile programs. This was the fourth such "complete disclosure" of biological weapons, the third for chemical weapons and the third for missiles. In no case was the disclosure full or final or complete.

In June 1997, Iraq threatened the safety of UNSCOM's helicopter crews and banned inspectors from certain sites. Another condemnatory resolution (1115) came from the council. In September, while seeking access to a site declared by Iraq to be "sensitive," UNSCOM inspectors filmed the movement of files, burning of documents and dumping of ash-filled cans in a nearby river.

Rolf Ekeus resigned and was succeeded in mid-1997 by Richard Butler, a strong-minded Australian diplomat with long experience in arms control. I had known Butler in Indochina as an outspoken and effective Australian ambassador. He brought a very different style to UNSCOM. Ekeus was an accomplished pianist and he played the Security Council like an étude. Butler marched to an insistent drum. He came to believe that Saddam Hussein was a monster and his spokesman Aziz a liar, and often he did not try to conceal this behind the diplomatic niceties that UN officials are wont to employ. He would say that in the twentieth century every civilization had thrown up a monster. The land of Schiller and Beethoven had produced Hitler, Russia Stalin, Asia Mao and Pol Pot, Africa Idi Amin—and now the Middle East had produced Saddam Hussein. He wrote later that the Iraqi leaders, in their green uniforms garnished with "pompous insignia," reminded him of the Nazis.

The Iraqis and their allies on the council did not appreciate such forthright views. But by the time Butler began his assignment, they had had enough of UNSCOM anyway. By now UNSCOM had completed its fifty-sixth biological weapons inspection, its sixty-first missile inspection and its forty-second chemical inspection. The inspectors were fairly confident that they had cleaned Iraq of most of its missiles (though not of its missile propellants or its indigenous production capabilities) and chemical weapons (barring the deadly nerve agent VX), but they were certain that Iraq had not come anywhere near clean on its biological weapons program. "Now we're into the hard yards," Butler said to me, "which is finding the bits that remain and then keeping them under indefinite monitoring. They're the bits they don't want us to be able to do. This massive intervention was tolerated for five years or so, but they've reached the point where they just don't want it anymore."

Butler thought UNSCOM had an importance far beyond Iraq: it was an integral part of a thirty-year struggle by the international community to create a tapestry of treaties to prevent the proliferation of weapons of mass destruction. At the same time a moral consensus had to be and largely was built that the use of nuclear, chemical and biological weapons was wrong. Saddam Hussein was one of the few dictators to defy that consensus in deed, particularly with regard to chemical weapons. "There's no one in history more prepared to use chemical weapons at home or abroad," said Butler. "For him chemical warfare is as normal as crowd control."

By the second half of 1997 the Iraqi regime had decided to go fully on the offensive against UNSCOM. In September it claimed a new kind of site—"presidential sites"—which it said were out of bounds to UNSCOM inspectors. Some of these were said to be "palaces" belonging to or occupied by Saddam Hussein. It was true that he had spent inordinate millions on building such structures while the country starved in the years since the Gulf war, but UN-SCOM knew that at least some of these eight new so-called presidential sites had more than residential or office uses.

Iraq received a clear signal that now was a good moment to press the edge of the envelope. On October 13, five members of the Security Council—Russia, China and France were joined by Egypt and Kenya—abstained rather than voting to accept Butler's first report. This dealt with Iraq's record of cooperation on access, and the imposition of a travel ban that was to have been put on those Iraqi officials responsible for blocking UNSCOM. Since the end of the Gulf war, the council had never been so split. This was the best vote Iraq had ever had.

Iraq began to press three lines of attack more vigorously than ever. The first was to ridicule and discredit—UNSCOM were cowboys, CIA agents, Zionists led by a "mad dog," Butler, who was in the pay of the Americans. The second device was to widen the base of political support for Iraq. The third was to provoke a military attack, which they were convinced they would survive and win, in the sense that their enemy would not get what he wanted.

It was the second line of attack—the political and diplomatic line—which was the most insidious and in a way the most depressing. By now any kind of unity on the Security Council was long gone; the French, Russians and Chinese were all tired of UNSCOM and wanted the oil embargo and sanctions lifted. There were sound reasons for disliking sanctions. It was true, of course, that over the last seven years sanctions had damaged above all ordinary Iraqi people, in particular the most vulnerable including children, and not their leaders. The continued intransigence of Saddam Hussein was

the strongest argument that sanctions do not impose changes on recalcitrant regimes.

For the Chinese the underlying issue was, as always, Tibet. They
never supported intervention. For France there was the promise of
commerce, particularly for French oil companies, once sanctions
were lifted, as well as an issue on which to oppose the United States
and its Anglo-Saxon ally, Britain. For the Russians there was the $8
billion which Iraq owed them and which could never be repaid until
sanctions were lifted. Iraq was traditionally part of the Russian
sphere of influence. Russia also saw the crisis as a way of reasserting
itself on the world stage and of diminishing the role of its rival, the
one remaining superpower. On that issue all three were united: none
liked the unipolar world dominated by the overwhelming power of
the United States.

The crisis that came to dominate Kofi Annan began in earnest at
the end of fall 1997. It may have been caused by the fact that UN-
SCOM was closing in on the last secret caches of biological weapons.
In late October, Tariq Aziz wrote to the Security Council demanding
that all American inspectors of UNSCOM leave Iraq within a week.
There were six Americans on the team in Iraq at that time. The
council condemned this breach of its resolutions, but the Iraqis ordered the Americans out nonetheless; simultaneously, Butler responded by withdrawing almost all the UNSCOM staff. One out, all
out. Annan and his senior officials thought he did this precipitously
and without adequate consultation. Annan thought it would be better to leave the bulk of the inspectors in place and to negotiate for
the return of the Americans. Butler disagreed; he argued that the
Americans had irreplaceable skills and that Iraq should not be allowed to dictate the composition of UNSCOM's teams.

U.S. air strikes loomed.

In early December, Iraq appeared to back down and allowed all
UNSCOM personnel, of whatever nationality, to come back. But
Aziz told Butler that from now on the new category of presidential
and sovereign sites would be absolutely off-limits forever. One such
presidential area contained hundreds of buildings in the downtown
Al Kark district of Baghdad. Altogether, the Iraqis were creating siz-
able sanctuaries free from inspection. Both Butler and the Security
Council refused to accept this new restriction. Married to it was a

new concept which the Iraqis demanded had to be respected. They already often invoked their national sovereignty and their national security; now there was also their "national dignity."

Tariq Aziz attempted to personalize the issue in order to deflect attention from the real problem—Iraq's continued programs of weapons of mass destruction. He said all that was needed was for Kofi Annan to remove Richard Butler. "After seven years of sanctions you get desperate . . . another wave of missiles makes no difference to the Iraqi people or the Iraqi government."

Annan thought military intervention was a bad idea and proposed to send a team to Iraq to ask them to lift the ban on access to presidential and sovereign sites. The British were cautious about this idea. The French and the Russians were more enthusiastic. The Americans were not happy. Clinton called Annan both to say that he was upset by the failure of Congress to pay U.S. arrears to the UN and to insist that the Iraqi regime must not be allowed the opportunity to rebuild its weapons of mass destruction.

Next Madeleine Albright called Annan to express U.S. concern about Butler's ability to work without any political pressure. It would be a disaster if the composition of UNSCOM's inspector teams was to change now, since it would look as if a deal had been struck with Iraq, she said. Annan agreed. Albright said the Russians did not like Butler, but the U.S. thought he was doing "an excellent job."

Annan did send his team to Baghdad; it achieved little. The crisis continued to develop. The Russians and the French sent in envoys. The Iraqis told the Russians they would open the palaces for a one-time inspection, by diplomats, not UNSCOM, and then they did not want to see anybody near the palaces again. The Arab League sent a delegation to Baghdad. The Turkish foreign minister told Annan that he was going to Baghdad as "a neighborhood initiative." He told Annan that it reflected Turkish concern about the threat to the region posed by Iraq's weapons of mass destruction. The Islamic Conference made efforts. Nothing was resolved. No one came up with a plan acceptable to Washington. The Russian position was colored by a fierce debate in the Duma, the lower chamber of the parliament, and in the media over how far the United States would and should go. What would happen if U.S. force against Iraq led Baghdad to attack Israel and the United States retaliated? Would the conflict become nuclear?

★ ★ ★

B y early 1998, U.S. and British warships were gathering in force in the Gulf. The round of talks between Richard Butler and Tariq Aziz in January was bitter. Aziz and other Iraqi delegates made long statements which the inspectors knew were totally untrue; they were personally abusive, and they put the entire blame on the UN for the fact that, seven years after the Gulf war, no end to the inspection regime was in sight.

Aziz claimed that Iraq had divested itself long ago of all its prohibited weapons. He insisted that Iraq "possesses no weapons of mass destruction, no major components, nor was it seeking to produce proscribed weapons." If the UN did not accept this assurance and if sanctions were not lifted, then "The Government of Iraq has no intention of continuing to work with the Commission. Iraq was ready to face the consequences, including war. The Executive Chairman should report this to the Security Council."

Butler wrote to the president of the Security Council that the Iraqi attitude was "disturbing and disappointing." He cited "specific grave instances" of Iraqi attempts to mislead the commission and the council. And he warned that Iraq was clearly "determined to withhold any further or new information from the Commission" and had refused the Security Council's demand for unconditional access in Iraq, as it was bound by international law to provide.

The issue remained access, without sanctuaries or special procedures, to the so-called palaces or presidential sites.

The United States continued to build up its forces in the Gulf and Annan came under increasing pressure—from around the world and from within himself—to act to try to still them. The pope asked him to go to Baghdad; so did John Cardinal O'Connor of New York during a service at St. Patrick's Cathedral in which Annan was himself participating. More pressure to act came from his own humanitarian workers in Baghdad. Denis Halliday, the head of the humanitarian team there, was concerned that military action might kill thousands and create tens of thousands of refugees.

There was a sharp and important cleavage between UNSCOM and the rest of the UN personnel in Baghdad; the humanitarians, traditional UN workers, loathed the aggressive attitude of UNSCOM. The humanitarians tended to call UNSCOM "cowboys," as the Iraqis did.

UNSCOM staff in turn mocked the humanitarians as "bunny huggers." This culture clash existed not just in the UN office in Baghdad, but also at headquarters in New York. UNSCOM inspectors, led by Butler, saw the resolutions under which they were acting as tablets of stone, international laws that must be enforced. Many senior UN officials, including some of those around Annan on the thirty-eighth floor, saw UNSCOM as a bunch of zealots who were too close to the Americans, whose activities were out of normal UN control and who were an infuriating obstacle to bringing Iraq back into the international fold. For their part, the inspectors eight floors below the secretary general and his staff felt that their extraordinary achievements in disarming Iraq were scorned by the "wet" diplomats above them, who were more interested in acquiescing to Iraq and its Russian, Chinese and French supporters in the council than in disarming a monstrously dangerous regime, as the council had originally demanded. This clash of views was fundamental and damaging.

On February 3, Annan pressed Aziz on the need for inspection of the presidential and sovereign sites. Aziz said inspection per se was acceptable, but Iraq's dignity must be preserved, not placed under continual assault by UNSCOM. The government was unable to work in presidential sites and ministry buildings under continual inspection.

The Russians then proposed that Annan establish a special group for surveying the eight presidential sites, to be headed by an eminent political figure. They proposed that inspections be conducted "without a pause," which meant just one-time visits, as opposed to the right to further inspections as required by the United States. On February 4, Boris Yeltsin said Clinton's actions could lead to a world war. "He's acting too loudly," he said. "One should be careful with such weapons. One can't say, 'Send the planes against them, bomb them.' "

Annan stayed in touch with all the governments that had sent envoys to Iraq. A message came from Yasser Arafat that Saddam definitely wanted a way out. Annan still saw his role as holding himself in reserve. "But if I had to intervene I had to know what was going on," he said. He thought he had to figure out how to get Security Council members into a process; because they were not engaged, they were not communicating. They all had different ideas on how to solve the crisis. The Russian and French proposals were not acceptable to the others.

On February 6, Annan told the Security Council he was ready to intervene. "I didn't want a mandate," he said. "I didn't want a message. I just wanted to have a broader understanding of what would constitute a settlement. If I had that, then I knew that at least my side was united. You don't go into battle with a divided side." He recalled he said: "We don't seem to be going anywhere, and I'm prepared to go to Baghdad," but he would want to have a common understanding among the council. "Without that, I don't think it would be appropriate for me to leave New York."

He produced a piece of paper intended to provoke ideas as to what could be the basis for a settlement. It cited free and unfettered access, and respect for Security Council resolutions. For the palaces it proposed a special regime, and a special group, called UNSCOM Plus—plus diplomats. It suggested that it might be necessary to treat the presidential palaces separately—to give them "a sort of, as it were, white glove inspection"—while everywhere else got the regular UNSCOM inspections. This, he thought, would respond to the questions the Iraqis had raised about their dignity. The whole approach was to remain firm in substance but flexible in form.

Annan's plan pleased the French and the Russians and many other members of the council, but alarmed the U.S. government. Bill Richardson, the U.S. representative to the UN who had been traveling the world trying to get support for the U.S. position against Iraq, said he hoped Annan would not go without the agreement of the permanent five. Albright called and said the United States was trying to find a coordinated position with other members of the Security Council. "We're trying but we're not exactly together." Annan assured her that he would not visit Baghdad until a solution was closer.

Albright said that one-time visits to the palaces would not be acceptable. Annan agreed. Albright stated she was not prepared to trust any document signed by Saddam Hussein; his actions had traumatized the world.

Annan said he was not seeking to diminish the authority or integrity of UNSCOM, but was exploring ways of getting the Iraqis to back down. It was essential to persuade them to respect council resolutions and to focus on disarmament. There had been progress. Iraq was no longer rejecting all access to the presidential sites. Albright said the bottom line was that a phony deal was unacceptable; the United States was trying hard to come up with a position.

Annan kept up the pressure. He insisted on sending a team to Iraq to map the disputed palaces. Albright told him she feared it was accommodating Iraq. Annan said he did not think so. The main aim was to sit with the Iraqi authorities and get them to provide maps, since the actual size of the presidential sites was in dispute. He was calling the Iraqi bluff. He was prepared to make the supply of maps a precondition if he was to undertake a trip to Baghdad. He confirmed that UNSCOM officials would be included in the team. "Okay," Albright replied. "Slow down, we can't work at your pace."

Iraq had led UNSCOM to believe that the total size of the "presidential areas" was some twenty-seven square miles. The Iraqis showed the mapping team areas totaling some twelve square miles. This meant that a smaller area would be excluded from the regular inspections, but it was still the equivalent of everything from Central Park to Battery Park in Manhattan. And the real issue was not the size and shape of the areas, but the need for "any time, any place" inspections, with no special treatment—as the resolutions required.

On February 13, Albright said she hoped that Annan would not travel to Baghdad before the permanent five had reached agreement on the approach. The secretary general responded that if agreement was not forthcoming that day, he would suggest another meeting on February 16. "I can assure you, you won't have an agreement today," said Albright.

Madeleine Albright also asked him a key question: "Would you go if we don't want you to go?"

Yes, replied Annan. "Do you realize what you're saying, if you say the SG [secretary general] should not go? I have a constitutional right to do this. Besides, do you know what it says about the organization or the secretary general's role? And do you realize what it's saying about your role? You're telling the whole world that you're seeking a diplomatic solution, but you say the SG shouldn't even try. How are you credible?"

Annan devised a system of rolling meetings with the permanent five. Each time he failed to reach an agreement, he fixed another meeting, hoping to create a dynamic. It seemed to work.

On Sunday, February 15, Madeleine Albright and Annan met for lunch at his home on Sutton Place. She read from a note stating what the U.S. problems were and she proposed the idea of "red lines"— lines over which Annan should not cross in any talks with Iraq. They included unfettered access to the palaces, which were to be open not just once but for reinspection, without time limits. "We should reserve the right to go back, and we should be able to go anywhere," Albright read.

Annan said afterwards that he was not trying to put pressure on the United States as such. "What I wanted was to get a common position with the permanent five. The U.S. was difficult to bring on board, but at the same time it didn't want to be isolated. I knew that, so that it was something I could play, at one stage making it clear that I have my role as SG, so I would go whether the five agreed or not.

"There was lots of pressure for me to jump on the plane and go— from the Russians, the French, the nonaligned, the pope. But I was determined not to go until I had all the elements in place."

The administration's rhetoric continued to be fierce. National Security Adviser Sandy Berger described Saddam's "reckless pursuit of weapons of mass destruction" as "one of the most dangerous security threats our people will face over the next generation." Clinton warned that if the world did not stop Saddam now, "he will conclude that the international community has lost its will. He will then conclude he can go right on and do more to rebuild an arsenal of devastating destruction. And someday, some way, I guarantee you, he will use that arsenal." Such warnings apparently did not convince all sections of the American public. The day after Clinton spoke, a bad-tempered crowd at Ohio State University jeered Albright, Berger and William Cohen live on CNN as they tried to explain U.S. policies toward Iraq. It was an unnerving moment and a public relations disaster; it led some administration officials to think that Annan's trip might be a better idea than they had originally believed. It could provide Washington with an escape route.

The last of Annan's meetings with the permanent five took place on the evening of Monday, February 16. The British ambassador to the UN, Sir John Weston, took the lead in this meeting. He had played a crucial and skilled role in the last fortnight, bridging gaps between members and in particular persuading Washington that enough common ground existed for them to unite with the other permanent members of the Security Council behind Annan's visit. He had now taken over the red lines.

Weston told his colleagues, including the Americans, "When we go in to see Kofi, I'm going to read out what I shall describe to him as the British speaking notes, following permanent five discussions. I'm going to tell him that I'm confident that none of you are going to disagree with this as he listens to it. You are not precluded from having your own say afterwards, but basically, the deal is, you're not going to disagree with me reading this out to Kofi as the agreed P5 advice."

The Americans said that so long as there was no piece of paper handed over the table, which would leak, they could live with this.

Weston replied that he would not hand a piece of paper over the table, but he would ensure that Annan "has a copy of this in his back pocket when he goes to Baghdad, so he's not in danger of forgetting."

That Monday evening, that was what happened. Weston set out the areas on which consensus had been achieved and the limit of concessions that the council would allow. The "red lines" stated that the inspections had to remain in the hands of the professionals, and the executive chairman, Richard Butler, had to have full operational control of the inspections, choosing the where, when and how. And all reporting and evaluation was to remain under Butler's control. The last sentence in Weston's statement said that any agreement that Annan brought back from Baghdad would be subject to the approval of the council in a new resolution, which would stipulate that any violation by Iraq of its commitments would have the severest consequences.

The Russians and the French agreed. The Russian ambassador, Sergei Lavrov, said, "If the Iraqis fuck this up and really violate it, that will mean a radical change in the Security Council."

Annan had something akin to marching orders, though he did not like to think of them as that. He now felt he could respond to the worldwide pressure and go. The permanent five had given him a workable formula to resolve the crisis. He had the support of the full council. He was going not as a messenger of the permanent five but as the secretary general elected by all 185 states. He thought he had carved out his own space. And he had assurances that he would be received well in Iraq.

The next day, February 17, Clinton called Annan to say, "I want a diplomatic solution as much as you, but it must be principled, have integrity." Complete access should be granted to UNSCOM and the integrity of the inspections process should be preserved. Annan agreed one had to be firm with Saddam Hussein.

"The whole world is running to satisfy this man," Clinton said.

"People have been asking what they could do to please someone who did not follow UN resolutions." He made a veiled warning to Annan. If UNSCOM and Butler were now weakened and the influence of the Security Council undermined, the effect in Washington would be almost incalculable, not just for Iraq but for U.S. relations with the UN. In other words, Annan could kiss goodbye to any hopes he had of getting America's back dues paid.

Clinton told him he should be putting pressure on Saddam Hussein, not the United States. He should not reduce the authority of UNSCOM, the Security Council or the secretary general. Saddam Hussein should not be given the impression that he had won a big victory. Clinton wanted to be sure where the secretary general stood. Annan replied he knew what the U.S. wanted from him, and he knew what to demand from President Hussein.

Annan had told the Iraqis he was coming for two days only; he would arrive on Friday, February 20, and leave on Sunday. On Thursday he flew to Paris on the Air France Concorde. That evening, President Chirac told him he was not sure Saddam was getting the full story. He was probably being told that the U.S. bombing could be stopped by other countries. Not only would they not be able to stop it, they would all join the consensus, once the U.S. had started to bomb.

Annan said he would make sure he told Saddam this. Chirac was concerned lest Iraq break up. He said that Iraq was a big and important country in the region—it had water, oil and twenty-two million people. One had to be careful not to decimate it. But a French envoy who had just returned from Baghdad said Tariq Aziz still would not agree to keeping the palaces open for more than one inspection.

The French warned Annan not to underestimate Saddam. They said Saddam was very reflective, poised and well informed, and he listened well. They told Annan that his meeting would be long because Saddam spoke slowly and with pauses. "Do not try to fill the gap, but engage him with eye contact."

On Friday morning Annan and his entourage flew to Baghdad in Chirac's presidential Falcon 900. When he landed he was surprised by the mob of reporters at the airport. He spoke with emotion of his "sacred duty" to come here to try to find a solution. He told me later that this striking phrase came to him spontaneously.

Next morning he met Aziz and gave him a draft memorandum of

understanding, along the lines he wanted to sign with Saddam. He told him of the red lines the permanent five had given him. Aziz replied, "Yes, we also have some red lines." These included the insistence that one-time inspections were all that was allowed. Annan saw right away that there was still a conflict.

All Saturday was taken up with arguments over the wording of a draft memorandum for Annan and Iraq to sign. The preamble to paragraph 4, dealing with the inspections, was a big problem. Aziz insisted that "inspection" was insulting to Iraq. He asked for the word "visit" instead.

Annan said, "You can't have 'visit.' People will wonder if we're coming for tea. That's a very weak word."

The talks continued, fruitlessly, all day Saturday. By 2 a.m. on Sunday there was still no agreement. The Iraqis would not commit to return inspections, or to removing the deadline, and they still wanted the word "visit." "This was for me a no-no. So we put everything in brackets," said Annan, who insisted on going to bed. Aziz suggested another meeting before Annan was due to meet with Saddam at midday. Annan said no. Next morning he ordered his staff to prepare two press releases—one announcing success, the other failure—and went to meet Saddam in a car sent by Saddam's own security detail.

Annan had no idea of where he was being taken. Saddam's whereabouts were always secret. The destination could have been in the desert or in a completely different part of the country. In fact it was near the villa in which he was staying, in one of the new palaces Saddam had built since the end of the Gulf war.

Annan carried a list of "talking points" prepared by his staff. They suggested he remind Saddam Hussein of the difficulties he had had in making this trip possible. He had come not as a messenger of anyone, but as the secretary general of the United Nations, "fully conscious of my moral and legal responsibility to help avoid tragedy."

When he returned to New York he had to report to the Security Council. "And I'll be faced with questions on practically every word and every comma of our agreement," his talking points advised him to say. "I appeal to your statesmanship, your courage, your wisdom and your vision to clear the remaining hurdles and enable me to go back to the UN HQ with an agreement that opens the way to the creation of those conditions that will allow Iraq to return to normality."

At that point his talking points suggested: "Listen to the president's reaction, which will probably focus on injustices perceived by Iraq, and may take a defiant line. Then resume: 'I understand your concerns about the situation you face, but our discussions over the last 2 days demonstrate that Iraq is now fully aware of what is at stake. The differences between us can be bridged.' "

THERE were guards everywhere. Some were in military garb and some were dressed like Swiss Guards in brightly colored uniforms with helmets. They held spears crossed archway fashion for Annan and his party to walk through.

Saddam greeted them, wearing what Annan described as an elegant double-breasted blue suit with matching tie. Annan was glad that Saddam was not, as often, in military dress.

When they began their tête-à-tête, Saddam said it was time sanctions were lifted. Annan said he could understand, but he told Saddam, "Basically it's in your hands. If you cooperate, then you will see light at the end of the tunnel. If we don't come to an agreement, the U.S. will use force and nobody can stop them. There are governments who say they support you, but they will not be able to stop the U.S."

Annan flattered Saddam. "You're a builder, you built modern Iraq. It was destroyed once. You've rebuilt it. Do you want to destroy it again? Look how you talk about the suffering of your people. It's in your hands, we can do something about this. If we can work out an agreement that will prevent military action and you would undertake to comply, it will save the day."

Annan went on to say that he had had many messages encouraging him to do what he could, from the pope among others. He repeated his words on arrival: "I feel I have a sacred duty to do whatever I can to avoid the bloodshed and tragedy, and you have to help me make that possible."

Annan recalled later that Hussein listened, then brought out his yellow pad and started making notes. This meant Annan could not speak eyeball to eyeball. On the other hand, he thought that perhaps something was getting through.

As they went over and over the issues, Annan told him that obviously all the governments which had approached him had friendly intentions. Saddam should take advantage of this by working with other governments to stabilize the region. Annan said, "You've taken some courageous decisions. Some of them have been miscalculated, but this time around there's history to consider. In 1991, you didn't know. Now you know what happened in '91. You know what has happened on several other occasions. And this time, let me tell you, you'll be hit and hit very hard. All the reconstruction you've done will be gone and you'll have to start again. Think of the suffering of your people. You say that an attack will end the inspections. Maybe, but the impact on your people, and on the region, will be disastrous."

It was becoming an exhausting encounter. Annan said later he felt he had to just try to reason with Saddam, to tell him what was at stake, to try to convince him. "I had to really draw on all my inner re-sources—creativity and stamina and almost a spiritual courage—to really engage him in this. So at the end it was very draining," Annan related.

At one point Hussein told Annan, "I know you're a courageous man."

This encouraged Annan to believe he was getting through to him. "He realized I had taken risks to do what I was doing."

After almost three hours Saddam said, "You seem determined to solve this problem. Many people have failed to solve it—the Russians, the French, the Egyptians, the Turks. If you manage to solve it, it will be your victory."

"No, Mr. President, it will not be my victory, it will be your vic-tory, your decision, it's in your hands. It will be victory for the Iraqi people, victory for the region. Not my victory. So let's do it together, let's find a solution. Work with me to find it."

They turned back to the draft memorandum. Saddam did not have an Arabic translation in his hand, but he spoke very precisely from memory. "When I look at the agreement, everything that is in the interests of the UN is written in crisp, sharp language." And he pointed to paragraph 3 in Annan's English text: "The government undertakes to accord immediate unconditional unrestricted access."

"But anything that affects Iraq is in wishy-washy, loose language. You offer me nothing."

One of the problems was still over the word "inspections" of the presidential sites. Saddam said, "Tariq has already told you, we can-not accept 'inspections'; we can use the word 'visits.' "

Annan replied, "I can't accept that. It's too loose, it will not be understood."

He reminded Saddam that he was speaking for the Security Council. "So you are negotiating not just with me but also with them. They are the ones I have to convince—and the rest of the international community. So you don't want 'inspections' and I don't accept 'visits'—and we have to find a formula."

Saddam said, "Okay, they can enter."

Annan recalled he then said, "That gives me an idea. Shall I try a formulation on you?"

Saddam replied, "Yes."

Annan said, "What if I use this phrase, 'initial and subsequent entries for the performance of the tasks mandated'?"

Saddam responded, "I agree."

Annan wrote it down and showed it to him.

He said, "Agreed."

Then Saddam complained about the word "diplomats" to refer to those being added to the team. He did not want any old diplomats. He wanted "ambassadors." They compromised on "senior diplomats."

Annan then said, "Mr. President, now that the two of us have cleared the text, can we call in the others and tell them that we have an agreement?"

Hussein replied, "Okay, call them in." Tariq Aziz and his colleagues, along with Annan's colleagues, returned.

Annan asked, "Do you go first or I go first?"

Saddam answered: "You go first."

"We have an agreement, we have a text," said Annan. He took them through the changes, and then Saddam said, "Fine, you and Tariq finalize it."

"And that was it," said Annan later. "After another orange juice, we shook hands and left."

As he said goodbye, Saddam said, "I want to thank you for coming to Baghdad personally. You must feel free to come here. You can even come for a holiday, if it won't embarrass you."

As he left, Annan felt elated but exhausted. "I was tired. In a strange sort of way I was very calm."

AFTER he returned to his villa, Annan spoke to several of the principals, including Madeleine Albright, Jacques Chirac, Yevgeni Primakov, Tony Blair and the president of the Security Council. He did not have a secure phone, so he just said, "We have a good text. I think we can leave with it and I think you'll be pleased with it."

He did not fax it to them at once because he knew he would get objections and demands for change. "That's why I had had the four meetings with them, to get their general understanding," Annan said. "Once I had that, I would be free."

Not really. Washington in particular kept pushing. On Sunday night Annan looked forward to his first decent night's sleep. At 2 a.m., Albright called. His staff tried to deflect her, saying he was exhausted and asleep. But the State Department insisted and eventually his staff woke Annan. Albright wanted the text. Half asleep, Annan refused.

"Even if it's unfinished," she said.

"No," he replied. Only after it was signed did he send it by cryptofax to all the Security Council members.

Albright complained about the spin that Annan's press people were putting on the story; he had three spokesmen in Iraq to deal with the hundreds of journalists who had flocked there for his visit, many of them flown in on special UN planes. She said that his people were leaking and saying all sorts of things to the press. "We don't know what's happening. Newt Gingrich and Jesse Helms etc. are going crazy and we can't respond."

The next morning the Iraqis tried to alter the text. Annan refused. He met briefly James Traub of the *New York Times* and said, "It's really quite something. The concentration and attention, the creativity that you need to move people along and to convince them. What comes out of this, in my sense, is, We say Iraq is isolated from the international community, but the international community is also isolated. We want them to comply, but I'm not sure we make the effort to understand what is going on. I believe that we have demonized Iraq, and maybe with some justification. But to not go beyond that. . . ." Engagement was essential, he felt.

Before he left, he had a quick meeting with Iraqi ministers to discuss the oil-for-food program and other aspects of sanctions. Oil for food was a device to mitigate the worst impact of sanctions on children and other vulnerable groups. Iraq was allowed to pump limited amounts of oil, and the revenue from its sale was to be used by the United Nations to buy food and medical supplies. Recently the Security Council had agreed to allow Iraq to pump another $5.2 billion of oil over the next six months. But Iraq had never taken full advantage of the program, and far less food and medicine had been imported than was possible. The Iraqi government's rationale was that the oil industry was in such a poor state of repair that it could not pump such quantities. Now one of the ministers complained to Annan about the agreement. Annan, tired, did not hide his irritation, saying, "I was so surprised and even frankly disappointed at the note which came after approval of the $5.2 billion. . . . After the discussions that we had gone through, I would have expected at least a little thank-you for those people here who worked hard and helped make it happen. You should try to moderate your language." The Iraqi ministers were surprised at his angry tone; so were some of Annan's staff. He was clearly correct: Iraq could have done far more to protect its most vulnerable citizens from sanctions, but the regime had no wish to do so.

Annan left for Paris on Chirac's plane. That night Chirac invited him to dinner at the Elysée Palace, and toasted him for having avoided a world war and for having pulled off a *coup de maître*—a master stroke. Chirac clearly saw Annan's achievement as a success for French diplomacy and joked, "My plane has never had so much publicity before I gave it to you. Each time I turn on the television, my plane is there."

Chirac also talked at some length about the differences between Catholics and Protestants. He thought that Protestants go to the bitter end, for punishment, justice and expiation, but Catholics are more in favor of redemption. This perhaps explained the difference in the Anglo-Saxon and French approaches to Iraq. Which was better, he asked, to have 100 percent control of Saddam or a system of about 60 percent control as now? It was not perfect, but if the U.S. bombed, they would have none because everything would collapse. It was clear to Annan's team that the French were irritated by Tony Blair's closeness to the American position.

The next morning Annan took the Concorde to New York. In the foyer of the United Nations building almost the entire staff had gathered to cheer him—the first secretary general since Dag Hammarskjöld to capture world imagination.

The UNSCOM staff did not attend the celebration. With the exception of Richard Butler, most of the inspectors were depressed, and some were shocked, by the memorandum of understanding.

They felt that by endorsing two separate categories of sites, the memorandum allowed the Iraqis to know in advance what kind of inspection was planned. If diplomats were involved, it must be a "presidential" site—if not, it would be an ordinary site. Either way, the Iraqis would have more time to conceal material.

Annan said he wanted to thank President Clinton and Prime Minister Blair for being "perfect peacemakers"; they were prepared to threaten force in order to achieve peace.

From the public embrace of his staff, Annan went straight into a meeting of the Security Council, where some of the ambassadors, in particular the U.S., Japanese and British, were far more skeptical of the deal he had reached. The encounter was somewhat disappointing for him. They questioned him about possible weaknesses in the text and about whether the Iraqis could claim that there were side understandings. Annan assured them that there were not. He was asked if there were any "constructive ambiguities." He said no. In the end the council unanimously approved his memorandum of understanding.

Afterwards, at a press conference, weary, he made a mistake. Asked if he could trust Saddam, he replied that Saddam was "a man I can do business with," perhaps unconsciously echoing Margaret Thatcher's famous remark on first meeting Mikhail Gorbachev in 1984. In a literal sense, Annan's remark was correct; he had just done business with Saddam, but the phrase had a resonance that sat uneasily with the reality of Saddam as an intransigent and brutal dictator. He also praised the Iraqi leadership for showing "courage, wisdom and flexibility."

Annan flew to Washington. If he had hoped that averting war in Iraq would win him new political support in the United States and persuade Congress to pay the massive arrears it owed the UN, he was disappointed. In Washington the Senate majority leader, Trent Lott, attacked Albright for subcontracting U.S. policy to the UN, and denounced Annan for "appeasement" of Saddam.

Clinton was more welcoming; he said that Annan "deserves the thanks of the American people," and that U.S. arrears to the UN should be paid. Senator Jesse Helms said, "Given what you had to work with, you did a very good job." This was kinder to the UN than Helms's usual style, but when a reporter asked him if the U.S. owed the UN a debt of gratitude, Helms responded, "The question is, does the UN owe the United States and American taxpayers a debt of gratitude?" Not much changed. Legislation authorizing back payments to the United Nations remained tied up in Congress, where Republicans had attached it to anti-abortion language that Clinton had promised to veto. Despite the institutional reforms in which Annan was engaged, despite the fact that he was far more sympathetic to the U.S. than Boutros-Ghali, despite even his trip to Baghdad which some saw as pulling U.S. chestnuts out of the fire, Washington remained defiant—and the UN remained bankrupt.

When I talked to Annan soon after his return from Baghdad, he was still confident that his agreement with Saddam Hussein would work. "I don't think the Iraqis can annoy us now. If they block UNSCOM again the mood in the council will be quite different; it would be much easier for the U.S. to get a consensus to hit them. My sense is that this agreement is qualitatively different because it is the first one Saddam himself has negotiated."

He thought that the Clinton administration also wanted to make it work. "So we all have to make sure we put in the systems to make it work and make sure that Richard [Butler] doesn't get too gung ho. It will be a tough one, come October, if they're concealing things we know they have. I encouraged them to come clean. Tariq said, 'We've already done so.' I said, 'That's not the record we have.' Unfortunately they've got into their heads that UNSCOM is dominated by the Americans, and they're using UNSCOM to look for Saddam."

I went to see Richard Butler also. His public support (despite complaints from his staff) of the memorandum of understanding was tempered by private concern. He said to me that at least the memorandum included "[the] highest level Iraqi commitment to obey the law. It doesn't create anything that should be of any concern." Of course, he said, there was a "notional text" of the memorandum that would have been technically better for UNSCOM, but clearly that would have been a text that Saddam was unlikely to sign. Butler thought that Annan and his staff were now using "diplomatic, sympathetic magic" to talk up the imperfect text in the hope that it would work and thus "by some kind of transmutation actually turns out to be or becomes that good text.

"Kofi takes immensely seriously his role as the person in charge of the maintenance of international peace and security. That goes with the turf. It's the nature of his office that while others consider the use of war, the world should have a voice extolling the virtues of peace. He is admirably suited to that and feels it deeply." But Butler felt that Annan had perhaps forgotten how long a spoon you need when you sup with the devil. "Saddam *is* the devil; his track record on keeping agreements is appalling. And he's a very unsentimental person. The instant he thinks it's in his interest, he will drop Kofi down the crocodile hole. It would be a tragedy if such a good man and his gifted initiatives for peace should then get trashed in the dustbin of history because he didn't realize the realities of dealing with the devil."

The realities quickly became clear. Even as Annan left Iraq, Tariq Aziz had sent him a letter which set out further "understandings." These were not included in the memorandum of understanding and were contrary to UNSCOM's established practices for inspections. For example, from now on any samples taken by UNSCOM would be tested only in the presence of Iraqis and "state documents shall not be subjected to the verification in question." Annan formally rejected this letter, but it showed the reality of Iraqi attitudes toward the memorandum of understanding.

Butler then mounted an aggressive inspection of the Ministry of Defense. It was completely empty. Iraqi officials told UNSCOM that, fearing bombing, they had moved everything out. The new procedures for inspecting the presidential palaces worked—up to a point. They were cumbersome, and some of the new diplomats on the teams (particularly the Russians) took Iraq's side and argued against UNSCOM in disputes on the ground. Most important, the inspectors found nothing. In April, UNSCOM reported that the sites it had visited had been cleansed: "In all the sites outside Baghdad, for example, there were no documents and no computers. The buildings were largely empty."

Now Iraq began to argue that it had done enough to fulfill its obligations under the memorandum.

All the delays meant that the UN's legal duty to determine whether or not Iraq still retained weapons of mass destruction had been stymied for the last six months. Annan's mission was shown merely to have postponed a military response. The Iraqis continued to try to frustrate UNSCOM and to discredit Richard Butler. The rest of 1998 was punctuated by crises with Iraq in one form or another.

But the secretary general also had to deal with other crises, including the nuclear explosions unleashed by Pakistan and India, war between Eritrea and Ethiopia, and the spread of fighting in Kosovo.

During the rest of 1998 and early 1999 most members of the Security Council, let alone of the General Assembly, grew more tired of confrontation with Iraq, as did most UN officials. The Iraqi government was more and more able to turn global opinion against further intervention, against the intrusions of UNSCOM and against the combative, straightforward leadership of Richard Butler. Its propaganda was, at one level, brilliant. Its purpose was to preserve what remained of its prohibited weapons.

By the end of 1998, UNSCOM inspectors still had good reason to believe that Iraq had not accounted for 2.5 tons of complex media, of which only tiny amounts are needed to create biological weapons, 200 tons of precursor chemicals for VX nerve gas production and the full extent of its capabilities to produce long-range missiles. In other words, Iraq could still have concealed systems to deliver sufficient anthrax and VX to cause immense, horrific damage to its neighbors. And the past had shown that Saddam Hussein was more than ready to use such weapons.

Even in the face of such a clearly documented threat from a warlord whom few governments had any reason to trust, the world was uncertain how to react. Indeed, its leading members in the Security Council were divided and inconstant. The French, the Russians and the Chinese still wanted a deal, whereas Madeleine Albright called Saddam "the most evil man since Hitler." Even allowing for a touch of hyperbole, there was no doubt that he is one of the most atrocious rulers of modern times. Sitting in Annan's dining room on the thirty-eighth floor of the United Nations, I asked him, How did a good man deal with devils?

"Well, who are the really bad people I've negotiated with? Aideed in Somalia was one. I didn't spend much time with Karadjic and Mladic. Mladic looks very mean. Karadjic has a funny air about him, sort of a bit arty, and if you are not careful, you might think he's an absentminded, elderly hippie. These people can be very deceptive. When you get one-on-one with them, they can be interesting and have an easy smile, yet you know what they're capable of. You think, How can they smile and yet do all these things?

"Saddam is very calm and polite. You wouldn't think he was capable of what he has done. One of my staff, a pastor's son, said that he felt that he was in front of an evil man. But I don't think the others had that feeling. He looks like somebody's uncle. But if you mistake his calmness, soft-spokenness for weakness, you're in trouble."

He recalled that his wife's uncle, Raoul Wallenberg, who had rescued thousands of Hungarian Jews from the Nazis in 1944, had said, "To do good one sometimes has to deal with the devil." He said, "What I find is that even with these evil ones, one can touch them, can reach them somehow. The French have a word, you have to get them *engagé* and persuade them it's in their self-interest to do what you want them to do. Self-interest propels them, so you need to find out what is important for them and then place it in the broader picture of what you're trying to do—is it their people, is it the palaces they are building, is it acceptance by the international community?—and then begin to work with those things. In the end, the only means I have is reason and persuasion. I cannot call on an air force or an army."

After his two-year term as chairman of UNSCOM expired in June 1999, Richard Butler accused Russia, China and France of deliberately trying to "kill" UNSCOM. "They wanted . . . to demonstrate that UNSCOM was an evil organization that misled the council."

He insisted that UNSCOM told the truth and criticized Kofi Annan's "misguided decisions." He accused Annan of trying to destroy UNSCOM because it was "too independent," and of trying to paper over Iraq's cheating on its disarmament obligations with diplomacy. "You may get a short-term diplomatic solution but the real problem—the weapons—will still be there, and they will come back to bite us in the future," he said.

Annan's view was that the only way to disarm Iraq was with inspectors on the ground, not by bombing from the air. "I hope we will be able to get back in and continue that work— it's essential," he said to me in response to Butler's criticism. He thought Butler should have realized, as Ekeus did, that UNSCOM could not succeed without the support of the council and the cooperation of Iraq. Butler argued that the days of relative cooperation by Iraq were long gone, and so, as a result, was unity in the council. But Annan had to try to reforge that. Some maintain that weapons are more important to Saddam than anything else. Annan said, "This may be so, but it ought to be possible to devise means to contain him and ensure that he does not rebuild his arsenal."

Annan had thought he could appeal to Saddam's vanity as the "builder of modern Iraq." He believed that Saddam's personal commitment to the secretary general would make a difference. It did not; his agreement to Annan's memorandum was merely tactical. Saddam continued to defy the international community, and the international community remained hesitant and divided on how to respond. The persisting crisis showed, in its most dramatic form, the dilemma at the heart of the world of Kofi Annan.

10

Into Africa

I N May 1998, Kofi Annan went to Africa as part of his attempt to focus the United Nations on the continent's problems. In his first year he had already visited South Africa and Angola. In Angola he had hoped to be present at the inauguration of a new government of national unity that embraced the existing government and the UNITA rebels led by Jonas Savimbi. The creation of the government, which was supposed to end an atrocious civil war in Angola, was delayed, so Annan had traveled to see Savimbi and had persuaded him to move ahead with the peace process. However, this apparent success was short-lived, and by mid-1998 Angola was shuddering back toward the abyss of all-out war for the fourth time. Now Annan was visiting some of the other African countries which had been most deeply struck by war in the last decade.

In early 1998 international attention was directed to Africa. In March, President Clinton, touring six countries, had apologized for the U.S. role in African slavery and had praised Africa's "new leaders" and their successes. He declared, "One hundred years from now your grandchildren and mine will look back and say, 'This was the beginning of a new African renaissance.' " Sadly, such optimism was not justified.

Annan had just published a report on the sources of conflict in Africa in which he pointed out that there, as elsewhere, the UN was increasingly being asked to respond to intrastate conflicts "in which the main aim, to an alarming degree, is the destruction not of armies but of civilians and entire ethnic groups. Preventing such wars is no longer a question of defending states or protecting allies. It is a question of defending humanity itself."

Annan was frank. He urged African leaders to stop blaming their problems on the colonial past. He proposed that Africa demonstrate the will to rely upon political rather than military responses to problems; he called on countries to cap their military spending at 1.5 percent of gross domestic product and to commit themselves to zero growth in their defense budgets for the next ten years. Africa must also abandon the old socialist command-and-control economic methods, and promote the reforms necessary for economic growth. He said governments must ensure respect for human rights and the rule of law, strengthen democratization and promote transparency—all of which added up to the newly fashionable term "good governance."

The day after Annan's report was published, bad governance triumphed in the Congo. Annan had to announce that the UN was abandoning its investigation of the suspected massacre of tens of thousands of Rwandan Hutu refugees thought to have been butchered in the last year as Laurent Kabila was swept to power with the backing of a regional Tutsi-led army. Ever since Annan had tried to set up the investigation in 1997, Kabila and his allies (especially in the Rwandan government) had tried to stymie it.

It was two weeks after delivering his report that Annan arrived in Ethiopia, where he had spent part of his early United Nations career before famine and Stalinist revolution had engulfed the country. After attending an Organization of African Unity meeting in Addis Ababa, Annan touched down for a night in Djibouti, a wretchedly poor outpost of the former French empire. Djibouti had done well during the relief efforts into Somalia and Ethiopia in the eighties and early nineties, when much of the food had been passed through its Red Sea port before distribution. Now there was almost nothing from which it might prosper. Government workers were rarely paid.

The prospect that France might reduce the size of its garrison from 2,000 to 1,200 troops was causing alarm.

The president, encased in his gloomy palace, sat with Annan in huge chairs placed so far apart that people could scarcely make themselves heard. Here, as elsewhere, the continuing wars in Somalia and Sudan were the subtexts of Annan's talks. In Somalia, the long factional or clan civil war, which the UN had tried and failed to solve in the early nineties, continued pointlessly. There were now initiatives from Egypt, Italy and Ethiopia to try to find a solution. These efforts sometimes seemed no better coordinated than the clans within Somalia itself. It was Annan's hope, on this journey, to try to impose some order upon them. He told all those he met that the Somalis exploited the divisions among the would-be peacemakers. They should be told that there was only one way forward, and that the international community would support only that. But, of course, before that could be done, the international community had to unite on a policy.

In Sudan, war and famine were still the scourges they had been in the 1980s. The ceaseless war of attrition waged by the Muslim fundamentalist northern government against the rebellious Christian and animist south was leading to yet another fearful assault by famine on the people of the south. In 1989, diplomatic pressure, especially from James Grant, the late executive director of UNICEF, had led to the opening of humanitarian corridors, known as "corridors of tranquillity," to take supplies to the southerners. But these supplies, known as Operation Lifeline, could never do more than save some lives, even while they may have helped prolong the conflict, as humanitarian aid so often does.

The next morning, after a hot night at the Djibouti Sheraton, Annan's convoy of white cars visited the UN compound, where careful preparations had been made for his brief visit. The secretary general was read a eulogy by the oldest man on the UN team and given a bouquet by the youngest woman on the staff. He thanked them, and we climbed back into the convoy to drive to the airport for the three-hour flight on the little turboprop Fokker F-27 which had come from the UN mission in Georgia to Nairobi, where the UN had its regional headquarters for Africa. The plane was like an old flying bus, slow and uncomfortable.

In Kenya, Annan was aware that the fifth consecutive election victory of Daniel arap Moi's KANU Party had not improved the country's political or economic situation. More violence had erupted in the Rift Valley, and KANU politicians and the government had been blamed. The opposition was getting stronger, but overarching problems of democratization and good governance prevented Kenya from having fully transparent relations with the donor community and international financial institutions. Police committed extra-judicial killings and torture and beat detainees. Arbitrary arrests took place, detentions were lengthy and prison conditions remained awful. The government interfered with the judiciary, intimidated opponents and limited freedom of speech and assembly. Kenya owed the UN a total of almost $140,000 on its contributions to the regular budget, for peacekeeping operations and for tribunals. On the other hand, the country was owed almost $7.5 million for its contribution of troops to UNPROFOR, the thankless UN mission to the former Yugoslavia.

Annan was not advised by his staff to raise any of these issues when he met President Moi at the statehouse on the hill in Nairobi the next morning. On the contrary, he was advised to thank Kenya for the hospitality it accorded the UN and to commend the president for his attempts to find peace in Sudan and Somalia.

On arrival at the front door of the statehouse, Annan signed the visitor's book with Moi standing, tall and unsmiling, behind him. The secretary general was led into the building, past two stuffed lions and two large elephant tusks mounted on the floor. He went into a private room to speak with the president. They discussed the large UN presence in Nairobi and conflicts in the Great Lakes area, Sudan and Somalia. "There were no sharp edges," said one of his aides after the meeting. "Perhaps there should have been."

Annan's entourage waited in a large reception room dominated by two rather crude paintings of Moi in a socialist realist style. One, depicting the president "participating in soil erosion control in 1983," showed him lifting a very large rock above his head in a river gorge, on the edge of which thousands of people watched in admiration. Annan's spokesman, Fred Eckhard, was reading a faxed copy of a *New Yorker* article, just published, by Philip Gourevitch criticizing Annan's failure to act more decisively to prevent the 1994 genocide in Rwanda. It quoted one of the January 1994 cables from General Roméo Dallaire, saying that an informant had warned of an impending genocide. Gourevitch suggested that Annan had not responded adequately to the cable and that had he done more in January 1994 the genocide of April might have been averted. Eckhard was wondering how to reply to it and whether he or Annan should not ask, Where was the moral leadership in the world then?

In his suite later that morning, Annan talked about the article, saying that Somalia and Bosnia both showed that where there was a will much could be done, but not where there was not. Also, the peacekeeping department always receives masses of information, not all of which proves to be accurate, and a commander's first responsibility has to be to his troops.

A meeting with UN staff that afternoon was peppered (as were all UN staff sessions on his trip) with complaints from local staff about their conditions of service. Then, at a press conference, Annan praised the government of Sudan for increasing the number of humanitarian aid flights that it would allow into the stricken south. What was needed now, he said, was more money. Only 20 percent of the $109 million appealed for had been pledged.

Questions on Sudan, Somalia and Congo were followed by a series of quite pointed, almost aggressive questions on Rwanda and Gourevitch's article. Annan finally replied rather emotionally that "some of the reports seem to forget the incredible circumstances under which Dallaire and the peacekeepers operated. At one point in the crisis he was left with only the Ghanaian battalion, when the Belgians had withdrawn and the Bangladeshis had gone. He put himself and these troops at great risk to protect people at the stadium and Hotel Mille Collines. We do not hear anything about that."

His voice almost cracking, he ended by saying that too much was being made of one cable and that if *information* was indeed the only problem, then peacekeeping would be much easier. "We would not be having problems in Kosovo because everybody *knows*. We would not have had a problem in Congo because everyone *knew* we had to separate the troops and the refugees. Why didn't it happen, despite the information? Later everybody *knew* that there were refugees left behind when a million went back to Rwanda. Why didn't that information make us go and save them? The information was there. We have to be logical."

From Kenya we flew the next morning direct to Arusha, the small town in Tanzania which was host to the international tribunal on war crimes in Rwanda. Annan was greeted in Arusha by a magnificent snake dance in which a substantial python, which appeared (fortunately) to be in a trance from the insistent music of drums, was entwined and stretched by its keeper. We then went to the tribunal, which had had problems ever since it was set up after the 1994 genocide. Tanzania had been chosen to host it, in part because it was close to Rwanda and therefore accessible to witnesses. There was also an empty conference center in Arusha which the government was pleased to rent to the United Nations, but other facilities were not good. At first the tribunal had lacked telephones, computers, a law library, even electric power. Progress was very slow through 1995, and early in his term Annan had ordered an investigation; as a result, some of the senior staff had been dismissed and a new registrar had been appointed. But there were still problems. Perhaps the most serious was security—two witnesses had been murdered. Costs were soaring (the budget was $59 million a year) as Tanzania raised rents and defense lawyers from the West submitted large fee bills. By the time Annan came to Arusha, there were twenty-three Hutus in custody awaiting trial, but there had not yet been a single verdict.

Past jewelers' shops and video shops in the hall of the conference center, we went into the little specially constructed courtroom. It was a long, narrow room, about twenty by fifty feet, with the judges, lawyers and accused separated from the spectators by a glass wall. The accused man sat in the dock with his back to us, while his defense lawyer complained about what he called prejudicial behavior by the prosecution.

Outside, Annan said that the court's efforts to end the culture of impunity were very important: "It is very moving and reassuring to see that justice can be done." From the court we were driven briefly to the prison where the accused Hutus were incarcerated. It was a small concrete building within larger walls. We passed through a series of high metal doors and walked quickly around. It was not a pleasant feeling. The prisoners had been ordered to stand outside their cells when the secretary general came by. They were sullen and silent as we passed, but when the gates banged shut behind us, they began to shout angrily and in unison.

That evening the foreign minister insisted on driving Annan and his party along appalling roads and down into an extinct volcano which was home to an exquisite wild game park where elephants and lions roamed.

The next day, when we touched down in Bujumbura, the capital of neighboring Burundi, the welcome was ecstatic. Three bands of traditional drummers met the secretary general at the airport, whooping and playing with cheerful abandon. He was given a hero's welcome by the government. Burundi was cut off from its neighbors by economic sanctions which they had imposed after General Pierre Buyoya seized power in 1996. The regime desperately sought international acceptance and hoped that Annan's visit might lead to the lifting of the sanctions.

Buyoya's seizure of power was undoubtedly illegal, but it had helped calm Burundi, which has a mixed Hutu and Tutsi population. The majority are Hutus, but the army and administration have been dominated by Tutsis since before independence in 1962. In 1993 Tutsi paratroopers assassinated the country's first democratically elected president, a Hutu, and since then more than 200,000 people, mostly Hutu civilians, had been killed in fighting between the Tutsi-dominated army and Hutu rebels. This so-called slow genocide had also caused at least half a million people to flee abroad or internally. Boutros-Ghali had called for some member state to take up the role of "lead country" and prepare a peacekeeping force. No nation saw any "vital interests" there and none came forward. Buyoya's coup reduced the killing—but the consequent sanctions imposed by the region in protest at his seizure of power were now ruining what little economy there was, and enriching officials in the nearby countries who helped enforce them.

On the tarmac I was pleased to meet an old friend whom I had known when he worked for UNICEF on the Thai-Cambodian border in the early eighties. "This is an extraordinary country," he said. "Everything changes every day. It's like a kaleidoscope. Without Buyoya there would have been an even worse bloodbath than before."

Burundi was still in civil war; on the road from the airport, soldiers stood guard facing out from the road all the way into town. The hotel where Annan met with Buyoya teemed with hundreds of plainclothes security men. In a dark and crowded room, Buyoya explained at some length that sanctions were destroying all hope of stabilizing the country. Annan's party and the local elite were then led into a dining room, where a buffet lunch more suitable for a five-star hotel in Paris than an impoverished little country on the Great Lakes awaited. After toasts between Annan and Buyoya, we rushed to the parliament, where there was a traffic jam of brand-new Mercedes 500 SEL sedans—bought, I supposed, with all the gains gotten from sanctions-busting. Annan was careful to promise nothing specific, but after his visit he wrote to Julius Nyerere, the former president of Tanzania, who had been one of the main organizers of the sanctions, recommending that they now be lifted. Nyerere agreed and a few months later they were.

Some countries generate immediate goodwill and sympathy. Burundi in all its fragility was one such. Annan was seen off as he had been welcomed—by enthusiastic drummers. The contrast with his reception in Rwanda, less than an hour's flight away, could not have been more startling. There he was ambushed. The representative of that amorphous creature, the international community, was insulted and abused for the failures of that community to take action to prevent the genocide which had devoured Rwanda in 1994.

WHEN we touched down in the dusk at Kigali, Annan was met by two little girls who handed him and his wife bunches of flowers. He was welcomed politely by the foreign minister, Anastase Gasana. There was the usual cortege of white UN four-wheel-drive cars—one for each of the senior UN persons on Annan's flight—Ethiopian, British, French, Algerian and others. In the lead car the minister told Annan that he knew how hard he had worked as head of peacekeeping to try to find international troops to stop the genocide. Later, Annan thought this was an attempt (largely successful) to lull him into a false sense of security.

The parliament building had been the scene of terrible massacres during the genocide; the fabric of the building had been ruined and it had since been rebuilt. It was a modest, poorly lit brick structure on a small hill. Annan's party walked into the dim chamber and he was taken to the podium, while his delegation was seated near the front of the hall. There was no clapping. The members of the parliament greeted his arrival in silence. Unlike everywhere else he had visited on this trip, there was no UN flag to be seen.

When they had taken their seats, the foreign minister delivered his

speech. It was a fierce attack on the League of Nations and the
United Nations for failing to prevent all acts of genocide in the country since the 1920s. He said that the United Nations had known all
about the genocide planned in 1994 and yet had done nothing. Why?
Who was it, he asked, who had lacked the political will?

Clapping greeted this question. The UN, Gasana went on, had
given the green light to the French government to mount Operation
Turquoise, the armed intervention in the middle of the genocide,
which many Tutsis saw as a French attempt to save their genocidal allies of the Hutu-dominated regime. Then, he said, the killers had
fled to the refugee camps sustained by the UN across the border in
Zaire. These had become havens for the forces of evil—and again the
UN bore a heavy responsibility. In all, he said, recent years had been a
disaster for Rwanda and for the UN itself. But I am sure, he concluded, that the secretary general will answer all these points.

Gasana's tirade was followed by a more soothing speech from the
chairman of the National Assembly. But Annan was clearly taken
aback by the attack. Before he began his own speech he said that he
had not expected to be publicly confronted like this in the assembly.
Politely he turned the question of responsibility back on Rwanda.
What is it in a society, he asked, which drives people to turn upon
each other violently? How can we be sure that we never have to live
through this pain again? "I did not come here to get into polemics
and I'm sure you all know the old saying that the guest is always prisoner of the host," he said.

His speech had gone through many drafts, agonized over by his
traveling team and his staff in New York. They had discussed at
length how apologetic Annan should be about the genocide and the
failure of the UN or the international community to prevent it.

In the end, those on the side of mild rhetoric rather than a full-
scale apology had won the day. Annan said that four years ago
Rwanda was "swept by a paroxysm of horror from which there is
only the longest and the most difficult of escapes." He then said—
and this angered his hosts—that "It was a horror that came from
within." The government preferred, as the foreign minister had just
done, to blame foreign forces for their disasters. But Annan believed
that if Rwandans continued to blame the world they would never be
able to deal with the poisoned relations between Hutu and Tutsi
within their country. "We must and do acknowledge that the world

failed Rwanda at that time of evil," Annan asserted. "The international community and the United Nations could not muster the political will to confront it. The world must deeply repent this failure. Rwanda's tragedy was the world's tragedy."

What Annan did not do was what President Clinton had done—make a personal mea culpa in a brief stopover at Kigali airport in March. Clinton had declined to venture a few yards down the road to a memorial created by the government especially for his visit. Lack of adequate security, said his Secret Service team. Standing on the airport tarmac he said that, back in spring 1994, he personally "did not fully appreciate the depth and the speed with which [Rwandans] were engulfed by this unimaginable terror." This statement was seared with hypocrisy. The terror was perhaps "unimaginable," but it was also undeniable, and manifest almost from the start. It was the United States, above all nations, which had resisted attempts to mount an international intervention in Rwanda. The Rwandan government made no criticism of Clinton.

Now, Annan did not choose to apologize on behalf of the United Nations. He felt that the failure to intervene amounted to a failure of political will by the member states—whom he could not criticize directly—rather than of those who worked for the UN Secretariat either as officials or as peacekeeping soldiers. His speech was subtle and rather brave; unlike Clinton, he did not play to the gallery.

After the speech there were a few questions from members of the assembly. Annan was asked about compensation, about why there was no Marshall Plan for Rwanda, about the UN's responsibility for the disaster and about his personal sense of responsibility. He made a distinction which is fundamental, but not always understood, and rarely appreciated. He said it was important to clarify, What is the UN? Who is the UN? "There are two UNs," he said. "There are governments—yours, mine and others, who give orders. And there is the Secretariat. In peacekeeping operations the UN borrows troops from governments under certain understandings. It is the independent decision of governments to send troops. It is not up to the secretary general."

From the parliament, Annan and his party drove briefly to the Hotel Mille Collines, which had itself seen horrors during the genocide. He then went to an open-air drinks party hosted for him by the president and vice president. They snubbed him by not turning up, so he soon left. Later that evening the presidential spokesman told the press that Annan's speech was "arrogant, insensitive and insulting." The spokesman was unable to say exactly what was wrong with the speech, but he did say that they particularly objected to Annan's unscripted remark about "polemics."

It was not now clear what if any program the government would allow for the following morning. Annan's advisers debated long into the night, calling New York, to decide what to do. In light of the public insults, should they advise the secretary general to abandon the visit and leave early next morning? In the morning one Western ambassador called to say that he had been assured by Rwandan military intelligence that the secretary general would not be humiliated by crowds of demonstrators, still less endangered, so they decided to carry on.

The government wanted Annan to visit two memorials of the genocide. We drove in the convoy of white UN cars to the first, a school a few miles from the center of Kigali. No one was there. Go to another site nearby, we were told. There on a bare hillside were hundreds of simple wooden crosses with names written on them in ink. A junior official read Annan a short explanation of how the people here had died: they had been awaiting rescue by United Nations troops. Annan laid a wreath on a marble mausoleum amid the graves. A local official told Annan politely, "We consider this site, like hundreds of others, to be a sanctuary for people who were abandoned. We believe four thousand people were killed here alone."

We then drove fast about eighteen miles through the gentle hills to another memorial site, where skulls are laid out along one side of a long, narrow corrugated-iron shed, and bones along the other. Annan, his wife, some of his staff and a group of journalists silently crowded into the shed to view this testimony to inhumanity. Outside about one hundred survivors of the genocide were gathered. The hostility was palpable.

Annan and his wife laid wreaths wrapped in cellophane and tied in purple ribbon. On the hillside, surrounded by survivors, the secretary general was then harangued over a loudspeaker by the local prefect, an aggressive-looking man who made a scripted, swinging attack on "the UN of Boutros-Ghali and Annan," blaming it for the genocide. He said that Annan's speech last night had "made us suffer a lot" and, in an extraordinarily brutal insult, he said that Annan had "added evil to evil."

Annan listened with his arms crossed tensely in front of him. His wife looked downcast. In reply he said, "What we have seen here today is one of the worst examples of man's inhumanity to man. All of us saw on our televisions what was going on in Rwanda. The international community could not muster the resources or the will to come to the aid of the Rwandan people as quickly as it should have. We should draw lessons from the past as we build on the future, as we build a society of tolerance, and the international community should give all support to the Rwandan people to pick up the pieces."

To the survivors he said, "Your tragedy is our tragedy, your pain is not limited to you. I and the whole international community share your pain, share your tragedy. Let's look forward, learn from the past and build a unified and tolerant society. You have a competent government, focused and determined to bring the society back."

Throughout, Annan was polite about the government that insulted him, though there were serious criticisms that could be made of its minority Tutsi rule over the Hutus. The government was guilty of human rights abuses both at home and abroad; in 1997 its troops and troops allied to it had hunted down and murdered tens of thousands of Hutu refugees in Zaire. Recently, it had ignored pleas from the pope, Annan and other world leaders and staged public executions of twenty-two people convicted of involvement in the 1994 genocide. Annan could also have pointed out that many servants of the UN had lost their lives in attempting to serve Rwanda. Ten Belgian soldiers were horribly mutilated and murdered in 1994. In 1997, seventeen UN officials or contract workers were killed there.

The motorcade then proceeded back through the fields to the main road and Kigali, where Annan had a brief lunch with members of the UN office. Over their sandwiches, members of the staff talked about the difficulties of working with this government, which gave the UN almost no cooperation. In particular, the Human Rights Commission staff were prevented from doing their job of monitoring abuses within the country, apparently for the simple reason that such abuses, by government officials and soldiers, against the Hutu majority were rampant, and the government wanted to keep them quiet. Indeed, the government was on the verge of expelling the UN Human Rights Commission's representative in Rwanda.

Annan then drove to the presidential palace. The guards at the side gate of the office were brusque to the point of rudeness, physically preventing anyone else from entering the building with him. Annan spent an hour and a half with President Pasteur Bizimungu and Vice President Paul Kagame, the real power in the land. The conversation began angrily and then softened somewhat. Kagame said that Rwanda had a complaint against the organization which Annan headed, not against him. But they did have complaints about Annan's speech, which they felt fell far short of what they had expected. They did not like his use of the word "polemic" or the idea that the problem was "internal." They felt that "the world must deeply repent" was not an adequate way for the secretary general to express the UN's duty to atone.

Annan said he had been misread and asked if they thought he would come to Rwanda to undermine the government or society. They said no.

They then had a long discussion on the dynamics of the Security Council and the way in which peacekeeping missions operate. Annan said he had called about a hundred countries in 1994 to try to raise troops for Rwanda, and had done everything he could to persuade the Ghanaian battalion to stay after the Belgians and Bangladeshis fled. Kagame admitted that General Dallaire had had far too few troops to fulfill his mandate.

Outside, one of Annan's staff said to me that Annan's great strength is that he has no ego and therefore no agenda. He never feels insulted and is humble enough to recognize mistakes. He negotiates from humility and offers hope.

At a brief press conference afterwards, President Bizimungu was asked by the Reuters correspondent why the government had not been as rude to President Clinton as to Kofi Annan. Bizimungu replied, lamely, that he thought they had been. In fact, they had made almost no criticism of Clinton; they would not dare—the personification of the international community is a much easier target than the president of the United States. Asked by a Rwandan journalist if he had any personal regrets, Annan said that he did regret that the United Nations could not have done more, could not convince member states to provide the resources needed: "But I also did say that your pain and your tragedy was that of the international community and mine as well because no one who understands the human condition and has compassion could have remained indifferent."

Then we rushed again to the airport. After a short but beautiful flight over Lake Victoria, we landed at Entebbe, Uganda. Annan drove straight into a television studio and told CNN's worldwide audience, "There is lots of anger in Rwanda against the international community and the UN and it is personified in me." He then dealt with questions about Cyprus, Iraq and other international problems.

That evening Annan had dinner with President Yoweri Museveni of Uganda, who told the secretary general that the other powers in the region were now "fed up with" President Kabila in Congo. "We put him in," said the Ugandan president. "But you are the world's policeman, so I shouldn't say that to you." He did not say that Uganda and Rwanda were about to invade Congo once again, this time to try to depose the man they had installed only a year before.

Just before we left Uganda, Annan gave a press conference at which he was asked why he had withdrawn his human rights investigation team from the Congo but still left UNSCOM in Iraq. He replied that the human rights investigators could not work without the cooperation of the Congo authorities, but UNSCOM was set up under Chapter VII of the UN Charter and members were determined to enforce it. Asked if the lesson of the last couple of days was not that the UN should stand up for itself better, he made an implicit criticism of Rwanda: "We will have to make choices because resources are limited, so we will work with governments which cooperate with us and which want to increase civil society. There may come a time when we just have to cut our losses and concentrate on where we can make a difference, not where we are thwarted."

From the press conference it was back into our convoy to the airport and the short march along another red carpet, and then into the cramped plane, where Annan and his wife sat day after day on the long, slow flights, surrounded by the journalists and staff traveling with them. The pilot headed north for the four-hour flight to Eritrea. I thought of the contrast between the way in which the secretary general of the United Nations and the president of the United States traveled. Clinton's most recent trip to Africa had involved fleets of planes and 1,300 fellow travelers, U.S. officials and others. It had cost

U.S. taxpayers $42.8 million. By contrast, the UN Secretariat informed me later that Annan's trip cost about $108,000.

During the flight, Annan reflected on Rwanda, saying that he thought it was important to tell the Rwandans the truth. "They have gone through an inhuman and traumatic experience, but now they need to move on. I have told them that in private. They identify with the Jews and Israel and believe that the international community should help them in a similar manner to Israel. That is not wise."

Storms shook us. The plane was not powerful enough to fly through or above them and the pilot announced he would have to make a detour and land in Khartoum, Sudan, to refuel. This meant that we would inevitably arrive late in Asmara, too late for the planned official dinner of welcome.

At Khartoum airport the night's dry forty-degree heat hit us as we landed almost unnoticed in a corner of the airfield and began to walk toward the terminal. A minibus rushed across the tarmac to pick us up and take us to the VIP lounge, where there was a prayer area among the heavy stuffed chairs, and a small duty-free shop selling large containers of baby milk, aftershave and stuffed baby alligators. The head of UN security in Sudan, a Fijian who had been a military observer in Somalia in 1992, came to meet Annan.

The refueling was soon done—two thousand liters (approximately five hundred gallons) for $400, plus $200 landing fee—but our departure was delayed for a few minutes while the foreign minister of Sudan's Islamic regime (reckoned by the United States to be a terrorist regime) rushed to greet his unexpected guest at the airport. He gave Annan a file containing Khartoum's latest position on the hideous war that the regime was pursuing against the south. The regime had been under pressure to allow humanitarian relief organizations more access to the millions of starving people in the south. The foreign minister promised this. The war continued.

Finally, we left for Eritrea. The country had won independence from Ethiopia in 1993 after a thirty-one-year war in which it had had support from neither East nor West and, consequently, almost no attention from the UN. Now the new government, made up mainly of former fighters from the Eritrean People's Liberation Front, was attempting to rebuild the country with minimal outside assistance.

President Issaias Afewerki was a clever and caustic former guerrilla who, despite the fact that he led a one-party state, was at this time a "new African leader" favored by Western governments. He had been scathing about aid and the international community. "Billions of dollars have been spent in cases like Somalia, Cambodia," he had said recently. "Where have these billions gone and how has society benefited? And what can the UN or the international community claim was achieved? Is it peace or the transformation of living standards? Nothing has changed. In fact, the international community has created institutions that give the false impression of resolving problems but in fact only perpetuate problems and create parasites."

When Annan landed, close to midnight, the president was polite but also clearly upset. The largest state dinner the new government had ever laid out had been ruined. To some Eritrean officials the delay must have looked like another example of UN indifference. At the dinner Annan had planned to say, "I am aware that Eritreans by and large believe that the United Nations did not support their struggle for independence," but he hoped there would now be a new partnership. He would have praised Eritrean self-reliance and emphasis on civil society and human resources. "In just a short period you have become a key voice in Africa and the region." Because of our delay, all of this was unsaid. Annan apologized to the president.

The next morning we flew by ancient helicopter down to the Red Sea port of Massawa, the scene of devastating fighting in the war against Ethiopia. The Ethiopian government had thought it was impregnable, but after fantastic losses on both sides, the Eritrean People's Liberation Front had captured it. The mayor's office was lined with photographs of the killing and destruction in the port.

Now a South Korean construction company was building a large housing and office complex on one side of the derelict port which, on this day, contained ships from Yemen, Poland and Saudi Arabia, and some modern luxury dhows with full air conditioning, berthed outside the Dahlak Hotel.

Some of the beautiful narrow streets around the old port were untouched except by decay. "Captain Faias Import Export" read one sign, "Red Sea Grocery" another, "Gaellatly Hankey Shipping Agency" a third. The *pièce de résistance* in the town was the war memorial, which consisted of two captured Ethiopian tanks, festooned with Eritrean flags, whose barrels produced an endless spout of water into a pool. It was a memorial well calculated to add insult to the injury of defeat.

Before leaving the country that evening Annan gave a short press conference with the president at the airport. Questions about Rwanda and General Dallaire's cable still dominated the agenda. Annan repeated that Dallaire had had neither the capacity nor the mandate to disarm the Hutu extremists. The secretary general said, "The impression has been given that it is because of this cable that the international community did not stop the genocide. I don't think anyone in the Security Council would claim lack of information. It was lack of will."

Annan was told that the UN had not been relevant to Africa. How would his reform proposals change that? Annan replied that the UN could do nothing alone but needed the cooperation of governments, civil society, nongovernmental organizations and the private sector. Donor contributions for assistance were declining, so other ways of energizing society had to be found. Asked why on this tour he had met only government leaders, not members of civil society, he replied that it was true that he should spend more time with leaders of civil society. His purpose on the trip was to engage governments in the search for peace in Sudan and Somalia.

The Agence France-Presse reporter Bertrand Rosenthal spoke out on behalf of Ruth Simon, a young correspondent of AFP who had been jailed, with her small child, without trial in Asmara for over a year. He asked President Afewerki of what she was accused and under what process she would be judged. The president replied with clear anger that she had committed an offense, and the government intended also to sue AFP itself for spreading false information about the conflict between Eritrea and Sudan. He went on in combative mode to say that the UN had been "irrelevant" and "discredited" in Africa. He hoped that Annan would help create a "serious United Nations" which could "participate not only in conflict prevention and resolution but also in development issues." But Africa had to keep its own houses in order and "we understand the bitterness towards the UN over Rwanda. The then secretary general dealt with Rwanda with apathy. But we are looking to the future."

The president said UN agencies must be more accountable, and attacked some agencies which had "big offices, very expensive cars and redundant people who could not find jobs in their own countries who come under the umbrella of those agencies to do very mediocre jobs."

   With this rebuke in his ears, Annan flew the last leg of the journey back to Djibouti, where he joined that evening's Air France flight to Paris. There he was given the warm welcome that the French now always accorded him. Having resisted his election on the grounds that he was from the wrong part of Africa—the Anglophone part, not the Francophone sector—President Chirac had been so delighted by Annan's deal with Saddam Hussein (and the fact that he went to Baghdad in Chirac's plane) that French officials were now beginning to talk of his having a second term.

   After a night in Paris seeing Chirac, other high officials and the Iraqi deputy prime minister, Tariq Aziz, who happened to be there, Annan was whisked to the Cannes Film Festival. There, flanked by Emma Thompson and John Travolta, he made a surprise appearance to speak briefly about the importance of human rights. He was given a standing ovation. The next day he flew back to New York.

   On May 11, India exploded a nuclear device and shortly afterwards Pakistan followed suit. They thus changed forever the security needs and the level of danger in the entire subcontinent. Then a border war, wholly unexpected, erupted between the first and last countries on Annan's trip, Ethiopia and Eritrea.

   Over the next year and a half the human costs of this war were horrendous as the two sides fought across their disputed, barren border. Tens of thousands of soldiers were killed in trench warfare that recalled the horrors of the First World War. Ethiopia deported fifty-two thousand Eritreans—men, women, children, even hospital patients—en masse. Several hundred thousand people were displaced along both sides of the disputed border by the fighting.

   The war also tore apart the image of both the Eritrean and Ethiopian presidents as leaders of the "African renaissance" of which President Clinton had spoken in March 1998. At the same time it damaged the alliance against the Islamic fundamentalist government of Sudan nurtured by Washington. Ethiopia moved toward Sudan, Eritrea toward Libya. Each side began to activate the other's dissidents. A peace proposal devised by the Organization of African Unity and supported by the United Nations was accepted by both sides in principle but not in fact. At the General Assembly in fall 1999, the foreign ministers of each country abused each other roundly. The killing continued.

11

Political Prison

Death stalks the United Nations.

On the evening of Friday, June 26, 1998, as Kofi Annan spoke to a distinguished audience in Ditchley Park, England, about the merits and the perils of intervention, a Beechcraft 200 light aircraft crashed in a coastal swamp twelve miles east of the airport of Abidjan, capital of the Ivory Coast. Everyone on board was killed. The group was led by Alioune Blondin Beye, a former foreign minister of Mali and the UN special envoy to Angola. There were five others aboard, including two South African pilots. Beye, aged fifty-nine, was a respected diplomat, legal scholar and politician, known as Maître Beye in recognition of his career as a lawyer in France and Mali. He was articulate and energetic, and usually wore flowing robes. Angola had been his life and his nightmare for the past four years.

Angola had been at war since the 1970s. When the Portuguese scuttled their colony in 1975, granting an ill-prepared independence, the country descended into a gruesome Cold War battlefield. The principal protagonists were UNITA, led by Jonas Savimbi and backed by the United States, and a Soviet-supported Marxist movement led by José Eduardo dos Santos and aided by Cuban troops. At the end of the Cold War, Savimbi's American supporters pressured him to accept a 1991 peace plan which called for elections. He agreed, until he lost those elections. Then he quit the peace process and started to refight the civil war.

This third Angolan war was even more destructive than the previous wars and was notable for systematic violations of the laws of war by both sides. A 1999 Human Rights Watch report noted, "Indiscriminate shelling of starving besieged cities by UNITA resulted in massive destruction, and the loss of untold numbers of civilian lives. Indiscriminate bombing by the government also took a high toll." The UN estimated that in mid-1993 as many as a thousand people were dying every day in Angola—far more than in any of the other conflicts in the world at that time, Bosnia and Somalia included.

The UN had been deeply involved in Angola since 1990. The task of its first force, the UN Angola Verification Mission (UNAVEM), had been to oversee the withdrawal of Cuban troops in 1991. UNAVEM II was then established to monitor the demobilization of both sides, but each side had demanded that the UN be denied the resources to enable it to do that job. The special representative, Margaret Anstee, compared her predicament to "fly[ing] a 747 with only the fuel for a DC-3." UNAVEM II was later described as "a textbook example of the sort of peacekeeping operation that should not occur."

In 1993, Anstee retired and Secretary General Boutros Boutros-Ghali asked Beye to lead new talks. In 1994 he helped persuade the two sides to sign a peace agreement in Lusaka. It called for UNITA's twenty thousand troops to be demobilized or absorbed into the Angolan national army. This time the UN was given more resources— UNAVEM III had an authorized military contingent of up to seven thousand personnel. They were deployed (slowly) during 1995 and 1996. The delays facilitated abuse of the Lusaka accords by the government and especially by UNITA, which refused to implement the agreement. The UN was also criticized for turning a blind eye to gross breaches of the accords and especially human rights abuses, for fear of undermining them completely. Human Rights Watch claimed that "this strategy of see no evil, speak no evil, appears to have backfired badly" and led to the complete collapse of the Lusaka accords.

The horror that Angola had become can be discerned just in the section headings of one chapter of the Human Rights Watch report.

Abuses Committed by UNITA:

Mutilations, Atrocities Against Children, Sexual Slavery, Abductions, Forced Labour and Forced Recruitment, Pillage, Indiscriminate Shelling, Killing of Government Officials, Killing of Traditional Chiefs, Lack of Freedom of Movement.

Abuses Committed by the Government:

Arbitrary Killings, Assault and Harassment of UNITA Supporters, Arrests After the Resumption of All-Out War, Forced Recruitment, Violations of the Laws of War, Pillage. . . .

Such evils were not confined to Angola in 1998.

In May 1998, Beye threatened to quit the stalled process. He then helped persuade the Security Council to impose new sanctions on UNITA and to allow more robust monitoring of violations of the Lusaka accords. But Savimbi warned that this would be seen as an assault on UNITA to which it would respond. In June, UNITA began to attack UN observers and army positions. Aid workers had been fired at, UN staff detained, and regions which had been handed over to the government reoccupied. The UN threatened to pull out its remaining 1,200 soldiers, military observers and police. Beye's fatal trip was part of a mission to try to persuade the leaders of the Ivory Coast and Togo, which were close to Savimbi, to pressure him to comply with the accords. Bill Richardson, the U.S. permanent representative to the UN, said Beye's death was a terrible loss to the peace process.

Boye's mission was one of the many sorts of "intervention" that Annan described and recommended in his speech in Ditchley. "Why was the United Nations established, if not to act as a benign policeman or doctor?" he asked. "Our job *is* to intervene: to prevent conflict where we can, to put a stop to it where it has broken out, or—when neither of those things is possible—at least to contain it and prevent it from spreading." He pointed out that not enough had been done to prevent tragedies in Bosnia and Rwanda—and that "the 'next time' may already be here," in Kosovo. "As in Bosnia, we have witnessed the shelling of towns and villages, indiscriminate attacks on civilians in the name of security, the separation of men from women and children and their summary execution, and the flight of thousands from their homes, many of them across an international border. In short, events reminiscent of the whole ghastly scenario of 'ethnic cleansing' again." He pointed out that a great deal was at stake in Kosovo: "All our professions of regret, all our expressions of determination to never again permit another Bosnia, all our hopes for a peaceful future for the Balkans will be cruelly mocked if we allow Kosovo to become another killing field."

After his speech Annan flew to Vienna to address a human rights conference. On Monday, June 29, speaking to UN staff there, he paid tribute to Maître Beye's courage and the sacrifice he had been called upon to make. He revealed that he was not leaving for New York as planned, but for Nigeria. Nigeria was one of the deepest black holes in Africa—the continent's most populous nation and certainly one of its worst governed. It was a country whose military leader, General Sani Abacha, had defied international opinion and executed all those critics he chose—until his own sudden death a few weeks earlier.

The Nigerian presidential Gulfstream was furnished in dictator-chic style, with beige leather seats, gold-plated seat buckles and other fittings, and gold taps in the lavatory. It had been sent to Vienna to pick up Annan by the new Nigerian president, General Abdulsalam Abubakar, who had invited Annan in an effort to end the country's isolation. There was a small VIP section at the front of the plane where Annan sat, a large TV screen before him. I wondered how many really bad people had sat in that seat. We took off, circled and headed south and west from Central Europe to West Africa. There was a Nigerian crew of four. Meals were served by a young steward and stewardess with enameled cutlery bearing the presidential seal— mini-pizzas, spring rolls, open sandwiches and a choice of steak or salmon—all washed down (if one chose) with a French vin du pays.

O N the plane I read from newspapers and UN analyses of the latest crises to swirl around the secretary general. The subtext of UN predicaments, past, present and future, rumbled across the air with us to Nigeria.

On Sunday, June 28, Slavko Dokmanovic, the Serb mayor of Vukovar, who was on trial before the UN war crimes tribunal in The Hague, charged with sending Croat patients in the hospital to their deaths at Serb hands in 1991, committed suicide. He hanged himself from a door hinge in his cell.

The former Yugoslavia was once again opening divisions between the United States and Europe. At this moment the conflict was over whether the Kosovo Liberation Army should be included in peace talks on the province's future. The American negotiator, Richard Holbrooke, argued that since the KLA held one third of the province, it made sense to try to talk to its leaders—if they could be found. Many Europeans officially believed that this would undermine the political leader, Ibrahim Rugova, who preached nonviolence. But they and everyone else in the international community had ignored Rugova's warnings of disaster for many years, until it was too late to act upon them. The European Union had just called on the Albanians as well as the Serbs to stop "violence and acts of terrorism." But an American official told the *New York Times,* "The Europeans didn't act fast enough to get Milosevic to stop the attacks so the rebels poured troops and arms in. Now we have a new situation to deal with."

That Monday, Olara Otunnu, whom Annan had appointed the new UN special representative for children in conflict, reported to the Security Council that two million children had been killed and another six million wounded in wars and civil wars during the nineties.

And, as ever, of course, there was Iraq. U.S. Army scientists had just discovered traces of VX nerve agent in Iraqi warheads sent abroad by UNSCOM for inspection. The chairman of UNSCOM, Richard Butler, had told the Security Council that he had no doubt that the findings were accurate, but he had asked French and Swiss laboratories for confirmation. If the findings were verified, this would prove yet another instance in which Iraq had outright lied over the extent of its weapons program; it had always denied weaponizing any missiles with VX gas.

Over the Mediterranean, I asked Annan about this latest assault upon the trust he had put in Saddam Hussein at his meeting in Baghdad. He replied, "In all honesty, we need to manage this in a competent, rational, wise manner, because if not we could have a disaster on our hands. In the end there will have to be a political judgment as to whether we have sufficiently disarmed them. We should then set up a mechanism to monitor and contain them."

We left the Mediterranean and flew over the Maghreb. Two of the countries below us were preoccupying the UN's secret diplomatic machine. Annan was trying to negotiate some kind of diplomatic breakthrough with Libya in the bombing of Pan Am Flight 103 over Lockerbie, Scotland, in December 1988. International sanctions had been imposed on Libya in 1992 to induce the state to hand over for trial two men indicted for the bombing. The sanctions were beginning to fray and Annan felt it important that an agreement be reached before they were flouted totally. He was also planning to send a high-level investigating mission to Algeria, where terrorism had killed at least sixty thousand people, nearly all of them innocent civilians, in the last few years.

As we flew over Western Sahara, the desert over whose future the UN was staging a referendum costing millions of dollars, I read about Nigeria's predicament and talked to Annan about his own involvement in the country. In recent years Nigeria had provided a clear example of the world's inability to act against or even to influence bloody and recalcitrant regimes. Few had been more recalcitrant than that of General Sani Abacha, though many were even more brutal.

In Nigeria, the army was the state. At about seventy-five thousand men, it was much the biggest in Africa. Defense absorbed 9.2 percent of total recurrent spending and 3.3 percent of capital expenditure. The military had dominated and abused Nigeria since it seized power in the sixties, never more so than in the last five years under Abacha. The military was now loathed, yet it was almost the only national institution in this vast and disparate country. The Yoruba in the southwest, the Hausa in the north and the Ibo in the southeast have always had difficulty in forging a common purpose. The Biafran war of secession by the Ibos in 1967 was only the most tragic example of the tendency to irredentism. One former leader once said, "West and East Nigeria are as different as Ireland from Germany, and the north is as different from either as China."

The army had always been controlled by the Hausa, and in recent years, as it abused power more and more, the people of the southwest suffered disproportionately.

Abacha had been the eighth military dictator that Nigeria had endured since independence in 1960 and the most intransigent. He had lived a life which can best be described as weird and which depended heavily on caricatures of despotism. His rule showed very clearly how difficult it is for the outside world, the international community, to intervene and change a government which is determined to pursue its own interests, however obnoxious these seem to much of the rest of the world.

Abacha's career path in Nigeria had been in the army. By the early 1990s he had become both army chief of staff and minister of defense. By now Nigeria was in a state of chaos, particularly because its succession of military dictators had used their power to ensure that the country's vast oil wealth profited themselves above all and no one else. Oil is Nigeria's most important industry, providing about 80 percent of government revenue, not to mention the personal revenues of top military officers. Corruption was not part of government in Nigeria; it was the object of government. The ruling clique had become more and more deeply involved in every stage of the petroleum business. Officers took kickbacks from foreign companies seeking to prospect for oil; they were bribed by the construction companies that won the contracts to build rigs and pipelines; they controlled almost every sale of Nigerian crude oil; and as if all this was not enough, in recent years they also had begun to siphon off the money used by Nigeria's oil refineries to turn crude into gasoline. As a result, the people of one of the world's largest oil-producing countries suffered crippling shortages of fuel.

The most important moment in Nigeria's descent into misrule came in 1993. General Ibrahim Babangida, the current dictator, was under huge international pressure to move the country back toward democracy, and he staged elections that year that were intended, the military said, to return the country to civilian rule.

Moshood Abiola's name was a byword for the extravagant acquisition of wealth in Africa. In the early nineties, he was so close to the military rulers of Nigeria that it was difficult to say which needed the other more. With their help, he bought an airline, farms, factories, a publishing house, a fifty-room ranch in a suburb of Lagos, with swimming pools, marbled halls and stretch limos, all protected by razor wire stretched atop high concrete walls.

In 1993, Babangida persuaded Abiola to use his position to run in the elections demanded by the outside world. He became leader of a newly formed Social Democratic Party, fighting the equally novel center-right party. The early returns showed him to be the winner, with support cutting across religious and tribal lines in a way which was unprecedented in Nigeria. The military then seemed to panic; the northern Hausa generals decided they could not bear the idea of a southern Yoruba president, even one as entrenched in the murkiness of the system as they were. Before the votes were all counted General Babangida canceled the elections, citing irregularities. No doubt some had taken place, but the election was thought to have been the fairest in Nigerian history. Abiola went back to making money.

Later that year Sani Abacha forced out President Babangida and made himself head of state. At once he dissolved the federal parliament, the thirty state governments and all local councils, and declared all political parties illegal for the next two years. But at first there were some reasons to hope, as he promised an early return to democracy. Nigeria was then in a chaos of corruption. Inflation was wildly out of control, some $8 billion of oil revenue was lost (stolen) according to the central bank, the country was at least $8.4 billion in arrears in paying just the interest on its huge debt, and the international price of oil (which accounts for 98 percent of Nigeria's exports) was at a ten-year low.

Abacha's prescriptions provided no cure. The financial crisis worsened, and he began to exhibit more and more of the paranoia which eventually consumed him and the country. Unrest grew, but the opposition was split and weak. Trade unions, once very powerful, were diminished by increased unemployment and falling real wages as well as poor leadership. In stepped Moshood Abiola again. On the first anniversary of his canceled election win, he appeared before a large crowd in Lagos and declared himself president, head of the army and head of government. He was arrested and charged with treason. Nigeria's oil workers then went on strike demanding his release. Abacha resisted them. Twenty people were killed in riots in Lagos. Public shootings took place all over the country. Abiola remained in jail, mostly in solitary confinement. He was mistreated if not tortured. He already suffered from diabetes and a weak heart. He was never given adequate medical care.

Nigeria plunged to ever lower depths of corruption and misrule. In January 1995, Abacha announced there had been another coup attempt and he let loose hit squads. Eighty or more army officers were killed. One general, Lawan Gwadebe, who was alleged to be a ringleader of the alleged plot, was hung upside down, had his fingernails torn out and was smeared with excrement.

Then, in another snub at the opinion of the international commu nity, Abacha arrested General Olusegun Obasanjo, head of state from 1976 to 1979 and the only military ruler ever to leave office voluntarily. He also intensified a campagn against the Ogoni tribe from southern Nigeria, which was protesting the exploitation of their land and resources by the Shell Oil Company. Protestors were shot or locked into detention camps, where the men were beaten and the women raped. General Obasanjo was sentenced to death along with many other senior former officials. Eventually most of these sentences were commuted to life imprisonment.

That October, Abacha announced a new three-year transition to civilian rule. But only a month later he committed the act which brought the furious condemnation of the outside world. He executed Ken Saro-wiwa, the Ogoni playwright and environmental activist, and eight other Ogoni activists. They had been tried on trumped-up charges of murdering their political opponents. Appeals for clemency came from all over the world, including from Boutros Boutros-Ghali and from the leaders of the Commonwealth, in particular South African president Nelson Mandela.

To show his contempt for outside opinion Abacha had the men executed while the Commonwealth heads of government were meeting in Auckland, New Zealand. As a result, Nigeria was suspended from the Commonwealth.

Abacha's brutality increased rather than diminished his sense of paranoia. Throughout 1995, 1996 and 1997 more military officers were dismissed or arrested on suspicion of disloyalty. Abacha spent much of his time secluded in the marble fortress he had built himself in the midst of the military complex of Aso Rock in the center of the new capital, Abuja. He trusted only the presidential guard; other brigades were deprived of ammunition so that they should not be threats. In December 1997, Abacha announced he had foiled another coup attempt, led by the deputy head of state, Lieutenant General Oladipo Diya, who, with eleven other officers, was arrested, tried, found guilty and sentenced to death.

Oddly enough, however, outside Nigeria, Abacha's rule had some good effects. In 1996, Nigeria brokered a peace agreement to end Liberia's appalling, nihilistic seven-year civil war. And in Sierra Leone, an intervention by ECOWAS, the Economic Community of West African States, was led by Nigeria and proved vital in helping restore the democratically elected government and overthrowing the

vicious rebel junta which specialized in cutting off the hands of peasants, though Nigeria suffered heavy casualties among its troops.

Many foreign interlocutors found Abacha reasonably pleasant to
meet. He always asked after people's families, and he did not behave
in a bombastic manner. He was deeply superstitious and spent a
general's ransom scouring Africa for the best marabouts, or fortune-
tellers.

Abacha depended heavily on a small coterie of foreign businessmen who made fortunes during his regime and, in turn, serviced his
needs. Those he favored had helped him accumulate a vast fortune
abroad, said to be over $6 billion. There was a Lebanese "mafia" that
is said to have made billions of dollars from its deals with the military. Its members would fly in and out of Abuja on private jets, bringing girls or whatever else Abacha and his cronies ordered. Other
prostitutes came in on state aircraft including, I imagined, the one on
which we were now flying.

Abacha functioned only at night. In the early hours the anterooms
of the garishly marbled statehouse would be lined with cabinet ministers, senior civil servants, foreign officials and businessmen all waiting nervously for an audience with the dictator, who would very
often be drunk and occupied with his imported prostitutes.

As we flew over the Sahara, Annan said he had been concerned
about Nigeria since becoming secretary general. Realizing that
Abacha was impervious to public criticism and deaf to public pleas,
he had tried to deal with him quietly.

A few weeks after his appointment, in January 1997, Annan had
flown to Lomé, the capital of Togo, to take part in a mini-summit
convened by President Gnassingbé Eyadema of Togo on the Zaire
crisis. At that time the rebels against Zaire's president, Mobutu Sese
Seko, backed if not controlled by such neighboring countries as
Rwanda and Uganda, were marching toward the capital, Kinshasa.

It was an odd encounter, Annan's first experience of President
Eyadema's cult of "authenticity." "You go to these meetings," Annan
said, "and the room is packed with more dancers and singers than
delegates. Whenever the president speaks they get up and cheer and
sing and dance, and cry that he is the greatest, and so on. The same
thing happens for other speakers, too. So it takes a long time."

Sani Abacha was taking part in the Togo summit and Annan used
the time to get into long discussions with him on the release of pris-

oners and the transition to democratic rule in Nigeria. I asked the secretary general what Abacha was like to deal with. He said he "was very mild mannered; you wouldn't think he had it in him to do all the things he had done. But then Saddam was equally calm, and so you wonder if their sensitivities get numbed."

With Abacha in Lomé was General Abdulsalam Abubakar, an officer who had served with UNIFIL, the UN peacekeeping force in South Lebanon. Annan thought him clearheaded; he spoke well and came across as a serious professional officer. When Abacha left the room, Annan told Abubakar that Nigeria had to break with the past, come back into the international community and play its role in Africa.

After that meeting in Lomé, Annan took to telephoning Abacha at regular intervals to try to persuade him of the need to release prisoners. Abacha would speak to him always very late at night Nigerian time. "He used to say, 'Maybe next year,' and I would say, 'Next year is too late,' " Annan related.

When Annan asked for clemency for General Diya and the other officers sentenced to death with him, Abacha replied that clemency was a mistake. If he had not shown clemency to Obasanjo and others arrested in the last few years then General Diya might not have plotted against him. Annan hastened to assure him that leniency had been right.

By now it was clear that Abacha's plans for the transition from military to civilian rule were devised so that he could "succeed himself." The five presidential parties he had allowed to be created had all adopted him as their presidential candidate. He had weathered the visit of and protests by the pope. He had arrested more critics without problem. The country's oil, squandered though it was, still allowed him to ignore the world. But then, suddenly and unexpectedly, on June 8, Abacha died.

The next day General Abubakar was installed as president. Annan called to congratulate him. The secretary general had agreed with Abacha before his death that he should send his foreign minister, Tom Ikimi, to New York to discuss the release of political prisoners. He now suggested to Abubakar that Ikimi should still come. Abubakar agreed. Annan went to sign the condolence book at the Nigerian mission at the UN.

A week after Abacha's death Abubakar began to release political prisoners. In a television broadcast he asked Nigerians to "give peace a chance. There is no nation in the world that does not make mistakes. When such mistakes are made there is no use crying over spilt milk." In the outside world he was knocking at an open door. The West considered the stakes in Nigeria enormous.

On June 22 Tom Ikimi came to see Annan secretly at the secretary general's residence on Sutton Place. He was a changed man. Gone was the arrogant spokesman of the military who would lecture all critics on the need not to interfere in Nigeria's internal affairs. Ikimi was now almost meek. He said that Abubakar thanked the secretary general for the two phone calls he had made and noted that Annan had signed the condolence register at the permanent mission. The death of General Abacha had been a shock to the entire country whatever one may have thought of him as an individual. Annan said Abacha had played an important regional role. He had in mind the Nigerian army's intervention on the side of the elected government in Sierra Leone.

Ikimi said Abubakar felt the secretary general could help Nigeria put behind it the difficult experiences of the last three or four years. He wanted to use the "window" of General Abacha's death to resolve Nigeria's fundamental concerns. Nigeria took seriously the comments of those who said it should resume its rightful place in Africa and play a role in the world. General Abubakar, he said, was committed to a transition to democratic rule but had to engage in "consultations" before proceeding. But Abubakar wanted the secretary general's support for an extension—not to extend his time in power but to ease the transition.

Looming over everything was the question of Abiola. When and under what conditions should he be released? And what then? His supporters, mainly from the southwest of the country, insisted either that he should assume the presidency as soon as he was released or at the very least that he should head a government of national unity. But an Abiola-led government would be hard if not impossible for the military and the five political parties that had agreed to support Abacha's presidential candidacy on August 1 to accept.

Annan asked about a government of national unity involving Abiola. Ikimi thought the idea unrealistic.

No one knew what Abiola himself felt about it all. In 1995 he had turned down the offer of being released on bail on condition that he

play no part in politics. One of the last people to see him in detention, his doctor, was quoted as saying that Abiola was singing religious songs to himself. Annan said that Abiola should be released as
soon as possible. He said that General Abubakar had already gener-
ated quite a lot of goodwill. The Canadians, as head of the Commonwealth Ministerial Action Group, were prepared to let bygones
be bygones and work with him, and so was the United States. Ikimi
said that if Annan went to Abuja to give Abubakar his blessing, Abiola would be released. Annan said that he wanted to help Nigeria's
transition to democracy.

The foreign minister offered to send Annan a plane. We were now
on it.

AFTER about a six-hour flight from Vienna, over the Mediterranean, Algeria and Niger, a country I had once crossed by car in
search of the camel caravans which still carry salt across the desert,
we arrived in Abuja, the purpose-built and thus rather aseptic capital
in the center of Nigeria. On the usual airport red carpet Annan was
met by Ikimi. Rather to Annan's surprise and the disappointment of
some of his staff there were no press or television cameras at the airport—no one to whom he could read the statement which they had
carefully prepared, stating that he was here to help the transition to
democracy. There was then a forty-minute drive along good, wide
empty roads into the town. In his suite Annan gathered his staff; they
marveled at the low-key nature of their arrival. There were not even
any messages from any leaders of civil society, heads of nongovernmental organizations or human rights groups. Annan said he wanted
to be sure he saw such people, but he wanted to choose them himself, not have the government select them.

His principal objective was to promote "an early, credible and genuine return to civilian rule." He would ask the general how he
planned to implement the commitment to return Nigeria to democracy, emphasize the importance of adhering to the October 1, 1998,
transition date, encourage specific confidence-building measures and
offer UN support for advancing these objectives.

Annan believed that Abiola's release posed a dilemma for
Abubakar. If Abiola was to become a conduit for "people power,"
Abubakar might either repress it, which would damage his standing,

or permit demonstrations, which would undermine his authority with the military. In any case there would be considerable legal grounds to say no to any move to make Abiola president at once, as his followers wished. The 1993 election, held under the 1989 constitution, had been annulled by decree before the final results could be tabulated or announced. The claim that Abiola was the winner was based on partial results. He had never taken the oath of office. Even if he had been elected and sworn in, his term of office would have ended in 1997. There was no legal, constitutional basis for declaring him president now. However, he should be released and allowed to play a part in the transition to democracy. Annan believed that if the military were to be persuaded to leave, some kind of protection had to be offered to them. The amnesty given to Chilean officers when the military relinquished power at the end of the 1980s offered a precedent.

Now in the gossipy atmosphere of Abuja, we began to hear more rumors about the circumstances of Abacha's death. Officially, he was said to have suffered a heart attack. Unofficially, Nigeria was alive with rumors that this attack was caused by overexertion in bed. Among the more lurid tales was that Abacha was on this occasion in bed with two women, one of whom ran screaming from the bedroom when he started having convulsions. There were other stories that he had taken an overdose of Viagra or that his Viagra had been laced. In early July one Nigerian magazine, *Newswatch*, reported that some of the rumors about Abacha's death "stretched the imagination quite a bit" and that his widow was sure that close friends had killed her husband.

The *New York Times* subsequently reported that U.S. intelligence analysts thought there was evidence that Abacha was poisoned by enemies in the military elite while in the company of three prostitutes. The *Times* reported that the poisoning might have been done by an officer or clique of officers "who believed that the general's hold on power was destroying what little good name the army had left." The cause of death was now less important than the effect. The end of Abacha had enabled Nigeria to come in from the cold.

The next morning Annan and his party were taken in a convoy of black Mercedes into the sprawling suburban fortress of Aso Rock, Abacha's heavily fortified lair. Behind white walls in carefully manicured gardens where gazelles and ostriches grazed, a series of huge white hydraulic gates blocked the road against cars and attack by armored vehicles. While Abacha was alive the gardens were studded with tanks and armored personnel carriers. The gazelles and ostriches had shared the grounds with what seemed like legions of men in trench coats and dark glasses, toting submachine guns. They were gone now. The mood inside the complex was relatively relaxed.

In the center of the fortress was a low building, white and slightly Moorish on the outside, heavily and garishly marbled inside. Annan and his team of UN officials were brought through a group of Nigerian photographers into an extraordinary paneled council chamber where Annan and Abubakar sat on twin throned leather chairs on a raised podium; Abubakar's people sat at a long desk running down one side of the room, Annan's on the other.

The first part of the meeting included senior military and police officers, secretaries of state and ambassadors. Nothing of interest was said. But when all the others were cleared out for the two principals to meet alone, the conversation was, said Annan later, "very frank." Annan became convinced that Abubakar was ready to hand over power, feeling that fate and historic accident had landed him in this job. The general said that only when he took over did he realize what a desperate situation Nigeria was in. The country was on the edge of explosion, he thought.

Annan asked Abubakar about his wife, a judge. Abubakar replied she *was* a judge, but there would have been an obvious conflict of interest so she had stepped down when he became president.

In the last three weeks Abubakar had consulted widely, with women's groups, trade unions, churches. Annan encouraged him to move fast; he told the general that he had done very well so far, and should now create a sense of momentum and inevitability. Abubakar said he was concerned that Nigerian civil society does not know what it wants. (But when does it ever? asked Annan later of his staff.)

Abubakar said he wanted to move ahead as soon as possible, but feared that October 1 would be too soon for credible elections. Annan responded that if he delayed them, he must set out clearly the reasons and establish a new timetable at once. The general said he was prepared to release Abiola, but only if he gave up his dreams of becoming president. If he would confirm in writing that he would renounce the mandate of 1993, he could be out tomorrow. Abubakar evidently hoped that Annan, the magician of the Iraq crisis, would try to persuade Abiola to do this. Annan said he hoped he could see Abiola quickly.

That evening Annan was secretly driven from the hotel back into Aso Rock and led to a villa near the statehouse where he had seen Abubakar. There he found Abiola watching the World Cup quarterfinal between England and Argentina, but with the sound turned off.

Annan shook hands and asked about his health. Abiola said he was fine, despite his long incarceration. Then he asked, "Who are you?"

"I am Kofi Annan, the secretary general of the United Nations."

"What happened to the Egyptian?"

Annan explained that he had taken over as secretary general from Boutros Boutros-Ghali at the beginning of 1997. Abiola rushed toward him and kissed his hand. He said he had been told only that he was being brought to meet "an important person."

Abiola's isolation had been almost total. He did not know that the pope had recently visited Nigeria and pleaded in vain for his release. And it was only the day before that he had been told that Abacha had died of a heart attack in early June. Annan asked a security guard to turn up the sound on the television so that he and Abiola could talk with less risk of being overheard. The guard fiddled with the remote control; nothing happened and he said the set was faulty. (It turned out that this was not true.) Abiola told Annan that he had had no radio since the summer of 1994. He had seen no one in his family since 1995. His guards refused to talk to him, so long ago he had given up trying to find out from them what was going on in the world. All he had to read were the Bible and the Koran. But he had been shown one newspaper story. It was about the death of one of his wives, Kudirat, who had campaigned for his release and was assassinated in 1996.

Annan asked Abiola what he would do if and when he was released. Would he claim the presidency as of right since 1993, and as many of his supporters demanded? Abiola said he had no such intention—that he knew the world had moved on since 1993. "I want to go to Mecca to give thanks for being alive," Abiola told Annan. "I do not have to be president to live my life." Annan was greatly encouraged, believing that he would be able to get Abiola quickly released.

Abiola astonished Annan. He seemed both humble and realistic despite his long and cruel isolation. But he did not want to make any commitments in writing at this stage. He said that if he signed anything rather than just give his word, he would be accused of cowardice "and I will be destroyed socially and politically. I'll become a leper." He said he would prefer to meet with Abubakar and give him the same assurance, on his word of honor, as he had given Annan.

THE lobby of the Hilton began to fill with people eager to see Annan. His surprise arrival was greeted with enormous enthusiasm by opponents of the regime. Everyone he met—the fabulously costumed traditional rulers; leaders of nongovernmental organizations; Nigeria's former leader General Yakubu Gowon, who had defeated the 1967 Biafran rebellion and been generous in victory; newly released political prisoners—was elated by his presence.

Staying in the same hotel were President Ahmad Tejan Kabbah of Sierra Leone and President Charles Taylor of Liberia. They had been invited to a "mini-summit" by Abubakar, particularly to see if they could, with Annan's help, bring an end to Sierra Leone's civil war, in which Liberia was aiding the nihilistic rebels. It was easy for me to arrange to see Kabbah, who explained the difficulties of rebuilding his country while the terror wrought by the rebels persisted. When I went down the opposite corridor to try to ask for a meeting with Taylor, the way was barred abusively by the thugs with whom he surrounds himself. Taylor, unlike Kabbah, is intransigent. The "mini-summit" was unable to resolve the crisis.

By Thursday morning it seemed that Abubakar was unable or unwilling to release Abiola while Annan was in Nigeria. Annan had a final meeting with the general. "I told him that he should release all political prisoners, including Abiola, at once and that I was about to announce in public that I expected him to do so," Annan said to his staff. Then, at a parting press conference Annan said, "All Nigerians insist on a return to democracy and . . . a peaceful, credible process leading to free and fair elections." He said that Abubakar had agreed to release all political prisoners, including Abiola, promptly. He revealed that Abiola had told him he would not seek the presidency as of right. In an oblique reference to some of Abiola's militant supporters, Annan said, "I found him in some ways more realistic than some of us outside."

We left Nigeria as we had arrived—on a Nigerian presidential jet bound for Ghana, Annan's homeland. Half an hour into the flight, the plane shuddered and slowed as the flaps extended and stuck. The pilot rushed into the cabin and announced that we had to turn around at once and land again in Abuja as quickly as possible. Some members of the party were visibly anxious. Not Annan, who continued talking and reading. When the plane landed safely he said, "I often tell my wife I am a happy fool."

Not much worked under the Nigerian military, but they had made sure of their own comfort. Another executive jet was available within minutes to carry us on to Accra, Ghana, where a full dress guard was lined up to meet the country's most famous son. He was then driven to the beautiful but run-down fort on the ocean where President Jerry Rawlings has his domain. After a long talk with Rawlings, and a night at a government guesthouse, we left on the Nigerian jet for London, where Annan reported to the British foreign secretary, Robin Cook, on the partial success of his visit and his belief that Abubakar was committed to ending military rule. They also discussed the secret moves in which Annan had been involved to find an end to the UN's impasse with Libya over the Lockerbie bombing. Shortly afterwards the British and American governments announced that they would now accept what they had hitherto always refused— a trial under Scottish law in a third country, the Netherlands.

General Abubakar was not as prompt in releasing Abiola as he had given Annan to believe. A week later, on July 7, while Abiola, still imprisoned, was meeting with Thomas Pickering, the U.S. under secretary of state, he collapsed. Pickering attempted artificial resuscitation, but Abiola died. There were inevitable suspicions among his family and supporters that he had been murdered, perhaps by poison. An autopsy conducted by an international team of pathologists found that his death was, in fact, caused by heart disease. But conspiracy theories remained rife and led to riots in which scores of people died.

What was clear was that by their malign neglect of Abiola's medical condition his jailers had hastened his death. If General Abubakar had released him to Annan as he had indicated, Abiola would have had medical attention which might have identified the gravity of his condition. The good offices of the secretary general had not been used well enough.

In other respects, General Abubakar kept his promises in a remarkable manner. He was indeed a bridge to democracy. Assembly elections were held at the end of 1998, and in May 1999 presidential elections followed. They were won by former military ruler and former political prisoner Olusegun Obasanjo, and he was inaugurated president.

General Abubakar faded into the background a year after he had unexpectedly come to power and sought Annan's assistance. The days of roadblocks manned by soldiers with submachine guns demanding bribes, of coups and rumors of coups, of international sanctions and pariah status, were gone. Obasanjo began to attack corruption. Nigeria was accepted back into the world. The International Monetary Fund and the World Bank resumed lending and the country was readmitted to the Commonwealth.

In June 1999, General Obasanjo became the first Nigerian leader in more than ten years to address the United Nations.

12

Iraq Again

I next ran into Annan in November 1998, when a new Iraq crisis interrupted his attempt to mediate in Western Sahara. This dispute, between Morocco and the Polisario guerrillas who sought independence, over a vast tract of desert stretching between Algeria, Morocco and Mauritania was one of the UN's longest and least successful peacekeeping problems.

The Iraq crisis that Annan had flown to Baghdad to resolve in February had not ended. Saddam Hussein had flouted the memorandum of understanding with Annan almost as soon as he had signed it. Perhaps Annan should have expected no less. As I have mentioned, the inspectors had made only one visit to the contentious palaces from which Iraq had demanded that they be excluded. The team had found them completely sanitized—even furniture and telephones had been removed. The Iraqis had told Charles Duelfer, the head of the team, that despite Saddam's agreement with Annan, there would be no further entry. Duelfer reported this to the Security Council. During the summer of 1998, Saddam had wooed more support for the lifting of sanctions, and probed for signs of American weakness. Throughout the period the United States and Britain were in a minority of two on the fifteen-member Security Council, with all others counseling at least caution if not concessions to Iraq. This conciliatory lobby was led by the French and the Russians. Saddam also had reason to think that with President Clinton in the toils of the Lewinsky scandal, Washington was in no position to respond to provocation.

In early August, exactly eight years after invading Kuwait, Iraq announced that it would no longer cooperate with UNSCOM with regard to its disarmament work. Then it curtailed even monitoring activity. Washington's response was surprisingly mild. Until now the U.S. had been pursuing a two-prong strategy against Saddam— mandatory UN inspections to find and eliminate his weapons of mass destruction, and comprehensive economic sanctions to deny Iraq access to funds and industrial equipment until it fulfilled the UN's requirements. The policy had failed to destroy Saddam or to discover all of his prohibited arms, and international patience was wearing thin. There was a growing feeling that sanctions were causing too much harm to ordinary Iraqis, especially children, and doing almost no damage to the corrupt and entrenched ruling clique around Saddam.

Then UNSCOM and the UN and the U.S. were seriously embarrassed by the resignation from UNSCOM of Major Scott Ritter, one of the most creative inspectors. Ritter, clearly angry, alleged that the Clinton administration had asked UNSCOM's chairman, Richard Butler, to soft-pedal the inspections in recent weeks, and to be careful not to provoke another real showdown with the Iraqis. Ritter also charged that the U.S. had placed its own intelligence agents in UNSCOM, and he described methods of investigation and contacts, which damaged UNSCOM. Ritter also revealed that the Israelis had given UNSCOM significant help in tracing prohibited weapons. This was seen as an embarrassment to UNSCOM, though all UN member states had an obligation to extend such assistance. Many, including some of the permanent five, had refused to honor this commitment.

Saddam's assault on UNSCOM's position did not incur the immediate wrath of Washington or its principal ally on Iraqi matters, Britain. It appeared that Washington did not want to create such an open and difficult crisis as in February. Saddam may well also have been emboldened by the fact that the U.S. failed to carry out threats to bomb Serb forces as they drove several hundred thousand ethnic Albanian villagers out of their homes and into the mountains of the Serbian province of Kosovo.

But it was worth recalling, as the *Washington Post* did in mid-August, that in February, National Security Adviser Sandy Berger had described Saddam as "one of the most dangerous security threats our people will face over the next generation." Now the Clinton administration appeared to be shifting from the certainties of a few months ago toward a more ambiguous response.

Annan believed that this new crisis had been provoked by the Iraqis' belief that whether or not they cooperated with UNSCOM, the United States had no intention of ever allowing the sanctions to be lifted. He and his staff sought to end the deadlock. He proposed a so-called comprehensive review of the relations between Iraq and the international agencies, within several weeks of UNSCOM's and the International Atomic Energy Agency's being allowed back to work. This review, he hoped, "would not only produce light at the end of the tunnel but, more importantly, facilitate business in the council and break the impasse."

At first, the United States reacted cautiously if not coldly to the idea. By the end of October, still faced with 13–2 votes against it in the Security Council, Washington agreed to allow the review to go forward on certain conditions. But the U.S. still would not countenance a timetable for the lifting of sanctions. On October 31 the Iraqi government ordered a halt to all of UNSCOM's work in Iraq.

This was an error. Usually Saddam had showed skill in the way he toyed with the international community. Not this time. Three days later the Democrats won a resounding victory in the midterm elections. This was taken to show how little the American people cared about the Lewinsky affair and how much more they were interested in preserving their president. Moreover, Clinton had gained some advantage in the Arab world by pushing through the Wye agreement between the Israelis and the Palestinians, under which Israel should promptly cede more land in the occupied West Bank.

Saddam had both humiliated Kofi Annan and destroyed his 13–2 advantage in the Security Council. Even the French and the Russians felt unable to condone, let alone support, such a flagrant breach of Security Council resolutions and Annan's memorandum of understanding. In response to the Iraqi halt to UNSCOM's work, the United States began a massive new buildup of its forces in the Gulf. The plan of attack called for waves of Tomahawk cruise missiles to be launched from carriers such as the USS *Eisenhower* and from B-52s flying out of the United States onto more than a hundred targets in Iraq. They would first be targeted on Iraqi ground-to-air defenses. Then E-2 Hawkeyes, the naval equivalent of AWACS observation planes, would be launched to provide early warning of Iraqi counter-attack, and to exercise command and control for the following waves of aircraft. EA-6B Prowlers would follow into the sky, equipped to close down communications within a city, and to jam Iraqi radar and electronic data links. Then the strike aircraft, FA-18 Hornets, would destroy any remaining air defenses before moving on to specified targets.

Officers claimed, as they do at the start of every war, that the equipment was far more sophisticated than anything that was available at the time of the last one: "In '91 what we dropped on Iraq was 'dumb' technology. It was like throwing the whole kitchen sink at Saddam," one veteran of Desert Storm told *The Times* of London. By the week of November 9, an American aerial bombardment, supported by Britain, was very close.

In Western Sahara, then in Marrakesh, then in Casablanca, Annan was constantly pursued by calls to and from Madeleine Albright; Robin Cook, the British foreign secretary; and Hubert Védrine, the French foreign minister. On Tuesday, November 10, Albright said she thought it would help if Annan issued a statement; her staff had prepared a draft and she would have it faxed to him. He replied he would think about it. "I've already made two statements," he said. "But if I do it, I'll have to do it my way."

Annan asked Albright what was happening in Washington and she replied that all options were on the table. Use of force was very possible, and the United States was asking all nonessential staff to leave Jerusalem and Tel Aviv in case of Iraqi counterattack. When Albright's draft arrived Annan felt it was too bellicose. She wanted him to say, inter alia, that he was "deeply concerned at" Iraq's decision of October 31 to suspend all cooperation with UNSCOM, and that this was a "flagrant violation" of the relevant resolutions. "President Saddam Hussein now bears a heavy responsibility. His actions have created a dangerous situation and time may be short. I appeal to him, in the name of the Iraqi people, to take this opportunity and to resume cooperation with UNSCOM and the IAEA."

Annan accepted some of the ideas suggested but, he told me in Morocco, "Member states or the council can play tough. I'm not in a position to do that. They have to let me do it in my way. They should not encourage me to be a Rambo—because I can never be a Rambo or use language that is not mine."

In Marrakesh he made a statement that he was "saddened and burdened" (rather than "deeply concerned") by Iraq's decision to stop cooperation. He urged Saddam Hussein and the Iraqi government to rescind the decision. The only way to get sanctions lifted was for Iraq to cooperate fully with the Security Council and wait for the results of the comprehensive review he had proposed. "This would be good for the Iraqi people, for the region and for the world," Annan said.

At about two the following morning, Wednesday, November 11, Annan was awakened to be told that Richard Butler had just ordered all UNSCOM personnel to leave Baghdad at once, after U.S. officials had warned him that an attack was imminent.

UNSCOM is answerable to the Security Council, not to the secretary general; Annan asked if the council had given permission for this wholescale withdrawal. He was told that Butler had consulted that month's president of the council. The presidency was held at this time by the United States, and it was its acting ambassador, Peter Burleigh, with whom Butler had consulted. Burleigh had given his permission at once. In Morocco, Annan immediately began to worry about the other UN staff in Baghdad. UNSCOM was only a third of the total, and he feared that if UNSCOM was withdrawn the others would panic that they were about to be subject to a massive attack.

The new German foreign minister, Joschka Fischer, who had recently come to see Annan in New York, called from Moscow to ask if the time had not come for Annan to take a new initiative. He replied, "Mr. Minister, to take an initiative one has to have elements to work with, and the will to deal and find a compromise must be there." Annan decided to fly straight back to New York.

I remarked to him, in his hotel room in Casablanca, that Saddam's behavior meant that the U.S. was in a much stronger position than in February. "He has torn up your deal."

Annan agreed. "Not only has he torn it up, but even people sympathetic to him in the Security Council are fed up with him." But that did not mean the Chinese, the Russians and the French were enthusiastic for bombing. "My concern is that if we hit him because he's been so stupid, stubborn and unreasonable, not only do we lose all rights to inspect and monitor, but oil for food may also cease and we will be accused of starving Iraqi children even more. Then what will happen to the Kurds above the 32nd parallel? We've been feeding the north with Iraqi oil-for-food money. We'd have to pull out and someone else will have to do it. The risk of a very weakened Iraq beginning to disintegrate is real."

Annan thought that bombing would make Saddam a hero in the Arab world for daring to defy the U.S. "Saddam has put everyone in an impossible situation now," Annan said. "I keep telling the Iraqis that the ball is in their court. It took months to get the Security Council to agree to a comprehensive review. Then the Iraqis blew it. I told Tariq that compared to February, when people were still standing up for Iraq, now there is a deafening silence." The secretary general agreed that the UN had to react, but he was nervous about bombing. "We have a saying in Ghana, 'The horse may be mad but the rider need not be.' Men like Saddam can make you do all sorts of crazy things in trying to punish them that are not in your own interest."

But, I pointed out, we could not go on playing Saddam's game forever, being continually jerked back and forth by him.

"I don't argue with that," Annan replied. "But the point is, if you can't play Saddam's game, how do you best hit him? I'm not convinced that massive use of force is the answer. I don't have the answer. My frustration with Saddam does not push me to support things that punish the people of Iraq. Bombing is a blunt instrument."

I asked the secretary general whether he felt personally betrayed by Saddam. "I really did see it as my duty to go in February," he responded. "When I was asked later what guarantees I had and what I would do if he broke his word, I replied that I went there to resolve a crisis, not to take personal responsibility for the behavior of Saddam Hussein. When we sign agreements, the other side may break them, but that says more about them than about us."

Quoting his remark on his return to New York after his February trip to procure an agreement that Saddam was "a man I can do business with," I suggested that it was now proved that you could *not* do business with him.

"It proves you cannot take his word," Annan said. "I used that phrase in that I got him to change his mind. I did not mean that he was a man of honor. You cannot rely on him."

Annan also pointed out that normally those defeated in war have to abide by the agreements imposed upon them. Look at Germany after World War II, he said. Moreover, defeat usually means a change of government. "Saddam would not have lasted any time in a democratic system," Annan reflected. "No one would have guessed he would still be in power eight years later. Sanctions work well against democratic regimes [where they aren't needed] but much less well against autocracies. They haven't worked in forty years against Castro."

WHILE Annan was in the air on the way back to New York, the U.S. armada, supplemented by a small but important British contingent, was gathering around Iraq. Of all the agencies, the Pentagon was the most eager to bomb on this occasion. This was not because the Pentagon is always hawkish. Indeed, in recent years it had been among the most cautious members of the U.S. national security establishment, particularly where the commitment of U.S. troops was concerned. But Secretary of Defense William Cohen had traveled to eleven Middle Eastern countries in the previous week, attempting to put together the best possible informal coalition of consent among Iraq's neighbors. He had to reassure all the regimes with which he met that this time the United States was not crying wolf; it was really serious in its determination to press its advantage and attack. "We will do it this time," Cohen had told all of his interlocutors.

President Yeltsin now sent a letter to Saddam urging him to back down, and Ambassador Lavrov, Russia's UN ambassador, informed the Security Council that Saddam's response was positive. He said that Iraq was now prepared to comply with Resolution 687, section C (the disarmament provision), in the expectation that as soon as the Security Council was satisfied that it was complying, it would begin a comprehensive review.

In Washington, it was decided that this was not enough—that all it amounted to was Lavrov's oral interpretation of what Saddam's aides had written in an unseen letter replying to an unknown missive. Acting U.S. UN ambassador Peter Burleigh said that the U.S. insisted on an unambiguous, authoritative, public and immediate statement that Iraq had rescinded its decisions of August 5 and October 31 unconditionally. The same message was sent through the Russians to Baghdad.

At this stage, as often these days, some U.S. officials deemed the Russians to be more helpful in searching for a solution than Iraq's other principal ally, the French. Whereas Russia's policy was both to oppose the use of force and to insist to Saddam that he had to comply, France seemed to spend much more time blocking the use of force than in trying to get the American message across to Iraq. Once again the Western alliance was shown to be in deep disarray, with the United States and Britain the only members of NATO who were really prepared to take military action.

During the course of Friday, Clinton had several conversations with Annan. There was, according to one senior U.S. official, "a real feeling of disappointment and even anger with him. We felt he was accepting the alleged reply to Yeltsin."

Through Friday afternoon, the Security Council continued wrangling on how to respond to the Russian initiative. They could not agree on what, if any, further communication should be sent to Saddam. With no progress in sight, Annan became somewhat exasperated, and at the end of the afternoon he said he would send a message under his own authority. He left the chamber, returned to his office and did just that. It was picked up by an official from the Iraqi mission.

Annan deliberately used only "language on which everyone had already signed off," writing that he had come from a four-hour meeting with the Security Council. "I can report to you that without exception, all the members of the Security Council expressed preference for a diplomatic solution of the crisis. As you are aware, I have made continuous efforts myself over the past three months to bring about such a solution." The Security Council, he wrote, also unanimously endorsed the appeal to Saddam he had made from Marrakesh. He repeated that appeal—that Iraq renew its cooperation with UNSCOM and the IAEA—and ended, "The Security Council remains actively seized of this matter. I should, therefore, be grateful for an early response to my appeal. Please accept, Excellency, the assurances of my highest consideration."

Annan's letter arrived in Baghdad in the middle of the night. It was at once seized by the Iraqis as a ladder down which to climb. Saddam met with members of his inner circle, the Revolutionary Command Council, and they instantly approved just such an apparent move. "The answer came faster than I expected," said Annan later. At 7:22 on Saturday morning in New York, Annan was awakened to be told that Deputy Prime Minister Tariq Aziz had replied. The secretary general's special representative in Iraq, Prakash Shah, said that he understood the reply was "positive." This characterization was immediately conveyed to Washington by telephone.

By this stage many of the principals in Washington thought they were past the fail-safe point for attack. The B-52s were long airborne, the gyroscopes on the cruise missiles had already been switched on. Pentagon officials had already told the principals that the point of no return had been reached at 3 a.m., and then again at 5 a.m. But still at 7:30 a.m., Clinton hesitated when he heard that a new letter had arrived.

The planned attack was less than an hour away. By 8:15 a.m. the White House still did not have the text of the letter. "It was touch and go," one senior official told the *New York Times.* "Sandy [Berger]'s there saying, 'Get me the text of that letter right now! Get what you can off the wires right now! We've got 60 minutes, 45 minutes left.' " The U.S. could not get much more information than that Iraq was saying it would rescind its decisions of August 5 and October 31, observe all relevant resolutions and allow UNSCOM back. In the next few minutes Clinton had to decide whether to proceed. There was nothing in the history of the last eight years to suggest that Saddam should be trusted. Indeed, every past crisis proved that he could not—that in order to achieve his ambition to build weapons of mass destruction he would utter any lie he deemed necessary. Even the summary of the letter put out by the Iraqis might well mislead; indeed, why should anyone think they might tell the truth?

Defense Secretary William Cohen thought the attack should go ahead. Secretary of State Albright was out of touch on a flight to Malaysia, despite all the communications facilities her plane boasted. Her aides said that she would want to attack.

At about 8:45 a.m., as seven B-52s approached Iraq and fourteen warships in the Gulf were poised to fire up to three hundred cruise missiles, Clinton aborted the assault. Later, to justify his decision, U.S. officials said ten thousand Iraqis might have died in an attack launched when much of the world would believe that Saddam had his hands up in surrender. No one had previously mentioned any possibility of such enormous casualties. A "White House official" explained to the *New York Times,* "Can you order a military mission that kills thousands of people if there is the possibility that your adversary is giving in to your demands? To my mind, he had no choice but to delay this thing." Some among the principals disagreed.

Clinton had asked whether it was possible to delay for three or four hours while the Iraqi letter was studied. He was told no by the joint chiefs, but another attack could be planned for twenty-four hours later, on Sunday. To emphasize that the attack was still on hold, Clinton canceled his own trip to Malaysia and sent Vice President Al Gore instead to join Madeleine Albright.

At 10 a.m. Iraqi ambassador Nizar Hamdoon brought the text of the Iraqi reply around to Annan's home on Sutton Place. Annan immediately sent a copy to the Security Council and, privately, to Washington. Hamdoon sat with him on the sofa in the first-floor reception room while the secretary general went through the letter. It read very differently to different people.

The "positive" reply, poorly translated and poorly typed, was in two parts—first a one-and-a-half-page letter signed by Tariq Aziz, saying that Iraq had no intention of flouting the UN. Attached to it was a list of nine changes in UN policy that Iraq wished to see. Aziz claimed that Iraq's decisions of August 5 and October 31 were not intended to sever the relationship with UNSCOM or the IAEA or to cease its obligations under Resolution 687. Iraq's objective is to end "the suffering of its embargoed people" and get sanctions lifted. "Due to its trust in you and your good faith," Iraq had dealt with Annan's initiative on the comprehensive review. But the Security Council had not acted fairly and objectively. "It is well known that the main reason for that was the American position, which does not represents [sic] the prevailing opinion on the Council. That position, contrary to your initiative, objected continuously to the presentation of any clarity in regard to the objective of the comprehensive review."

Now "on the basis of what was stated in your letter" and because of Boris Yeltsin's letter "and the positive positions expressed and conveyed to us by China, France, Brazil and other States, and in order to give a further chance to achieve justice by lifting sanctions," Iraq had decided to resume working with UNSCOM and the IAEA "and to allow them to perform their normal duties. We offer this chance not out of fear of the aggressive American campaign and the threat to commit a new aggression against Iraq, but as an expression of our feeling of responsibility, and in response to your appeal and those of our friends."

The kicker came in the penultimate paragraph, in which Aziz said that "we rightly believe" that if the comprehensive review "were not to be a mere formality and to be free from the influences of the tendentious purposes" then the nine points in the attached annex "will render the review serious, fair and fruitful." The letter concluded with what read like a warning to Annan. "We expect that you will continue with your efforts to lay down the bases and the correct procedures for the review and so as to commence with as soon as possible."

Annan thought that the letter as such was acceptable. But as he turned to the nine-point annex he became more concerned. This stated that the comprehensive review "be carried out within a very short time" after UNSCOM and the IAEA had resumed their normal duties. ("Normal" was nowhere defined and was clearly one of the definitions which would give rise to endless argument.) In the second phase of the review no matters should be raised which were "contrary to the legal interpretation of the resolutions." Members of the Security Council, especially the permanent members, must "abide by international law. . . ." (By most definitions it was Iraq that was acting outside the law.)

Most ominously, perhaps, "the question of Butler and the structure of UNSCOM and its practices are important matters. The Council is to consider them seriously in order to ensure a good relationship in the future." Finally, "It is necessary that these assurances be communicated directly to the leadership in Baghdad either by the Secretary General or by a delegation from the Council." No lesser emissary would do.

Annan was immediately concerned that this list comprised conditions for the apparent backing down in the letter. Aziz called him from

Baghdad and assured him that this was not so. The annex was merely a "wish list" of "positions" for the Security Council's "consideration."

Some of Annan's staff, eager to find a solution, said they thought the annex had been attached to pacify domestic Iraqi opinion, though Saddam Hussein is not known for showing concern for the opinions of the Iraqi people. After Tariq Aziz told him the nine points were for consideration, and were not conditions, Annan welcomed the letter publicly as "a positive step" and said that "in my opinion" it met UN demands.

I asked him later why Saddam had apparently backed down.

"I think because they realized their total isolation this time."

But wasn't the way in which Saddam behaved as a puppet master to the UN and its secretary general destructive?

"Yes, it's very destructive," Annan agreed. "We have to lead and manage better. We shouldn't let Saddam lead. The initiative should never be with him."

Therein lay the core of the problem: how do you lead and manage a recalcitrant dictator, particularly when the Security Council is divided, as it often will be?

I suggested to Annan, "You have let him off the hook again."

He replied, "But the entire Security Council said they wanted a diplomatic solution. The UN is not in the business of waging war if it can be avoided. I have already been criticized as being the 'human shield' for Saddam, but I have a mandate, I have a conscience, and I fervently believe in the ideals of the UN."

In Washington, officials were less sanguine than Annan. Aziz's letter created a day-long argument. One senior official said, "You had to have a grudging admiration. It was full of bombast but was legalistically very clever. It made it very hard for us to argue that they were in noncompliance, but it left them lots of room to maneuver."

All day Saturday the debate raged back and forth in Washington and between Washington, New York, London and other capitals: could they, should they, bomb on Sunday, having aborted the Saturday strike?

George Tenet, the Central Intelligence Agency director, said that the letter guaranteed nothing except that Saddam would likely cooperate for a few more weeks and then throw another monkey wrench into the process as he had always done before. As soon as the inspectors got close to any weapons systems that Saddam wanted to conceal, they would be thwarted again. According to the *New York Times*, Clinton said, after Washington had analyzed the letter, "I'm not going to accept this." Plans for an attack the next day, Sunday, were resumed.

At 5:30 p.m. National Security Council Adviser Sandy Berger emerged from a five-hour principals' meeting to tell the press that the letter was "neither unequivocal nor unconditional; it is unacceptable." The annex in particular "has more holes than Swiss cheese." The U.S., he said, *"was* poised to take military action and *is* poised to take action. We will proceed on our own timetable."

By this stage, as is inevitable in such crises, everyone was locked into personal roles in the drama. Annan was working for a peaceful solution; many of the U.S. principals were arguing for war. William Cohen, in particular, felt that unlike the Grand Old Duke of York, he could not go on marching his men up and down the hill indefinitely. Also aggressive was the British prime minister, Tony Blair. He wanted war, unless the guarantees from Saddam could at least be presented as cast iron.

Washington told Annan to seek "clarifications" from Aziz directly or through Iraq's UN ambassador, Nizar Hamdoon. Further demands should be made of the Iraqis. The Americans called this "raising the bar." The U.S. insisted that all contacts be made through the secretary general. They wanted to emphasize the role (and responsibility) of the UN in this matter.

Ambassador Hamdoon, wearing an open-necked shirt, hovered around the periphery of the Security Council all day long, looking increasingly nervous. On Saturday evening two more letters arrived at the White House. Hamdoon had been in touch with Aziz by telephone and had help in writing the final drafts from a senior member of Annan's staff. In the first letter, received in Washington at 7:20 p.m., Aziz withdrew all the nine qualifications, conditions or "considerations" in the annex. That was not enough for Clinton or for Tony Blair. They both insisted that Iraq must specifically renounce its August 5 and October 31 refusals to comply with the weapons inspectors.

Annan's staff helped Hamdoon write another letter which did just that.

There were several principals in Washington who still argued that Saddam's concessions were inadequate, even with the Hamdoon emendations. But Blair's view was now important in Washington. In the course of several conversations on Saturday night, he and Clinton decided that at last Iraq could be said to have met their demands. It was an important partnership, as with Kosovo. On both occasions the U.S. and its principal ally struck a balance between the opportunities of multilateral diplomacy led by the UN and unilateral force led by the U.S. and the UK. But the corollary was also that they were isolated within the alliance.

Shortly after midnight it seemed that Clinton, Blair, Cohen, Albright and Berger were agreed that the planes must be turned back. Iraq had apparently agreed to comply, once again, with the resolutions and the secretary general's February memorandum of understanding. At a Sunday morning press conference Clinton said the strikes were on hold and enumerated what Saddam must do to be in compliance. "The world is watching to see if the words he uttered will be followed by deeds," the president stated. In fact, the world was watching Clinton just as closely—to see if he was ever prepared to carry out the threats he was prepared to make. There were those who believed that, as in February, Kofi Annan had given Clinton as well as Saddam Hussein a ladder to scramble down.

In London, Blair said that if Iraq made trouble again it would be attacked "without warning." This was not quite true. Warning would inevitably be given by the evacuation from Iraq of UN officials before any attack. What he might have meant was "without diplomacy." Even that was unlikely. Diplomacy, conducted by Annan, the Russians, the French and the Chinese, would inevitably follow the warning of an attack conveyed by the removal of UN officials. As ever, the U.S. and Britain would be placed under great diplomatic pressure to back down again.

Both Blair and Clinton embraced a new policy—encouraging the Iraqi opposition to overthrow Saddam. Blair claimed in the *New York Times* to have detected growing opposition to Saddam, though he did not make clear what it was. Everyone knew that such Iraqi opposition to Saddam as did exist was hopelessly fragmented and also infiltrated by Saddam's agents. What the week had also shown again was the fragility of the Western alliance at the core of what we call the international community. In rhetorical terms, the alliance that confronted Soviet hegemony and faced it down has new and equally vital tasks—to deal with threats from vicious new nationalisms, grotesque tyrants and the proliferation of weapons of mass destruction. But unity and consistency of purpose are far harder to maintain than they were during the Cold War.

UNSCOM officials returned to Baghdad. Perhaps inevitably and certainly not surprisingly, they were soon in a new dispute with the regime. Iraqi officials refused to hand over specific documents requested by Butler on chemical and biological weapons, one of which had even been mentioned as essential by President Clinton on Sunday. As Annan prepared to resume his interrupted tour of Western Sahara, the specter of yet another confrontation loomed.

13

Desert Encounters

B Y the end of 1998 carnage was sweeping Africa, from the Horn south. Almost a third of sub-Saharan Africa's countries were consumed by wars—civil, international, guerrilla or merely nihilistically criminal.

It seemed far longer than just over half a year ago that President Clinton had made his carefully calibrated swing through six countries in March, praising Africa's "new leaders" and "African renaissance." Since then war had spread across the continent. Some countries were mere victims of fighting and lacked strong institutions with which to defend themselves. But suddenly more and more states were sending troops they could not afford to sustain across national boundaries. In a real and awful sense, by the end of 1998 there was a new world war in Africa. Invasion and intervention were now the name of the game. Ethiopia and Eritrea were still at each other's throats. And at least eight countries were now fighting in Congo.

A new war had begun in Congo in early August when Rwanda and Uganda launched a covert invasion in order to overthrow the man they had installed just over a year before, Laurent Kabila. In response, Kabila called upon other countries to fight to save his regime.

Even for his allies, Kabila had been a disastrous disappointment.
Mobutu had been rightly accused over the years of serious human
rights abuses but, as we have seen, Kabila had waded to power with
blood on all his garments.

Now, to conceal their invasion and confuse the outside world, the
Rwandans and Ugandans recruited a collection of Banyamulenge
(Congolese Tutsis), some ex-Mobutu civilian and military officials,
and a handful of frustrated political aspirants and academics from
the diaspora. These were made to pose as rebels. They accused Kabila of both tribalism and corruption. Each was undoubtedly true. As
the invasion gathered force and began to threaten Kinshasa, the capital of Congo, Kabila denounced the Tutsis, last year's allies, in the
same hysterical, racial tone as the Hutus of Rwanda had denounced
them during the genocide of 1994.

Parts of the country, especially the east and south, became more
and more lawless. Some four thousand rebels were thought to be
roaming south of the Matadi-Kinshasa road from their hideouts in
the UNITA-controlled areas of Angola.

The invasion, obvious though it was, was not denounced by the
United Nations. But Kabila toured the region enlisting support from
Chad, Zimbabwe, Angola and Namibia, all of which intervened on
his behalf. In doing this Kabila split SADEC, the Southern African
Development Community, which had been set up in 1980 to reduce
the area's economic dependency on apartheid South Africa, and of
which South Africa was now the dominant member. South Africa
tried but failed to stop other members from sending troops to help
Kabila. The combatants all had different motives and were rewarded
in different ways. In November, Kabila thanked Zimbabwean president Robert Mugabe and his Zimbabwe by naming a prominent
Zimbabwean businessman and ally of Mugabe as head of Congo's
state-owned mining company.

In Congo itself the social and economic fabric was already in tat-
ters when Kabila drove out President Mobutu. Nothing he had done
since had improved matters. The state's treasury was empty. Civil
servants and soldiers had not been paid for months. As the exchange
rate of the franc congolais had deteriorated, soldiers had refused to
accept their pay at official rates. One of the few sources of government revenue was diamonds, but the government had recently introduced a state monopoly, which had the effect of driving the industry

underground. Industrial production collapsed and so did investor confidence.

In the early weeks of the invasion food prices climbed four to five times in Kinshasa. By November these had fallen back, but food was probably still twice as expensive as before the new war began. One result was that few people could still afford to send their children to school; there is no state system in Congo. At the beginning of the new school year only about 25 percent of places in the school system were filled. Kabila attempted to ingratiate himself with the people of Kinshasa by announcing that they would receive three months of free electricity and water.

CONGO was the major topic of concern at the last Franco-African summit before the millennium, held in Paris at the end of November 1998. It was the largest ever, and designed to show that the old Francophonie was more all-embracing than before. The French were still a substantial power in Africa, despite American competition and despite the fact that they had now cut back their troop commitment to the continent to only a little over five thousand men. Forty-nine countries were represented in Paris and fully thirty-four of them sent their heads of state. It was the first Franco-African summit attended by a secretary general of the United Nations.

The conference gathered as former president Augusto Pinochet of Chile was being held in London while the courts grappled with a request for his extradition to Spain. Inspired by this example, two French human rights groups demanded that French prosecutors begin criminal proceedings against Laurent Kabila on torture charges when he arrived in Paris for the summit. The French government gave him immunity as head of state. An editorial in the newspaper *Libération* angrily compared the treatment of Kabila to that of Pinochet in Britain. "Are there two categories of international criminals as far as our leaders are concerned?" the paper asked. "Those who are 'useless,' without power, whose crimes deserve to be punished, and those who are 'useful' . . . who are granted impunity for political, diplomatic or commercial reasons?" The answer was yes.

In response to such feelings, President Chirac, who had praised the arrest of Pinochet, greeted Kabila only perfunctorily in public.

And he noted, in an oblique criticism of the United States, that France did not bring Kabila to power. The French still believed that Mobutu, an old client of the Quai d'Orsay, the French ministry of foreign affairs, was preferable to the former nightclub owner, gold trafficker and self-styled Marxist, Kabila. The truth was that both France and the United States were also interested in the vast mineral reserves of Congo.

After an unsatisfactory and inconclusive first plenary session, Annan called a private meeting with the leaders of both sides in the Congo war for the following morning. "This was the first time they were all in the same room," Annan said later. "They really felt awkward. Museveni of Uganda said, 'I didn't want to fight.' Mugabe looked at Museveni and said, 'He was an ally, now he's an ex-ally.' "

They all said they wanted to settle the issue politically and peacefully, and Annan got them to agree to an immediate cessation of hostilities and to sign a cease-fire agreement by December 14. He said, "Let's not get into the question of who was the aggressor and who was invited. We can take care of that with the phrasing of the withdrawal. You've all agreed to leave; that's what's important."

Back in the plenary session, Annan reported on what they had achieved. Chirac was pleased; it looked as if the Paris conference had achieved something. "Kofi Annan," he said, "is a wise man. The world needs him."

But the agreement had little substance. It was flawed if only because the rebels, who did have some independent life and who now occupied about a third of the country, were not part of it. Annan hoped that if the leaders all agreed they might be able to deliver the rebels. They could not.

In Paris, Annan gave an interview to a French radio station. He was asked if next time there was a crisis with Iraq, the U.S. and UK would definitely bomb. He said yes and there would be no warning. This caused an outcry in Iraq. The government declared that it used to trust him but no longer did.

ON Sunday, November 29, Annan flew to Algiers in the Gulfstream jet of the Algerian president, to resume the trip through Western Sahara that Saddam Hussein had interrupted two weeks before. The day he arrived, local Algerian newspapers revealed that another six civilians had been killed in recent terrorist attacks. Three civilians had been shot dead on Friday when they were caught at a fake roadblock put up by suspected Muslim fundamentalist rebels in Ain Defla province, about 81 miles southwest of Algiers. In another incident in Saïda, about 212 miles southwest of Algiers, Muslim guerrillas were thought to have murdered two shepherds; they slit their throats in order to steal their sheep to feed fellow guerrillas.

No one knew how many people had died since Algeria was plunged into civil war after the military authorities canceled the general election in which radical Islamists had taken the lead in 1992. It was widely believed that there had been at least sixty-five thousand victims, perhaps eighty thousand. In 1997, Annan had offered his services as a mediator, saying, "The killing has gone on too long." This had elicited an Algerian response to the effect that the country's problems could only be "resolved by Algerians themselves away from all external interference of whatever source." Annan had replied to that rebuke by saying, "No one can fight with me for defending the sanctity of life and the fundamental rights of individuals."

But that was as far as he got. In November 1997, Amnesty International criticized the international community for having deliberately avoided action. Amnesty alleged that the victims, most of whom were civilians, including many thousands of women and children, had been killed both by fundamentalist Muslim rebels and by government forces trying to wipe out those rebels. The government had managed to silence the world by using its influence among nonaligned countries, the Organization of African Unity and even the European Union. The decapitations, slitting of throats and burnings alive had continued. In summer 1998, Annan finally persuaded the government to accept a high-level UN fact-finding team under Portugal's former president Mario Soares.

After a two-week visit Soares and his team argued that the Algerian government deserved "the support of the international community" in its efforts to combat terrorism, but said that all such efforts had to take place within the framework of "legality, proportionality and respect for the fundamental human rights of the Algerian population." The panel did not apportion blame or take a position on many of the statements it gathered. It said that "energetic efforts" should be made to entrench in society and all public institutions a state of legality and respect for the rule of law, as well as to encourage more political openness. "It is important to work resolutely for a change of mentality in the judiciary, the institutions responsible for upholding human rights, in the police and the army, and in the Algerian body politic as a whole."

The report was criticized by Amnesty International and other human rights organizations for being insufficiently tough on the Algerian authorities. And it had little impact in the country itself. The killings continued apace.

After Annan and his party had landed in the early evening in Algiers, their motorcade drove under heavy police escort through deserted streets to the presidential guesthouse in a park on the hillside above the harbor. Next morning he flew again on the president's Gulfstream to Tindouf, the small town in the Western Sahara where the UN peacekeeping operation MINURSO (United Nations Mission for the Referendum in Western Sahara) had its Algerian headquarters.

Western Sahara had been "annexed" by Morocco twenty-two years before, when Spain, after the end of France's dictatorship, gave up its colony. Resistance to Morocco was built up by the Popular Front for the Liberation of Saguia el Hamra and Rio de Oro (Polisario), and over 100,000 Western Saharan (Sahrawi) refugees had fled to southwestern Algeria, where they were confined to tent camps.

In 1988, Morocco and the Polisario agreed to a UN settlement plan, which was approved by the Security Council in April 1991. The plan called for a referendum to be conducted by MINURSO. It would ask the Sahrawis to choose between independence and integration into Morocco. The UN was to carry out an identification process to determine who was entitled to vote in the referendum. Since then Morocco had constantly frustrated the process.

Annan's mission had begun in November in Mauritania, the southern end of Western Sahara, from where he flew up to Laayoune, the dusty capital of Western Sahara. There he was mobbed by a throng of tribesmen and their families. It was a moving, splendid sight, and it was easy to overlook the fact that many of them had been bused in by the Moroccan Ministry of the Interior to cheer Annan and protest their eternal loyalty to King Hassan. In Marrakesh, Annan had made new proposals to the king on how disputed voters might be registered. Since then Morocco had quietly rejected them. In the Moroccan view, they disenfranchised too many of those who Morocco thought should be entitled to vote. Annan was now "hopeful" but not "optimistic" about reaching some sort of agreement, said his spokesman, Fred Eckhard.

When we landed in Tindouf, we were greeted by a debonair Austrian general, MINURSO's commander. A Russian colonel gave a quick briefing. A cheerful Macedonian civil affairs officer informed Annan that in the days when this was a French outpost, TINDOUF was said to mean *"Tout Individu Normal Devient Obligatoirement Fou"* (every normal individual becomes crazy as a matter of course). Not much, he seemed to say, had changed.

At the MINURSO office Annan told the staff they could be proud that MINURSO had kept the cease-fire agreement for seven years after fifteen years of war. But once again he said there was a question of whether the two parties had the will to make peace. "We can't impose peace." By now, it seemed, this was becoming Annan's refrain in almost every one of the apparently endless and insoluble situations he faced. It was an entirely understandable complaint, but it obviously also raised the question of whether and how political will could be summoned where it was lacking.

We boarded a couple of old Russian helicopters, chartered to the UN, for the short flight over the desert to the Polisario camp at Smara. There a stunning welcome had been arranged. Annan and his wife were driven half a mile or so along a path through the sand lined by hundreds of Polisario's green, black, red and white flags with crescent and star flapping noisily in the desert wind. Under the flags, Annan passed first through the Polisario army, standing stiffly in dark green fatigues by the side of the track. Many men looked old and exhausted; many had no weapons.

Beyond the army were the crowds—thousands of women and children shouting, laughing, chanting, carrying little signs on which they had written JUSTICE; PEACE PLAN; COLONIALISM—NO; UN IS OUR HOPE; WHERE ARE THE DISAPPEARED SAHRAOUIS?; FAIR REFERENDUM. (In a mirror image, posters in Laayoune a few weeks before had complained about the "PRISONERS OF THE POLISARIO"—exactly the people Annan was seeing now.)

When Annan arrived at the camp itself, he and his wife were given three pigeons to release into the air. They were swept by the crowd around the parade ground in the center of the camp past a circle of great tents, whose canvases were billowing in the wind. Mobbed by men, women and children, the Annans were borne along on the surge, with cameramen dashing around the periphery attempting to film the extraordinary spectacle. It was exhilarating, breathtaking— and very dusty. Though clearly the event had been scripted by the Polisario leaders, the enthusiasm seemed genuine, an astonishing vision of the trust that ordinary and, in this case, luckless people have in the United Nations. Too quickly, it seemed, the wave of people crashed against a gate at one end of the ground through which Annan and his party were squeezed by Polisario guards. When the gates were closed the crowd dispersed to the tents.

For the next few hours, Annan talked with Polisario officials, was entertained at a vast and splendid lunch for about two hundred people—of camel, goat, vegetables, fruit, and much more. In a bright orange tent, he addressed the sheikhs of the tribes under Polisario control. One sheikh stood up and said that two previous secretaries general had been to Tindouf promising progress, but still there was no movement. He asked if Morocco's delaying tactics would ever end. He said of Annan's plans, "We will do everything we can to make it a success, not just because we have given so much for it, but also because you are a son of Africa and a judge of this planet."

After lunch Annan met with the Polisario leadership in a dark room with sand-colored walls and red ochre doors and windows. To his evident pleasure, they said that they, unlike the Moroccans, accepted his proposal. A referendum was the only solution. Western Sahara had only two choices—either to be independent or a part of Morocco. They asked Annan why the UN was prepared to threaten force in Kosovo and Iraq but not in Western Sahara. He explained that unlike the other two, Western Sahara was subject to Chapter VI resolutions, which depend on cooperation to be implemented. If the UN were to apply Chapter VII enforcement to impose a referendum on Western Sahara, how many men would be needed? How many would be killed? How would the force leave? Again he stressed that what was needed was the political will of both the parties.

But this raised another question. What if, as in this case, one party had the will but the other did not? Must the UN be held hostage indefinitely to the intransigence of Morocco? And must MINURSO, which was costing $4.5 million a month, stay forever because of Morocco's refusal to abide by its agreements? Some senior UN officials felt that MINURSO should now withdraw, or at least be reduced to a much smaller presence. The team had ten international mechanics for its cars; was this really necessary? And over two hundred military observers to monitor the cease-fire agreement. Could this not be cut back radically? Annan spoke often of the need for UN reform and MINURSO seemed in many ways an obvious candidate for change. One senior official complained to me that the organization had a Pakistani demining unit which cost $300,000 a month and was completely incompetent. But nothing could be done about it: the Pakistani government wanted its men here, and it was always difficult to criticize troop contributors. Annan said he had no intention of taking the troops out at this time.

The talks concluded, Annan made his way back to the helicopters. Once again the track over the dunes was lined with thousands of cheering people and the sad soldiers. We were struck, above all, by the number of children in Tindouf: one entire generation had already grown up in the camps and now another generation was beginning to do so—an awful reflection on man's inability to resolve such issues.

Before he left Algiers the next day, Annan met with his principal advisers on Western Sahara; they were now of the view that the UN should challenge rather than accept Morocco's delaying tactics. There was complacency in the present situation, they thought; an endless process was in Morocco's interests—the UN should call Morocco's bluff. The secretary general should call King Hassan and say how disappointed he was. Only the king could decide to compromise; it was his dossier. Annan did not think Morocco had yet decided to abandon the whole UN strategy. He quickly quashed the proposal that MINURSO be reduced, and departed for the airport and Tunisia.

WHEREVER Annan traveled, his communications expert, Americo Canepa, an amiable Peruvian, went with him. Wherever the secre-

tary general stopped, faxes and E-mails followed. Piles of coded cables from UN offices or missions around the world were delivered
every day, as were even larger piles of press clippings regarding new
or lingering crises. While Annan was moving across North Africa,
the subtext was changing constantly. On the flight from Algiers to
Tunis, I read my way through some of these piles.

Le Monde on December 1 quoted a senior Moroccan official at the
Paris conference the weekend before as saying that if the UN went
forward with Annan's plan and published the list of electors approved by MINURSO, "there will be troubles in the Sahara because
the people excluded by MINURSO will certainly react."

In Bosnia, General Radislav Krstic, the Serb general in command
of the Drina Corps, was arrested after a secret indictment and flown
to The Hague, charged with "direct personal involvement" in the
massacre of thousands of Bosnian men at Srebrenica. At the same
time it was revealed that the United States had put a price of up to
$5 million on the heads of Ratko Mladic and Radovan Karadzic.
NATO troops continued to be reluctant to attempt their arrests. In
Serbia itself President Milosevic had just conducted a wholesale
purge of his inner circle, dismissing the leaders of the army, air force
and intelligence service. It was clearly linked to his reluctant agreement in October to pull troops out of Kosovo and it seemed to many
to be a sign of desperation which might well mark the beginning of
the end of his regime. "Increasingly insecure, even paranoid" was
how he was described by the *New York Times*. Increasingly under the
influence of his hard-line wife also, it seemed; she was now being
freely compared to Madame Ceauşescu.

At the same time, in Iraq, UNSCOM, which still had not been
given the documents it had requested in November, now embarked
on challenge inspections. These would be much more difficult than
the monitoring which inspectors had been conducting since their return two weeks before.

In Nigeria, the first free local elections in many years were being
held. They were a great success and provided extraordinary evidence
of the achievements of General Abubakar as he moved the country
back toward democracy, as he had promised Annan in July.

In Angola, Jonas Savimbi's rebel group UNITA was holding fifteen
UN military observers hostage in its central highland strongholds.

Annan made a public statement putting the full responsibility for their safety on Savimbi himself. Annan also called Savimbi to warn him personally. A few days later they were released.

In Somalia, now in its seventh year without a central government, four people died in continuing interclan violence in the town of Sakow on the night of November 28. The quarrel was said to be over the sharing of aid donated by a Western humanitarian organization. The fighting in Sakow had left two hundred families homeless and without food, according to one clan politician.

Burundian politicians were cheered by the news that Tanzania's former president Julius Nyerere was ready to recommend the lifting of the sanctions imposed against President Pierre Buyoya's regime in 1996 at the insistence of Nyerere himself and others.

In Cambodia, the last Khmer Rouge general still dug into the Thai-Cambodian border finally surrendered to the new government led by Hun Sen, in which his rival, Prince Ranariddh, had agreed to be president of the National Assembly, instead of number-one prime minister, as he had been before. Ranariddh's own commander, General Nhek Bunchay, also surrendered. Finally, it seemed, the long civil war in Cambodia might be over—and the undisputed victor was Hun Sen, the man whose imposition on the country by Hanoi in the early 1980s the West had resisted so long, the former Khmer Rouge who had lost the only free elections Cambodia had ever enjoyed, those staged by the UN in 1993, the man who had beaten his way back to power by violence ever since.

From China came reports that, on the eve of the fiftieth anniversary of the signing of the Universal Declaration of Human Rights, the Chinese government had rounded up nine dissidents, including Xu Wenli, one of the most famous opposition figures still living in the country. He had spent a year in prison for his part in the Democracy Wall movement at the end of the seventies. Now, despite the fact that China had recently signed the UN International Covenant on Civil and Political Rights, the Foreign Ministry declared that he was "suspected of activities which have harmed national security" and "his acts have violated relevant criminal codes of the People's Republic of China."

In Senegal, about two thousand delegates from 190 nations and

500 nongovernmental organizations were meeting to discuss the threat of desertification at a UN-sponsored conference in Dakar. The encroaching deserts, it was alleged, could threaten the livelihoods of almost a billion people around the world.

In Cairo, Eritrean president Issaias Afewerki accused Ethiopia of setting "unacceptable conditions" for the settlement of the border conflict which had burst into flames in May. "The problem arises from the expansionist ideas of the Ethiopian regime and the impossible conditions they set," he said at a meeting with the head of the Arab League, Esmat Abdel Meguid. "Ethiopia wants to encircle us and make our territory an object of bargaining, and those are unacceptable conditions." He also declared that Sudan was trying to impose its ideology by force on Eritrea.

From Congo came repeated assertions by the rebels fighting against Laurent Kabila's regime that they would not accept any cease-fire agreement like that which Annan had negotiated in Paris, unless it included them.

Many of these problems required calls or faxes from the traveling roadshow. Meanwhile Annan's staff were staying up till all hours of the night preparing or finessing speeches for him to make along the route, and in particular for the end of the trip in Paris where he was due to speak about human rights to UNESCO, Amnesty International and the French National Assembly.

In Tunisia, Annan had no urgent business other than to report to his hosts on his discussions about Western Sahara, Africa and Iraq, and prepare for a still secret trip next door to Libya to discuss a resolution of the Lockerbie affair with Colonel Muammar al-Gaddafi. This had been an astonishingly complex case, as well as one filled with ten years of grief for all those seeking justice for relatives or friends murdered in the bomb attack, Britain's worst terrorist outrage.

Pan Am Flight 103 was blown up over the little town of Lockerbie, Scotland, on December 21, 1988, killing 270 people, including 11 on the ground. A long and controversial investigation followed the bombing. At one stage the finger was pointed at Syria, not Libya. But Western intelligence agencies gradually became convinced that the bomb was checked onto a flight from Malta to join the Pan Am flight in Frankfurt by two Libyan intelligence agents, Abdel Basset Ali al-Megrahi and Al-Amin Khalifa Fhimah.

In 1992 the UN Security Council imposed sanctions on Libya, the most damaging of which was a ban on all international flights in and out of the country. Sanctions were to remain in place until Libya handed over the two men for trial in Britain. Gaddafi ignored them with contempt. Boutros-Ghali tried hard but failed to resolve the impasse.

When Annan became secretary general of the UN in January 1997, he began to look at how he could address the issue. By the judicial distribution of largesse, Gaddafi had managed to persuade a growing number of African countries to ignore the flight sanctions. Instead of flying to Egypt or Tunisia and then traveling overland to Libya, as the sanctions demanded, African leaders began to fly direct to Tripoli in defiance of the UN. Even Nelson Mandela, whose struggle against apartheid Gaddafi had aided, did so, incurring the public anger of the United States. Gaddafi had special medals minted with which he decorated all those VIPs who arrived by plane. In the summer of 1998, the Organization of African Unity formally voted to ignore the ban on flying to Libya. In other words, one of the world's most important regional blocs, the one of which Libya was a member, decided to defy the Security Council.

Among Annan's staff Libya was often called "the L country," as secret negotiations began. As I have mentioned, in July, after Annan visited Nigeria, he talked to the British foreign secretary, Robin Cook, about the problem. He stressed, as had Sir John Weston, the British ambassador to the UN, that support in the UN for the U.S. and UK position was eroding fast. Libya had already said that it would agree to the two suspects being tried in a third country, but not in Britain or America. Annan urged Cook to accept this proposal. In August the British and American governments did so. They took up a Dutch offer that the two men be tried in the Netherlands by a panel of Scottish judges, acting in accordance with Scottish law, on territory that would be declared Scottish for the duration of the trial.

But then the Libyans had wavered, saying they needed "guarantees" about the treatment of the two men, should they be convicted, and that they must not serve any sentences in Britain. Britain and the United States announced that they would not agree to any more conditions. Annan arranged for secret negotiations to be conducted in

New York between a Libyan legal team and the UN's legal counsel, Hans Corell.

Libya's able ambassador to the UN, Abouzeid Dorda, a former prime minister of the country, played an important part in these talks. It was his job to try to persuade the Leader, as Gaddafi liked to be called, that the issue of where the two men might serve their sentence should not be a deal breaker.

While these talks were proceeding, Annan sent two delegations to Libya. One was instructed to look at the humanitarian impact of the sanctions, because the Libyans alleged that these were greatly harming their hospitals. The second had a still harder mission: to try to discover whether or not the Libyans were still engaged in terrorism. Under the 1992 resolution the Security Council could lift the sanctions only if the secretary general reported that Libya had abandoned state-sponsored terrorism. This was a strange commission to give to the secretary general because the UN has no intelligence arm. It was almost impossible for Annan to make a judgment.

Under pressure to get a deal—and get the men to Holland—before the tenth anniversary of the disaster, which would be marked by a large requiem mass in Westminster Abbey, the British government made further concessions to the Libyans. They were told that Libya could open an office in Scotland, and Libyan officials could visit the men in prison, assuming they were convicted. Their families could visit, too. So could UN or other international observers, to make sure the men were being held in humane conditions. Their Islamic faith would be accommodated. As for sanctions, once they were suspended, it would be very hard to get them reimposed; that would take a majority vote in the Security Council which Britain and the United States could probably not muster, ten years after the outrage. Memories and political convictions are not as long as that.

Until the moment that he left Tunis, Annan was not clear what would happen when he arrived in Libya. He had sent a senior UN official, Rolf Knutsson, who had been deeply involved in the negotiations, as an advance party, but Gaddafi was totally unpredictable.

I asked Annan in Tunis if he would still go even if he had word back from Libya that Gaddafi might not cooperate. He said, "I think I will still go. If I go, there is a chance he will change his mind. If I don't go, he will say, 'This guy is next door and he doesn't even come to talk to me.' That could complicate things. So either way there is an advantage in going."

Annan was taking an obvious risk. But he seemed to see it as the point, if not the duty, of his office to do just that.

On December 4, the evening before he left Tunis, Annan still had no idea what to expect. He had a message from Madeleine Albright and a call from Robin Cook. They were very different. Albright said that he should not proceed unless he really thought he was going to get something from Gaddafi, and the United States had no indication that he would. She reminded him that he had no authority to negotiate, that he should make no deals: "We do not want a package."

Cook, by contrast, was keen for Annan to proceed. Like Albright he reminded Annan that he had no room to negotiate, but he thought that Annan's act of going might be enough to sway Gaddafi. Cook assured Annan that the UK was well intentioned. The British believed that they had offered all the clarifications that the Libyans had sought.

There was a discussion of whether Annan could bring the two men out with him, if that was offered. This was a nonstarter; the UN Office of Legal Affairs had devised an elaborate plan for the legal transfer of the prisoners to Holland. If the two suspects were effectively expelled by Gaddafi from Libya on Annan's plane, they might ask for asylum in the Netherlands. Moreover, no one knew what state they would be in. They needed to be protected from themselves, and the aircraft needed to be protected from them also. This had been arranged discreetly on the UN plane. It could not be done if Annan suddenly had them on the Tunisair plane out of Libya. How would the Tunisians react?

The next morning Annan took off with his staff and some eight journalists, expecting to fly direct to Sirte in Libya. He had obtained the permission of the UN sanctions committee. He said that after ten years he thought the families wanted to put this behind them. "I hope when I have met with Colonel Gaddafi I can come up with a solution which is satisfactory to all concerned." But he would not speculate.

As soon as the Tunisair plane was over Libyan territory came the first surprise of the day. Libyan air traffic control ordered the pilot to divert at once to Tripoli. There most of the journalists were forced to remain.

We took off again in Gaddafi's own plane, a venerable 707 fitted out with a little fake grotto with plastic rocks and trees, private bedroom, shower and sitting room, a glass-fronted bookcase filled with Gaddafi's collected works and an ancient telecommunications facility which apparently no longer worked. The plane was under the command of Captain Chub, a mild, sad-eyed man who said he had been Gaddafi's pilot for twenty-nine years, ever since he became Leader. The plane had been his personal carrier since 1976.

At Sirte airport Annan was welcomed by the foreign minister, Omar al-Muntasser, and a somewhat bedraggled guard of honor. In the VIP lounge the foreign minister offered Annan coffee. "Real coffee, not the sort of black water you get in America," he said. An avuncular figure, with a walrus mustache and an easy manner in his comfortable tweed jacket, al-Muntasser said he used to roam all over the States, but now he was confined by sanctions to the five boroughs of New York City when he went there. "Maybe that will soon change," said Annan. After ten minutes of small talk we set off in a fleet of black Volvos and Mercedes to drive at a steady fifty miles an hour along an excellent, empty road through the desert.

Sirte is a modern, pleasant-looking town with some rather fine administrative buildings. We were taken to the conference center and hotel. In the upstairs sitting room he had been assigned, Annan turned up the volume of CNN on the television and spoke to his delegation, saying, "I hope to meet the Leader alone because then he will not have to act out for an audience."

Rolf Knutsson, who had met us in Sirte, said that the real problem appeared to be the Libyans' fear that sanctions would not actually be lifted ninety days after the two men were surrendered. They felt they could no longer count on the Russians, who were so dependent on IMF assistance, or on the French, to veto the possible reimposition of sanctions after their suspension. Gaddafi was angry with the Arab leaders also, because none of them had broken the sanctions to fly to him, unlike so many Africans. He had disbanded the Ministry of Arab Affairs and now considered Libya an African country. The

Libyans did not trust anyone except Annan. "They think he's a magician," said Knutsson. "If he can convince them, then maybe there is hope."

At a formal meeting with Omar al-Muntasser, Annan said that both the Americans and the British had assured him that they were not about to cast a wider net over Libya to try to catch more senior Libyans. Absolute guarantees were not easy for him to offer. "But I think all who have dealt with me have done so in good faith," he asserted. "I think none of them wants to put the secretary general in an impossible position."

The foreign minister complained that the Western press had set a deadline of December 21. He even had the temerity to say, "This is worse than killing people. This is terrorism by another method."

He complained that Libya had made many compromises, especially in allowing the men to be tried abroad. When they agreed to the Netherlands they expected the venue would be The Hague, not a former U.S. military base. They were worried the Americans might try to kidnap the two men. Then, "the place of detention is very important to us. We feel it should be in Libya, under UN supervision of course."

Annan said that Libya had indeed made concessions, but so had Britain. "You should not underestimate the major shift in the UK and U.S. to agree to have the trial moved to a third country. It was a major thing for them. I don't want to call it a revolution, but . . ." The trial would be in the full glare of the media, he said; no one would allow it to be held in camera. "We're also dealing with a country with a strong legal tradition. Prosecutors and judges will not want to embarrass themselves." But in regard to the place of sentence, the U.S. and UK governments were adamant. It had to be in Scotland.

Then Annan said something which he both believed and was trying to promote. "We live in an age of readers, not leaders." Governments are influenced much more than ever before by the effect that the media have on their electors. As for suspension of sanctions, the secretary general told the foreign minister, that would be automatic as soon as the two men arrived in the Netherlands. All concerned, he said, wanted to resolve this issue as quickly as possible. "We have many other difficult problems. No one wants to drag it out. You referred to the ultimatum of December 21. I don't think they see it as an ultimatum. They want to make progress. You know what these anniversaries are like. Also, the press is not always accurate. Writers have to have imagination."

The minister asked again how they could overcome the problem of the place of detention.

Annan replied, "On that I have no room for maneuver. We have had assurances that the imprisonment will be open and transparent, and you and the families can visit. What we can ask for is fair treatment. Once you've taken the major step of accepting a Scottish trial, the rest follows. A lot of governments which have supported you will be very disappointed if you allow it to stick now."

Then the foreign minister said that any concession on the place of imprisonment would have to be agreed to by the People's Congress, which was meeting the following week, on December 8. "People talk about Gaddafi as the president, but he has no power at all in this."

Once again the foreign minister asked if Annan did not have something up his sleeve regarding detention.

"No," replied Annan. "I'm not a magician."

Then there was another long wait. CNN broadcast the news from Atlanta that the Libyan News Agency had announced that Annan might not be able to meet with the Leader at all. Annan remained certain he would. "These regimes work at their own speed and with their own realities," he said. He was correct.

At about 6 p.m. the black cars arrived to take him and just a few of his staff into the desert to the colonel. A few miles out of town everyone was told to get out of the cars and climb into four-wheel drives. At this point most of those still with the secretary general were separated from him and compelled to stand out in the cold until they became so angry with the brusque Libyan officials that they were driven to the airport to await him.

Gaddafi is said to spend as much time as possible in the desert; he apparently lives in a mobile trailer with female security guards. He likes to receive foreign dignitaries in a large tent. Annan was driven there through the dark. The tent was a rather garish affair, heated by a bonfire on the open windward side of it. The Leader greeted him on a crutch, the result of a recent injury.

Annan had been told that the Leader had two personalities— the outside, bombastic one and the private, rational one. This was the one on display to the secretary general. According to Annan,

Gaddafi appeared in command of himself and referred to specific clauses of the UN resolutions, saying that the wording was so stringent that Libya might never be able to prove it was in compliance. He said he feared an Iraq-type situation where sanctions were never lifted.

Sitting opposite the colonel on a sofa, with the interpreter on an ugly white plastic chair between them, Annan assured him that the British and Americans were acting in good faith and wanted to resolve this painful matter after ten years. He said that the Scottish legal system was open and fair. He also stressed that it was clear that once the sanctions were suspended it would be almost impossible for the Security Council to reimpose them.

Gaddafi complained that the embargo on spare parts for planes had caused a plane crash which killed 140 people. How could people with conscience do this? He told Annan, as the foreign minister had already done, that the decision would have to be made by the People's Congress, which would meet next week. He claimed that decisions of this nature were not imposed by him but were made by the people.

Gaddafi asked what guarantees Libya had that the UK and U.S. did not have other tricks up their sleeves, and that they would not find new reasons not to lift sanctions. Annan acknowledged these concerns. Appealing to Gaddafi's vanity, he said, "In life sometimes we have to have the courage and the vision and wisdom to do what is good for our people and nation. You have been leader for a long time, you have tried to build this nation, and you've taken some tough decisions and I think you are capable of one more. I would encourage and urge you to do it."

Gaddafi also got into a discussion of what it meant to be "a terrorist." He said he had always been passionately anti-colonial and did work with freedom fighters. "I helped Mandela for a long time, I helped Museveni by airdropping weapons to him close to Kampala, I helped Mugabe, I helped Sam Nujoma [of Namibia], I helped [Joachím Alberto] Chissanó of Mozambique. All these people I helped now travel around the world as heads of state and are kissed by the same people who call me a terrorist!"

"But what about Lockerbie?" I asked Annan afterwards.

"Ah, but they deny that," he replied.

"We had a healthy discussion," Annan said later. "At the end of it, he said, 'I am prepared to try and work this out with you, not because you are the secretary general or because of threats against us, but because of the man you are, a brother African from a friendly state.' "

Annan was driven back to Sirte airport, where he made a brief statement to the cameras: "I found the Leader in good health. Thank you very much."

"In good health?" I asked Annan later. He said that that was what he had agreed with the Leader he would say, especially to Libyan television, so that it would not look as if Gaddafi had been unduly influenced on Lockerbie by Annan's visit.

Annan left Sirte in good spirits. "I saw this part of the process as confidence building," he said. Libyan officials and lawyers who had been working to break the deadlock seemed to agree. The Foreign Ministry said that a settlement was "close" after Annan's talks. Near the little plastic grotto on Gaddafi's old 707 to Tripoli I sat next to one of the Libyan lawyers who had been negotiating in New York. He told me that he thought that now the only issue was sanctions. Libya was prepared to concede that the two men would be imprisoned in Scotland if found guilty.

On the flight out from Tripoli on the Tunisair plane, the crew provided champagne. Annan talked to the journalists who had been confined to Tripoli all day and said he regarded this visit, his first to Libya, as part of a long process. "Gaddafi doesn't want to be seen to impose a decision. He wants it to look as if it came through the Congress."

Annan was, as ever, the opposite of confrontational. "We don't make these societies," he said afterwards. "We have to deal with them as they are. They live their own realities. They have their own way of taking decisions and preparing their people for them. You have to leave it to them to find their own way of doing it. You have to leave it to them."

Putting trust in dictators does not always work, as the way in which Saddam Hussein tore up the agreement he made with Annan in February 1998 demonstrated. Annan was criticized at once for this trip by the *New York Times,* which pointed out that this was the third time in his first two years as secretary general that he had taken political risks to try to reach a compromise with a dictatorial leader. The first was when Laurent Kabila refused to assist the UN Human Rights Commission investigate the mass murders of Hutus in eastern Congo; the second was with Saddam. "In both cases his agreements were not honored," said the *Times*.

But given the weird, brutal and opaque nature of Gaddafi's rule, Annan's method of calm persuasion may well have been the only way of trying to ensure that some of those believed to be guilty of the terrible crime of Lockerbie were finally brought to justice.

FROM Tunisia, Annan flew for a twenty-four-hour visit to Abu Dhabi for the opening of the Gulf Cooperation Council. The sheikh sent his personal plane, not an executive jet but a wide-bodied Airbus, sumptuously decorated as, literally, a flying palace, complete with miles of gold-plated filigree ceilings weighing several tons, gold telephones and a throne room. In Abu Dhabi, Annan met with President Mandela of South Africa, who was still one of Gaddafi's most prominent supporters.

Annan recounted the story of his meeting with the Leader forty-eight hours before. Mandela said that until now he had supported Gaddafi's refusal to hand over the two suspects. But having heard Annan's account of his visit, he would change his mind and urge the Libyans to hand the men over to the Netherlands. Annan also saw Crown Prince Abdullah, the acting ruler of Saudi Arabia, and asked him to support his effort on Libya. Abdullah agreed. A few weeks later Mandela and the Saudis sent a joint delegation to Libya. In early March 1999, Gaddafi declared on Libyan television, "Mandela's word is stronger than a Security Council resolution and stronger than any other commitments." Gaddafi said he had received a letter from Abdullah that "includes guarantees and assurances. The most important thing is Mandela's credibility. . . . If the credibility of Saudi Arabia and Mandela is sacrificed and if they too are betrayed, then nothing matters."

The combination of Annan, Mandela and the Saudis did bear eventual fruit and on April 5, 1999, the two suspects were flown on a specially chartered UN plane to the Netherlands for trial, just over a decade after Pan Am 103 had been blown out of the sky.

* * *

BEFORE he left Abu Dhabi, Annan had a hectic dash of conversations with senior officials of the Gulf Cooperation Council all gathered in one hotel, and then addressed them in the hotel's huge conference center. This was an extraordinary session, with all the rulers and their officials dressed in their white kaffiyehs; the only women to be seen were two in Annan's delegation. Then it was back on the ruler's Airbus overnight to Paris, where Annan made his speeches in defense of human rights. And then he went to New York, where the simmering crisis in Iraq finally exploded into military action.

Once again Iraq had failed to carry out the promises it had made to the secretary general and the Security Council. On December 9 it refused UNSCOM inspectors access to a suspected site in Baghdad. Madeleine Albright called Annan to ask what he thought Saddam was doing. Did he not realize that this time the United States was serious and there would be bombing with no warning?

Annan said he had repeated this reality in several of his meetings in Abu Dhabi. He agreed that whereas after his visit in February there had been some cooperation from Iraq, since the November crisis there had been none.

On December 15, Richard Butler delivered a report to the Security Council in which he documented how Iraq had frustrated UNSCOM's work despite its recent promise to cooperate fully. This time, bombing appeared to be inevitable. Butler ordered all UNSCOM staff to leave Baghdad at once. For some reason, no such warning was given to the humanitarian staff, which increased the bitterness between the two groups.

On December 16 in New York, members of the Security Council were debating the crisis when suddenly the cell phones of all the ambassadors started ringing almost in unison—the attack had been launched. Some, particularly the Russian, Sergei Lavrov, and the French, Alain Dejammet, were furious. Annan himself was distressed. He made a short statement saying, "This is a sad day for the United Nations, and for the world. . . . It is also a very sad day for me personally." There were those who thought he should also have condemned Iraq for its flagrant abuse of international law embodied in the council resolutions. Subsequently he did describe Iraq's behavior

since his visit to Baghdad as "a flagrant and deeply troubling violation of both the Memorandum of Understanding that I secured *and*
Iraq's long-standing obligations to the Security Council."

The bombing campaign, named Desert Fox, continued for four
days until the start of Ramadan. The impact of the bombing on the
infrastructure of Iraq was no doubt significant, though Iraq did not
claim that there were ten thousand casualties as some U.S. officials
had warned in November. The most obvious effect of the bombing
was to put an end to UNSCOM's work in Iraq and cast doubt on its
ability ever to resume any monitoring or investigations there.

The Butler report, which proved the casus belli, evoked very
mixed reactions. The Americans and the British approved it; Tony
Blair told Annan that it had been "the last straw." But the French saw
it as a provocation, and stepped up their campaign to get rid of Butler. President Chirac called Clinton, Blair, Yeltsin and Annan, among
others, to complain about him. He told Annan he thought Butler was
probably acting under the orders of Washington. Butler had organized a real coup d'état and was a dangerous personality who must
be replaced; the French would officially demand it. Chirac and
Annan talked about future methods of monitoring after UNSCOM
and Chirac asked about sanctions. Annan replied that he did not
think the United States would allow them to be lifted while Saddam
was still in power.

Chirac thought there were three victims of the bombing: the Iraqi
people, the Security Council and Clinton. He said the French did not
want to attack Clinton because one does not attack a wounded man.
As for the council, the Americans must not get the impression they
could act in its place. It was very important not to create a precedent.

Chirac thought it was now important to set up a new system of
monitoring Iraq that would avoid these constant crises. New men
were needed; it was absolutely essential to get rid of Butler. Once he
had gone, they could put in place a "polite" system and hope that the
Iraqi regime would accept it. In that case there would be no more
bombing. They also needed to devise a policy to improve the daily
life of the Iraqi people, which would mean lifting the oil embargo
and sanctions.

The French foreign minister, Hubert Védrine, was even more ex-
plicit. He asked Annan if the U.S. and UK were thinking of keeping
UNSCOM in its present form. Annan said he thought they were be-

ginning to think about the changes which were necessary. But they were preoccupied by the divisions in the council. Védrine said that the British and Americans were now more isolated than they thought and were hardly supported by any other country. Even Germany had been very cautious.

The British foreign secretary, Robin Cook, on the other hand, was at this stage still supportive of Butler. He thought the criticism of him was unfair and was being orchestrated by Baghdad. Annan said that if Butler had lost the confidence of three of the permanent five it would be impossible for him to function, but Butler was not and should not be made the issue. Cook agreed. To question Butler's status now would raise questions about the correctness of the U.S. and UK's military action, which was based on his report.

Cook said creative thinking on the way ahead with Iraq was required. He was concerned about French talk that the time had come to move from intrusive inspections to monitoring and to lift the oil embargo. Annan said he thought it was important not to provoke greater intransigence on the part of Iraq. Announcing that the United States would bomb again could do just that and could have the result that those wanting a peaceful solution would feel "trapped" into using force. What had this bombing achieved? It could not be repeated again and again. Cook agreed, but said that Iraq still had to be contained and military pressure must be maintained. If the oil embargo was relaxed, Saddam could simply use the money on rebuilding his weapons systems. But the UK was also eager to meet the humanitarian needs of the Iraqi people. A way had to be found of overcoming the obstacles put up by the regime.

It bears repeating that Annan's predicament reflected clearly the disjunction between the idealistic beliefs that millions of people had in the UN (which he himself had imbibed) and the reality of power on the Security Council. Annan liked to hope that his moral authority could override the realities of politics. This was questionable. The Security Council did not have the will to act against all tyrants. In the case of Saddam Hussein it did, yet it was divided on whether that authority should be used. There was little doubt that the U.S.-British view, that Iraq was in breach on international law, was correct. Yet eight years of war, sanctions, inspections and now bombing had failed to persuade the Iraqi dictatorship to abide by the rulings of the Security Council and forswear its weapons of mass destruction.

Annan argued that his office and indeed the United Nations itself should be judged with "a sense of reality," above all in its responsibility to try to serve the interests of *all* states, not one state or group of states. The end of the Cold War had transformed the moral premise of the office of secretary general, and in his first two years Annan had tried to make it a bully pulpit for the promotion of human rights, democracy and good governance. He had also tried to use it as a bridge between recalcitrant parties to try to find peaceful resolution of disputes; hence his various missions, in particular to Iraq. He said that he had often been as skeptical as anyone else about a leader's true intentions, "and I have entered every war zone without illusions." But he had persisted because he must deal with the world not as he would wish it to be but as it is. "Does that make me morally blind?" he asked. "Can a secretary general not tell good from evil, or victim from aggressor? Of course he can. . . . Impartiality does not and must not mean neutrality in the face of evil; it means strict and unbiased adherence to the principles of the charter—nothing more, and nothing less."

This statement goes to the heart of the matter. Does the UN Charter, or the way it is enacted through the UN machinery, actually provide any adequate defense against evil? The UN succeeded in helping to bring peace to various places in the 1990s—to Namibia, Mozambique and Central America. In others the story of the last decade is less encouraging. As 1998 ended, and the final year of the old millennium began, the two warlords who had most successfully tortured their own people and the institutions of the world for the last decade, Saddam Hussein and Slobodan Milosevic, were still in power. Nothing that the international community had been able to do, either by using or by circumventing the charter, had succeeded in dislodging them.

14

From Kosovo to East Timor

I N the last months of the old millennium crises in two obscure provinces at different ends of the world, Kosovo and East Timor, challenged what we now so easily call the international community and its perception of its duties of humanitarian intervention.

Between them they dramatize most of the dilemmas that have troubled the protagonists of this book. Both featured brutal ethnic cleansing, the deliberate denial of rights to the people of a small territory by the forces of the larger power of which it was a part, the forced creation of refugees and mass murder. In both cases the international community was forced to confront a humanitarian disaster which was in part the product of its own neglect, and had to decide what price it was prepared to pay to right it. How and when can the rich and powerful countries of the international community actually intervene? How can they obtain the support of their citizenry? What is commensurate force? And does their desire to intervene—but only with minimal risk to themselves—actually expose the subjects of their concern, the victims on the ground, to still greater danger?

As I completed this book, those questions had been posed more starkly than before, and many of the consequences of intervention had been made manifest, but the fundamental questions were still unanswered. Was the quality of mercy really "twice blessed"? Did it really bless "him that gives and him that takes"? Such questions can never find a general reply; they have to be asked time and again, and answers sought always.

On March 24, 1999, NATO began to bomb Yugoslavia, a member of the United Nations. It was perhaps a logical but certainly a controversial conclusion to this decade of intervention.

NATO's action was justified by humanitarianism; its leaders said it was intended to stop Yugoslav security forces from indulging in ethnic cleansing and murder of the Albanian Muslim majority in Kosovo.

This was the first sustained use of force by NATO in its fifty-year history; the first time force was used to implement Security Council resolutions without specific authorization from the council; the first time a major bombing campaign was launched against a sovereign country to stop crimes against humanity within that country; and the first time that a bombing campaign alone, without the assistance of ground troops, appeared to succeed in its aims.

To repeat Boutros Boutros-Ghali's notorious remark about Bosnia, there were probably ten places in the world that were worse off than Kosovo at that time. Tens of thousands of Eritreans and Ethiopians were still dying unseen in desert trenches. Sudan was still bleeding, and being fed by UN food supplies as it bled. Afghanistan was still at war with itself. Africa's "Great War" had spread all around Congo. In Sierra Leone, children and their parents were still having their hands and lips chopped off by the rebels.

But Kosovo was seen by the United States and its allies to be different: Kosovo was in Europe, surrounded by members of both NATO and the European Union. To ignore what was happening there would be to ignore the fundamental precepts of those two flourishing organizations of democracies—and would appear to be a repeat of Western inaction over Bosnia.

In his televised address explaining why the United States and its allies had to fight this war, President Clinton announced that Kosovo was important because it was only an hour away from where Americans went on vacation. His sense of history was uncertain. He declared: "We act to prevent a wider war, to defuse a powder keg at the heart of Europe that has exploded twice before in this century with catastrophic results." In fact, Kosovo had scant connection with the outbreak of the First World War and none with the Second, which started in Poland. "By acting now, we are upholding our values," he declared. "Ending this tragedy is a moral imperative."

Clinton would later affirm: "If somebody comes after innocent civilians and tries to kill them en masse because of their race, their ethnic background or their religion, and it is within our power to stop it, we will stop it." Such claims were grand. While well-meaning, they were not unlimited and risked seeming hypocritical.

Clinton said that the world had not acted early enough in Bosnia. "And let's not forget what happened: innocent people herded into concentration camps; children gunned down by snipers on their way to school; soccer fields and parks turned into cemeteries; a quarter of a million people killed. . . . At the time, many people believed nothing could be done to end the bloodshed in Bosnia. They said, 'Well, that's just the way those people in the Balkans are.' "

"Who were some of those many people?" asked the American writer Mark Danner in a critique of Clinton's speech. "Well, one of them was Bill Clinton, who had said of Bosnia early in his administration, 'The hatred between all three groups is almost unbelievable . . . it's almost terrifying. . . . That really is a problem from hell.' " By 1999 attitudes had changed.

Other allied leaders tried to maintain that this was a new kind of war. Tony Blair called it the first "progressive" war. He claimed that unlike all previous wars, which were fought on grounds of realpolitik or national self-interest, this war "was fought for a fundamental principle necessary for humanity's progress: that every human being regardless of race, religion or birth has an inalienable right to live free from persecution."

Chancellor Gerhard Schroeder of Germany said: "The Alliance had to demonstrate . . . that the weak have in NATO a strong friend and ally ready and willing to defend their human rights."

In starting their war, the NATO powers—the most powerful members of the international community—largely cut the UN out of the process. Then, at the end of the war, after NATO had suc-

ceeded in expelling Serbian forces from Kosovo, the UN was handed
the responsibility of administering the shattered province, and American officials soon began to say that if it failed, it would never be entrusted with any major task again.

K o s o v o was the crisis that everyone expected, but, as so often happens, no one prepared for it until it was too late to prevent.

Slobodan Milosevic had begun his rise to power by promising to
protect the Orthodox Kosovar Serbs from the huge and growing
Muslim Albanian majority in what Serbs regarded as their traditional
heartland. In 1989 he abolished the autonomy that Tito had given
Kosovo within the Yugoslav federation, dismissed Albanian teachers
from schools and universities, introduced a new Serbocentric cur-
riculum, made it illegal for Albanians to buy and sell property without permission, imposed a brutal Serbian police rule and encouraged
a form of apartheid in which the Albanian majority had no power.

Ever since, and even while the crises in Croatia and Bosnia grew,
Kosovo was seen as a more dangerous threat. War there could easily
involve Albania itself, destitute and destroyed after forty years of
Stalinism, and Kosovo's other neighbor, the fragile new state of
Macedonia, where Albanians, Slavs, Turks, Serbs, Vlachs, Roma and
others lived together in a fragile new polity.

Independence for Kosovo seemed even more dangerous; it could
lead to demands for a Greater Albania and the change of all borders
in the area, causing wide conflagration.

At the end of 1992, in the last weeks of his administration, President George Bush had warned Milosevic not to attack the Kosovar
Albanians. Milosevic did not, and for the first half of the decade the
Kosovars practiced an extraordinary form of passive resistance under
the leader they had themselves elected, a modest academic named
Ibrahim Rugova. When I visited Kosovo at the end of 1993, I was astonished by the stoicism of the Albanians. In small houses in Pristina,
the capital, I saw schools and clinics which the Kosovars had established for themselves to replace those that had been either removed
or corrupted by the Belgrade government. The Kosovars eschewed
violence as a way of regaining the rights of which Milosevic had
stripped them. They hoped that the international community would
act to resolve the impasse. Nothing happened.

As I have mentioned, Kosovo was not discussed at Dayton in 1995. Richard Holbrooke's reluctance to complicate his task there was understandable, but the international community (in this case, NATO and the EU) was complacent over the next two years. Little was done to try to alleviate the crisis of the Kosovar Albanians or to address the legitimate fears of the Serb minority in the province. Inevitably, Albanians began to lose patience with Ibrahim Rugova. In 1996 an armed resistance movement, the Kosovo Liberation Army (KLA), or Ushtria Clirimtare e Kosoves, was formed. It immediately targeted Serb policemen in Kosovo and began to attract support among the Kosovar young, at home and in the vast Albanian diaspora.

By early 1998 the KLA had become a real irritant to the Serbs. The international community, led uncertainly by President Clinton at the beginning of the Monica Lewinsky scandal, was still ambivalent. In February, Robert Gelbard, the U.S. special envoy to the Balkans, praised Milosevic's adherence to the Dayton accords and denounced the KLA as "without any question a terrorist organization." Within days the Serbs had responded by attacking two suspected KLA villages, Cirez and Likosane, killing twenty-six villagers. In protest some fifty thousand Albanians took to the streets of Pristina and were dispersed by Serb water cannon and tear gas.

The crisis grew throughout the spring and summer of 1998. Mary Robinson, the UN high commissioner for human rights, said later that that period was the moment of lost opportunity. Like the UN High Commissioner for Refugees (UNHCR), she tried to draw attention to the spread of fighting within Kosovo; the Serbs were burning down villages suspected of harboring KLA and thousands of refugees were fleeing into the hills. "No one was listening to us," she said. The worsening crisis was, in the words of the *New York Times,* "noticed but not dramatized."

President Clinton promised that the United States would not allow Kosovo to become another Bosnia. But how to prevent that was the problem. Western policy was still that Kosovo should remain part of Serbia. Sanctions against Belgrade were reduced and the West continued to brand the KLA as terrorists, which some of them certainly were in terms of their methods against the Serbs, who left Kosovo in large numbers.

In June, Morton Abramowitz, the founder of the International

Crisis Group, warned that Milosevic "can effectively control the territory for the long term in only one way—by driving out the bulk of the 2 million Albanians who live there. He may still try to do that."

UNHCR officials argue that they did what they could to alert the international community about what was happening, to the extent of being criticized by the Russians and the Chinese, as well as the Serbs, for overstepping their humanitarian mandate. In September, UNHCR gave a closed briefing to the Security Council. The council's president reported that UNHCR "used stark words to make clear that the international community was facing a humanitarian disaster in Kosovo as a result of the Serb offensive. Following that briefing, the majority of council members had underlined the need to take action."

By this time Serb forces had driven about 200,000 Albanians out of their villages and into the hills. Winter was descending fast, and the council accepted the warnings of Sadako Ogata and others that disaster loomed. On September 23 the Security Council adopted Resolution 1199, which demanded that the Yugoslav security forces withdraw from Kosovo. Next day NATO warned Milosevic to stop the violence in Kosovo or face air strikes. Russia made its opposition to that clear. The same day, Ogata was in Belgrade and Milosevic complained to her that UNHCR's "exaggerated" reports had been used as propaganda to justify the resolution and NATO threats.

Richard Holbrooke, languishing as Clinton's nominee for the job of U.S. ambassador to the UN—an appointment delayed both by opposition from Senator Jesse Helms, the chairman of the Senate Foreign Relations Committee, and by the unwillingness of both the president and the secretary of state, Madeleine Albright, to fight for their nominee—took up the Kosovo challenge. He spent most of October negotiating with Milosevic.

Holbrooke himself wanted armed peacekeepers deployed in Kosovo. He said: "I have stated repeatedly Albanians and Serbs would not be able to live together in peace in Kosovo until they had had a period of time with international security forces to keep them from tearing each other to pieces." Washington would not support him. "We made numerous mistakes," Holbrooke noted.

Nonetheless, in October, under threat of NATO bombing, Holbrooke persuaded Milosevic to accept a cease-fire with the KLA and to agree that his security forces be reduced to pre-conflict strengths.

Milosevic also agreed to the stationing in Kosovo of two thousand unarmed monitors from the Organization for Security and Cooperation in Europe (OSCE). The monitors were supposed to supervise the cease-fire and to enable Kosovars to return to their villages with some measure of safety.

Inevitably, it took many weeks to recruit and deploy the monitors; by January 1999 only some eight hundred of them were on the ground. They worked hard and bravely, and were able to limit and to document some of the excesses on both sides. But killings and forced displacement continued.

The U.S. ambassador to Macedonia, Christopher Hill, intensified his shuttle diplomacy between Pristina and Belgrade to try to devise a political solution. The Albanian side wanted a return to the pre-1989 autonomy of Kosovo, guarantees that the Serbs would not launch further attacks and a referendum in three years on the final status of the province. Belgrade was prepared to accept nothing but limited autonomy within Serbia. The KLA was confident that despite Serb assaults upon them, they were growing stronger all the time. Belgrade also appeared to believe this.

On January 8, KLA fighters murdered four Serbian policemen, and in revenge Yugoslav forces mounted a ferocious attack on the village of Racak, where they believed some of the KLA killers lived. They laid siege to the village with mortar and artillery fire, then stormed it and murdered at least forty-five villagers. The murders in Racak, condemned at once by the OSCE monitors, led to war.

In February, both sides were summoned to talks at the French castle of Rambouillet outside Paris, where the French and British hoped to impose a settlement just as the Americans had done at Dayton. It was an unhappy and unsuccessful encounter. The most important player, Milosevic himself, refused to come, perhaps in part because he feared indictment by the international war crimes tribunal in The Hague and arrest. The Albanian side was constantly divided. At Dayton, all the principals had attended and Holbrooke had used the reality of U.S. power to threaten and cajole. Neither French nor British officials could speak with such authority. The Americans spent most of their energy persuading the Albanians to sign on to the agreement so that the Serbs could be clearly cast as the spoilers.

It is also arguable that Milosevic could neither have accepted NATO's demands nor pushed them through the Serbian parliament.

The essential elements, eventually accepted by the KLA but rejected by the Serbs, included an international military presence; a three-year interim administration to be followed by a referendum (in which the Albanian majority would undoubtedly have voted for independence); and unrestricted freedom of movement for NATO troops throughout Yugoslavia, which both diminished Serbian sovereignty and would have appeared to suspicious Serb leaders as a mechanism for snatching them to face trial in The Hague. Henry Kissinger, the former secretary of state, argued that the Rambouillet text was "a provocation, an excuse to start bombing. Rambouillet is not a document that an angelic Serb could have accepted. It was a terrible diplomatic document that should not have been presented in that form."

A critical moment arrived on March 20 as the OSCE verifiers started to leave Kosovo. NATO recommended that UNHCR and other UN personnel withdraw also. During the conflict in Bosnia, as long as international personnel had been on the ground, the Serbs had reason to believe that NATO would not attack them. (It was only when Rupert Smith withdrew all the potential UN hostages from the safe areas that NATO attacks began in earnest in 1995.) As the international officials drove out, Milosevic began to move more troops into the province.

That day Annan talked to Robin Cook, the British foreign secretary. Cook said the situation was very grim. The Serbs had made no attempt to negotiate in good faith at Rambouillet. He and the French had been reluctant to stop the talks, but they had been close to becoming a farce and there had been a risk that the Albanian side would disintegrate. There was still time for Milosevic to cut a deal, but military action against him was very close. Annan agreed it was remarkable how stubborn Milosevic had been until now. He thought that sometimes people who always tried to take an issue to the brink did not know when they were actually there; they miscalculated.

On the evening of March 23, Richard Holbrooke had a final meeting with Milosevic. Holbrooke said afterwards that the Serb leader was completely unrealistic and claimed that CNN, fed by KLA disinformation, had invented the Serb offensive against the Kosovars. Holbrooke recommended that the talks be terminated. "We could not allow the talks to be dragged out while the Yugoslav security forces rolled up villages. They would simply have become a smokescreen for delaying NATO action."

When Holbrooke told the Yugoslav president it was the end and bombing would begin, Milosevic was calm; he compared his defiance of the West to that of Tito against Stalin. He said, "I wonder if we will ever see each other again." To which Holbrooke replied, "That depends on your actions, Mr. President."

That evening Holbrooke flew from Belgrade to Brussels to inform NATO leaders that Milosevic would not accept any kind of international force in Kosovo. NATO's secretary general, Javier Solana, now had the authority to launch a military operation. He told Annan he might have to do so that night. It was a bad development, but it was the only remaining possibility. "We have done everything."

NATO was determined not to seek a Security Council resolution because it would certainly have been vetoed by China or Russia. Annan had to decide how to respond. In earlier statements he had admitted the possibility of the use of force as a last resort. (In February 1998, one might recall, he had praised Clinton and Blair as "perfect peacemakers" for their readiness to use force to induce Saddam Hussein to make concessions.) Now he was in a dilemma. He could not be seen to support Milosevic by insisting on the need for Security Council authorization of the use of force. Nor could he encourage the apparent disregard of international law by allowing NATO to act without such authorization.

In other words, Annan had to balance two moralities—the assault on civilians against the demands of the UN Charter. Strictly speaking, the use of force by NATO could not be justified as self-defense under Article 51 and would contravene Article 53 on the need for the Security Council to authorize the use of force. But the U.S. and other NATO powers could and did argue that NATO already had Security Council authority to act under Resolution 1199 of 1998, in which the council had affirmed that the deterioration of the situation in Kosovo constituted a threat to peace and security in the region, and demanded that all parties cease hostilities and maintain a cease-fire there. Then Resolution 1303 had reaffirmed the analysis and the demands. Such decisions of the council were binding and Yugoslavia's failure to comply placed it in violation of its obligations under the charter.

Albright called Annan to say that Milosevic was intransigent and had violated the cease-fire agreement systematically; up to seventy-five thousand people had been displaced in Kosovo since the Rambouillet talks began, including thirty thousand in the past week. There was a massive humanitarian crisis. NATO was compelled to act.

Albright knew that the Russians were unhappy, but they had been just as frustrated with Milosevic as the U.S. She asked Annan to try to minimize divisive actions in the Security Council. Annan said the council should be involved when it came to the use of force. Albright replied, "We don't agree."

She acknowledged: "You are the secretary general of the UN and I am the secretary of state of the United States. That's life. But if we had to put this to a council vote the Russians would have vetoed it, and people would have continued to die."

Annan did not dispute that for practical and operational reasons the U.S. was not able to go to the council on this occasion. But he could not argue that it should be ignored. In his carefully crafted statement Annan said: "I deeply regret that in spite of all the efforts made by the international community, the Yugoslav authorities have persisted in their rejection of a political settlement which would have halted the bloodshed in Kosovo and secured an equable peace for the population there. It is indeed tragic that diplomacy has failed, but there are times when the use of force may be legitimate in the pursuit of peace." He balanced this, however, by pointing out that under the charter the Security Council should be involved in any decision to resort to the use of force.

AIRPOWER has always had the voice of a siren, promising war without pain, victory without casualties. General Colin Powell recalls in his memoirs that after the Iraqi invasion of Kuwait in August 1990, President Bush said to him, "Colin, these guys have never seriously been bombed. [Prince] Bandar [the Saudi ambassador to the U.S.] tells me, 'A couple of bombs and they'll fold.' Mubarak, [Turgut] Ozal in Turkey, they all tell me the same thing. We can knock 'em out in 24 hours."

Powell disagreed and remembers that he replied, "The trouble with air power is that you leave the initiative in the hands of your enemy. He gets to decide when he's had enough." Such warnings were evidently either not given to President Clinton and the eighteen other NATO leaders in spring 1999 or were not adequately heeded.

Apparently, Bosnia in September 1995 was taken as a precedent. Senior U.S. officials had convinced themselves that the Serbs were bombed to the negotiating table at Dayton. So, they argued, the threat of bombing would now compel Milosevic to accept the demands of the international community. In fact, in 1995 there had been other pressures on Milosevic which were more significant than bombing. First, by then the Croatian army had defeated the Croatian Serbs in western Slavonia and in Krajina, and were moving fast against Serb positions in Bosnia itself. Second, the bombing was against targets in Bosnia, not in Serbia itself, and the Serb leaders were themselves completely divided. Milosevic was exasperated with the Bosnian Serb leadership and had been pressing them to accept 49 percent of Bosnia-Herzegovina as a basis for settlement since the end of 1993. Third, the new British and French Rapid Reaction Force (in particular its artillery) in Bosnia was capable of hitting Serb positions with great accuracy regardless of weather conditions, especially around Sarajevo. In other words, in 1995 airpower had not worked alone; it had had crucial land-based reinforcements.

NATO leaders made a fundamental mistake: they believed that a few days of bombing would bring about Belgrade's surrender. Indeed, one fashionable conceit was that Milosevic needed at least a small NATO attack to convince his political allies and enemies at home that acquiescence to NATO's demands was the better part of valor. This mistake was compounded by the fact that Clinton and other leaders repeatedly assured their own public, and therefore the Serbs, that there would be no land war whatsoever. This meant that the Yugoslav forces in Kosovo could concentrate on killing and concealment rather than defense, while in Belgrade the government could hope simply to sit out the bombing.

Bombing sorties look impressive on television: fighters are seen roaring off carriers, B-52s lumber off distant airfields, and cruise missiles snake toward their targets. Just a few such shots manage to convey the impression that a massive air campaign has been launched.

But the first week of the campaign against Serbia was anything but massive. On the first night only thirty sites were targeted. In the first five nights only 100 cruise missiles were launched (compared with 425 against Iraq in December 1995), the B-52s dropped only 64 bombs, and the total number of sorties by all NATO fighter bombers was only 450. This, as the military strategist Edward Luttwak pointed out, was one day's work for a medium-sized air force such as the French or the Israeli. The fragile nature of the NATO alliance forbade any such serious attacks as those inflicted on Baghdad at the beginning of the Gulf war in 1991—systematic bombing of electrical power grids, telephone exchanges, radio and television transmitters and "presidential" buildings.

This pinprick bombing certainly did not have the desired effect of driving Milosevic to the negotiating table. But it may have had the undesirable effect of worsening the plight of the people it was supposed to protect. As soon as the bombing began, Serb forces in Kosovo were launched en masse against Albanians; hundreds of people were murdered in the first few days; many thousands of people were driven from their homes; houses, villages and districts were burned and emptied.

About 2,500 Kosovars had been killed in the twelve months before the NATO bombing began; in the next eleven weeks it is believed that at least 10,000 more died violently, most murdered by the Serbs.

UNHCR reckoned that by March 24 over 260,000 Albanians had been driven out of their homes in Kosovo itself and another 200,000 were refugees abroad. In the four weeks after the bombing began, well over half a million more people were forced to flee into neighboring countries. By June that figure had risen to a million. Milosevic was to blame. But whether or not he had planned such a total solution to "the Albanian problem" in Kosovo anyway, it is reasonable to believe that the bombing increased both the scale and the viciousness of the assault. War unleashes brutality. One Kosovar refugee told the *Washington Post,* "The Serbs can't fight NATO, so now they are after us." But it is important to stress that Kosovar refugees almost all supported NATO's action unreservedly.

The appalling television images of vast armies of refugees being forced at gunpoint across European borders—crucial now as always to Western demands that "something must be done"—meant that Western opinion coalesced around NATO. But it could be fickle. Milosevic did not crumble. As the bombing was extended, NATO made errors, what was called "collateral damage" occurred and civilians were killed. A column of refugees was hit. Critics in the NATO countries began to decry the Third Way in which Clinton and Blair claimed they were making war—by resisting ethnic cleansing in a way which carried the least jeopardy to allied troops but thereby added to the dangers faced by the victims. The rhetoric was far ahead of the real commitment made by NATO.

But early in the war the *Wall Street Journal,* never a home to liberal pieties, recognized the dilemma and the changes in an editorial entitled "Why Kosovo?": "In today's world of instant communication, foreign policy cannot succeed without making a place for human rights. We suspect, indeed, that the key foreign policy issue of the new millennium will be defining the role of humanitarianism."

With a world filled with barbarity, the *Wall Street Journal* editorial continued, "it is clearly not feasible to redress every wrong with military might . . . [but] Kosovo lies in a part of the world where inevitably we will be involved whether we like it or not. Europe is different not because the inhabitants are white as is so crudely suggested, but because it has been at the core of this century's immense bloodshed and now holds such promise as a growing zone of peace."

And there were obvious linkages to some of the other crises mentioned in this book. Milosevic's fate would be studied by barbarians throughout the world, the *Wall Street Journal* went on. "He himself trimmed his sails in the immediate aftermath of the Gulf war, but now sees Saddam Hussein still in power and working on weapons of mass destruction after absorbing the full brunt of Western military power. Saddam, in turn, is no doubt digesting reports of depletion of cruise missile stocks, as are the North Koreans, Libyans and others."

o

THE rest of the world did not stand still for Kosovo.

Saddam Hussein and his allies took advantage of the shift in international media attention to Kosovo and Milosevic's replacement of him once again as the chief international demon. On Wednesday, April 7, the Russian delegation to the UN barred Richard Butler, the chairman of UNSCOM, from even entering the UN Security Council chamber, where UNSCOM and possible alternative methods of assessing Iraqi disarmament were to be discussed. The Russian ambassador to the UN, Sergei Lavrov, said afterwards that he would continue to bar Butler. "We don't consider him as someone doing anything on Iraq." France, Russia and China were still trying to get Butler dismissed before his planned departure at the end of June because of his December 1998 report which concluded that Baghdad was still not cooperating with UN arms inspectors, thereby triggering Desert Fox.

Lavrov's ban on Butler was hailed in the Iraqi press. "The expulsion of the spy Butler from Security Council meetings is an important step to restore respect to the Council which has become one of the sections of the U.S. State Department," said the government newspaper *al-Jumhouriya.**

In Geneva on April 7, Annan called Colonel Gaddafi in Libya to thank him for the release of the Lockerbie suspects, who on April 5 had been flown by special UN plane to face trial in Holland. Gaddafi replied it was all due to Annan; Libya had been justified in placing its trust in him. He then said what was taking place in Kosovo was very dangerous. The NATO action violated the UN Charter. Even if Milosevic could be accused of committing massacres, the NATO action gave pretext and cover for those massacres, and set a serious precedent which had implications for peace and security. Gaddafi noted that Libya had been a friend of the Serbs since the days of Tito and was also close to its Muslim brothers in Kosovo. Libya had influence over both. This was a card the secretary general could keep in mind, the Libyan leader said.

Among other initiatives of which Annan was informed in Geneva was a plan to end the war between Eritrea and Ethiopia, a draft resolution on ending the war in Congo and a West African plan to destroy weapons seized in Liberia, one of the region's most fractious and brutal societies.

---

* The reality of Iraq, behind its self-congratulatory propaganda, was, as usual, more grim. On February 19, Grand Ayatollah Mohammed Mohammed Sadeq al-Sadr, a popular religious leader in Najaf, a holy city to the Shia, was murdered, almost certainly by government agents. His death led to the most intense riots in Iraq since the uprisings of the Shia Muslims and the Kurds in 1991. They were crushed by Saddam's security forces, who were reported to be accompanied by troops in white uniforms with gas masks. Citizens of Najaf immediately feared that Saddam was about to use poison gas against them—that same poison gas that UNSCOM had been trying to eliminate. In other cities more traditional methods of repression were used. According to exile groups, assaults on suspected opposition forces in the south of the country became even more brutal in spring 1999—just as the Western world was transfixed by the drama in Kosovo.

At the same time the secretary general was becoming more concerned with the growing crisis in East Timor, the territory invaded in 1975 and annexed in 1976 by Indonesia after Portugal scuttled this and other colonies. The annexation was briefly recognized by Australia, Indonesia's nervous neighbor, but by no other country and not by the United Nations. Nor did any Western country seriously protest the conduct of Indonesia, the world's largest Muslim country and a strategic ally in the Cold War. The Indonesian army behaved brutally toward the local population; massacres and famine killed up to 250,000 people, about a third of the population, after the annexation. Although it invested substantial economic resources, Jakarta ruled the territory harshly thereafter; indeed, it became a fief of the Kopassus special forces, but even they were unable to destroy the small guerrilla movement fighting for independence. In 1996 two East Timorese leaders were given the Nobel Peace Prize, Bishop Carlos Ximenes Belo and José Ramos-Horta.

In January 1999, President Suharto's somewhat capricious successor, B. J. Habibie, proposed a referendum under UN auspices in which the inhabitants of East Timor could vote either for wide-ranging autonomy within Indonesia or for independence. Habibie seemed to believe that the inhabitants would vote to stay within Indonesia; many others had little doubt that the vote would go for independence. If so, the danger was that this would be resisted by the large, vicious, semi-official Indonesian militias, linked to the Kopassus, who were entrenched on the territory.

Annan was now in frequent contact with José "Xanana" Gusmão, the principal Timorese pro-independence leader, who was able to speak to him only from house arrest in Jakarta, and who was eager for the proposed referendum to take place. Habibie's offer was seen by many East Timorese, and in the wider world, as a window of opportunity that might well soon be closed.

Negotiations over the referendum were conducted between Indonesia and Portugal, the former colonial power, with the United Nations overseeing the talks in consultation with the East Timorese. The UN tried to insist on disarming the militias and confining Indonesian soldiers to barracks during the referendum. The Indonesians refused. They also refused any idea that foreign troops be allowed into East Timor; they insisted that security would remain in the hands of the Indonesian police—who were controlled by the army. Only three hundred unarmed UN civilian police (CivPol) would be allowed to patrol. During April militia violence increased.

But East Timor was on the back burner. Inevitably Kosovo dominated the secretary general's agenda. By the first week of April, Annan felt he should get the UN back into the picture and make a statement of his position. Albright called to say it was important to stress that Milosevic must live up to his obligations. She felt he should blame Milosevic clearly. The U.S. position could be summed up as "Forces out, refugees in, international force in."

Annan did not want to attack Milosevic directly; he wanted to give him a ladder to climb down. The secretary general's statement called upon the Yugoslav authorities to end the security forces' campaign of intimidation, to withdraw those forces, to allow the return of refugees, to accept the deployment of an international military force and to allow the international community to verify compliance with these undertakings. When this was done, NATO should end its bombing. Annan's spokesman said that the UN and NATO Charters both called for Security Council approval for any intervention by a regional force.

On the weekend of April 10, Russian president Boris Yeltsin used the Kosovo crisis to stave off the threat of impeachment in the Duma, and warned that if NATO was not careful, Russia would be dragged into the conflict and a new world war would loom. But Clinton told Annan that notwithstanding Yeltsin's attack, he thought there was a good chance of forming a united diplomatic front. He hoped that Annan's statement would enable the Russians to "get back in the hunt."

By starting the campaign with no backup role being given to ground forces, the alliance had only ever-increasing airpower to rely on. By the end of the third week of the bombing, NATO announced that the U.S. would send another eighty-two aircraft to the theater, bringing the total to around six hundred.

Annan flew to Brussels, where he met Javier Solana at the airport rather than at NATO headquarters. Solana was holding the alliance together with consummate skill. He said that NATO's position was that the ethnic cleansing had to be reversed; this meant Yugoslav troops had to be withdrawn and an international force deployed. The Russians had to be involved in order to diminish the divisions in the

Security Council. Annan wondered what would happen when NATO ran out of targets to bomb; Solana said not to worry, there were still plenty.

On his way to the Lipsius building of the European Union, Annan took a call from Madeleine Albright on his car phone. She was worried that he might go to Belgrade as he had to Baghdad; Annan assured her he had no such intention. She said she had had a good meeting with the Russian foreign minister, Igor Ivanov, who wanted to be part of the solution. The next call was from Ivanov himself, who confirmed that his meeting with Albright had been useful.

Annan then saw Tony Blair, who had called in *Newsweek* for "a new internationalism" which would not tolerate those dictators who "visit horrific punishments on their own people to stay in power." This seemed to imply that the Western democracies should take up the cudgels on behalf of oppressed people everywhere. This was a radical proposal and Blair said again that it stemmed from the fact that Western governments were now run by people like him and Clinton—"a new generation of leaders in the United States and Europe who were born after World War II, who hail from the progressive side of politics, but who are as prepared as any of our predecessors right or left in seeing this thing through."

Like Clinton, Blair compared Milosevic to Hitler. The analogy was unhelpful; there was no way in which the aspirations of Milosevic, a Balkan thug, should be compared to those of Hitler, who wished to tyrannize the world, not just his own country.

In Brussels, Blair told Annan that the UK's position was "to hang very tough indeed." The most horrible things were happening in Kosovo. Ethnic cleansing had to be defeated; the international community could not compromise. Annan said everyone wanted to get the refugees home, which meant an agreement with Milosevic. Blair stated it was important that the details be worked out clearly so that Milosevic could not "take us for a ride, like Saddam Hussein."

Annan jumped at the opportunity of saying he wanted to talk to Blair about Iraq one day. The international community was at an impasse; there was a need for creative thinking. This was not a post–World War II situation in which the Allies had an occupying force in Germany; nothing could be done without Iraq's cooperation. The secretary general said Iraq was like an albatross around the UN's neck—one that was getting heavier every day.

Annan then went into a meeting of European leaders, who expressed clear differences of opinion as to how far the bombing should be stepped up. Toward the end of the meeting the secretary general said this was a race against time. There were two ways of helping to get the refugees home—by military methods and by political means—and they were not mutually exclusive. There was a danger of NATO taking over too much of the relief effort; humanitarian assistance should not be militarized.

By now the secretary general was beginning to worry that NATO's reliance on bombing coupled with Milosevic's intransigence might mean that no solution would be found, or no peace imposed, before winter descended upon the refugee camps in Macedonia and Albania. And he knew that eventually the crisis would be turned over to the UN.

Annan decided that to keep the UN actively involved he would appoint two peace envoys, arguing that it would help to have someone apart from the Russians engaging with Milosevic. After casting around, he settled upon Carl Bildt, the former Swedish prime minister who had been the high representative in Bosnia after Dayton, and Eduard Kukan, the foreign minister of Slovakia. Annan's proposal was not well received in Washington or London. The U.S. and Britain were concerned that the whole idea would seem to Milosevic to be a crack in the wall against him. While they had no objection to Kukan, they did object to Bildt, who had publicly criticized the bombing.

At the end of April, Annan decided to go to Moscow. Washington was nervous. Albright told him that while the U.S. appreciated his role, they did not want a repeat of the Iraq problem: they did not want him to make agreements the U.S. could not accept. Annan assured her that was not going to happen.

Before traveling to Moscow the secretary general issued a new statement: "Since the beginning of the conflict, we've all been concerned with the tragedy of the Kosovo Albanians. But as the conflict escalates, we see the negative impact spreading through the sub-region. The human cost of the violence is unacceptably high. . . . Once again, innocent civilians are paying the price for unresolved political conflict. We must be bold and imaginative in the search for a lasting political solution, which cannot be won on the battlefield."

Predictably, the Russians liked this statement. Also predictably,

Madeleine Albright did not. Annan's response was that he did not work for the U.S. government; he was secretary general of the UN, and as such he needed room to maneuver.

At the Kremlin, Boris Yeltsin spoke entirely from cue cards. He and all the other Russian leaders assured Annan that Milosevic would never surrender. They also trotted out the familiar line that if Milosevic did accede to NATO demands, he would probably be overthrown and replaced by someone even worse. This argument was increasingly unpersuasive since it was hard to see anything worse than what had already happened to Kosovo. As Yeltsin said goodbye to Annan, he became animated and said spontaneously, "Together, you and I are invincible. Together we can end this war."

When I saw Annan in London after his return from Moscow he said, "The frightening thing is that unless a solution is found quickly, there will be a major humanitarian disaster in Yugoslavia. Winter will come and, with refineries gone, bridges gone, electricity gone, water gone, you could have a mass exodus, this time from Serbia. It would be another catastrophe."

Just before and just after his trip to Moscow, Annan saw Strobe Talbott, the U.S. deputy secretary of state who was now leading the American diplomatic effort with the Russians. Talbott had been a prominent Russian expert ever since he was chosen by *Time-Life* to translate the memoirs of Nikita Khrushchev while he was still a student in 1969. He had spent the seventies and eighties as a senior correspondent for *Time* magazine, and had written several distinguished books on arms control. He had been a friend of Bill Clinton since they were Rhodes scholars together at Oxford and had left *Time* to join the administration in 1993. Since then he had been Clinton's point man dealing with Russia until he was promoted to deputy secretary.

Now Talbott was embarked on what was, in a way, the culmination of his life's work to date—a nine-week shuttle between the U.S., Western Europe and Russia to try to persuade the Russians to ally themselves to the aims of NATO to defeat their old ally Milosevic. By the beginning of May, Talbott was convinced that no matter what they said to Annan and for public consumption, the Russians were being pragmatic if not yet fully supportive. Talbott argued that the Yeltsin government had contained rather than exploited the domestic uproar over the NATO bombing. It had not given outright assistance to Serbia. It was evidently prepared to engage in diplomacy to end the war. And it had said that it would participate in the eventual peacekeeping operation.

It was true that the Russians tried, as usual, to weaken the alliance by splitting France from *"les anglo-saxons."* On this occasion that failed. When, on April 21, Yeltsin nominated former prime minister Viktor Chernomyrdin to handle the crisis, thus removing it from the Foreign Ministry, Talbott saw this as a hopeful sign that Yeltsin wanted a solution. The U.S. strategy was to convince the Kremlin that its objective—the end of the bombing—could be achieved only if Russia stopped defending Milosevic and joined the consensus of the international community that his ethnic cleansing policies must be reversed, that the refugees be allowed to return, and that Yugoslav security forces withdraw from Kosovo. These were NATO terms, but they had been accepted by the EU and by Annan.

On May 2, Washington was heartened when Milosevic released to the Reverend Jesse Jackson three U.S. soldiers captured along the Kosovo-Macedonian border. Two days later a breakthrough occurred. Viktor Chernomyrdin had breakfast with Vice President Al Gore, Albright, Sandy Berger and Talbott at Gore's Washington residence. The Russian said he needed a person of international stature at his side when Milosevic surrendered, if only to cover his own flank with the nationalists in the Duma. This person should not be a Russian, should not be an American, should not be from a NATO country and should not be a German. When the Americans suggested the Finnish president, Marti Ahtisaari, Chernomyrdin's eyes apparently lit up. Ahtisaari, a seasoned diplomat as well as a politician, had good relations with the Russians and a long history with the UN, and was widely seen as a capable and independent leader.

Ahtisaari was happy to become Chernomyrdin's partner. He felt NATO's terms had to be met without question or compromise. Washington called the new Chernomyrdin-Ahtisaari axis "hammer and anvil." Chernomyrdin would be the hammer, Ahtisaari the anvil, and Milosevic would be beaten in between. On his shuttle to meet the two of them and other Russian and European leaders, Talbott tried to persuade Chernomyrdin to bring Russia's position as close as possible to NATO's, with Ahtisaari acting as honest broker, representing the incoming presidency of the EU and a neutral, nonaligned (non-NATO) country which could argue objectively for NATO's terms.

Washington then tried to persuade Annan to appoint Ahtisaari as his special envoy in this joint effort with Moscow. The secretary general had high regard for Ahtisaari but he demurred, and his conversations with Albright on this topic became tense in early May. Talbott told Annan that the U.S. plan was not an attempt to sideline the UN but to try to breathe life into a basically Russian proposal. He asked Annan at the very least to bless Ahtisaari's appointment. The secretary general appointed his own envoys, Carl Bildt and Eduard Kukan, anyway. They were sidelined by the speed with which the Ahtisaari-Chernomyrdin machine moved ahead. Annan kept in touch with Ahtisaari and met with him twice during the next critical weeks.

On May 7, the forty-fifth day of NATO's air campaign against Yugoslavia, U.S. bombs hit the Chinese embassy in central Belgrade, killing three Chinese said to be journalists. The embassy had apparently been targeted by mistake, though that was not widely believed in China. Beijing went out of its way to stoke populist anger against the United States, and suspended talks about human rights, arms control and trade. It was another low point of the war.

IN early May, I traveled through Albania and Montenegro to visit Kosovar refugee camps with Dennis McNamara, the senior official of the UN High Commissioner for Refugees in the Balkans. UNHCR was in trouble.

The agency had been at the center of the maelstrom of the decade. It was the agency most used by peacemakers and most abused by warlords. When Turkey closed its borders to 400,000 Iraqi Kurds in 1991, and the Allied forces created safe havens for them in northern Iraq, UNHCR had to help them down the mountains and back into the homes they had fled in fear of Saddam Hussein. In Cambodia, it had succeeded in repatriating more than 300,000 people from the Thai border in time for the 1993 election, though many of them languished in poverty on indifferent land thereafter. In Bosnia, it had run the convoys which kept the beleaguered populations alive for several years—and also supplied the warriors. The disaster of Srebrenica showed the difficulty of ensuring protection if safe areas are the objective of territorial claims in fierce intergroup conflicts. As

Sadako Ogata, the high commissioner, put it, "By definition the protection of the inhabitants of such areas cannot be neutral *a fortiori*
when they are demilitarized."

Throughout the decade one of the worst problems with which
UNHCR had to contend was the militarization of camps. In the
eighties this had been the exception, as in the Khmer Rouge and
other armed Cambodian camps along the Thai border. In the
nineties it became commonplace. The issue was at its most stark in
Zaire and Tanzania, where UNHCR had been forced between 1994
and 1996 to preside over camps which no government would help
clear of the Hutu killers who terrorized ordinary refugees. Beyond
that, in countries like Liberia and Sierra Leone, UNHCR and other
agencies had to deal with crises in which state structures had unrav-
eled and violence had become an end in itself, profiting warlords and
their factions. This type of conflict had spread through the decade
and, indeed, was one reason for the sweep of war around and in
Congo. The nefarious proliferation of cheap small arms since the
end of the Cold War had vastly worsened the problem and spread violence to children. "For many children today," said Ogata, "thou
shalt not kill is no longer the norm; it is not even a pious wish."

In the 1990s humanitarianism had become politicized as never before. Now, in Kosovo, humanitarianism was being militarized as well.
Like every Western government, every journalist and every other humanitarian agency, UNHCR was surprised by the scale of the exodus
in March, April and May. No one expected such a mass expulsion.
UNHCR had expected about 100,000 refugees, but 360,000 came by
the end of April.

UNHCR was fiercely attacked by governments and other agencies
for its unreadiness. But until days before the exodus began the international community, especially the key Western governments, was
banking on peace and urging UNHCR and others to prepare for the
early implementation of the Rambouillet accords. It was unlikely
that these governments would have responded to a request from
UNHCR for massive contingency preparations predicated on the failure of their own peace efforts. Nonetheless, there were valid criticisms of UNHCR to be made. In particular, the agency had not
staffed its field offices adequately. When the crisis broke and refugees
began to flood into Albania and Macedonia, there were too few effec-

tive UNHCR officials on the spot to carry out the agency's most vital functions—protection and assistance. The agency then caught up—but it should not have been caught out.

UNHCR suddenly found itself engaged in an operation as complex as it had ever faced. Among the most serious problems were the reluctance of Macedonia to give asylum; security concerns in Montenegro, where the government was ready to aid the refugees but where Yugoslav forces were a real threat; recruitment by the KLA; and finding the many missing members of families.

UNHCR and governments turned to NATO for help. During April, NATO troops built camps in Macedonia, relocated refugees and sent eight thousand troops to Albania to assist the Kosovars who had fled there. It was, to say the least, unusual for one of the parties to a combat to undertake vast humanitarian actions of this sort. UNHCR was criticized by some humanitarian officials for allowing NATO to take the lead. But there was no alternative. Hundreds of thousands of people suddenly needed assistance. Macedonia demanded that NATO build camps and that an immediate evacuation program be begun as part of its agreement to allow the refugees asylum.

By mid-April the atrocious scenes in Macedonia and Albania of hundreds of thousands of refugees struggling terrified out of Kosovo conjured up the images of previous mass exoduses from brutal regimes, and the way in which the world had tried to deal with them. But although the nature of the human suffering was similar, and the TV pictures were at least as ghastly, there were important differences from previous crises.

Perhaps the nearest parallel was when the Croatian army ethnically cleansed Krajina, the Serb area of Croatia, in August 1995. In three days, 250,000 Serbs, mostly peasants not involved in wrongdoing, were driven out of the homes they had lived in for centuries. There was far less outcry over their fate than over that of the Kosovars because no Serbs, however innocent, aroused much sympathy by the mid-nineties, and because the Croatian assault was supported by the United States as an essential part of its plan to end the war in Bosnia.

In terms of numbers, the Kosovar refugee crisis was not as horrendous as others with which the international community has had to deal in recent years. In April 1994 about 250,000 Rwandans crossed into Tanzania in the space of twenty-four hours. Over the next three days another 250,000 came. That July almost a million more crossed in four days. Altogether two million people fled from Rwanda during a five-month period of 1994. Cholera broke out and 50,000 people died in four horrible weeks at the height of the disaster.

As we saw, for the next three years genuine Rwandan refugees remained terrorized under the control of Hutu militias responsible for the worst of the killing. The Kosovars did not have to suffer under the same sort of military thuggery in their camps, though Annan warned that the KLA's power would undoubtedly grow the longer the camps remained. In mid-May he visited the camps in Macedonia and Albania, and was moved by the enormity of the tragedy of what he saw. These refugees suffered from a new and ominous menace: the Serbs had stripped many of them of their identities, stealing all papers, tractor license plates and everything else that might prove they were residents of Kosovo. The Serbs were trying to create mass statelessness.

There were also differences between the Kosovo and Bosnian crises. In Bosnia, the UNHCR operation had been a substitute for political action, and governments wanted it to seem a success. By contrast, the Kosovo exodus and humanitarian crisis were, at least in part, a consequence of actions by the international community, which needed to be seen to contain it. Instead of hiding behind UNHCR, as in Bosnia, donor governments tried to launch their own actions and take credit for themselves. In Bosnia, UNHCR had controlled the humanitarian operations; in the Kosovo crisis, it was virtually a free-for-all. Germany, Italy, Denmark and the United Arab Emirates all built their own refugee camps in Albania. Governments made their own arrangements with nongovernmental organizations, kept UNHCR short of cash and then complained when the agency was unable to coordinate effectively. The standards of assistance from nongovernmental organizations varied widely. Some that had never before been active in Kosovo arrived to help; some insisted on high visibility, without always a clear understanding of the context or needs.

In the refugee camps I was struck, as I have been in many such camps around the world, by the appalling waste and frustration. Until very recently these people had lived normally (insofar as life under the Serbs could be normal), taking their children to school, going to work, shopping, eating at home. Now most of them were nameless as well as stateless, their future dependent upon the success of NATO.

In northwestern Albania, a country whose poverty was startling and reminded me of Cambodia, I visited an abandoned tobacco factory in the derelict town of Shkodër, a place of vast potholes and tiny ponies and traps, where industry and almost all government had collapsed, where gangs ruled. Eight thousand refugees had been brought to the tobacco factory. With its dark, satanic windows, crazily tilting chimneys and crumbling redbrick walls, it looked more like a grainy motion picture of a concentration camp than a refugee camp. But order and some sustenance were being brought by a small group of Western aid officials from UNHCR, Médecins sans Frontières and the Spanish group MPDL.

Huge warehouses where tobacco leaf used to be stored had been turned into dormitories, divided with plastic stretched over crude wooden frames into family cubicles where everyone slept on pallets. What is the major health problem? I asked one young Albanian relief worker. "Promiscuity," she replied.

Victory in Kosovo meant above all the return home of these and all other refugees before winter. But at least, unlike in most other camps throughout the world, the international community was battling on their behalf, and the exile was likely to be measured in weeks, not years or even decades. Around Congo now, refugees from bloody and unnoticed battles were squatting in cholera- and malaria-infested camps which were awful beyond belief, where assistance from and the interest of the world were small.

By mid-May, NATO pilots were running out of targets; the same empty Yugoslav army barracks were being bombed again and again. But more and more damage was being done to Serbia's infrastructure as bridges, factories and other utilities were destroyed. General Wesley Clark, the NATO supreme commander, still bullish, told Annan's envoy Eduard Kukan that he had spent hundreds of hours with Milosevic and thought he could read him like a book. Till now Milosevic had always gotten what he wanted and defeated every international organization. He had humiliated UNPROFOR in Bosnia and run the OSCE out of Kosovo. But now NATO was taking out his houses, bunkers, industry and command system. He was dependent on the military structure for his power and he was beginning to lose that. Clark quoted a Yugoslav woman who said, "Fighting with NATO is like fighting with God." This was Europe, he said, and one million people could not be driven out of their homes without consequences. This was not Africa, it was not even Chechnya. There could be no compromise. Milosevic had to give in.

Ground troops remained a painful issue. Tony Blair had been rebuked by American officials for trying to get the alliance to announce it might send in ground troops. But then Colin Powell publicly attacked Clinton for refusing to do so and the Joint Chiefs were said to be moving in favor of it. At last on May 19, Clinton suggested for the first time that he would consider it. Then NATO approved a plan to expand the projected size of the force eventually to go into Kosovo to fifty thousand, and the U.S. government finally gave Wesley Clark permission to widen and reinforce the road through Albania up to the border with Kosovo. All of these moves apparently convinced Milosevic that the use of NATO ground troops was no longer out of the question. By the end of May, KLA operations close to the Albanian border forced Yugoslav troops out into the open, where NATO planes could bomb them.

On May 27, Milosevic and four of his senior colleagues were indicted by the Yugoslav war crimes tribunal on the basis of evidence, including intelligence intercepts, recently provided it by the allied powers. (One should note the risk this demonstrated of the new international war crimes processes being politicized. The tribunal had long been requesting such evidence. Till now the allied powers had withheld it because they hoped to continue to work with Milosevic.)

Behind the scenes Washington was still trying to persuade the secretary general to appoint Ahtisaari (an old friend of Annan) as his personal envoy, to strengthen his hand in the talks he and Chernomyrdin were conducting with Milosevic. Mindful that he had already appointed two envoys, Annan continued to demur—to the irritation of Madeleine Albright.

Marti Ahtisaari was now well into the hunt for a solution. He was a robust negotiator. He had no patience with Milosevic's attempt to dictate which countries could take part in an eventual occupation of Kosovo. He recalled that when he had served with the UN in

Namibia, the South Africans wanted Israel and Taiwan to be in the peacekeeping force, while SWAPO, the Namibian independence fighters, wanted Iraq and Libya. None of these was chosen. As far as Ahtisaari was concerned Milosevic had no choice but to accept NATO troops in Kosovo. "These moralistic arguments about excluding participants from the bombing are not of this world," he stated. The Russians had suggested a Finnish commander for the occupation force. He had slapped that one down, saying, "No, thank you very much. What would he be? A Father Christmas?"

Nor did he have any time for the concept of a bombing pause, which Milosevic and some UN officials were pushing; Milosevic would use it to prolong the talks forever, Ahtisaari told Eduard Kukan at the end of May. He thought the Russians were being increasingly realistic. At the same time he was pushing the Americans to accept the UN as the entity that should take over the postwar administration of Kosovo once NATO had driven out the Yugoslav army. Albright was digging in her heels against this, but it was crucial to Russia.

Through the night of June 1, Chernomyrdin and Ahtisaari and Talbott met at the Petersberg, an official guesthouse on the Rhine outside Bonn, and negotiated exactly what the hammer and anvil would do and say when they flew next day for their first visit to Milosevic. Chernomyrdin was already close to the NATO position, but had not yet agreed with the NATO demand for the total withdrawal of all Serb forces from Kosovo. Now, to the surprise of the Americans and, apparently, of the military members of his own delegation, he suddenly also accepted Talbott's argument that nothing less would enable NATO to stop the bombing. Chernomyrdin and Ahtisaari flew to Belgrade with a common position; there was no gap between the hammer and the anvil.

On June 3, after seventy-two days of NATO bombing, Milosevic suddenly and unexpectedly capitulated and signed a settlement with Chernomyrdin and Ahtisaari which allowed an international force with NATO at its core into Kosovo. This led, after some considerable further difficulties, to a military agreement signed at Kumanovo air base in Macedonia on June 9, and to Security Council Resolution 1244 the next day.

The abruptness of Milosevic's surrender took everyone by surprise, particularly when it became apparent by the number of unscathed tanks and troops which drove out of Kosovo that the bombing had damaged his military machine far less than NATO had claimed. But the bombing had clearly inflicted serious damage on Yugoslavia's civilian infrastructure, and as the military analyst Adam Roberts pointed out, this meant that "the disturbing lesson of the air campaign may be that its most effective aspect involved hurting Serbia proper (including its population and government) rather than directly attacking Serb forces in Kosovo and protecting the Kosovars."

Almost as soon as KFOR (NATO's Kosovo Force) had driven unopposed into Kosovo, refugees began to return en masse and with great joy. But as NATO and Russian troops deployed around the province (Russian troops had made a dash from Bosnia to seize Pristina airport in advance of NATO's arrival) and the United Nations prepared to take over the civilian administration, it became clear that the peace would be even more difficult than the war. The international community, in the guise of the NATO powers plus Russia, which had ignored the UN during the war, now turned to it to enforce the peace. One senior UN official said, "It was a NATO war, it will be a UN peace."

T H E meaning of NATO's victory was inevitably disputed. Its costs were high. Far more Kosovars had been killed and driven out of their homes than had ever happened before it started. The manner in which NATO had chosen to fight, only from fifteen thousand feet, had saved NATO lives—not one NATO soldier had died in combat—but had cost the lives of those whom the war was supposed to save, the Kosovars. Both Kosovo and Serbia had been devastated, albeit in different ways and for different reasons. But NATO had been coherent and consistent, and had driven Milosevic and the Serb military out of Kosovo as it had determined to do. Arguments over how the crisis of March 1999 could have been avoided will continue for years, but when Milosevic refused Holbrooke's proposals on March 23, NATO had no alternative but to do what it did and, once committed, it had to win. It did.

In the opinion of Czech president Václav Havel, the war showed that the "glory" of the nation-state had passed its peak because "human beings are more important than the state." He believed that in the next century "the condition toward which humanity will and, in the interests of its survival must, move will probably be characterized by a universal or global respect for human rights, by universal civic equality and by a global civil society."

A gloomier assessment came from former U.S. secretary of state Henry Kissinger, who warned that the doctrine of national sovereignty and the doctrine of noninterference emerged "at the end of the devastating Thirty Years' War, to inhibit a repetition of the depredations of the 17th century, during which perhaps 40% of the population of Central Europe perished in the name of competing versions of universal truth. Once the doctrine of universal intervention spreads and competing truths contest, we risk entering a world in which, in G. K. Chesterton's phrase, virtue runs amok."

President Clinton, by contrast, declared: "There is an enormous opportunity to be seized here, a chance to shift our focus from defeating something evil to building something good." It was reasonable enough for Clinton to be glad and relieved but, as one writer pointed out, "evil is not so smoothly defeated and good is not so smoothly built. Evil is cunning and clings to life." Milosevic was certainly still clinging to office. The peace attained by Chernomyrdin and Ahtisaari left him in place despite the fact that Blair, Clinton and others had compared him to Hitler. For a decade Milosevic's ambitions had ruined what was Yugoslavia and severely strained the international system that had been trying to evolve from forty years of Cold War confrontation into more flexible structures. Hundreds of thousands of people had died and many more had been made refugees. The Serbs were not alone in their brutality. But Serbian ambitions, stoked and exploited by Slobodan Milosevic, had been at the core of the wars of Yugoslav succession for over a decade. The Serbs had suffered from them, too; they had lost their territories in Croatia, most of Bosnia and now Kosovo. There were at least 250,000 Serbian refugees from Krajina languishing in miserable conditions in Serbia, and now they were joined daily by hundreds more as Serbs from Kosovo fled the vengeance of the Kosovars which they feared NATO would not be able to control.

But the removal of this latter-day "Hitler," even though he was indicted by the court in The Hague during the war, was not a war aim of the Clinton administration, any more than the removal of Saddam Hussein had been a war aim of George Bush in the Gulf war of 1991. Milosevic's brooding presence would certainly complicate the implementation of the UN peace. Strobe Talbott pointed out that NATO's intervention had been intended to save both the Albanian community from expulsion and Yugoslavia from further dismemberment. "That latter goal, however, will be feasible only if Serbia saves itself from tyranny and warlordism of the kind personified by Milosevic."

KOFI Annan had set up a Kosovo task force back in March to devise the best postwar "architecture" for the international presence in Kosovo. Chaired by his deputy Louise Fréchette, it proposed an interim UN administration under a special representative of the secretary general who would have four deputies. As usual, every capital wanted to use the UN.

Clinton called to say that although the Europeans would be paying most of the bill for the reconstruction of Kosovo (the U.S. having flown and paid for 90 percent of the bombing missions), he recommended that Annan appoint an American as his special representative. The man he proposed was Jacques Klein, who had distinguished himself as deputy high representative in Bosnia and as head of the UN mission in eastern Croatia. He was undoubtedly very well qualified to run Kosovo.

The Europeans were having none of that. The Italians proposed Emma Bonino, the outgoing EU humanitarian affairs commissioner. Tony Blair called to suggest that Paddy Ashdown, the retiring leader of the Liberal Democrat Party in Britain, should have the job. French president Jacques Chirac called and proposed Bernard Kouchner, the former minister for humanitarian affairs who had co-founded Médecins sans Frontières. The French also argued that since a British general, Mike Jackson, was already commander of KFOR, the civilian job should go to another nationality. France won the day and Annan appointed Kouchner as his special representative.

Kouchner had four deputies from different organizations. The High Commissioner for Refugees was to be in charge of humanitarian relief, the EU was responsible for reconstruction, the UN itself had control of the civil administration and the police, and the Organization for Security and Cooperation in Europe was responsible for institution-building and preparing for elections.

As with almost all UN missions, the real difficulty lay in finding good personnel quickly. They had to be assigned by the member states. Governments were slow, but the UN was blamed. There was supposed to be an international police force of over 3,000 officers; by August only 156 had arrived in Kosovo, and by December only 1,800.

Other agencies had no such problems. As soon as KFOR was established a "Scramble for Kosovo" began as literally hundreds of nongovernmental organizations, all with their own acronyms, mandates and ambitions, tried to secure a piece of the peace. It would not be easy for the UN to find a way to coordinate all these ambitious rivals, let alone control the triumphant Kosovo Liberation Army.

By the end of July, the KLA had in effect staged a silent coup. Kosovo was supposed to be administered by the United Nations, but the KLA had already established a network of ministries and councils, had seized businesses and apartments, and were collecting taxes. It was, in the words of *New York Times* reporter Chris Hedges, a *"fait accompli."*

The provisional government was headed by Hashim Thaci, a KLA commander who had appointed himself prime minister and assigned departments to his friends and relatives. His orders were apparently delivered around town by armed young men who warned that failure to carry them out would lead to beatings or death.

The KLA coup was eased by the fact that the moderate Kosovar leaders, from Ibrahim Rugova down, were in disarray. Bernard Kouchner said that things would take time and that the UN had to work with the KLA in order to establish law and order. Violence against those Serbs who had chosen to remain increased steadily. On July 23, fourteen Serb farmers were murdered in the fields as they harvested.

The Kosovars were using the same tactics against the Serbs as had been used against them. Serb houses were being seized or burned down. In Prizren, as in many other towns, all the administrative offices were now in the hands of KLA fighters. In Pristina, wrote Hedges, "small cafes, shops, apartments and the huge shopping center are in the hands of KLA members." Significantly, "most of these new entrepreneurs come from the rural areas and have nothing but disdain for the urban Albanian elite who, they say, failed to drive away the Serbs under Ibrahim Rugova."

By the end of July it seemed that the province which Milosevic had tried to empty of Albanians was now likely to be virtually emptied of Serbs. One cleansing had replaced the other.

There was reason to fear that NATO would have to remain in Kosovo at least as long as it was in Bosnia, which probably meant decades, not years.

o

IN a macabre coincidence, the costly victory over terrorism in Kosovo was followed swiftly by what promised to be a costly connivance with terrorism in Sierra Leone. The elected government of President Ahmad Tejan Kabbah was compelled on July 7 to form a coalition with the rebels. At Christmas 1998 they had run amok in the capital, Freetown, and abducted up to four thousand children to serve in their army. They had killed at least two thousand people in a few days. The finance minister pointed out at the time that this was about the same number as had been killed in Kosovo in all of 1998.

Now Kabbah was compelled to make this agreement because the rebels had been uncontained and undefeated since the withdrawal of the South African mercenary group Executive Outcomes at the end of 1996 as part of a peace agreement. The Nigerian-led peacekeeping force had failed to subdue the rebels and the Nigerians wanted to pull out. Kabbah was told by his neighbors in the region, by the international community and by Annan himself that since the rebel terrorists could not be defeated, they must be brought into the government. The rebel leader, Foday Sankoh, demanded and received crucial portfolios in the new government, including for himself minister of mines, which gave him control of the diamond mines, the source of Sierra Leone's potential wealth and actual misery.

At the beginning of July, Annan went on a trip around West Africa which included a short visit to Freetown. He and his wife and staff were horrified; Annan said that nothing, not even visiting the sites of genocide in Rwanda or the victims of ethnic cleansing in Kosovo, had prepared him for what he now saw. He visited a "rehabilitation center" for amputees with almost no resources with which these people could be rehabilitated. It was filled with people whom the rebel movement, now part of the government, had forced to lie on the ground while their limbs and other parts of their bodies were chopped off, often with blunt farm instruments. "I saw an eighty-six-year-old woman who had lost her feet in this way," Annan related. "I held in my arms a two-year-old girl whose right arm had been cut off." Such inexplicable acts, thought Annan, "make all our fine speeches about peace and humanity seem inadequate, even futile."

By now at least a quarter of Sierra Leone's 4.5 million people had fled as refugees and Annan met some of them in camps in neighboring Guinea. They sang songs about Sierra Leone and, he wrote, "they rejoiced at the help that their 'brothers and sisters' in Kosovo were getting, and hoped their own plight would now receive similar attention." The secretary general knew that that would never happen, even if Kosovo had not diverted politicians and resources from other crises around the world.

Annan found himself locked in another painful dilemma. "Peace" had been agreed to even if it had not yet arrived in Sierra Leone. But it had been achieved on paper only by rewarding the perpetrators of evil. The mutilators would now share government with those who had been properly elected "and be given charge of gold and diamonds—the country's economic lifeline." How could this possibly be reconciled with "ending the culture of impunity" which Annan saw as one of the principal tasks of his term of office? How could the Sierra Leoneans be forced to accept this kind of solution, when the world had set up special tribunals for Rwanda and the former Yugoslavia, and was constructing an international criminal court? At exactly the same time as NATO, the enforcement arm of the international community, was hunting those guilty of crimes against the Albanians in Kosovo, the same community was offering no alternative to the Sierra Leoneans but to share power with those guilty of similar crimes against them.

Annan had instructed his special representative, Francis Okelo, to enter a reservation when he signed the peace agreement that for the United Nations the amnesty could not cover crimes such as genocide and other grave breaches of international humanitarian law. This was window dressing. The fact was that the government of Sierra Leone was in effect forced to embrace the murderers and mutilators by the international community, because that community was not interested enough to try to seek a more just solution.

Annan wrote that the United Nations "cannot stand between Sierra Leone's people and their only hope of ending such a long and brutal conflict." But the people of Sierra Leone had had no say in the matter, and the UN had actually been midwife to the agreement. It could be argued that there was no alternative because no developed country was prepared to send peacekeeping troops which could have dealt with the rebels more efficiently than the West Africans.

Annan acknowledged, "No one can feel happy about a peace obtained on such terms," but he argued that immense effort by other African countries had gone into it and that if Africans "got the international support that the people of Kosovo are now getting, Africa would have a real chance to turn the corner." Boy soldiers could be demobilized and educated—if only there were schools. "So many things have to be built or rebuilt, in such a short time. Without timely help, countries like Sierra Leone may soon fall back into the cycle of violence and despair." Subsequently Annan recommended that the UN establish a peacekeeping force of more than six thousand troops for Sierra Leone.

o

A T the end of August, Annan's attention—and the world's—was wrenched eastward toward East Timor, where the lessons and the apparent promises of Kosovo were severely tested—and found wanting.

A small UN mission known as UNAMET, the UN Assistance Mission in East Timor, was now preparing for the referendum to choose between independence and autonomy proposed in January by the Indonesian president, B. J. Habibie, and agreed to with the UN and Portugal on May 5, at the height of the war in Kosovo.

By that time the UN's $50 million program of voter education and electoral processes was well under way. UN officials and workers at every level were dedicated to making the vote a success. So, even more importantly, were East Timorese local workers. But no armed troops were deployed with UNAMET; the UN's mandate was weak because the Indonesian government would not accept a stronger one and had assured Annan that its army and police could and would provide security. This was a promise that could not have been kept.

During the summer Kofi Annan had to postpone the vote twice because, despite its promises, the Indonesian government failed to control the violence of the pro-integration Indonesian militiamen who, in league with the army, roamed and terrorized the territory, picking especially on independence activists. By summer 1999 aid organizations reckoned that up to fifty-nine thousand people had been driven out of their homes by the militias, and five thousand people had been murdered since the start of the year.

Still, the Timorese were clearly eager to vote, the UN's registration process went well and Annan eventually decided that the referendum should go ahead. The risks were reminiscent of the 1993 election in Cambodia, but the difference was that in Cambodia there was a huge UN peacekeeping force to keep at bay the Khmer Rouge and others bent on destroying the democratic process. In East Timor the UN had virtually nobody.

The vote was finally set for August 30. On August 24, Annan asked President Habibie to make sure that the military got the militias under control. Habibie said he would; he wanted to give the East Timorese a fair chance to decide on their own future. "We pray to God that he leads them in the right direction." He apparently still believed that the Timorese would vote to stay within Indonesia.

The day before the vote Ian Martin, Annan's special representative in Dili, the capital of East Timor, was cautiously optimistic that the vote would go well. It did. On August 30 an astonishing 98 percent of the electorate voted (even more than in Cambodia). Enthusiasm, even joy, was widespread, as it always seems to be when people are given the first chance in their lives to vote.

It was clear which way the vote would go, and as soon as the polls closed Kopassus and the militias launched a horrifying assault on the population. Tens of thousands of people were chased from their homes. Many were forced over the border into West Timor. Thousands were either shot or slashed to death by men wielding machetes. Hundreds sought refuge in the UNAMET compound, throwing their children over the razor wire on the walls, cutting themselves badly in their desperate search for safety.

Annan decided to announce the result of the vote as soon as the count was complete. On September 4 the UN announced that almost 80 percent of the voters had chosen independence, rejecting autonomy within Indonesia. Under the agreement between the UN and Indonesia, Indonesia would remain in charge of security until its parliament rescinded the 1976 annexation of East Timor, probably in November.

President Habibie accepted the result and ordered the military to maintain order. But the militias, who had good reason to fear independence and reprisals against them, increased their attacks, killing local UN officials and East Timorese. Thousands of locally recruited East Timorese soldiers and police mutinied and joined the militias. The UN's unarmed CivPol were quite unable to keep order. By now it was clear that only an international force could control the violence. From house arrest in Jakarta, José "Xanana" Gusmão appealed to the secretary general to help the East Timorese people and stop "a new genocide."

Australia and other countries began to call for intervention by a UN peacekeeping force. The Indonesian government refused to agree. Without such consent, at least two of the permanent five members of the Security Council—China and the U.S.—refused to consider it. In any case, no government would provide troops without Indonesia's agreement.

Annan saw his task as coaxing Habibie toward accepting intervention, by means of both private persuasion and public exhortation, while also trying to muster volunteers for intervention—a "coalition of the willing." In this case there was an obvious leader for such a force. Australia had an uneasy relationship with Indonesia, but it possessed not only the means but also the interest to try to prevent the collapse of its neighbor, which would cause a wave of refugees. John Howard, the Australian prime minister, told Annan that Australia would be prepared to lead such a force if it had Indonesia's consent. Annan said he did not want to go public with the proposal as yet for fear of undermining President Habibie.

He called Habibie again. Habibie said everything was under control, and anyway it would be faster and cheaper to introduce martial law or declare a military emergency. But he agreed that if this did not work, "we will say the UN is coming in as a friend." Recognizing the gravity of the situation, the UN Security Council voted to send a mission of ambassadors to Indonesia.

September 6 was worse, with more and more people being hacked to death. The university in Dili was set on fire, along with many other buildings. The city center was looted, stripped and burned by the militias; telephone, water and electricity services were shut down. Militiamen stole UN vehicles and careered around town in them, triumphant. They targeted UN officials, foreign aid workers and journalists in an attempt to terrorize all observers out of the territory. They largely succeeded.

Prime Minister Howard called Annan to say that he was on the point of having to pull out the Australian consulate in Dili. It was "five minutes to midnight" for getting action out of President Habibie. The prime minister was planning to ask Clinton to pressure Habibie to allow in an international force.

The Portuguese government was pushed toward panic by an outraged press emphasizing Portugal's residual responsibilities for the disaster. The prime minister, António Guterres, told Annan that Portugal was prepared to take part in a multinational force—or not, whatever was best.

In the next few days, hundreds of East Timorese were murdered and tens of thousands were driven from their burning homes by the militias. Two thousand people seeking refuge in Bishop Carlos Belo's house were driven out and Belo was forced to flee to Australia. The head of the East Timorese Protestant Church, Arlindo Marcal, was less fortunate: he was hacked to death in a militia-controlled refugee camp in West Timor. By September 8, three thousand refugees an hour were being trucked into West Timor by militias. It was ethnic cleansing Indonesia style. UN officials said they feared that at least a third of the population of East Timor might be forced out.

Richard Holbrooke called Annan. To him, as to everyone else, there were echoes of recent disasters. Holbrooke knew that Madeleine Albright was very aware of the Rwanda analogy—when the U.S. opposed UN action to halt the genocide—and she did not want the same thing to happen again.

Having been at the center of the Yugoslav storm, Holbrooke drew parallels with the Balkans. He was worried about the reports of people being taken away in buses from Bishop Belo's residence. Could this be a repeat of Srebrenica? Holbrooke thought East Timor must be contained. Otherwise other parts of Indonesia could explode. The death toll would be much greater than in Yugoslavia and the international community would find it much harder to respond, if only because of Indonesia's geography.

There was yet another troubling echo. The scene of hundreds of foreigners and East Timorese crammed into the refuge of the UN compound in Dili was eerily like the French embassy in Phnom Penh in April 1975 just after the Khmer Rouge victory. Then the Khmer Rouge had forced the French to expel hundreds of Cambodians from the compound (the drama portrayed at the center of the film *The*

Killing Fields) in order to save the lives of foreigners. Many Cambodians had walked out to their deaths. No one wanted that to happen again in Dili.

Inevitably, also, comparisons were being made with Kosovo and the rhetoric with which Clinton, Blair and other leaders of the international community had embellished their "progressive" crusade there. After Kosovo, Clinton said, "Whether you live in Africa, in Central Europe or anywhere else, if someone intends to commit massive crimes against innocent civilians, he should know that, to the limit of our capacities, we will prevent it." But when Annan told President Clinton that the Australians wanted the U.S. to participate in an international force, Clinton worried about the reaction in Congress and feared that people would say that East Timor was a long way away and the United States could not be the world's policeman.

If ethnic cleansing was to be stopped by military force and with Security Council approval in Europe, why not in Southeast Asia? One easy answer was that Yugoslavia is a friendless, poor and only medium-sized country from which not too much need be feared. Even its principal supporter, Russia, could be wooed away from it. Indonesia, on the other hand, is one of the largest countries in the world and has the support of China in resisting foreign intervention. One diplomat told the *Financial Times:* "The dilemma is that Indonesia matters and East Timor doesn't." The very weakness of President Habibie, clearly facing an insurrection in the armed forces, inhibited the world in its response. The disintegration of Indonesia would be catastrophic.

Over the next thirty-six hours the mayhem and the killings became even more insupportable. The military and the militias were clearly determined to destroy the territory that had had the temerity to vote for independence. And rather like the Khmer Rouge who, back in the 1970s, had murdered people connected with the former regime (and those who wore glasses—because they were "intellectuals"), so the militias were now reported to be murdering the leaders of East Timor society—independence activists, doctors, priests, nuns. One specialist on East Timor, Peter Carey, called this "a policy of political genocide, eliminating all members of the pro-independence intelligentsia."

Annan woke after 3 a.m. on September 8 to talk with Habibie, who rambled for almost an hour. Habibie said the army was finally asserting control; Annan told him that was just not so, and that the situation was so bad that UNAMET would have to be evacuated. The Australians would assist if Indonesia cooperated. Habibie said any involvement by Australia—whose public supported East Timorese independence, to the anger of at least Indonesia's ruling elite—would destabilize not only East Timor but also other parts of Indonesia.

Later that morning Annan briefed the Security Council and told them that no government wanted to deploy troops in an international force without the consent of Indonesia. He did not want to pull UNAMET out and leave the East Timorese who had sought the UN's protection to be cut to pieces. He authorized only a partial withdrawal and told UNAMET to seek volunteers to stay behind to extend the UN's protective presence. There was no shortage of volunteers.

From Lisbon the prime minister called with the news that he had just taken part in a six-mile human chain stretching through Lisbon to demand action. He had also made fervent appeals to Clinton and Blair on the need for action. Clinton promised to try to give "material support" to the force. The U.S. cut all military contacts with Indonesia and threatened to veto further International Monetary Fund and World Bank loans.

The Security Council mission had now reached Jakarta and reported to Annan that the situation was "surreal." Habibie seemed to be operating in a universe of his own and was certainly not in charge. The people who were in charge were telling lies. The violence was clearly orchestrated. The issue of crimes against humanity would be raised. Things were happening which were reminiscent of Rwanda. Mass graves would be found. The secretary general should warn the Indonesian military that they would be held responsible under international law.

Annan made a strong public statement on September 10 declaring that Indonesia had failed in its responsibilities and "the time has clearly come for [it] to seek help from the international community." He said if crimes against humanity had been committed those responsible must be held to account. The issue of Kosovo was not completely irrelevant. And he said, "No one in their wildest dreams thought that what we are witnessing could have happened."

September 11 was a crucial day. The Security Council mission flew with the head of the Indonesian army, General Wiranto, to Dili. The general was humiliated and the foreigners were appalled by the level of destruction and violence. In their compound UNAMET officials were understandably nervous. The British ambassador to the UN, Sir Jeremy Greenstock, called Annan to say it was a "ghastly scene" and that Wiranto was so shocked he was now considering the need for an international force. But the Indonesians wanted it to be led by an Asian, not by a white Australian. Till now Asian countries had been reluctant to get involved, but Thailand and Singapore were both moving toward providing troops.

On Sunday, September 12, Habibie called Annan to say he was speaking to him "as a personal friend and as a friend of Indonesia" and asked for the deployment of a multinational force "as soon as possible." There were no conditions. It could be led by Australia. He was going to announce it on television. Annan thanked him and at once called Howard, who congratulated him.

Later that morning Annan talked to Habibie again and said he had seen his announcement on CNN; he thanked him for his courage. Habibie said it was a good feeling to know that he and Indonesia had such a good friend in the secretary general. "May God bless you in your work and me in my efforts to bring peace and human rights and the 'superhighway' of democracy to Indonesia and the region." Annan agreed with the need for the blessings of God. On September 15 the Security Council passed a resolution authorizing an Australian-led force of eight thousand soldiers to use "all necessary means" to restore law and order in the territory. This was a significant achievement for Annan—with unprecedented speed, the Security Council had unanimously approved a Chapter VII peace enforcement intervention in a member state.

On September 20 the first of the multinational force, led by Australia's Darwin brigade, arrived in the ruins of Dili. It became clear at once that the mere presence of the force would not end the violence. Militiamen vowed to kill Westerners, whom they accused of helping East Timor break free. On September 21, Sander Thoenes, a young correspondent who covered Indonesia with aplomb for the *Financial Times,* had been in Dili less than two hours when he was murdered by Indonesian policemen at a roadblock. Jon Swain of the London *Sunday Times* narrowly escaped a similar death; his driver had one eye gouged out by a militiaman enraged that he was helping a foreign journalist.

The level of viciousness was hard to believe. Paul Alexander of the

Associated Press, who had covered Somalia, compared the two situations—ominously. In Somalia, too, the intervention was intended to save innocent lives and foster a sense of nationhood. In both places law and order had collapsed and the peacekeepers faced vicious attacks from armed militias. Both Somalia and East Timor were utterly impoverished, with little infrastructure. In Somalia, the peacekeepers were very vulnerable to clan militias who fought low-intensity warfare in the streets. In East Timor, the head of the Australian-led operation, Major General Peter Cosgrove, arrived with only 3,500 men who were stretched very thin through a country which seemed almost empty of people.

Keith Richburg of the *Washington Post* wrote: "The young men at the roadblock, with the machetes and the daggers, had beer on their breath and anger in their eyes." He had written that first in Rwanda in 1994; now he was seeing it again in East Timor. A veteran of Africa's wars, Richburg observed that "after seeing the brutality that befell East Timor, I see how the evil really lurks within, respecting no boundaries of race, geography or culture."

Epilogue

At the end of 1999, old crises and old interventions loomed again or rumbled on, unseen, forgotten.

The Russian army mounted a brutal new assault on Chechnya, in a reprise of the 1994–96 war in which at least eighty thousand people had been killed, among them Fred Cuny, whom I described in the prologue. Russia's leaders justified the assault by declaring that Chechnya was an outlaw state, and, indeed, the Chechen authorities had lost control to armed extremists; Chechen bandits had invaded the republic of Dagestan in August and Chechen terrorists were believed to be responsible for bombing three apartment buildings and an officers' barracks in Russia. The war was immensely popular in Russia; even Aleksandr Solzhenitsyn said, "We have been attacked. We have been retreating for fifteen years and we need to stop somewhere. . . ."

But the impact was terrible. By the end of November at least 200,000 refugees had fled to the neighboring republic of Ingushetia and were shivering in railroad cars and other makeshift shelters with inadequate assistance. After Kofi Annan intervened with the Russian prime minister, Vladimir Putin, Sadako Ogata, the high commissioner for refugees, was allowed to visit the camps, and the United

Nations attempted to increase deliveries of tents and other supplies to the refugees.

On December 6, Russia's military command delivered an ultimatum to the Chechens who remained in the city of Grozny. It stated that a "humanitarian corridor" would remain open until December 11 and after that all those who remained in the capital "will be viewed as terrorists and bandits and will be destroyed by artillery and aviation." There were at that time thought to be about fifty thousand residents of Grozny, many of them too sick, old or impoverished to be able to leave in the depths of a winter siege. By any standards the Russian ultimatum was an outrage.

Western complaints about this new humanitarian disaster were muted; whereas in Kosovo and East Timor the international community had intervened with the full force of both rhetoric and arms, in the case of Russia there was no such possibility. But the Russians saw a symmetry between Chechnya and Kosovo. Just as the West had ignored Russian complaints about NATO's bombing of Yugoslavia in spring 1999, so Russia now ignored Western complaints about the humanitarian disaster that its attack on Chechnya created. Foreign Minister Igor Ivanov accused the West of showing little interest in the humanitarian problems in Yugoslavia after eleven weeks of NATO bombing.

As Michael Wines reported from Moscow in the *New York Times*, "Now, in Russian eyes, Moscow's day-and-night attacks on Chechnya mirror NATO's round-the-clock raids, but without the West's smart bombs and accurate missiles that minimized civilian deaths in Serbia and Kosovo." Chechnya in fact showed the limits of the new humanitarianism extolled by both Bill Clinton and Tony Blair.

In Cambodia, whose tribulations first interested me in international intervention, Hun Sen had consolidated his power by force and by guile. Now sole prime minister, over the last three years he had imprisoned, exiled or cowed the opposition in the royalist Funcinpec Party, the winner of the 1993 UN election. In 1997 he had finally destroyed the coalition with Funcinpec that he had barely endured since 1993 and took full control in a coup d'état. He consolidated his power in 1998 by winning elections which were by no means as free and fair as those staged by UNTAC.

Pol Pot had died, and among the other principal Khmer Rouge leaders a few were arrested, but most had been given amnesties by

the government and still enjoyed valuable timber and gem concessions. The United Nations wanted to stage an international trial of
other Khmer Rouge officials, but Hun Sen insisted that any trial had
to be under Cambodian procedures, in which few people had much
faith. Referring to the United Nations refusal to recognize his Viet-
namese-dominated regime in the 1980s, he warned, "Those who
maltreated Hun Sen should not criticize or teach Hun Sen how to
have a trial of the Khmer Rouge leaders."

But there was now a form of stability in Cambodia and UNTAC's
achievements were not all lost. The peace process had sown the
seeds of civil society, which had survived in the form of independent
human rights groups, newspapers and other free associations. Sam
Rainsy, the leader of the Khmer Nation Party, the most effective opposition group, continued to oppose the Hun Sen regime with great
courage. But the nature of governance in Cambodia depended on
Hun Sen, whose power was more and more extensive and whose
conduct was, as always, unpredictable. At the end of 1999 he maintained that there was no longer any need for even a small UN presence in Cambodia. But given the continued abuse of human rights,
in particular by Hun Sen's agents, the continued presence of the UN
and its human rights office seemed essential.

In Somalia, there was still no state. Mohammed Aideed was dead,
but, except in Somaliland in the north, the clan leaders still fought
bitterly at the expense of the population. This suggested that even
with wiser priorities the United Nations could not have rebuilt the
failed state in 1992 or 1993. In 1999, Somalia was still as far from becoming a "functioning and viable member of the community of nations" (Madeleine Albright's hope for Somalia in 1993) as ever.
Nonetheless, hundreds of thousands of people were alive who
would not have been but for the world's efforts in the early nineties.

In Bosnia, Dayton had been a success as a cease-fire, but it had
failed as a peace agreement. The fighting, mercifully, had been
stopped, but almost nothing had been achieved in terms of building
a democratic multi-ethnic state.

The original, well-intentioned concept of Dayton, "one state, two
entities and three peoples," had failed. Dayton's electoral system had
confirmed the power of the Muslim, Serb and Croat blocs. At the end
of 1999, the International Crisis Group pointed out, Bosnia had three
de facto mono-ethnic entities, three separate armies, three separate

police forces and a national government that existed on paper but scarcely anywhere else. International police monitors, under UN control, were unable to dilute the nationalist ethics of the police forces.

Few of those indicted for war crimes had been arrested (in particular, not such ringleaders as Radovan Karadzic and General Ratko Mladic). Political power still remained in the hands of hard-line nationalists who often collaborated with police and local extremists. They prevented refugees from areas where they were not in the ethnic majority from returning to their prewar homes. At least one million Bosnians were still without permanent housing. The NATO-led international force (SFOR) refused to fulfill its mandate and act as an implementing agent. The Serbs and the Croats were awaiting a lessening of international interest. Local leaders demanded aid as the price of even minimum compliance with Dayton's plans. As donor fatigue increased, so compliance receded.

The gloomy conclusion was that the ethnic cleansers had won: Bosnia was ethnically divided. The international community's principal achievement of the last four years was to have suppressed the fighting. This was essential but inadequate. If and when NATO troops withdrew, it seemed probable that war would begin again.

In Kosovo, the rights of the majority were now assured. But NATO troops held uneasy sway over a territory in which fewer and fewer Serbs dared to live (150,000 had been "cleansed" or fled since NATO's victory). Perhaps even more sinister, the enmity between Albanians and Serbs was echoed by a struggle between those Albanians who wanted to create a tolerant and multi-ethnic society and those who opposed it. At the end of 1999 the latter were in the ascendancy and the UN/NATO ambition of creating democratic, pluralistic institutions was far from being realized. Indeed, Kosovo appeared to be moving in the opposite direction, toward more violent intolerance.

And there was another uncomfortable paradox. The policy of the international community was that Kosovo should remain part of Serbia, but the overwhelming majority of Kosovars wanted total independence. The UN's mandate was therefore almost impossible to carry out. NATO troops, the liberators of the Kosovars, would soon be seen by those same Kosovars as the principal obstacle to the freedom that they sought. This was a strange dilemma for an organization of democracies intent on promoting the virtues of that system.

There was an even more serious problem for Kosovo by the end of

1999; the international community had forgotten it. That might not be the view of those who struggled to obtain funds for relief and development in a dozen African crises. But it was certainly felt by those fighting to maintain commitments to Kosovo. Steven Erlanger wrote in the *New York Times* in November 1999 that the UN government was "starved of funds by the countries that fought and had won the war." It could not even pay the salaries of the public employees it was supposed to hire and control. Serbs were still being killed with the same sort of impunity that had previously attended murders of Albanians; the reality of revenge and intolerance was eroding the UN's dreams of a multiethnic society. There were forty-two thousand Western soldiers and more than three hundred aid agencies in Kosovo, and yet the basics of a new state still had not been created. There was still no justice, no police, no power, no water, and there were not even any new identity documents to replace those the Serbs had stolen in the spring.

Bernard Kouchner, Annan's representative in Kosovo, complained that he was having to beg for money and police officers. Without them, he could not begin to restore a semblance of normal life. The international community just would not provide the $25 million needed for 1999's budget shortfall, let alone 2000's estimated $150 million budget gap. Compared with the costs of the bombing, the amounts were small. Without investment, the attempt to rebuild Kosovo would fail. "It is ridiculous and a scandal," complained Kouchner in December 1999. "If the nations of the world fighting to protect minorities altogether cannot send me six thousand police officers, what kind of a world is it?" The international community which had devoted its energies to winning the war was, as so often, far less obviously committed to the peace.

Serbia itself had been set back years, some said fifty years, by the bombing. Kofi Annan warned of a humanitarian crisis there unless food and heating oil were provided. Slobodan Milosevic, under indictment from The Hague, was facing increasing though still divided opposition. His ventures over the last decade had created catastrophe for all around. One of the leading Serb opposition leaders, Vuk Draskovic, said in October that the Milosevic regime was "an empire of evil, which allows nothing to grow in Serbia, which every day creates death and which will itself be destroyed."

Around the Great Lakes of Central Africa, war and terror still raged. In autumn 1999 the rebels trying to overthrow President Laurent Kabila of Congo signed a cease-fire agreement in "the Great War of Africa" involving many of the countries around Congo; fighting slowed but did not end. Everyone had switched sides. Now the remnants of the Hutu army which Kabila and his Rwandan and Ugandan allies had tried to exterminate in 1997 were fighting for him against his former allies. By November 1999, the cease-fire seemed to be on the point of total breakdown, as each side accused the other of violations. Kabila denounced his erstwhile allies as "Rwanda's dogs" and insisted he would crush them.

Much of the continued warfare in the region stemmed from the failure of the world to stop the genocide in Rwanda in 1994. And now Kosovo had diverted resources from this and other African crises. By fall 1999, UNHCR had most of the money it needed for Kosovo refugees, but only 60 percent of the funds needed for African refugees. The World Food Program had to cut its programs in three of the poorest African countries, Guinea, Liberia and Sierra Leone, because of lack of donor interest.

In October, Hutu rebels murdered UNICEF's representative, Luis Zuniga, and the World Food Program's logistics officer, Saskia von Meijenfeldt, in Burundi, which was still teetering on the edge of disaster. Several other UN workers just escaped. Their deaths came just one day after a UN official, Valentin Krumov, was murdered in Kosovo (a Bulgarian, Krumov was apparently mistaken for a Serb) and a month after a UNICEF doctor was murdered in Somalia. Throughout this decade UN and other aid officials have become more and more vulnerable. They used to be "off-limits"; in the new wars they are often targets. In 1998, for the first time in history, more UN civilian workers were killed in the line of duty—twenty-four— than peacekeeping soldiers. Perhaps more shocking still is that whereas governments went to great lengths to protect their troops (witness NATO in Kosovo), the deaths of UN civilians provoked little public outcry.

In 1999, the figures were even worse than the year before. By the end of November, twenty-eight civilian UN workers had been killed around the world. Fifteen of them died in the crash of a World Food Program plane in Kosovo which killed all twenty-four aboard, eight were shot to death and others died as the result of bombings and stabbings.

In Iraq, Saddam Hussein could still claim victory; for over a year there had been no inspections and no monitoring whatsoever of his attempts to create new weapons of mass destruction. According to the Pentagon, he was rebuilding his war machine, perhaps to the extent of building new chemical or biological weapons, in brazen defiance of the United Nations and international law.

The Security Council had been completely divided on how monitoring should be restored in line with successive resolutions. Iraq's friends on the council sought a far more lenient regime than that embodied by Richard Butler and the tough investigators from UNSCOM, one that would be answerable to the Secretariat rather than the council. The Russians had demanded that if and when new inspection teams (sometimes called "UNSCOM Lite") were allowed in, sanctions should immediately be lifted. The United States and Britain resisted this.

The consequences of the council's failure to agree stretched far beyond Iraq and the region, serious though they were there. The UN's basic responsibility for the "maintenance of international peace and security" was undermined by the fact that its unique lawmaking and law-enforcement power was being defied by a dictator of whose malign intent there was no doubt.

In Sierra Leone, the rebel leader, Foday Sankoh, had returned in triumph. The citizens of Freetown seemed prepared, for the moment, to give the peace accord which brought the rebels into government the benefit of the doubt. Kofi Annan had called for a peacekeeping force to be deployed there as envisaged under the accord, but unlike with East Timor, the troops and funds were hard to find, slow to come.

At the end of November, at the beginning of the largest peacekeeping operation in Africa in two years, 130 Kenyan troops arrived. In all there were to be 6,000 peacekeepers, under the command of an Indian general. Their task was very hard. At the airport ceremony to welcome the Kenyans, there was no representative of Sankoh. Despite the fact that he had signed the peace agreement authorizing their intervention, he had recently criticized their deployment saying, "It's up to Sierra Leoneans to solve their own problems," and accusing the peacekeepers of living on "blood money."

Only a handful of Sankoh's brutal troops had voluntarily disarmed, as they were all supposed to do under the peace agreement. Many of those who had laid down their arms were child soldiers. Tens of thousands of others remained in the bush and, according to United Nations officials, they were still killing, maiming, raping and abducting people in the countryside, even as their leaders became accustomed to the trappings of power in the capital.

In East Timor, independence was assured, but the future of Indonesia seemed more problematic. The East Timor peacekeeping force, INTERFET, had established order and thousands of people had returned from the hills to the wrecked towns. But unknown thousands were still missing. Many had been deported by the militias and the Indonesian army to West Timor or other parts of the Indonesian archipelago before INTERFET arrived.

In Afghanistan, the war between the Taliban and their enemies, together with opium traffic, religious extremism and gross human rights violations, particularly of women, still threatened the country's own people as well as its neighbors.

UN-sponsored peace talks had collapsed, and in an annual report to the General Assembly, Annan said that "Afghanistan is becoming a breeding ground for religious extremism and sectarian violence as well as various types of international terrorism." The Taliban government, he said, had been conducting "vicious attacks" against civilians, including executions of women and children, looting, burning, forced labor and driving thousands of people from their homes and land. In the Shomali plains in July, the Taliban had terrorized civilians, recruited children as soldiers, destroyed agriculture and cut down fruit trees. In September the Taliban had destroyed statues of Buddha in the Bamian area. The secretary general said the involvement of thousands of foreign "volunteers," including children under fourteen from religious schools in Pakistan, was unacceptable. "There is every indication that the fire has begun to spread in all directions."

In Haiti, which I visited again at the end of 1999, there seemed sadly little to show for the multi-billion-dollar U.S. invasion of 1994 that had been intended to restore democracy. Economic sanctions had helped lower per capita income to $250, the lowest in the Western Hemisphere. Leadership was nonexistent, and the country's political style remained intransigence. The UN had managed to create the country's first demilitarized national police—but the new force

had been unable to combat a crime wave which included serious out-
breaks of political violence. But the U.S.–UN intervention had
achieved at least an end to the systematic abuse of human rights in
the country. It had less success with politics. For more than two
years, the parliament had not functioned. Elections for a new parliament and local councils had slipped from 1998 through 1999 to
March 2000, a date widely questioned despite the efforts of an electoral council of integrity but dubious capability. U.S. troops, military
engineers and medical specialists had succeeded in alleviating for
some people the awful conditions in which almost everyone lived,
but the last few hundred were now about to leave. All in all, the U.S.
ambassador, Timothy Carney, admitted, Haiti was not a success
story, but he said that some international expectations had been unrealistic. A widely shared analysis was that Haitians had created the
norms of democracy, but were unable to realize those norms because Haitian leaders, in particular Jean-Bertrand Aristide, the former and perhaps future president, were unwilling to shed the
country's old autocratic, predatory political style. The hope that
Aristide had represented at the end of the 1980s was now entirely dis-
sipated across Haiti's political and middle classes and attenuated even
in the slums in which the vast majority of Haitians still lived. Like
Cambodia, the case of Haiti seemed to show that the international
community can put nations into the process of transition, but effect-
ing the transition depends on the indigenous leaders and political
class.

At the end of November 1999 the Security Council agreed to extend the police training program till March 2000, pending transformation of the human rights and police training into a new mission
which would add the vital dimension of judicial reform. Responsibility for Haiti was moved to the General Assembly because China had
threatened to veto any further police role on the island, in retaliation
for its links to Taiwan.

In the United States there was still argument over its debt to the
United Nations, reckoned at $1.5 billion by the UN—or 80 percent of
all unpaid assessments for the UN's regular budget and peacekeeping
operations. In mid-November the White House and Congress
reached a compromise under which the U.S. would pay $926 million
to the United Nations—about two thirds of what the UN believed the
U.S. owed. Annan said that the offer was a step in the right direction,

but it was not much more. The money was much less than hoped for, and Congress imposed other conditions, insisting that even this reduced amount would not be paid unless the UN accepted it in full payment, agreed to a permanent cut in the U.S. share of the UN's operating budget from 25 percent to 22 percent and pledged that the UN's administrative budget would not rise over the next two years. These conditions were onerous for the UN and its members to accept.

The U.S. ambassador, Richard Holbrooke, said, "This is not a diktat from Washington; this is an effort at persuasion. It will take a long time, it won't be easy. . . ." He repeated the mantra that U.S. payments were linked to UN reform. Kofi Annan agreed that he had not yet been able to remove "the overly burdensome and overly intrusive" management systems, which he blamed on "a plethora of resolutions and responsibilities handed down by the member states over the years, layer on layer."

Instead of the grand reform schemes proposed by Boutros Boutros-Ghali, Annan was now attempting to work through the existing structures, in particular, through regional organizations. Having infuriated senior U.S. officials by his ultimately unsuccessful attempts to deal with Saddam Hussein and stop the bombing of Iraq in 1998, Annan was now seen in Washington, as well as in other capitals of the permanent five, as an increasingly skilled builder of consensus on the Security Council. There were criticisms that he was too cautious and too averse to confrontation, but he could point out that confrontational policies had got Boutros-Ghali and the UN nowhere. He had begun to introduce a more transparent culture at the United Nations, which was best illustrated by his report on Srebrenica, published in November 1999. While it was painfully honest about the failures of the Secretariat and UNPROFOR troops, the report did not hesitate to blame the Security Council and member states for imposing totally inappropriate mandates which were bound to do more harm than good to the very people they were intended to help. He had also commissioned a report on Rwanda.

The report was published in the middle of December 1999, as this book was going to press. Like the report on Srebrenica, it was startling for its candor. Both were searing examinations of the flaws of the Secretariat and of member states. Annan had allowed the inquiry team, headed by former Swedish prime minister Ingvar Carlsson, complete access to the UN archives and to UN officials, past and present. The report was critical of everyone, including Boutros Boutros-Ghali, Annan himself, and officials in UNAMIR. It also identified much broader failures by the council itself and by individual nations, particularly the U.S., Belgium and France.

The report showed how the reluctance of the international community, led by the U.S., to "cross the Mogadishu line" led to bad decision making. UNAMIR was set up too slowly, too cheaply, with unrealistic optimism about the peace process, was "beset by debilitating administrative difficulties" and was unable to function as a cohesive mission. Annan and his peacekeeping department were criticized for not taking Dallaire's January 11, 1994, cable warning of massacres of Tutsis by Hutu extremists more seriously. The secretary general and the Security Council should have been directly informed. The three governments—the United States, Belgium and France— whom the peacekeeping department did inform took no action. When the genocide began in April 1994, some UNAMIR soldiers were courageous, but they also stood by virtually helpless as butchery spread across the country. The Belgians abandoned two thousand civilians hiding in a technical school after promising to protect them.

The inquiry called attempts by the U.S. and other governments to deny the genocide "deplorable." But it had much less detailed criticisms of the U.S. and other member states than of the Secretariat— because, unlike Annan, Albright and other senior U.S. officials declined to be questioned. The inquiry found that the overriding failure in the UN's response lay in both its lack of resources and its lack of political will; it declared that the UN Secretariat and its member states should have apologized more fully, more frankly, much earlier. Annan saw the finished report only shortly before it was published. He issued a statement saying that he accepted its findings unconditionally. "On behalf of the United Nations, I acknowledge this failure and express my deep remorse." At a press conference, Carlsson said wisely, "There is no mathematical formula for apportioning blame. We have not avoided telling the truth, but hindsight is easy."

The Rwanda and Srebrenica reports together showed a new culture of openness at the United Nations under Annan. Flora Lewis declared in the *New York Times* that Annan had made "a big breakthrough for simple honesty." The reports revealed, in excruciating detail, how very hard it is for the international community to respond with necessary speed to unfolding humanitarian disasters—for both organizational and political reasons. The bottom line in both crises was that major governments did not want to do more. And in both Bosnia and Rwanda, the United Nations tried to maintain the neutrality of peacekeeping longer than could be justified by the horror around. The Carlsson inquiry underscored Annan's assertion that when the international community promises to protect people, "it must be willing to back its promises with the necessary means." Far too often in the nineties there was a gulf between mandate and means. Partly as a result, thousands of people died.

Annan was praised not only for his openness, but also for many of his appointments, among them Louise Fréchette, who brought vigor to the new post of deputy secretary general; Pino Arlacchi, the Italian anti-mafia prosecutor, to run the UN's Drug Control Program; Mark Malloch Brown, who left the World Bank to become administrator of the UN Development Program and begin its long overdue reform; and Sérgio Vieira de Mello, the UNHCR official who was now the special representative in East Timor.

Rather than demand grandiose new global orders, he played his strongest card, himself, using his innate powers of persuasion to try to effect change. He had not publicly criticized NATO's actions in Kosovo, and he had helped persuade both the Chinese and the Russians to accept Chapter VII intervention in East Timor—no mean feat. *The Economist*'s Foreign Report stated in September 1999 that "Annan may be remembered as the UN's most ingenious leader." By the end of the year, he was three years into his five-year term and there seemed to be a growing consensus among the permanent five that he should be asked to stay on for a second term. Given the fantastic pressures of the job, in which one crisis tumbles always on top of another, and given the conflicting demands that are made daily on the secretary general from different and distant corners of the earth, that was a daunting prospect. But Annan now personified the spirit of the international community, with all its hopes, heroism and disappointments, more than any secretary general since Dag Hammarskjöld. Whether or not to stay on was a decision that he would soon have to face.

***

DELIVERANCE from evil was the theme of Kofi Annan's address on September 20, 1999, to the last UN General Assembly session of the twentieth century. Humanitarian intervention in the twenty-first century was his subject.

He pointed out that the notion of state sovereignty—central to the concept of the United Nations—is being redefined by the forces of globalization and international cooperation. Individual rights are being seen as more and more important, so we have to think anew about how the world responds to political, human rights and humanitarian crises.

We are doing so. A new global architecture is being built upon the international system that was constructed after the Second World War. The final structure is still unknown, but the shape is becoming clearer. It includes humanitarian rather than strategic intervention; the ad hoc war crimes tribunals dealing with the former Yugoslavia and Rwanda, which in turn have led to the birth of the International Criminal Court; and other changes which diminish national sovereignty.

The overall aim is to protect the rights of individuals and to limit the impunity of dictators. Whether they will all succeed in doing so is another matter. Justice and peace do not always march hand in hand. Is armed intervention and the imposition of cease-fires always the best road to peace? Or is it sometimes the case, as the strategist Edward Luttwak has observed, that only the evil of war can resolve a political conflict and bring about peace? In a provocative essay on Kosovo in *Foreign Affairs* entitled "Give War a Chance," Luttwak argued that governments should resist "the emotional impulse to intervene in other people's wars—not because they are indifferent to human suffering but precisely because they care about it and want to facilitate the advent of peace."

Will warlords in the future limit their atrocities for fear of international prosecution, or will they be even more determined to hang on to power? Put another way, has the indictment of leaders in the Yugoslav tragedy both helped end that tragedy and deterred other warlords? Or does the fact that, until early 1999, NATO governments withheld from the tribunal the evidence necessary to form an indictment of Milosevic suggest that politics lie, as ever, behind the pieties?

Would Sierra Leone have been better served by the international community if Foday Sankoh had been hunted down and brought to trial rather than made minister for diamonds?

The nature of the world today does not allow us to ignore the disasters that others suffer, but we are aware only of some. Many crises call for attention, but there are only limited resources and limited desire to meet them. Our choice of where to intervene is often driven by the capricious nature of television and the interests of major Western governments.

There is an uncomfortable paradox. We want more to be put right, but we are prepared to sacrifice less. To put this another way, Western television audiences want to stop seeing children dying on their screens, but many political leaders believe we do not want our own soldiers (our own children) to be put at risk to rescue them. That could change if political leaders (in particular the U.S. president) were prepared to argue that intervention cannot be cost free—but that was not the case in the 1990s.

The television cry "something must be done" can be irresponsible and fickle. Too many of the efforts I have described were forgotten as soon as victory was declared. (Even Kosovo had virtually disappeared from newspapers and screens by October 1999.) A commitment to peace is as important as a commitment to war, but it is far more difficult to sustain. Is there not sometimes a risk that by trying to do good halfheartedly or on the basis of emotion, we can actually do more harm?

Such questions are raised by the events of the last decade. Annan discussed them in his speech to the General Assembly. "From Sierra Leone to the Sudan," he said, "to Angola to the Balkans to Cambodia and to Afghanistan, there are a great number of peoples who need more than just words of sympathy from the international community."

He spoke of our partial vision: "our willingness to act in some areas of conflict, while limiting ourselves to humanitarian palliatives in many other crises whose daily toll of death and suffering ought to shame us into action." The truth is that national interest (or the perception of its own wide interests by the international community) and geography will determine that some crises get more attention than others.

Annan pointed out that Rwanda provides the most terrible example. The genocide there defines for this generation the consequences of inaction in the face of mass murder. By contrast, NATO's war against Serbia—with serious humanitarian reason but without Security Council approval—showed regional organizations acting unilaterally in a good cause. Which was preferable?

Some people (and many states) argued that the use of force without Security Council approval was the greatest threat to the imperfect but resilient security system created after World War II. Annan himself had been against NATO's unilateral action. But remember Rwanda, he said. "If, in those dark days and hours leading up to the 1994 genocide, a coalition of states had been prepared to act in defense of the Tutsi population, but did not receive prompt council authorization, should such a coalition have stood aside as the horror unfolded?" The implication was no.

He suggested that "if we are given the means—in Kosovo *and* in Sierra Leone, in East Timor *and* in Angola—we have a real opportunity to break the cycles of violence, once and for all."

As those and other examples show, that is astonishingly hard to achieve. Adequate means will never be available everywhere. Critics warned that Annan could be proposing everlasting humanitarian war. But Annan was right to stress the vital nature of the debate, and President Bill Clinton also told the General Assembly that the UN must strengthen its capacity to intervene.

I have described fragments of the last decade and some of the problems encountered by interventions. But overall this is a hopeful story. The crises with which the world has had to deal since the end of the Cold War are not new. Ethnic cleansing happened on a vast scale at the breakup of the Ottoman Empire, when there was no international community to do anything about it. Now there is and, with fits and starts, this community is making progress.

The decade began with paralysis in Bosnia, overambition in Somalia, a blind eye in Rwanda. It ended with Russia tolerating international action in Kosovo and joining with China to approve a peacemaking force in East Timor. But it ended also with the West attempting to downplay Russia's brutality in Chechnya. The new "humanitarian" foreign policy trumpeted by Clinton and Blair over Chechnya inevitably had pragmatic limits.

The interventions that I have described have attempted to make the world a little less horrible in the last decade. Similar interventions will almost certainly be needed in the next ten years.

The decisions of the men and women working as servants of that fickle master, the international community, revealed in the fragments of history which I have tried to describe here, were sometimes flawed by their own mistakes. More often they were hindered by the strictures and limits placed upon them by their master. To be humane, humanitarianism must last for more than the fifteen minutes of attention that each crisis is accorded these days. Intervention can assist people when they are desperate. But if it is to be more than a sop to our own guilt, intervention must be commensurate and consistent; it must be followed through. That is how more people can be delivered from evil and peacekeepers can prevail more often over warlords. As Annan put it in his report on Srebrenica, "When the international community makes a solemn promise to safeguard and protect innocent civilians from massacre, then it must be willing to back its promise with the necessary means. Otherwise it is surely better not to raise hopes in the first place."

But humility is important. Not everything can be achieved, not every wrong can be righted simply because the international community desires it. We cannot suddenly rebuild failed states or failing territories in our own image; Bosnia will not become Michigan, nor Sierra Leone the Netherlands, just because we would like to see visions of harmony on our television screens.

In a more religious time it was only God whom we asked to deliver us from evil. Now we call upon our own man-made institutions for such deliverance. That is sometimes to ask for miracles.

December 1999
London

Notes

A NOTE ON SOURCES

Throughout writing this book I have talked to many officials of the
United Nations, at all levels, many times. Among those who have
informed many different chapters are Boutros Boutros-Ghali, Kofi
Annan, Sadako Ogata, Marrack Goulding, Kieran Prendergast,
Shashi Tharoor, Elisabeth Lindenmayer, Edward Mortimer, Sylvana Foa and Fred Eckhard. Conversations cited between UN officials and others are based on UN documents or my reporting,
unless otherwise indicated.

PROLOGUE: THE WORLD'S TEXAN

Much of this chapter is based on my trip to Sarajevo in December
1993 and interviews with Fred Cuny, George Soros, Aryeh Neier
and Lionel Rosenblatt.

Strobe Talbott's remarks: interview with the author, July 14, 1999.

Michael Howard on the American Civil War: "Managing Conflict in
the Post–Cold War Era: The Role of Intervention" (Aspen, Colo.:
Report of the Aspen Conference, Aug. 2–6, 1995).

CHAPTER ONE: ANOTHER WORLD WAR

A. M. Rosenthal on Annan: *New York Times,* Jan. 15, 1999.

David Rieff on Annan: *The New Republic,* Feb. 1, 1999.

Fighting in Kosovo: author's interview with Richard Holbrooke and published sources.

Crisis in Sierra Leone: author's interviews with UN officials and UN documents; also Stuart Freedman, *The Independent on Sunday* (London), Oct. 17, 1999.

President Kabbah on Western double standards: *The Times* (London), Jan. 16, 1999.

Eric Morris, *The Limits of Mercy: Ethnopolitical Conflict and Humanitarian Action* (Cambridge, Mass.: MIT Center for International Studies, 1997).

CHAPTER TWO: FROM PHNOM PENH TO SARAJEVO

Hugo Slim on Dante: Hugo Slim, "Relief Agencies and Moral Standing in War: Principles of Humanity, Neutrality, Impartiality and Solidarity," *Development in Practice,* vol. 7, no. 4 (Nov. 1997) (published by Oxfam). See also David Rieff, "The Humanitarian Trap," *World Policy Journal,* Winter 1995–96; Adam Roberts, *Humanitarian Action in War,* Adelphi Paper No. 305 (London: International Institute for Strategic Studies, 1996); Larry Minear, Jeffrey Clark, Roberta Cohen, Dennis Gallagher, Iain Guest and Thomas G. Weiss, *Humanitarian Action in the Former Yugoslavia: The UN's Role 1991–1993* (Providence, R.I.: Thomas J. Watson Jr. Institute for International Studies, Brown University, and the Refugee Policy Group, 1994).

Boutros-Ghali's background: Boutros Boutros-Ghali, *Unvanquished: A U.S.-U.N. Saga* (New York: Random House, 1999); Stanley Meisler, *United Nations: The First Fifty Years* (New York: Atlantic Monthly Press, 1995).

The beginnings of UNTAC: author's interviews with Yasushi Akashi and UNTAC documents. See also my pamphlet *Cambodia's New Deal* (Washington, D.C.: Brookings Institution Press, 1994), in which I similarly reported on UNTAC.

Boutros-Ghali and the Dutch battalion: UNTAC documents.

Marrack Goulding in the former Yugoslavia: author's interviews with Marrack Goulding.

Breakup of Yugoslavia: conversations with Lord Carrington and

Susan Williams; Charles King, "Where the West Went Wrong," *Times Literary Supplement* (London), May 7, 1999.

Boutros-Ghali's concerns about the UN and Yugoslavia: author's interviews with Boutros-Ghali and other UN officials; Boutros-Ghali, *Unvanquished,* pp. 36–53.

Kofi Annan's self-critical report: Kofi Annan, "Srebrenica Report," published pursuant to General Assembly Resolution 55/35 (1998), Nov. 15, 1999.

CHAPTER THREE: REMAKING CAMBODIA

General Men Ron and UNTAC: UNTAC documents and author's interviews with UN military observers.

Indonesian battalion and the Khmer Rouge: UNTAC documents and author's interviews with UN military observers.

CHAPTER FOUR: CROSSING THE MOGADISHU LINE

I have consulted John L. Hirsch and Robert B. Oakley, *Somalia and Operation Restore Hope* (Washington, D.C.: U.S. Institute of Peace Press, 1995); and Elizabeth Drew, *On the Edge: The Clinton Presidency* (New York: Simon & Schuster, 1994). See also Ken Menkhaus and John Prendergast, "Political Economy of Post-Intervention Somalia," Somalia Task Force Issue Paper #3, (Unpublished, April 1995); Frederick C. Cuny, "How the US Military Could Assist Relief Operations in Somalia," (unpublished, Aug. 14, 1992); and "U.N. Peacekeeping: Lessons Learned in Managing Recent Missions," Report to Congressional Requesters (Washington, D.C.: General Accounting Office, December 1993).

Haiti crisis: see David M. Malone, *Decision Making in the UN Security Council* (Oxford, UK: Clarendon, 1998).

CHAPTER FIVE: GENOCIDE IN OUR TIME

Principal publications consulted: Alison Des Forges, *Leave None to Tell the Story* (New York: Human Rights Watch, 1999)—a superb documentation; and Philip Gourevitch, *We wish to inform you that tomorrow we will be killed with our families* (New York: Farrar, Straus, Giroux, 1998). See also Boutros-Ghali, *Unvanquished,* pp. 129–52; Alison Des Forges, "The Rwandan Crisis," Jennifer M. Olson, "Rural Poverty and Politics in Rwanda, 1990–94," and Catherine

Newbury and David Newbury, "Crisis in Rwanda: Political and Economic Roots to Genocide," papers delivered at the Conference on Sources of Conflict in Rwanda, U.S. Department of State, Oct. 17, 1994.

Many of General Dallaire's comments are from his essay "The End of Innocence: Rwanda 1994," in Jonathan Moore, ed., *Hard Choices: Moral Dilemmas in Humanitarian Intervention* (Geneva: International Committee of the Red Cross, 1998); see also the speech by General Roméo Dallaire, Nov. 14, 1994.

For an examination of Dallaire's belief that five thousand troops could have prevented most of the killing in Rwanda, see Scott R. Feil, *Preventing Genocide: How the Early Use of Force Might Have Succeeded in Rwanda* (New York: Carnegie Commission on Preventing Deadly Conflict, 1998).

French–Anglo-Saxon relations: see, for example, Asteris C. Huliaras, "The 'Anglosaxon Conspiracy': French Perceptions of the Great Lakes Crisis," *The Journal of Modern African Studies*, vol. 36, no. 4 (1998), pp. 593–609.

CHAPTER SIX: BOSNIAN ENDGAME

The principal published sources which I have used include Boutros-Ghali, *Unvanquished;* Jan Willem Honig and Norbert Both, *Srebrenica: Record of a War Crime* (New York: Penguin, 1996; Harmondsworth, UK: Penguin, 1997); Richard Holbrooke, *To End a War* (New York: Random House, 1998); Mark Danner's excellent series on the former Yugoslavia in the *New York Review of Books,* 1997–99; and Annan, "Srebrenica Report."

For a discussion of the efficacy of airpower see *The Use of Air Power in Peace Operations* (Oslo: Norwegian Institute of International Affairs, 1997).

Hasan Nuhanovic's lament: Nick Fraser, *Sunday Telegraph* (London), Nov. 21, 1999. This interview was part of the film "Cry from the Grave," *Storyville*, BBC2, Nov. 27, 1999.

Boutros-Ghali to Michael Ignatieff: see Ignatieff, *The Warrior's Honour: Ethnic War and the Modern Conscience* (London: Chatto & Windus, 1998).

Chapter Seven: Cultures of Impunity

Much of the material in this chapter was derived from my trips to Sierra Leone and Cambodia in 1996. See also International Crisis Group papers prepared by David Shearer and Alice Jay, 1996. I am also grateful to Ambassador John L. Hirsch for advice and assistance.

Howard French of the *New York Times* interview with Foday Sankoh: *International Herald Tribune,* June 24, 1996.

Sierra Leone: see reports by BBC special correspondent Feargal Keane—for example, in *The Independent* (London), March 6, 1999, and the *Sunday Telegraph* (London), March 7, 1999.

For a discussion of the use of mercenaries, see David Shearer, *Private Armies and Military Intervention,* Adelphi Paper No. 316 (London: International Institute for Strategic Studies, 1998).

Chapter Eight: Uniting Nations

Kofi Annan's background: author's interviews with Annan. See also James Traub, "Kofi Annan's Next Test," *New York Times Magazine,* March 29, 1998.

Mats Berdal on Boutros-Ghali: *Survival: The IISS Quarterly,* vol. 41, no. 3 (Autumn 1999).

Zaire-Rwanda crisis: interviews with Sadako Ogata, Sérgio Vieira de Mello, Dennis McNamara, Nicholas Morris, Filippo Grandi, Pierce Gerety and David Shearer.

Hutu refugees "airbrushed from history": Jeff Crisp, "Who Has Counted the Refugees? UNHCR and the Politics of Numbers," New Issues in Refugee Research, Working Paper No. 12, UNHCR Policy Research Unit, June 1999.

Spread of small arms: see, for example, Jeffrey Boutwell and Michael Klare, "Small Arms and Light Weapons: Controlling the Real Instruments of War," *Arms Control Today,* August/September 1998.

UNHCR on Zairean camps: Testimony of Dennis McNamara, director of the Division of International Protection, UNHCR, to the Committee on International Relations, Subcommittee on International Operations and Human Rights, U.S. House of Representatives, May 5, 1998.

France and the U.S. passing of blame: *Wall Street Journal,* May 12, 1998.

UNHCR and Kabila massacres: *Refugees,* Winter 1997 (published by UNHCR, Geneva).

Rwandan army's role in eastern Zaire: Lynne Duke, *Washington Post,*
July 14, 1998. For other material on the Great Lakes, I am grateful
for the reporting of others, especially John Pomfret and James Rupert of the *Washington Post.*

Kabila's atrocities and attempts to conceal them: "Democratic Re-
public of the Congo: What Kabila Is Hiding: Civilian Killings and
Impunity in Congo," *Human Rights Watch Reports,* vol. 9, no. 5(A)
(October 1997); Sue Lautze, Bruce D. Jones and Mark Duffield,
"Strategic Humanitarian Coordination in the Great Lakes Region
1996–1997," an Independent Study for the Inter-Agency Standing
Committee, United Nations Office for the Coordination of Hu-
manitarian Affairs, March 1998; Barbara Crossette, "UN Suspends
Inquiry into Hutu Deaths," *International Herald Tribune,* April 4,
1998.

Chapter Nine: Sunday in Baghdad

Principal published sources include UNSCOM reports to the Security
Council. See also Kenneth R. Timmerman, *The Death Lobby: How
the West Armed Iraq* (New York: Bantam Books, 1992); Wendy
Barnaby, *The Plague Makers* (London: Vision, 1997); and Scott Ritter, *Endgame: Solving the Iraq Problem—Once and For All* (New York:
Simon & Schuster, 1999). Other material is derived from published
reports and author's interviews.

Richard Butler on UNSCOM and Annan: *Talk,* September 1999.

Chapter Ten: Into Africa

This chapter is based largely on my trip around East Africa with Kofi
Annan and his senior officials in May 1998.

Cost of Annan's African trip: the figure of $108,000 relates to the
costs incurred by Annan, his staff and others in the office of the
secretary general. It does not include the costs of some other officials, such as those from the Department of Public Information,
who were paid from other accounts.

Cost of Clinton's Africa trip: *New York Times,* Sept. 22, 1999.

Eritrea-Ethiopia war: Martin Plaut and Patrick Gilkes, "Conflict in
the Horn: Why Eritrea and Ethiopia Are at War," Briefing Paper
No. 1 (New Series), Royal Institute of International Affairs, London, March 1999.

CHAPTER ELEVEN: POLITICAL PRISON

The Human Rights Watch report on Angola to which I refer is *Angola Unravels: The Rise and Fall of the Lusaka Peace Process* (New York: Human Rights Watch, September 1999).

Abacha's corruption: "Abacha's Wobbly Throne," *The Economist,* May 30, 1998; James Rupert, *International Herald Tribune,* June 10, 1998; "The Last Days of Abacha," *Newswatch* (Lagos, Nigeria), July 6, 1998.

CHAPTER TWELVE: IRAQ AGAIN

Western Sahara: "Keeping It Secret: The United Nations Operation in the Western Sahara," Human Rights Watch Report, October 1995; Report of the Secretary General on the Situation Concerning Western Sahara, Oct. 26, 1998; *The Economist,* Nov. 14, 1998.

CHAPTER THIRTEEN: DESERT ENCOUNTERS

Annan in Paris and Congo diplomacy: Karl Vick, *Washington Post,* Nov. 30, 1998; *Le Nouvel Observateur,* Dec. 9, 1998; *La Croix,* Nov. 28, 1998; *Le Monde,* Nov. 28, 1998; *Jeune Afrique,* Dec. 1–7, 1998; *The Times* (London), Nov. 30, 1998.

For an excellent description of Colonel Gaddafi's rule, see Milton Viorst, "The Colonel in His Labyrinth," *Foreign Affairs,* March/ April 1999.

Annan's visit to Gaddafi: *The Guardian* (London), Dec. 7, 1998; *The Independent* (London), Dec. 7, 1998.

CHAPTER FOURTEEN: FROM KOSOVO TO EAST TIMOR

The Observer (London), July 18, 1999, published an excellent history of the Kosovo war; so did *The Times* (London) on July 15, 1999. I have drawn on both for this chapter.

Sierra Leone's unhappy peace agreement: see James Rupert, "Diamond Hunters Fuel Africa's Brutal Wars," *Washington Post,* Oct. 16, 1999.

Kosovo's peace: I am indebted to Steven Erlanger, whose superb reporting for the *New York Times* on the Kosovo crisis throughout 1999 has helped inform my summary. See, for example, "Chaos and Revenge Erode Kosovo Peace," *International Herald Tribune,* Nov. 23, 1999.

Select Bibliography

Many authors have dealt in much greater detail with some of the stories I have covered here. Among the publications to which I am grateful are:

Bennett, Christopher. *Yugoslavia's Bloody Collapse.* London: C. Hurst, 1995.

Benton, Barbara, ed. *Soldiers for Peace.* New York: Facts on File, 1996.

Boutros-Ghali, Boutros. *Unvanquished: A U.S.-U.N. Saga.* New York: Random House, 1999.

Cahill, Kevin, ed. *Preventive Diplomacy: Stopping Wars Before They Start.* New York: BasicBooks, 1996.

Callahan, David. *Unwinnable Wars: American Power and Ethnic Conflict.* New York: Twentieth Century Fund, 1997.

Carnegie Commission on Preventing Deadly Conflict. *Preventing Deadly Conflict.* New York: Carnegie Commission on Preventing Deadly Conflict, 1997.

Carnegie Endowment for International Peace. *Unfinished Peace: Report of the International Commission on the Balkans.* Washington, D.C.: Carnegie Endowment for International Peace, 1996.

Chandler, David. *Facing the Cambodian Past.* Bangkok: Silkworm, 1996.

Danner, Mark. Series on the fall of Yugoslavia, *New York Review of Books*, 1997–99.

Des Forges, Alison. *Leave None to Tell the Story*. New York: Human Rights Watch, 1999.

Drew, Elizabeth. *On the Edge: The Clinton Presidency*. New York: Simon & Schuster, 1994.

Glenny, Misha. *The Fall of Yugoslavia: The Third Balkan War*. New York: Penguin, 1992.

Gourevitch, Philip. *We wish to inform you that tomorrow we will be killed with our families*. New York: Farrar, Straus, Giroux, 1998.

Hirsch, John L., and Robert B. Oakley. *Somalia and Operation Restore Hope*. Washington, D.C.: U.S. Institute of Peace Press, 1995.

Ignatieff, Michael. *Blood and Belonging: Journeys into the New Nationalism*. London: Chatto & Windus, 1993.

————. *The Warrior's Honour: Ethnic War and the Modern Conscience*. London: Chatto & Windus, 1998.

Meisler, Stanley. *United Nations: The First Fifty Years*. New York: Atlantic Monthly Press, 1995.

Rieff, David. *Slaughterhouse: Bosnia and the Failure of the West*. New York: Simon & Schuster, 1995.

Roberts, Adam. *Humanitarian Action in War*. Adelphi Paper 305. London: Institute of Strategic Studies, 1996.

Rohde, David. *Endgame: The Betrayal and Fall of Srebenica, Europe's Worst Massacre Since World War II*. New York: Farrar, Straus, Giroux, 1997.

Rose, Sir Michael. *Fighting for Peace*. London: Harvill, 1998.

Silber, Laura, and Allan Little. *The Death of Yugoslavia*. London: Penguin, 1995.

Acknowledgments

I first became interested in the way in which the world responds to disasters when writing my book *The Quality of Mercy*, about the world and Cambodia in the early 1980s. Many of the UN officials whom I talked to then also played a part in the crises covered in this book. There are literally hundreds of people I should thank; I list some of them here.

First of all, UN Secretary General Kofi Annan, for the assistance he has given me. The conclusions I have derived from this are entirely my own. Many other UN officials, past and present, senior and junior, have also given time and access. Again, they are not responsible for my conclusions. Among those I thank are former Secretary General Boutros Boutros-Ghali, Deputy Secretary General Louise Fréchette, and Sadako Ogata, High Commissioner for Refugees, who invited me to serve on her informal advisory group. I also thank Nane Annan for all the time I have taken. I was helped by many others who have worked in the UN, in many different ways; they include: Isabelle Abric, Salman Ahmed, Yasushi Akashi, Hedi Anabi, Dame Margaret Anstee, Wagaye Assebe, Reg Austin, Tony Banbury, Martin Barber, Anne Willem Bijleveld, Jeff Bloor, Lakhdar Brahimi,

Neil Briscoe, Ewen Buchanan, Richard Butler, Americo Canepa, Tim Carney, Jay Carter, Johan Cels, Hans Corell, Jeff Crisp, Brigadier Tim Cross, Manoel de Almeida e Silva, Tasa Delenda, Sérgio Vieira de Mello, Berhanu Dinka, Charles Duelfer, Fred Eckhard, Rolf Ekeus, Ahmad Fawzi, Mary Fisk, Sylvana Foa, Andrew Gilmour, Sir Marrack Goulding, Martin Griffiths, Jaque Grinberg, Hope Hanlan, Peter Harland, Julian Harston, John Horekens, Anne-Marie Ibanez, Pierre Jambor, Kris Janowski, Soren Jessen-Petersen, Ian Johnstone, Michael Keating, Rolf Knutsson, Ulf Kristofferson, Karin Langren, Judy Ledgerwood, Elisabeth Lindenmayer, Andrew Mack, Michael McCann, Dennis McNamara, Mark Malloch Brown, Eric Morris, Nicholas Morris, Edward Mortimer, Izume Nakamitsu, Olara Otunnu, Nick Panzarino, Christophe Peschoux, Albert-Alain Peters, Sir Kieran Prendergast, Iqbal Riza, General Sir Michael Rose, John Ruggie, General John Sanderson, Emma Shitakha, Lamin Sisse, General Sir Rupert Smith, Gillian Sorensen, David Stephen, Peter Swarbrick, Terry Taylor, Min Thant, Shashi Tharoor, Tim Trevan, Mourhad Wahba, Michael Ward, Benny Widyono, Michael Williams, Susan Woodward, Nadia Younes, Kirsten Young and Prince Saeed Zeid-Raad.

At Simon & Schuster, I am grateful to Alice Mayhew, Roger Labrie and Brenda Copeland, and Charlotte Gross and Steve Messina, who copyedited with skill and patience; my thanks also to Carolyn Reidy and Victoria Meyer. At Bloomsbury, to Bill Swainson, Nigel Newton and Liz Calder. I am grateful also to my literary agents, Lynn Nesbit in New York and Carol Heaton in London.

For many different sorts of conversation, help, hospitality or encouragement, I am grateful to Mort Abramowitz, Sheppie Abramowitz, Anne-Douglas Atherton, Harry Atherton, Hrair Balian, Zeinab Bangura, Peter Barthu, Elizabeth Becker, Jacques Bekaert, Chris Bennett, Mats Berdal, Jane Beresford, Rudi von Bernuth, Christiane Besse, Tony Besse, Xandra Bingley, Urs Boegli, Eilean Boniface, Emma Bonino, Norbert Both, Rosie Boycott, Ben Bradlee, Caroline Brooke, Peter Buckle, Kevin Buckley, David and Inger Burns, Vicky Butler, David Chandler, Carole Corcoran, Chris Cuny, Gene and Charlotte Cuny, Alison Des Forges, Sue Downie, Michael Elliott, Karen Emmons, Gareth Evans, Sir David Frost, Sir Martin Garrod, Adama Gaye, Christopher Geidt, Janine di Giovanni, Ed Girardet, Misha Glenny, Nik Gowing, Anne Grant, Iain Guest, Roy Gutman,

David Hamburg, Sir David Hannay, Steve Heder, Lindsey Hilsum, Richard Holbrooke, John Holloway, Anna Husarska, Michael Ignatieff, Alice Jay, Julio Jeldres, Roland Joffé, Randolph Kent, Carole Kismaric, Anne Lapping, Heather Laughton, Sochua Mu Leiper, Mary-Kay Magistad, Kishore Mahbubami, Kati Marton, Tom Maslund, Leonard Mayhew, Stanley Meisler, Judy Miller, Jonathan Mirsky, Jonathan Moore, Stephen Morris, Aryeh Neier, Dame Pauline Neville Jones, Kathleen Newland, Susan Osnos, Kevin O'Sullivan, Lord Owen, Tim Page, Coral Pepper, Gretchen Peters, Samantha Power, Sally Quinn, Charles Radcliffe, Ahmed Rashid, Tony Rennell, Paul Revay, David Rieff, Adam Roberts, Filippo di Robillant, Michael Robinson, Elizabeth Rubin, Sydney Rubin, John Sanday, Richard Sennett, Brooke Shearer, David Shearer, Lloyd Shearer, Marva Shearer, Robert Silvers, Steve Solarz, Mark Storella, Demelza Stubbings, Jon Swain, Julia Taft, Strobe Talbott, Tiziano and Angela Terzani, Nate Thayer, Jules Thomas, Dessa Trevisan, Charles Twining, Bob Tyrer, Salim Vahidy, Nick Warner, Rob Watson, Edouard Wattez, Sir John Weston.

An inordinate number of UN, ICRC and NGO officials have died or been killed while I was writing this book. Several were friends who helped me. They include Fred Cuny, with whose story I began this book; Nicholas Hinton, the first president of the International Crisis Group, who died of a heart attack while on assignment in Croatia; Yvette Pierpaoli, dedicated to refugee welfare since Cambodia in the 1970s, who was killed in a car crash in Albania during the Kosovo war while on a mission for Refugees International. With her died Penny and David McCall and their Albanian driver. Pierce Gerety, a courageous UNHCR field worker, survived great danger in the Great Lakes crisis only to die in the Swissair Atlantic crash in 1998. All these, and others, are remembered with gratitude.

Finally, and above all, I thank my wife, Olga, and my children, Conrad and Ellie, and stepdaughters, Alex and Charlie, for enduring this work.